पुरातत्त्व
PURĀTATTVA

Bulletin of the Indian Archaeological Society

No. 13 & 14 1981-82 & 1982-83

Indian Archaeological Perspective of India Since Independence

Editor
K. N. Dikshit

D.K. Printworld (P) Ltd.
New Delhi

Cataloging in Publication Data — DK
[Courtesy : D.K. Agencies (P) Ltd. <docinfo@dkagencies.com>]

Indian archaeological perspective of India since independence / editor, K.N. Dikshit.
p. cm.
Includes bibliographical references.
ISBN 8124602891

1. Archaeology — India 2. India — Antiquities. 3. India — History — 1947- I. Dikshit, K.N. II. Purātattva : bulletin of the Indian Archaeological Society, nos. 13-14, (1981-82 & 1982/83). III. Indian Archaeological Society.

First Published in 1985
First Reprinted in 2005
ISBN 81-246-0289-1
Price for volume 13 & 14 (1981-82) & (1982-83): Rs. 800 US $ 40

Reprint authorised by
Indian Archaeological Society
New Delhi - 110 016

Purātattva is published annually.

Manuscripts (whether in the form of articles or notes or book reviews) offered for publication should be sent to the Editor, Purātattva, Indian Archaeological Society, B-17, Qutab Institutional Area, New Delhi - 110 016.

Published and printed by:
D.K. Printworld (P) Ltd.
'Srikunj,' F-52, Bali Nagar
New Delhi – 110015
Phone : (011) 2545 3975, 2546 6019 Fax : (011) 2546 5926
E-mail : dkprintworld@vsnl.net
www. dkprintworld.com

CONTENTS

EDITORIAL

The book substantially incorporates the proceedings of International Seminar of the Indian Archaeological Society during its XIV Conference that met in New Delhi on the 25-27th October, 1982. For obvious reasons and relevance, the key papers on the various topics dealt with during the Conference Seminar are alone included, as even these are sufficiently bulky. They cover Prehistoric Stages, Protohistoric Cultures, the Harappan Culture, Iron Age Stages, Early historic and Mediaeval Archaeology and Archaeological Techniques.

It is a matter of great pleasure and previlege for the Society also to record that the above Seminar—whose key papers now stand published—was in honour of Professor B.B. Lal, one of the senior-most Archaeologists of the country and a doyen among the International fraternity on this discipline. The Society takes the opportunity of offering its respectful congratulations to Prof. B.B. Lal and wishes him further fruitful activities.

The publication of this book has been made possible mainly on account of the munificent grant for this purpose made by the Archaeological Survey of India.

* * * * * *

Archaeologists would be very glad also to learn that a Centre for Training and Research in History, Archaeology and Palaeoenvironment is under way, located in New Delhi, The Indian Archaeological Society with the full cooperation of the Indian Society for Prehistoric and Quaternary Studies and the Indian History and Cultural Society have already acquired the necessary land south of I.I.T. in New Delhi. This beginning has been made possible mainly due to the very kind gift of Prof. Devahuti and Prof. D.P. Singhal to the Indian Archaeological Society, from the proceeds of which this land, measuring 1.54 acres and costing of Rs. 9.25 lakhs, had been acquired. It is hoped that further steps will be progressively initiated towards establishing the nucleus structure of the Centre, for which further appropriate announcements would be made and cooperation of patrons, academic minded entrepreneuers and the knowledgeable public will be sought.

The Indian Archaeological Society will be called upon, in the future years, in the context of the above Centre to offer its unstinted services towards the programmes of training and grooming young archaeologists in various parts of the country and belonging to different Institutions be they States, Universities or learned bodies.

K.N.D

Prof. B.B. Lal

:rudition and contribution to ancient Indian y and archaeology the Nava Nalanda Mahavihara rred on him in 1979 the title of Vidyā Vāridhi. 82, the Darbhanga University honoured him with itle of Mahāmahopadhyaya. However, whereever appens to talk to Professor Lal about his achieve-s, he always repeats what he had stated as an gue to his *Indian Archaeology Since Independence*:

"What has been done is but a part of
of what remains, things all apart,
Let not a praise then make us burst,
Complacency the spade nor rust."

Prof. Lal is now 63 and 'still digging'. We all join to felicitate him and pray God for many more years of active field-work which he cherishes so much.

Braj Basi Lal

A top Indian archaeologist of international repute, Professor B.B. Lal was Director General, Archaeological Survey of India, from 1968-1972. He gave this up at the early age of 51 the better to pursue his researches. After a spell at Jiwaji University, Gwalior, where he was the Head of the School of Historical Studies, he became a Fellow, and from 1977 to mid-1984 Director of the Indian Institute of Advanced Study, Simla.

Born in 1921 at Jhansi in Uttar Pradesh, Prof. B.B. Lal received his higher education at the University of Allahabad. He won merit Scholarships all through his career which culminated in a first class first at the M.A. examination.

Professor Lal was trained by Sir Mortimer Wheeler at Taxila in 1944, and later dug with him at Arikamedu, Harappa and Brahmagiri. We well recall the warm regard of Sir Mortimer for B.B. Lal. After 1947 he carried out independent excavations with great distinction at Hastinapur in Uttar Pradesh, Birbhanpur in West Bengal; Sisupalgarh in Orissa, Gilund and Kalibangan in Rajasthan, Gupteswar in Madhya Pradesh, etc. This is besides a large number of epoch-making explorations, such as those conducted at and near Guler in Himachal Pradesh for Lower Palaeolithic cultures and in the Gangetic basin for the Copper Hoard and Ochre Coloured War sites. He also led the Indian party to the UNESCO-sponsored operations in Nubia, Egypt.

Prof. Lal is devoting all his time now to one of his old passions—whether or not there is any historical basis for the two Indian Epics, the *Mahabharata* and the *Ramayana*, sponsored as a national project, entitled 'Archaeology of the Ramayana Sites', which he is heading. The excavations have been completed at Ayodhya, Nandigram, Pariar and Bharadwaj Ashram at Allahabad. The work at Sringaverapura is on hand, and that at Chitrakuta is to be taken up shortly.

Prof. Lal has been associated with many national and international organizations in one capacity or another. To name some, he h
of the Indian Archaeological Soci
ral Secretary of International
Archaelogy, New Delhi, 1961-69;
and Proto-history Section, Second
rence on Asian Archaeology, Colo
Egyptology Section, XXVI Intern
Orientalists, New Delhi, 1964: Pr
Section, XXIV All India Oriental C
1968, President, Salvage Archaeolo
International Conference of Architec
of Ancient Monuments, Venice,
President, Indian National Commissi
Council of Monuments and Sites; M
Council, International Committee
Artistic and Historical Sites and Arch
vations; and Permanent Member, Ex
tee, International Congress of
Photohistoric Sciences.

Prof. Lal led an Indian Delegation o
archaeologists to the UNESCO-sponsor
Symposium on Ethnic Problems of the A
of Central Asia, held at Dushambe in

Prof. Lal was also instrumental in
first regular School of Archaeology at Ne
the overall charge of the Archaeolog
India, in 1959. He was its first Director,
he held till 1965.

Prof. Lal does not appear to believe i
inclusive books, although he did publish
viz. *Indian Archaeology since Independence*
he has written over a hundred and fifty
Indian and foreign journals, most of which
lasting contribution to our knowledge.

In fact, it was in recognition of this grea
tion to Indian Archaeology that in 1975, Pro
was honoured by the Asiatic Society of B
awarding him the S.C. Chakrabarti Medal. A

The Lower Palaeolithic in India

G.C. MOHAPATRA
Panjab University, Chandigarh

THE Lower Palaeolithic in India as we know today vis-a-vis the age, character, and context of the lower Palaeolithic in other parts of the world demands deliberation. Indian pre-historic research being as old as of any other region, may be older than most, deserves as *a priori*, assertion of its position in the global development in this field. But the problem is: where to begin about the pre-historic beginnings in India? Age in absolute years we do not know; character of its earliest culture is nebulous; contexts haphazard; and above all the MAN whose culture we are trying to understand has so far remained completely untraced.

Despite all these handicaps, we do possess a vast array of data gathered in a span of a century or more. From these, howsoever disorganised they may appear, I have chosen a few points which I believe to be fundamental in nature. I propose to deal with them as one does the ginning of a pile of virgin cotton. I hope the problems and perspectives will eventually emerge like the seeds from the fibres of cotton.

I. TRACING THE BEGINNING

Stone artifacts that occur in the earliest member among the whole series of quaternary deposits represent the earliest evidence of man in India and hence are designated as Lower Palaeolithic. The highest of the five river terraces in the western Sub-Himalaya, the lowest of the two or three gravel deposits in the peninsular river cliff sections, the detrital (secondary) laterite, and the bottom-most of the archaeological strata in some of the caves and rock-shelters like Bhimbetka and Adamgarh are now recognised as the stratigraphic horizons of such artifacts. Neither these horizons are necessarily the earliest of the Quaternary deposits of the regions concerned nor are the lithic artifactual remains same in all of them.

In the Sub-Himalayan region the river terraces are second order Quaternary deposits; the first being the Upper Siwaliks. Both being the results of almost identical aggradational process compliment each other in the same order as regards age. In peninsular India the detrital laterite and the first river gravel have no such context. Nor is there a correlation between the two excepting that both yield Acheulian artifacts. What are the relative positions of these two in the whole range of Quaternary formations of the peninsular India is unknown because no one knows for certain the exact nature of the formation that should be considered as the first post-Neogene deposit in this region. While the disputable nature of the Neogene-Quaternary boundary problem is as much sensitive in peninsular India as anywhere else, the difference is that until recently in peninsular India not even a faint delineation of the Lower Pleistocene was available which had frustrated even initiation of a primary enquiry into the problem.

As regards the caves and rock-shelters the human occupation in them could have begun at any period, and for dating the culture in these deposits, while no geo-stratigraphic help is possible, absolute dating methods are being applied whose results tend to diminish the antiquity of the artifacts in relation to the lower age limit of the Lower Palaeolithic in Africa, Europe and certain other parts of Asia.

As for the lithic material it is well known that the western Sub-Himalayan region had a distinct lithic cultural tradition throughout the Pleistocene. This tradition which is known by the name "Soanian" evolves at least through three stages beginning with the

Middle Pleistocene and ending up with the Pleistocene itself or a little later. Since there are some geo-stratigraphic basis behind the dating of the sub-Himalayan river terraces (Mohapatra 1976: 31-59), the first stage of the Soanian cultural evolution appears to belong to the Middle Pleistocene like most of the Lower Palaeolithic cultures of the Old World sans Africa. On the other hand the peninsular detrital laterite and the first river gravels contain a different type of lithic material which by and large goes by the name 'the Acheulian'. The similarity in their lithic contents is the strongest of all evidences for clubbing the two formations together chronologically. Till recently no convincing data were available to establish direct links between them. I shall presently review the results of a recent study undertaken to delineate the Neogene-Quaternary boundary in a part of the peninsular shield which throws interesting sidelights on this problem. So long, the general consensus was that, hypothetically the detrital laterite could be considered as Middle Pleistocene in age because of the environmental factors involved in its weathering and transportation from the parent formations of primary laterite. But the very fact that it does not appear in any river valley deposit despite such wide distribution, was most intriguing. However, the first river gravel with its characteristic bouldery form, cemented nature, and widespread occurrence was surely a phenomenon equal in magnitude to the detrital laterite. The stratigraphy noted at Vadamadurai and Kuliana/Kamarpal have unfortunately remained neglected but one gets a hunch that at these places the two formations probably compliment each other. It cannot be true that the first river gravels could be deposited only after the detrital laterites were eroded from the valleys because it will not only create an anomalous situation as regards their lithic contents but also deny the detrital laterite from its secondary origin and sedimentary character.

Tracing the beginning of the Quaternary

In this context a recent investigation in the Kasai basin in West Bengal undertaken in connection with the Neogene-Quaternary boundary has emerged as a very important piece of original research. This work, probably the only of its kind so far, records a sequence of Quaternary tectonic and sedimentary events like those in the western Sub-Himalaya, which can be arranged chronologically for the first time in an area in the peninsular shield.

Although the upland West Bengal is at the fringe of the peninsular India, still what had happened here might not have been in isolation from the identical geo-environments in Singhbhum and Mayurbhanj or for that matter from the whole of the contiguous laterite uplands covering parts of the eastern and central India. Detailed geomorphological, litho-stratigraphic, and morpho-tectonic studies undertaken by the geologists of the Geological Survey of India in the Kasai basin (Ghosh and Majumdar 1981: 63-74) reveal that at the end of the Neogene an intense orogenic movement caused differential uplift and tilting of parts of the local shield area. As a consequence, large scale erosion at the uplifted headwater region took place which was further intensified by a pluvial condition. This is attested by the occurrence of extensive deposition of coarse clastics in the form of a thick conglomerate. Besides a clearly noticeable unconformity between the Pliocene Upper Bhairab Banki formation, and this first Quaternary formation named as the Lower Lalgarh formation (conglomerate) in the Kasai basin, the latter contains Pre-Cambrian rocks, pre-Tertiary laterites, petrified wood of Mio-Pliocene period (*Pahudioxylon bankurensis*), and balls of white clay of probable Lower Bahirab Banki (Miocene) affinity, which are proof enough for its post-Neogene age. The river Kasai attained its present drainage configuration by occupying a structurally weak zone and superimposing the eroded surface of the Pre-Cambrian and Tertiary rocks caused by the terminal Neogene orogeny. Further relative vertical uplift of the basin occurred during the late phase of the early Pleistocene period when a sort of table land of lateritised boulder conglomerate (Lower Lalgarh) was produced. Ferrugination and lateritisation of the Lower Lalgarh conglomerate *in situ* and pedalfer pedogenesis took place under a hot tropical climatic condition coinciding with the uplift. At places, thick hard lateritic crusts more than 2 m were formed, whereas at the other points only rubification and red ferrugination of the sediments took place. It is important to note here that this evidence is the only one of its kind in India so far documenting the process of lateritisation during the Lower Pleistocene. Undoubtedly it is primary laterite because the petrological character and process of its formation are the same as those primary laterites of the Phulkusuma formation (Kasai basin) seen over the Pre-Cambrian rocks and dating to the pre-Tertiary to early Tertiary periods. Thus the primary lateritised boulder conglomerate of the Lower Lalgarh formation carries a lot of significance for the prehistorian. It tells us of a tectonic uplift of the parts of the peninsular shield at the end of the Neogene, an ensuing short phase of dryness and desiccation followed by another uplift accompanied by hot/humid pluvial type of tropical climate—all during the Lower Pleistocene. Excepting the petrified *dicotyledonous* wood of Miocene age no other palaeo-floral or any palaeo-faunal evidence occur in the Lower Lalgarh formation and interestingly too no Stone Age artifacts.

The next sedimentary unit named the Upper Lalgarh formation is seen conformably overlying the Lower Lalgarh formation. It is composed of secondary lateritic conglomerate which is slightly calcareous indicating incomplete pedocalcic pedogenesis; apparently a derivative of the earlier conglomerate (Lower Lalgarh). It contains fossils of *Antelope cervicapra*, *Boselaphas sp.*, *Equus sp.*, and some of the Bovidae family, all however range from Middle to Upper Pleistocene in age. Associated with these are large number of the much sought after Lower Palaeolithic tools. The contents of the Upper Lalgarh formation, therefore, are of great importance to the prehistorians. For the first time it reveals a well documented and conclusive correlation between the first river gravel horizon with the secondary laterite formation which had been a problem so far, as discussed above. The weathering of the Lower Lalgarh formation, its erosion and re-deposition as Upper Lalgarh formation indicate first a dry climate and then a pluvial condition both subsequent to the first pluvial period when the primary laterite of the Lower Lalgarh was formed. More than a century back Robert Bruce Foote in one of his writings almost prophetically anticipated the laterites of this region to hold clues for the solution of the problem of relative chronology between the laterites of the "high ground and the lateritic conglomerate in the valley (Atrampakkam)" (Foote 1866). In his own words '. . . the laterite passes down from the high grounds, disappears under the local alluvium and reappears again on the opposite side of the valley. A similar phenomenon is stated to be of common occurrence in the laterite of Bancoorah district in S.W. Bengal. This point must remain for future explorers to explain definitely by the discovery of better sections' (Foote 1866: 6).

The above piece of pure geological research in the Kasai basin has proved itself invaluable to the pre-historians at least on four counts.

(A) For the first time besides determining the boundary between the Neogene and the Quaternary, details of tectonic, climatic and sedimentological data pertaining to the Lower Pleistocene in peninsular India have been brought out.

(B) It has conclusively shown that in the Kasai Basin formation of primary laterite took place during the Lower Pleistocene and it is unimplementiferous as in other parts of the peninsula.

(C) There appears to be strong interrelationship between major phases of alluviation and the tectonic uplifts (usually preceding). This point should be borne in mind while dealing with the two prominent alluvial phases of peninsular India i.e., the Older Alluvium and the Newer Alluvium, which contain most of the pre-historic evidence. In the Kasai basin the last and the latest phase of tectonic activity seems to have taken place during early Holocene. Therefore, the second (late Lower Pleistocene) and the third (early Holocene) tectonic activities may coincide with the ages of the Older and the Newer Alluvium respectively.

(D) Also it shows existence of close connection between the cyclic pattern of sedimentation noticed in the peninsular river cliff sections and the two forms of laterites with a possibility of a third one as noticed at Attirampakkam on the terraces of the Budida Manu Vanka and the Gudiyam cave (*IAR 1964-65*: 3, and *IAR 1963-64*: 32-34) and at Bonai in Orissa (Mohapatra 1962). The first is without human remains (cultural), the second containing the Lower Palaeolithic, and the third with Middle Palaeolithic (Mousteroid facies).

Neo-tectonics and Quaternary Sedimentary Cycle

Most of the infra-continental river basins like that of the Narmada, the Son, the Tapti, the Pranhita-Godavari, and the Krishna owe their present pattern of drainage and position to the neo-tectonic movements which occurred at the end of the Neogene (Roy and Ghosh 1981: 153-58). In case of the Kasai it is well documented. While all these rivers besides the Kasai do not record the initial Quaternary (Lower) deposits in the inland areas, some points bordering the peninsular uplands like the deltas of the Godavari and the Krishna in the east coast, and the lower Narmada basin, Saurashtra and Rajasthan region on the west can be expected to contain a complete record of tectonic and sedimentary events of the Quaternary as has been noted in the shelf area of the Bengal Basin. Therefore, if concerted effort is made in the Cambay and the Godavari grabens, conclusive results can be expected on the lines of those noted in the north-western Siwalik geosyncline and the Bengal-Assam hinge-belt geosyncline.

The most voluminous among the peninsular rivers is the Narmada. Our expectations from its deposits, which were proportionately voluminous too, to provide a complete sequence of the Quaternary, are being reduced progressively with every new investigation undertaken. Datings, absolute or relative, have so far shown Narmada to contain deposits not older than late Middle Pleistocene (Biswas and Dassharma 1981: 15-20). Why is it so? The answer may be a neo-tectonic movement which probably occurred at the end of the Lower Pleistocene like the one noted in the Kasai basin preceding the Upper Lalgarh stage. It is well known that the Narmada and the Tapti lineaments have been active since Upper Mesozoic times and the top of the Neogene has been depressed by 150 to 175 m along 100 to 150 km wide zone along these lineaments (Niyogi 1981: 117-20). In the Lower Narmada valley traces of neo-tectonism are clearly noticeable (Allchin and Hegde 1969). The Kutch-Cambay region was uplifted to the present level during the Quaternary (Krishnan 1966). "The erosion surface in the Cuddapah basin at 488 to 609 m suggests uplift in the early Pleistocene, concomitant with the rise of the Mysore Plateau" (Vaidhyanathan 1954).

In almost all peninsular river valleys Middle Pleistocene and later sediments occur over the Pre-Cambrian rocks. Apparently this massive lithographic gap in the river valley morphology could not be due to anything else but a series of tectonic uplifts and erosion, the last of which caused Lower Pleistocene sediments to be eroded away from the valley floor while bringing about massive changes in the course of the rivers (only large ones which were antecedent to this uplift). This event was also responsible in giving rise to new drainages as can be seen in case of the Luni (Ghosh 1977: 157-66), and large scale changes in stream regimen noticed in the Tapti, the Mahanadi, the Wainganga etc. (Pitale 1977: 243-50). Therefore, it is likely that the factor which was responsible in obliterating all Neogene rocks from the peninsular river valleys re-operated at the end of the Lower Pleistocene producing the same erosional results. Hence the moral is to look for evidence of the Quaternary neo-tectonic events in the peninsular valleys for working out a reasonably scientific order in the sediments thus contributing to the establishment of a more reliable chronology for the lithic industries; particularly for the Lower Palaeolithic, rather than to beat around the bush with sediments alone which often are as vexatious as those at Mahadeopiparia.

Man in the Peninsula in Lower Pleistocene

The above lengthy discussion on the Lower Pleistocene was necessary in the context of the abrupt appearance of the Acheulian in its fairly developed manifestations as the first Stone Age culture of the peninsula without any convincible antecedents. It is apparent that we do not have yet much data on the Lower Pleistocene. Hence it is neither possible nor is desirable to vouch that man did not appear in the peninsular region earlier to the period of the detrital laterite and the first river gravel. It will be more scientific to keep the problem open because from purely deductive reasoning point there appears to be a negative possibility. The origin and composition of these two first tool-bearing Quaternary formations, suggest their derivation, at least partly, from older (Pleistocene) formations through fluvial re-working processes. The artifacts with their abraded physical condition and deep embedded nature within the matrix of the sediments suggest that their occurrence in these horizons is positively secondary in nature. In the light of this can one afford to totally over-rule possible derivation of some of the tools from the same older formations that supplied most of the sediments for these two horizons, or from the surfaces older, which could be their primary or the original *in situ* position? Purely dialectic in approach this reasoning has a subtle force which the Indian prehistory will ill-afford to ignore.

Before closing this discussion on the Lower Pleistocene it is appropriate to point out that the Lower Lalgarh conglomerate belonging to this period in the Kasai basin has its counterpart at the opposite end of the peninsular shield (which was to be expected for reasons discussed above). It is the massive gravel ridge around Jayal in Nagaur district of Rajasthan. "The gravel formation represents a palaeobraided drainage of western Rajasthan of later Neogene of early Pleistocene age. Though the climate was semi-arid (as suggested by calcretes associated with gravel) (note: equivalent to lateritisation in the Lower Lalgarh—author) the monsoonal precipitation was more than that of today" (Misra, *et al.* 1980: 25). Lower Palaeolithic tools are confined to the top 40 cm of this ridge which itself is nearly 20 m above the surface and another 40 m or more below. At places there occurs a massive band of calcrete deposit in between the implementiferous and the unimplementiferous horizons of this gravel deposit which further lends correlation with both Upper and Lower Lalgarh formations respectively.

From the studies conducted in the Kasai basin in the east, in the Jayal formation in the west, and the western Sub-Himalayan region on the north, we are in a somewhat better position to delineate the Lower Pleistocene in India now than what was possible a decade back specially as far as the peninsula was concerned. It is rather heartening to note that these studies clearly suggest where to search and what to expect. The southern part of the peninsular shield is likely to reveal better documented data regarding this period, specially in the deltas of the Godavari and the Krishna bordering the peninsular uplands as suggested above, which will have additional benefit of correlations with the Quaternary sea-level changes. Thus data from north, south, east, and west could be weaved into one fabric and I am pretty sure they will compliment one another. The entire region from the Siwaliks to the Cape Comorin and from the Rann of Kutch to Sunderbans is one big stretch of monsoonal land. It was so in the past (Pleistocene) despite the presence of paired terraces in the Sub-Himalayan valleys often considered as typical of a periglacial condition, or the occurrence of the Bain Boulder Bed alleged to be glacial in origin.

Evidences from Western Sub-Himalaya

The problem in the western Sub-Himalaya is not the same. Though the first and the earliest of the terraces does contain substantial quantity of eroded clastics from an older formation i.e., the Upper Siwalik Boulder Conglomerate datable to the time of the second Himalayan glaciation, it has been fairly established by thorough and repeated checking that neither the Boulder Conglomerate nor the other two Upper Siwalik formations (Tatrot and Pinjore) ascribable to the Lower Pleistocene and possibly partly to the terminal Neogene, contain any lithic artifacts. For verifying this, the advantages in the western Sub-Himalaya over the peninsular region is that these Lower Pleistocene Upper Siwaliks are massive formations often seen as hills which are visible, accessible, and invetigable. All recent investigators are unanimous in casting doubts on the existence of a lithic industry encountered by DeTerra and Paterson in the Upper Siwalik Boulder Conglomerate in the Potwar region which they designated as the Pre-Soan. Even if we do conceed its existence for the sake of argument, still in the western Sub-Himalaya antiquity of man does not extend anterior to the Middle Pleistocene. Hence the benefit of doubt enjoyed by the peninsular India on two counts i.e., the possibility of discovering lot more Lower Pleistocene deposits, and the absence of the antecedents of the Acheulian, does not accure to the western Sub-Himalaya in the light of data we have at present. While there is a likelihood of the initial developmental stages of the Acheulian in the peninsular India to stretch back in time (unless proved as a late intrusion), in the western Sub-Himalaya the first Stone Age culture (Early Soan) clearly appears to make its rudimentary beginning from the post-Siwalik period (Middle Pleistocene), and proceeds from then through a sequence of evolutionary stages till the end of the Pleistocene (or even to the early Holocene). Thus showing a complete and uninterrupted picture of the development of a regional lithic tradition in the local perspectives the Soanian unlike the peninsular Acheulian leaves little scope to speculate on its possible Lower Pleistocene origins. In the peninsula the Acheulian may or may not have given rise to the Middle Palaeolithic, but it is fairly certain that it did continue till the Upper Pleistocene which gives it a different personality when we try to group the Early Soan and the peninsular Acheulian in one broad culture complex of the Indian Lower Palaeolithic.

II. THE CULTURAL MOSAIC

All of us are aware that there are technological and morphological differences among the industries found in the first river gravels. If a detailed analysis is done over each such industry it will clearly show some with archaic characters but most others with very advanced traits that again are different from one to other. Similarly differences exist among industries found in the detrital laterite and also in among those found in the caves and rock-shelters like Bhimbetka and Adamgarh. On the other hand when the three groups as separate units are compared with one another, there also their group differences become obvious. Apparently all these differences in among the various Lower Palaeolithic industries of the peninsular India could not have come in the form of a package-deal under some cultural exchange programme. A temporal staggering of both, the stratigraphic context and the industries, should therefore be the *prime desideratum* in The Lower

Palaeolithic in India.

Age and pattern of the Indian Lower Palaeolithic as seen at present

We know that the traits noticed in the Lower Palaeolithic culture of India did continue as late as 40,000 years B.P. Therefore, from the Didwana Lower Palaeolithic (Misra, *et al.* 1982: 19-31) to Mula-Mutha Lower Palaeolithic (Gupte and Rajaguru 1971: 686-95) the story appears to be very long in time. Not only spatially but also temporally several types of environment must have played their roles in shaping the characters of this culture found so widely distributed over several ecosystems in the subcontinent. While it is neither possible nor necessary to elaborate this point by citing each and every example, I specially wish to draw your attention to the recent Acheulian discoveries in the western Sub-Himalaya as the most illustrative case. In brief, the Acheulian artifacts are found in the Siwalik Frontal Range (hills) whose final uplift and geomorphological developments can not go anterior to the Middle Pleistocene. The Acheulian artifacts are found scattered over its surface and not one has so far been found in any stratified deposit. Contrary to this the Soanian ones do occur in a post-Siwalik stratified context in this range. Further, in the valleys (*duns*) behind the Siwalik range where terraces occur, only the Soanian artifacts are encountered. These Soanian artifacts belong to the Sirsa valley indutry which I am inclined to equate with the Late Soan A of Potwar. The Sub-Himalayan Acheulian is a very developed manifestation of the culture (Mohapatra 1981a: 433-35) in which cleavers are in 3:1 ratio to the bifaces (handaxes). Three main observations could be made from this. (i) The stratified nature of the Late Soan A type of tools and the loose occurrence of the Acheulians in the same area (the Siwalik Frontal Range only) and some time at the same site suggests the age of the Acheulian to be posterior to that of the Late Soan A, i.e., the third Himalayan glacial. (ii) The Late Soan A being later than the Early Soan, the Sub-Himalayan Acheulian appears to belong to a much younger age very remote from the Early Soan. In the light of this can we include the Early Soan and the western Sub-Himalayan Acheulian within one culture-bracket? Or, for that matter, can we equate with the Early Soan (in age) any peninsular Acheulian industry that appears similar to the Sub-Himalayan one for the purpose of delineating the Lower Palaeolithic in the subcontinent? (iii) The third point is that, the distribution of the Acheulian in the western Sub-Himalaya is confined to the Siwalik Frontal Range. They are not found in the valleys (*duns*). Does it not suggest a separate identity, that too in a late context of the age of the Siwalik Frontal Range and the Late Soan A industry vis-a-vis the Early Soan? Environmentally the Early Soan appears to have preferred the valleys whereas the Acheulian the hills.

These are but a few points by way of illustrating the diverse nature of several disparate industries that we are now grouping as the Lower Palaeolithic in India. Survivals, intrusions, migrations, and isolations in the geo-ecological pockets in this vast sub-continent apparently constitute considerable portion of the totality of this culture in India. Despite diversities the Acheulian, whether late or early, is a Lower Palaeolithic culture the beginnings of which goes to more than a million years back as noted at the base of Bed II (Hominid 16) in Olduvai. The Acheulian industry at Didwana (Misra, *et al.* 1982: 72-86) or that which occurs below the milliolite horizons of Saurashtra coast (Joshi 1980) hold out promises of great antiquity. If we turn to western Sub-Himalaya, palaeo-magnetic dates of the Upper Siwalik Boulder Conglomerate (Yokoyama 1981: 217-22) suggest that the first river terraces probably date close to 0.7 million years (Mohapatra 1981b: 90-130) and we, therefore, have a reasonable ground to assign that date to the beginning of the Early Saon notwithstanding the Pre-Soan controversy.

Authorship in global perspective and the Indian context

Having discussed the problems concerning the beginning, probable antiquity, and very briefly touching the pattern, I would implore you to devote a little more time in considering the authorship of this culture in India.

Acheulian assemblages from various parts of India including western Sub-Himalaya hardly show any Early Acheulian or the so-called Abbevillian character. Their typology and technique are reminiscent of Middle to Late Acheulian and in many cases Acheulian-Mousterian and Acheulian-Levalloisean. In Europe, the earlier phase of the Acheulian and the stage previously known as the Abbevillian is very limited. In the light of this the almost abrupt appearence of *Homo erectus* (in contrast to the gradual evolutionary picture of the Plio-Pleistocene hominids in East and South Africa and South-east Asia (Indonesia) along with an equally abrupt appearance of Middle Acheulian in this continent during the Middle Pleistocene are suggestive of a close link between the two evidences i.e., the cultural and the physical. Absolute datations provide a wholesome personality to the history of Early Man of this period in Europe. But in India whatever handful of dates we possess show that most part of this culture belongs to a very late phase of the Pleistocene when in Europe, Africa and certain other parts of Asia new species of fossil man (*Homo sapiens* and *Homo sapiens sapiens*) had appeared. *Homo erectus* spans a period roughly one and a half million to half a million years B.P. An archaic form of the *Homo erectus* (formerly known as *Sinanthropus pekinensis*) was the author of a handaxe-free pebble/cobble and flake based culture (Choukoutienian) in China in early Middle Pleistocene period which is usually included within the group of 'Pebble-Cultures' to which the Soanian also belongs. There are other evidences from Java, Morocco, Israel, France, Spain and Czechoslovakia which along with African evidences show that the Lower Palaeolithic cultures of the Old World have been authored by two main hominid species, the *Australopithecus* and the *Homo erectus*, which together span the period from late Pliocene (2.6 my—Lake Rudolf) to the end of the Middle Pleistocene. But unlike the Pliocene-Pleistocene hominids, human fore-runners in the Middle Pleistocene belonged to one species, i.e. *Homo erectus* (Pilbeam 1972).

Some of the Acheulian industries in India are so late in age that it is impossible to correlate them by no stretch of imagination with the Acheulian authored by the *Homo erectus* in Africa and Europe during the Middle Pleistocene. But in the Sub-Himalaya the possibility of doing so in case of the Early Soan exists because of three reasons:

(1) The Early Soan may come closer to at least half a million years in antiquity as suggested by the palaeomagnetic date of the Upper Siwalik Boulder Conglomerate, and the age range of the *Homo erectus* does extend to this time.

(2) Sub-Himalaya's close proximity to and cultural similarity with *Homo erectus* areas in China and Indonesia.

(3) Its mid-way situation between the two major *Homo erectus* areas i.e., Western Asia-Africa, and S.E. Asia along a continuous chain of submontane terrain and Simons' studies suggest that 'at the end of the Miocene the region comprising East Africa, Arabia, and India formed a large and relatively continuous faunal zone that was largely forested' (Simons 1969).

The authorship of those Acheulian industries which date to 100,000 years ago can be construed from the following:

Brothwell (1963) had proposed that the area of East Africa, Arabia, Western Asia, and India was the 'cradle' of *Homo sapiens*, although such a hypothesis is based on almost no concrete data. However, it is probable that during the period between 100,000 and 50,000 years ago many populations within this area did evolve in the direction of modern man, the change being confined mainly to the skull, face, jaw and teeth. Shifts in social organization and also in social behaviour, probably occurred during this time, perhaps associated with an increasing frequency of hunting large herd mammals (Pilbeam 1972: 187-88).

Do the last four words explain the appearance of large bifaces along with the tools of Mousterian and Levalloisean facies in such late contexts in India which we now group with the real Lower Palaeolithic Acheulian?

III CONCLUSIONS

Keeping aside the morphological and technological parameters, which, however, are excercises in futility in view of the present position of the data, if we apply the occurrence in the earliest member in among the whole series of Quaternary deposits in a region as the criterion for determining the first Stone Age Culture or if we prefer to call it the Lower Palaeolithic, it will appear to have three clear contexts: (i) The detrital (secondary) laterite. (ii) The first river gravel. (iii) The first Sub-Himalayan river terrace. Although circumstances of their formation lead us to believe that all the three are Middle Pleistocene in age, what precise data do we have to club the industries contained in them as contemporaneous to one another? Can we vouch that the secondary laterite Lower Palaeolithic men, the first river gravel Lower Palaeolithic men, and the first Sub-Himalayan terrace Lower Palaeolithic men occupying three different ecozones lived at one and the same time? Did they all belong to one and the same fossil hominid species? The Sub-Himalayan lithic beginnings being so different from the peninsular area cast a big doubt on this matter. Apparently the mosaic of cultural pattern over the whole of the subcontinent at the very begining of the appearance of man can be brought out clearly only when our knowledge of the whole and complete range of Quaternary formations is precise. If work in any other region of the world is to provide a lead for us on these problems, it is Africa where neither the Lower Palaeolithic was confined to the Middle Pleistocene (it is now being traced from terminal Pliocene—Lake Rudolf evidences) nor was it authored by one single fossil hominid species, and very interestingly, like India, it did have two mutually exclusive lithic traits.

Therefore, at this matured stage of Indian Prehistoric research when it is paused for a dynamic multipronged proliferation our aims as regards the Lower Palaeolithic should be to search for the antecedents of the Acheulian on the one hand, which will mean documenting all earlier Quaternary deposits of the subcontinent, and assessing its temporal staggering vis-a-vis that of the Soanian on the other. For the latter, I am sure that like the Soanian evolving through three stages from Middle to Upper Pleistocene, the Acheulian too does the same. So far we have not looked into the culture from this angle. Instead we had always remained bogged down to the 'single or double' culture controversy.

Is the Lower Palaeolithic going to mean anything sans its implied antiquity and position in the lithic cultures hierarchy? Can't we have a Middle Palaeolithic Acheulian or an Upper Palaeolithic Acheulian if the dominant culture of the period is the Middle or the Upper Palaeolithic?

REFERENCES

Allchin, B. and K.T.M. Hegde. 1968. The background of Early Man in the Narmada valley, Gujarat: A preliminary report of the 1961 season's field work, *Journal of the M.S. University of Baroda* XII, (1).

Biswas, S. and D.C. Dassharma. 1981. A new species of *Stegodon* from the alluvial deposits of Narmada valley in peninsular India, *Field Conference on Neogene-Quaternary boundary, India, 1979, Proceedings*. Edited M.V.A. Sastry, *et al*, eds. Geological Survey of India, Calcutta.

Brothwell, D.R. 1963. Where and when did man become wise? *Discovery*, London.

Foote, Robert Bruce, 1866. On the occurrence of stone implements in the lateritic formations in various parts of Madras and North Arcot Districts, *Madras Journal of Literature and Science* 2, Reproduced in *Studies in Prehistory*, D. Sen and A.K. Ghosh, eds., Firma K.L. Mukhopadhyay, Calcutta.

Ghosh, R.N. 1977. Photogeological studies on ancient water regimes of Rajasthan rivers, *Ecology and Archaeology of Western India*, D.P. Agrawal and B.M. Pande, eds., Concept Publishing House, Delhi.

Ghosh, R.N. and S. Majumdar, 1981. Neogene/Quaternary sequence of Kasai Basin, West Bengal, India, *Field Confrence on Neogene-Quaternary boundary, India 1979, Proceedings*, M.V.A. Sastry, *et al.*, eds., Geological Survey of India, Calcutta.

Gupte, R.B., and Rajaguru S. N., 1971. Late Pleistocene geomorphological history of rivers of western Maharashtra, *Bulletin Volcanologique* XXXV (3)

Indian Archaeology, A Review. 1963-64, and 1964-65.

Joshi, R.V. 1980. Pleistocene and early Holocene stratigraphy environment and chronology in India. Paper presented at Seminar on Indian Prehistory. Nov. 29 to Dec. 3, Allahabad.

Krishnan, M. 1966. *Geology of India and Burma*, Higginbotham Ltd., Madras.

Misra, V.N., S.N. Rajaguru, D.P. Agrawal, P.K. Thomas, Zahid Husain, and P.S. Dutta. 1980. Prehistory and palaeoenvironment of Jayat, western Rajasthan, *Man and Environment* IV.

Misra, V.N., S.N. Rajaguru, D.R. Raju, Hema Raghavan and Claire Gaillard, 1982. Acheulian occupation and evolving landscape around Didwana in the Thar desert, India. *Man and Environment* VI.

Mohapatra, G.C. 1982. *The Stone Age cultures of Orissa*, Deccan College Research Institute, poona.

Mohapatra, G.C. 1976. Geo-tectonic developments, Sub-Himalayan lithic complex, and post-Siwalik sediments, *Union Internationale des Sciences Prehistoriques et Protohistoriques, Colloque VII*, Nice.

Mohapatra, G.C. 1981a. Acheulian discoveries in the Siwalik Frontal Range. *Current Anthropology* 22(4).

Mohapatra, G.C. 1981b. Environment and culture of Early Man in the valley of the rivers Chenab and Ravi, western Sub-Himalaya, *Union International de Ciencias Prehistoricas Protohistoricas, Commission* IX, Mexico City.

Niyogi, D. 1981, Geomorphology and morphotectonics of the Neogene-Quaternary sediments in India, *Field conference on Neogene-Quaternary boundary, India, 1979, Proceedings*. M.V.A. Sastry, *et al.*, eds.

Pilbeam, David. 1972. *The ascent of man*, Macmillan Co., New York.

Pitale, U.L. 1977, Quaternary climatic studies in Central India, *Ecology and Archaeology of Western India*. D.P. Agrawal and B.M. Pande, eds. Concept Publishing House, Delhi.

Roy, R.K. and B.K. Ghosh, 1981. Quaternary morpho-stratigraphy and neo-tectonic framework of the southern Ganga valley, *Field Conference on Neogene Qauternary boundary, India, 1979, Proceedings*, M.V.A. Sastry, *et al.*, eds., Geological Survey of India, Calcutta.

Simons, E.L. 1969. Late Miocene hominid from Fort Ternan, Kenya, *Nature 221*: 448.

Vaidhyanathan, R. 1954. Geomorphology of Cuddapah Basin, *Journal of Indian Geologists Association* 4.

Yokoyama, Takuo, 1981. Palaeomagnetic study of Tatrot and Pinjor formations, Upper Siwaliks, east of Chandigarh, North-West India, *Field Conference on Neogene-Quaternary boundary, India, 1979, Proceedings*. M.V.A. Sastry, *et al.*, eds., Geological Survey of India, Calcutta.

Middle Palaeolithic in India

K.V. SOUNDARARAJAN
Archaeological Survey of India,
New Delhi

ARCHAEOLOGICAL research on the prehistoric side, has sufficiently well established the soundness of the three-age system for the Quaternary in terms of human cultures. These were variously called Early, Middle and Late Stone Age, mostly in Africa, or Lower Middle and Upper Palaeolithic, mostly in Europe and West Asia, and in an earlier period of nonage in India, they were numerically designated Series I-IV, which was typoligically agreeable but chronologically and ecologically discordant with the three-age system and thus the Indian situation for the adoption of the former or latter system has yet been debated.

The Middle Palaeolithic or, more preferably, Middle Stone Age, by its very concept, is the period of continuance and transition from Early Stone Age towards Late Stone Age (or Lower Palaeolithic towards the Upper Palaeolithic). It is the full efflorescene of the Lower into a dynamic cultural motivation for the expanded activity range of Early man, but has not yet become the sedate, and sophisticated mental make-up of the primate blossoming into the *Homo Sapiens* which for the first time happens in the upper Palaeolithic or the end of the Middle Stone Age. The Middle thus is a continuing part of the early Stage, well within the Pleistocene, but ecologically not fully out of the woods, and bio-cranically still primitive. The Neanderthal *homo* of the digressive stem from the Lower Stone Age has still not yet been interlocked firmly with the *Homo Sapiens*. Typology is yet a useful media for identifying this stage, but technology is the back bone. Often in the development of tool outfit, it is comparative merit and the search for alternatives that is the base of the innovative skill. Mousterian culture is now diagnosed as the hallmark of the beginning of middle Stone Age with Neanderthaler as its human author.

The Indian system appears to be the microcosmic analogue to the Eurafrican, where the Mediterranian and North African tool industries and context are still moored to the European Acheulian—Tayacian—Levalloisean—Mousterian tool ranges and with a break between the Mousterian and the Upper Palaeolithic chatelperron—Aurignacian—Magdalenian sequence. In central and southern Africa, particularly the eastern belt from Ethiopia (including the most recent spectacular discoveries of the *homo* and his cultures in the Awash Valley there (J.E. Kelb *et al.* 1982) down to the Drakensburg mountain of South Africa, was located the ideal belt for the development of the Hominid stem and its Stone Age Cultures in the changing pluvial and inter pluvial climates relatable to the European Glacial and Inter-glacials. The Oldowan, the Stellenbosch, Fauresmith, Sangoan—and still pay sequence, in parts, in various zones there, inter-locking mainly the Early and Middle Stone Age tools in the Pleistocene are found to be the tool cultures between the Mindel-Riss great Interglacial and the Last glacial corresponding to the Kamasian and Gamblian pluvials of Africa.

A study of the physico-ecological provenance of Stone of Stone Age relics of both man and his handworks in Africa reveals that the eastern longitudinal belt along with the cost upto the line drawn from Libya to eastern part of South Africa, all along the Strikes of ranges of Ethiopia, Uganda, Kenya, Tanzania, Zambia-Mozambique and the Drakensberg mountains of South Africa mountains where the pre-hominid stems have been identified and where the early *homo* stages, as at Rudolf, Olduvai and Sterkfrontain, belong to a stage earlier than the second or great Inter glacial time-locus, were discovered. This is, again, where the Pre-Neanderthal hominid fossils themselves are seen in Africa. The

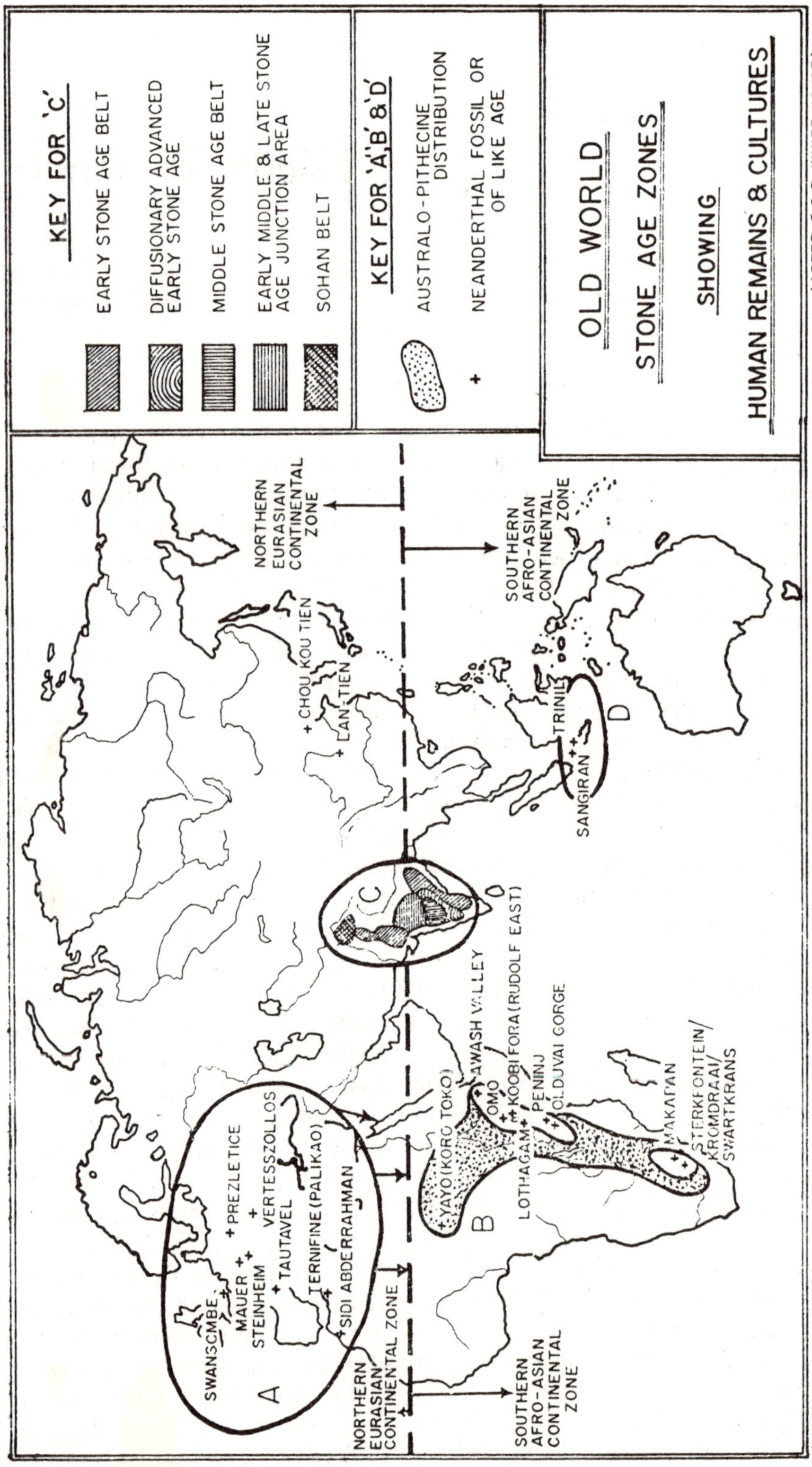
KEY FOR 'C'
EARLY STONE AGE BELT
DIFFUSIONARY ADVANCED EARLY STONE AGE
MIDDLE STONE AGE BELT
EARLY MIDDLE & LATE STONE AGE JUNCTION AREA
SOHAN BELT
KEY FOR 'A','B' & 'D'
AUSTRALO-PITHECINE DISTRIBUTION
NEANDERTHAL FOSSIL OR OF LIKE AGE
OLD WORLD
STONE AGE ZONES
SHOWING
HUMAN REMAINS & CULTURES
(AFTER D & R. WHITE HOUSE)
NORTHERN EURASIAN CONTINENTAL ZONE
SOUTHERN AFRO-ASIAN CONTINENTAL ZONE
A
B
C
D
SWANSCOMBE
MAUER
STEINHEIM
TAUTAVEL
PREZLETICE
VERTESSZOLLOS
TERNIFINE (PALIKAO)
SIDI ABDERRAHMAN
YAYO (KORO TOKO)
OMO
AWASH VALLEY
KOOBI FORA (RUDOLF EAST)
LOTHAGAM
PENINJ
OLDUVAI GORGE
MAKAPAN
STERKFONTEIN/
KROMDRAAI/
SWARTKRANS
CHOU KOU TIEN
LANTIEN
TRINIL
SANGIRAN

Fig. 1.

corresponding western part seems to have essentially manifested the continuance of the cultures and human species, taking the African Late Acheulian tool cultures as late as 50,000 B.C. in the sub-saharan site of Kalambo falls (J.D. Glarke 1965).

It is sometimes urged even in India, as Wainwright (1966) had done that the Late Acheulian hand axe industry of Lower Narmada may be datable upto the last interglacial and should truly belong to the 'upper Palaeolithic' or near adjacent stage culturally. Recent discoveries of rich Acheulian tools even in the west Sub-Himalayan Front Siwaliks in Hosiarpur District of Punjab (Mohapatra 1982) tend to show that this technology might have continued quite late in the quaternary sequence, though not necessarily upsetting any regional stratigraphical or cultural sequence. If we divide the Indian ocean area climatically, then we may think that eastern Africa, southern part of India and the east Indies including Java, may come under the sub-tropical belt, while the upper part of the Himalayan India would be in the sub-temperate and temperate belt and the Pleistocene ecology and culture sequence may have a great bearing on this. Further within India, from a geo-climatic or geo-environmental contexts, the Sahyadris on the west, the plateau in the middle, and piedmonts and the coastal belts to the east had seemingly their own contribution to the distribution as well as stages-of motivation of Stone Age life. Obviously, the faunal floral patterns had widely differed between lower south Indian, Deccan and mid Indian Vindhya Zones, and this should have a close relationship to the contemporary activities and aptitudes of hunting societies. We seem to find that from Orissa downward to the north of Tamil Nadu, an early Stone Age belt is identifiable wherein essentially two Stone-Age sequence is especially well defined, alternating with two wet and two dry phases, and culturally taking the tool range from proto-Acheulian to the post Acheulian flake and blade stage, whether at Kamarpal in Orissa or in Kurnool sites or in Chittor or at Attirampakkam. The so-called 'upper Palaeolithic' definitionally relatable to the European taxonomy—is seemingly found only in special pockets in two distinctive unmixed belts, one from Malwa to Mirzapur and Chotanagpur area of U.P. and another from Kurnool to Chittor belt of Andhra Pradesh and heretoo, the typology and contexts are limited to specific localities, both of the open station type and of the cave type in both the belts.[1] These are datable also from about 38,000 B.C. to 17,000 B.C. and so far as the early Stone Age is concerned, the time span is much larger from Middle-late Pleistocene with faunal assemblages continuously associated with this entire span, either reflecting contempraneity or as redeposits stratigraphically.

On the closer examination of the tool typology peneplanation of the area and correlations of the data (see Appendix), it is seen that the picture, as shown in Fig. 1, will have prevailed. The lowest south India (of lower Andhra and Tamil Nadu) and the Orissan-Vidhyan zones of lower Palaeolithic cultures would have been relatively earlier, and perhaps moved into Karnataka and the fringe of South Bihar respectively, where the Acheulian Industry tends to be more and more on flakes and advanced Acheulian stage generally forms the basal stage. The Middle Stone Age had entirely prevailed in northern part of Karnataka and Maharashtra, with a hiatus from early Stone Age and an upper Palaeolithic cave habitat-cum-open-air specialization is seen motivated only in the Vindhyan-Malwa belt, as in Patne or Bhimbetka, and lower Andhra belt (as in Kurnool-Chittor), and the late Stone Age Cultures thereafter are seen lingering in atavistic mesolithic stages upto the tribal cultural residue of the present day. This also leads to the hypothesis that the subsequent Neolithic revolution itself would have been caused by new stimuli on some specified locations under adventitious circumstances. Here again, Bellary (Sanganakallu, Tekkalakota, Bargur), Chittor belt turn out to be the Neolithic type zones for lower south, and Chotanagpur and Southern U.P. in the trans Vindhyan zone, for central India. In the north west, similarly, the Gujarat Stone Age ends virtually with Middle Stone Age after atavistic trends in the Mesolithic, triggers the Neolithic activity as at Bagor. It is without any upper Palaeolithic cultural stage as such. The Indo-Gangetic alluvial divide, in the Pleistocene was totally unfit for any kind of activity, being marshly and lagooned, and the sub-Himalayan Sohan which had prevailed in two zones on the Indian and Pakistani tracts could have contacts only of the Middle Palaeolithic Acheulian as may have reached from Rajasthan there in various stages—both early and very late—depending upon the morphological contact zones of diffusion feasible for this.

With such a situation, the regional study of the faunal, floral, climatic and raw material source components which together yielded firm zonations of early Palaeolithic becomes an imperative exercise through multi-disciplinary teams, in preference to a typological

1. Belan valley, Bhimbetka, Patne, Mucchantla, Chantamanu cave and sites near Renigunta.

studies.

In Africa, the Mousterian is generally well preceding the Aterian and is datable to 43,000 B.C. (and in Riss-Wurm Interglacial or European sequence) as from Libya, while in southern Africa, the Fauresmith and Sangaon take the place of Middle Stone Age, after Stellenbosch series. They are datable to 38,000 B.C. approximately. All of them belong to Gamblian Pluvial.

The Middle Stone Age in India is at present an adjunct and successor to the Acheuleo-Levalloisean series, but it displays progressive technical features only where the raw material is either of softer categories like chert/agate/jasper. It does not occur in areas where the lower Palaeolithic is not present, as it has no tradition and habitational familiarity there. It is not necessarily succeeded by any upper Palaeolithic in all the areas but rather into discrete Late Stone Microlithic traditions.

On the whole, the present picture legitimately underscore the fact that, for Indian Stone Age sequence, the African system of Early, Middle and Late Stone Age categories is more applicable, but with the qualification that what is technologically a true upper Palaeolithic in the European connotation may be highlighted only in very limited zones, as in M.P., U.P. and Bihar (all on the Vindhyan fringes on either sides) and in the Kurnool—Chittor zone of lower southern peninsula—which form, thus, unique ecological tracts, whose diffusionary relationship with the rest of the Stone Age life around, especially their links with the Middle Stone Age, requires to be carefully analysed by intensive field studies in team work. An automatic assumption of an 'upper Palaeolithic' in India, as a counterpart to the European system appears to be negated on present evidence. This is all more emphasized by the fact that in the lower south India, as in the Teris (hardened coastal dunes)—taken to be comparable to the Atlantean phase of the Monasterian sea level changes of the Mediterranean, and datable to *circa* 4,000 B.C.—we have fine feather-edgeflake points—in the Solutrean tradition—though on rather miminutive sizes and the whole activity was littoral, or oasis-based and only of the later Mesolithic Stage. As long as the Middle Stone Age counter parts, it would be of dubious importance to pose it an 'upper Palaeolithic stage, as such, in the Late Pleistocene of India, merely on the basis of Blade and Burin typology. Its functional ecological context is yet obscure. No engraved bones or even Mesolithic art has yet been identified. Let us hope the climato-cultural link studies, together with more intensive search for authentic habitat would advance our knowledge or what happened at the beginning and end of the Middle Stone Age of India.

APPENDIX

Comparative sequence of the Early & Middle Stone Cultures of Southern India

ORISSA		
Kamarpal		**Culture sequence**
General climate & Stratification	Dry (red weathered silt)	II (Late Acheulian flakes)
	Wet (smaller gravel)	I Stone Age (Acheulian)
	Dry (Silt)	Silt or alluvium
	Wet (sheet gravel)	Boulder Conglomerate clay
	Dry (claey layer)	Calcareous bed
	Wet (primary laterite)	
ANDHRA PRADESH		**Late Stone Age at other sites**
(Central area)		III (Blade and Burin in cave site of Muchantla Chantamanu)
	Fine gravel non-lateritic	Middle Palaeolithic

	Fine gravel and clay		Advanced Handaxe and Levellois flakes
	Coarse river gravel		End of Handaxe Culture I
	Coastal laterite		No tools
(Southern area) Chittoor (Reniguntal)	Blade & Burin (unmixed) III		
	Middle Stone Age Factory *Site III* Red silt (Wet Phase) Dry Phase Handaxe—Chopper (rolled in pebbly cemented gravel) I Laterite (Wet phase)		2 cycles of deposition. Older deposits only occasionally visible in the area. Early Stone Age tools only from loose gravels. No stratigraphic evidence of the total sequence.
Cuddaph	Close of Early Stone Age Levallois technique flakes Handaxes by Vaal technique Handaxes and cleavers on flakes		Similar to Karnataka sequence (Old Stone Age only represented)
TAMIL NADU			
	Terrace	**Penenplanation**	**Cultures**
(Courtalayar Terrace sequence and Regional Penenplanational sequence)	T_8 Middle Stone Age & Late Acheulian	17 m	Middle Palaeolithic fiake. scraper, point-II (mixed)
	T_{20} Late Acheulian & Flakes	30 m	
	T_{60} Late Acheulian (Ramakrishnapuram)	45 m	Early Palaeolithic I
	T_{100}		(Patination typology of Abbevilleo-Acheulian stages at Vadamadurai) (Dominand handaxecleaver of Bifacial Vaal techniques, scrapers, and points. Levallois technique)
		Neolithic	
KARNATAKA	**Late Stone Age**	**Pre-neolithic**	
Malaprabha Ghataprabha rivers	Middle Stone Age open sites (Salvadgi)	II	Middle Stone Age only in open sites and rare ? (True points absent)
Khyad	Advanced Acheulian Cleavers on flakes	I	
	Acheulian		Mainly *two* stages of Stone Age represented within the Pleistocene,

MAHARASHTRA		
Nevasa	Mostly of Middle Stone Age Silt *2nd gravel*	(Hathi well site, Nevasa)
	Silt (Brownish-thick) Gravel (Cemented) I	Middle Stone Age (Material change)
	(No direct stratigraphic succession of I & II)	Points—15.7 %—Tangid also 26 % Scrapers—57.3 %—side, end, below and Enticulate Scrapers Borers—24.9 % Scraper-cum-borer—2.1 % (True Aurignacian type nosed end scrapers absent)

Upper Palaeolithic Culture in India

M.L.K. MURTY
Deccan College, Pune

UPPER Palaeolithic culture has a wide distribution in Europe and is characterized by a diversity of regional sub-cultural phases, each displaying its own peculiarities. The chief diagnostic features of the Upper Palaeolithic, for the sake of definition are: (1) lithic blade tool technology (though blade artifacts occur in Mousterian and pre-Mousterian contexts), (2) bone tool technology, (3) mobile and parietal art, (4) Late/Terminal Pleistocene age, and (5) the humankind extant during this cultural phase belonged to *Homo sapiens* sapiens, which is in no way different from us.

It was earlier thought that there was not much evidence for distinguishing Upper Palaeolithic in the Indian Stone Age sequence. Recent discoveries of artifact assemblages based on blade tool technology, occurring in post-Middle Stone Age (synonymous with the Middle Palaeolithic) and pre-Late Stone Age (Mesolithic) contexts in different parts of India, the bone tools obtained from the Kurnool caves, the faunal associations at some sites and the available radiocarbon dates favour the recognition of Upper Palaeolithic also in the Indian sequence.

Sporadic discoveries of blade artifacts and assemblages, some from a stratified sequence, were made as early as the last part of the last century (to cite an instance see Brown 1889: 134-39). In fact Foote (1884a: 27-34, 1884b: 200-208, 1885: 227-35) noted that the bone implements recovered (by him and his son Henry Bruce Foote) from excavations in the Billa Surgam caves, which became popular as Kurnool caves (Kurnool District, Andhra Pradesh), included forms comparable to the Magdalenian types. The credit goes to Cammiade and Burkitt (1930: 327-39), who, by their pioneering studies of stratified riverine sequences (also in the Kurnool district) on the southeast coast, proposed for the first time, a four-fold lithic sequence in a stratigraphic, palaeoclimatological and technological context. They termed these lithic industries Series I-IV, which are synonymous with Lower, Middle and Upper Palaeolithic, and Mesolithic, respectively. Gordon (1950: 65) evaluated the stratified evidence recorded thus far by (1) Carlyle's excavations of Marhana (Morhana) Pahar cave shelter in Madhya Pradesh in 1880-81 (cited in Brown 1881), (2) Cammiade and Burkitt (1930) on the southeast coast of India, and (3) Todd (1939: 257-72) from Kandivili and Marve near Bombay, and observed that "... in India as elsewhere, there was a late Upper Palaeolithic blade and burin industry corresponding to Late Magdalenian, followed in succession by larger less geometric and smaller more geometric microliths". Soundara Rajan (1952: 71) who brought to light interesting evidence on the Stone Age succession at Giddalur (Kurnool district) compared the assemblage from Giddalur II to Series III of Cammiade and Burkitt, called it Upper Palaeolithic, and what is more, he saw Epipalaeolithic features in the quartz industry at the same site. And Lal (1958: 37) while discussing the antiquity of the Birbhanpur industry (West Bengal) stated that the Birbhanpur microlithic industry would appear to claim for itself a very early position-in fact at the very emergence of the microlithic from the proceeding blade and burin industry.

Among the noteworthy discoveries that gave a stimulus for research in this direction at the turn of the second half of this century, mention should be made of (1) the assemblage with Upper Palaeolithic traits brought to light by Sankalia (1956: 35-53) from the river Pravara (Maharashtra); (2) discoveries of Sharma in the Belan valley, Uttar Pradesh (1955-56); (3) discoveries of Soundara Rajan (1968) from Nagarjunakonda (Andhra Pradesh); (4) discoveries of Isaac (1960) in the

Kurnool district (Andhra Pradesh), confirming the findings of Cammiade and Burkitt; (5) Sen (IAR 1960-61: 60) and Ghosh (1961) on the river Banjer in Mandla district (Bihar); and (6) the blade and burin industry from Salvadgi in Bijapur district (Karnataka) described by Seshadri (1962). Subsequent findings made around this time from sites around Renigunta in Chittoor district, Andhra Pradesh (Murty 1966) and in Salvadgi and Meralbhavi (Bijapur and Gulbarga districts, Karnataka) Paddayya (1968) widened the scope for a fresh evaluation of the data in a pan-Indian context.

There is now a general consensus among serious researchers involved in Indian Stone Age studies that the discoveries being made especially since the last two decades warrant a provision for the Upper Palaeolithic in the Indian sequence (see comments of Sankalia on the discussion on terminology in Agrawal and Ghosh 1973: 509; Sankalia 1974: 207-30; Allchin and Allchin 1982).

The Lithic Industries

The diagnostic attribute of the industries under discussion is the blade tool technology; nevertheless, a variety of artifact types made on flake, flake-blade and nucleus form an important element. In the flake tool variants can in fact be seen the persistence of Middle Palaeolithic technological traditions. This is a common feature even in the classical Upper Palaeolithic cultures of France, as for example the Perigordian, which is strongly marked by Mousterian features in its numerous and varied scrapers, Mousterian points, Levallois flakes and Mousterian style denticulates (Bordes 1968: 147). Similarly, in a recent review of the Soviet Central Asian Palaeolithic Ranov and Davis (1979) have drawn attention to the fact that most of the technological characteristics of the Upper Palaeolithic in Soviet Central Asia were already present in the developed Mousterian and that many Mousterian elements like points, denticulates, side scrapers and Levallois technique remain in the Upper Palaeolithic. Coming to the Indian context, in the unexploited cores (abandoned after primary dressing because of faulty nature of raw material) at sites on the southeast coast, one can notice that the prismatic core technique for the production of blade artifacts in the Upper Palaeolithic is a developed version of the prepared core technique. In so far as blades are concerned, they do occur in varying sizes and proportions in the Acheulian and Middle Palaeolithic as at Gudiyam rockshelter site (*IAR* 1962-63, 63-64) in Tamil Nadu and Bhimbetka (Misra 1982: 7-13) in Madhya Pradesh; all the same, their representation can be considered relatively low, and what is more, the methods of delicate retouch and blunting to finish blade blanks into shaped tools as a technocultural attribute appear only in the Upper Palaeolithic.

On the basis of typo-technological criterion, the Upper Palaeolithic assemblages under discussion can be tentatively divided into three major groups: (1) flake-blade group, (2) blade tool group, and (3) blade and burin group. (Fig. 1 and Tables 1-3). It should be pointed out at the outset that they neither represent a succession of lithic phases nor indicate a relative antiquity in that order: they are only suggestive of regional elaboration of blade tool based complexes in association with the flake tool element during post-Middle Palaeolithic times.

Flake-Blade Group

These display a crude stage of blade technology as they are characterized by thick and broad, almost flake like blades but with parallel negative scars on the dorsal surfaces. Scrapers, points and borers made mostly on flake and flake-blade are the common types with scraper being the predominant element. The other forms are blades, knives, burins and small choppers. Assemblages of the flake-blade facies are well known from about 15 open-air river valley sites in the Singhbhum district of Bihar (Ghosh 1970: 1-60). Details of this group as given by their discoveries are given in Table 1.

Blade Tool Group (Figs. 1 and Pl. II)

A striking feature of this group is regularization of blade tool technology since there is a significant increase in the occurrence of standardised blades and retouched blade tools. These comprise large to small size blades; backed blade tools; and scrapers, points, awls and burins on flake-blade, flake and blade. Blade tool industries have a wide geographical distribution and are known from several open air sites in secondary as well as primary contexts in the states of Karnataka, Maharashtra, and Uttar Pradesh and both open-air and cave sites in Andhra Pradesh and Madhya Pradesh. The best known evidence is from Karnataka (Paddayya 1970), Andhra Pradesh (Murty and Thimma Reddy 1976: 214-26) and Maharashtra (Joshi and Pappu 1979: 86-91). A basic homogenity with some inter-site artifact variability can be seen in this complex in Maharashtra, Karnataka and Telangana (Andhra Pradesh) zones where crypto-crystalline rocks like

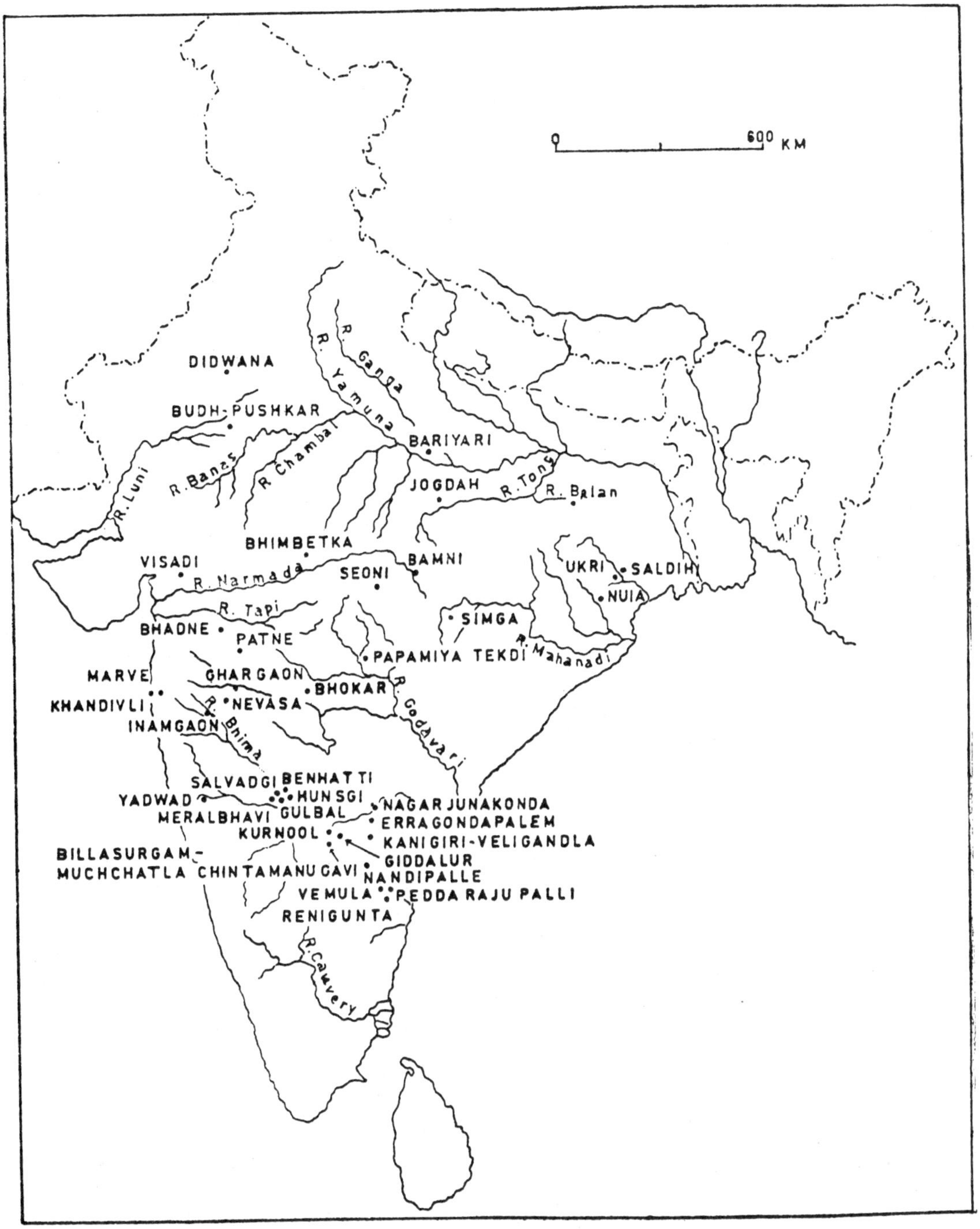
0
600 KM
DIDWANA
BUDH-PUSHKAR
R. Ganga
R. Yamuna
R. Chambal
R. Banas
R. Luni
BARIYARI
JOGDAH
R. Tons
R. Balan
BHIMBETKA
VISADI
R. Narmada
SEONI
BAMNI
UKRI
SALDIH
NUIA
R. Tapi
SIMGA
R. Mahanadi
BHADNE
PATNE
PAPAMIYA TEKDI
MARVE
GHARGAON
BHOKAR
KHANDIVLI
R. Bhima
NEVASA
R. Godavari
INAMGAON
SALVADGI
BENHATTI
HUNSGI
YADWAD
NAGARJUNAKONDA
MERALBHAVI
GULBAL
ERRAGONDAPALEM
KURNOOL
KANIGIRI-VELIGANDLA
BILLASURGAM-
MUCHCHATLA
CHINTAMANU GAVI
GIDDALUR
NANDIPALLE
VEMULA
PEDDA RAJU PALLI
RENIGUNTA
R. Cauvery

Fig. 2.

chert, jasper and chalcedony formed the chief raw materials.

Evidence from Kurnool caves points out that chert and jasper nucleii were quarried from outside from the veins in banded limestones, brought to the cave and subjected to fire treatment for production of artifacts. Here, a horseshoe shaped fireplace measuring 1.6 m in length and 0.70 m interior breadth, occurring in the Upper Palaeolithic levels (1.5 m to 1.8 m) yielded nucleii of green and chocolate coloured chert, primary flakes on chert showing evidence of fire-treatment, as well as burnt bone fragments which are completely lithified due to long association with carbonate rich cave sediments. This fireplace apparently was used for roasting meat and also for fire treatment of chert nodules for production of artifacts.

Details of the blade tool group as furnished by their discoverers are given in Table 2.

Blade and Burin Group (Figs. 4 and 5)

These are marked by a distinctive blade, backed blade and burin elements and finished forms on flake, flake-blade and nucleii also form an important component. The artifact types are large to small sized blades; backed blade tools (especially curved back and straight back points); scrapers (end, side, keeled, notched etc.); points (simple flake points recalling Levallois points and shouldered, tanged, unifacial and bifacial points). burins; awls; and small choppers. Several burnt nodules of quartzite and primary flakes with burnt external surfaces recovered from Upper Palaeolithic occurrences at Renigunta and Pedda Raju Palli (Andhra Pradesh) indicate that raw materials were fire treated for the production of artifacts. These two sites have also yielded bored stones, grindstones and pitted anvils. It is important to focus attention on the fact that a distinctive facies of the blade and burin complex with some intersite variation in the artifact forms and predominantly based on fine grained quartzite and lydianite is known from extensive occupation scatters from riverine ecotones of the Eastern Hill ranges. The most well known sites are situated in the Swarnamukhi, Gunjana, Paleru and Gundlakamma valleys. Similarly the assemblages from Patne in the central Tapti basin (Maharashtra) and Simga in the Mahanadi valley (Madhya Pradesh) (Pandey 1982), based on cryptocrystalline rocks, are suggestive of another variant. Owing to the nature of raw material, the latter show low mean values in length, breadth and thickness when compared to the quartzite forms on the south-east coast. An (Upper Palaeolithic) assemblage recovered by Banerjee *et al.* (*IAR* 1968-69) from trial digs at Battalavallam (Satyavedu Taluq, Chittor district, Andhra Pradesh) which reveals a transitional phase between the Middle Stone Age and Late Stone Age is suggestive of the southern extension of this facies. Another neteworthy feature that can be seen in the Pedda Raju Palli, Patne IID and Chopani Mando facies in the Belan valley is an increasing tendency towards microlithisation. They may well represent the Indian Epi-Palaeolithic. Details of this group as provided by their discoverers are given in Table 3.

Bone Tool Industry (Fig. 6)

As referred to earlier, excavations by Foote in the Billa Surgum caves yielded bone implements in association with Late Pleistocene fauna (Lydekker 1886: 22-58). The bone artifactual remains consisted of 1700 specimens of worked and cut bones, of which 200 were implements. These implements as described by Foote were awls, barbed and unbarbed arrowheads, daggers, scraper-knives, scrapers, chisels, gouge, wedges, axeheads and sockets. Recent excavations of a cave site (Murty 1974: 196-230) known as Muchchatla Chintamanu Gavi, about 6 km south-east of Bill Surgam not only yielded bone tools (confirming Foote's findings) but also blade artifacts and remains of Late Pleistocene fauna (Murty 1975: 132-38). The bone tools from this cave comprise scrapers, perforators, chisels, shouldered points, spatulae, worked bones, bone blanks, broken and cut bones and splinters—the finished forms amounting to 7.60%. The perforators, some of them made on bone blanks removed from ungulate phalanges have fire hardened tips. The bone artifacts from this cave as a whole are crude but since this cave represents a transitory encampment, one cannot expect finished forms. Excavations which are in progress in the adjoining long term campsite are likely to yield the range of finished types.

Chronology

The stratified evidence of the Upper Palaeolithic at sites in the Singhbhum district, the Belan valley, central Indian cave sites, Patne and in the river valley sites in the Kurnool district, indicate that they postdate the Middle Palaeolithic and predate the Mesolithic. At Renigunta Upper Palaeolithic occurrences are found on the ancient alluvium preceding the quartz microlithic assemblages.

Geomorphological investigations conducted by

Rajaguru in northern Deccan have shown that the stratigraphic units of the ancient alluvium which are associated with the Middle Palaeolithic of the Godavari, the Krishna and the Bhima river systems belong to an initial phase of the aggradation; and the known radiocarbon dates for this phase suggest that the Middle Palaeolithic in the northern Deccan is older than 40,000 B.P. and its upper limit cannot be later than 20,000 B.P. A radiocarbon date from Nandipalle, a site on the south-east coast, for the silt/clay horizon overlying the Middle Palaeolithic gravel is suggestive that the Middle Palaeolithic also on the south-east coast predates *circa* 23,000 B.P. Coming back to the river systems in the northern Deccan, the sediments that are either directly associated with the Upper Palaeolithic as at Inamgaon or that display comparable lithological and geomorphological features as at Ghargaon and Asla, belong to the later phases of that aggradation (referred to above), the sediments of the initial phases of which are associated with the Middle Palaeolithic. Radiocarbon dates of these deposits from Inamgaon, Ghargaon and Asla ascribe this phase associated with the Upper Palaeolithic to *circa* 20,000 B.P. to 10,000 B.P. Radiocarbon dated from the Belan valley (Varma and Pal, n.d.), Patne (Sali 1980), Didwana (Misra : personal communication) and the TL date for the Upper Palaeolithic fireplace in the Kurnool caves (Nambi and Murty 1981 : 945-46) indicate a time range of *circa* 30,000 B.P. to 10,000 B.P. Two more recent radiocarbon dates for ostrich eggshells for the Upper Palaeolithic horizon (succeeding the Middle Palaeolithic and preceding the Mesolithic) at Chandresal (Kota district, Rajasthan) on the river Chandoli which are in the range of *circa* 36,000 B.P. to 38,000 B.P., (Wakankar: personal communication) are suggestive of an earlier date for the Upper Palaeolithic, in some regions.

Palaeoecology

Observations on the possible types of Late/Terminal Pleistocene ecosystems can be made for some regions like the Deccan, which have yielded fossil fauna indicating the distribution of animal life. The Kurnool cave fauna comprises several species belonging to the orders Primates, Carnivora, Insectivors, Chiroptera, Rodentia, Perrisodactyla, Artiodactyla, Crocodilia etc. (Lydekker 1886; Murty 1975). Some of these species, especially those belonging to the orders Perrisodactyla and Artiodactyla which live in herds, indicate, being their favouted habitats, a savannah and grassland country. The faunal remains recovered from the Ghod valley from alluvial fills ascribed to *circa* 20,000 B.P. (Kajale *et al.* 1976: 122-32) include *Hexaprotodon Palaeindicus*, *Equus namadicus*, *Elephas* sp., *Bos* sp., *Bubalus* sp. and *Cervus* sp. What is interesting is the evidence pointing to the presence of rhinoceros (*Rhinoceros karnuliensis*) in the Kurnool cave areas and hippopotamus (*Hexaprotodon* sp.) in the Ghod valley zones, which, today, represent typical semi-arid environments with rainfall less than 750 mm. There is yet another but indirect evidence from which it can be conjectured that rich faunal life also existed on the hill ranges around Renigunta. This is the reference to the existence of elephants in the Mamandur forest (close to Renigunta) in 17th A.D. made by Baptist Travernier, a French traveller, in his diary dated 27th August 1652. If these hill ranges provided favourable habitats for elephants in 17th Century A.D., which are now confined to the reserved forests in the adjoining Mysore plateaux, it is likely that their habitation range could have extended into the forested ranges of Eastern Hills during early Holocene and Pleistocene times. The fossil fauna associated with the Upper palaeolithic horizon in the Belan valley are also rich and comprise cattle, antilope, sheep/goat, hippopotamus and elephant.

Whatever be the climatic types, the forest formations must have been extensive with ever green, deciduous, woodland, savannah woodland and thorny thicket zones in different parts of peninsular India and provided ideal niches in varied topographical settings with plentiful game, avifauna and aquatic fauna for these Late/Terminal Pleistocene hunter-gatherers.

Art

Excepting a bone figurine from the Belan valley and fragments of ostrich egg shell with engravings in a criss-cross pattern from Patne, no other objects indicating *mobile* art have as yet come to light.

Numerous examples of *parietal* art ranging from the Stone Age to historical times are known from the central Indian cave sites and rockshelters (Wakankar and Brooks 1976; Mathpal 1978). Though there is no dispute about the Mesolithic age of some of the paintings, it is quite likely, as Wakankar has shown, that some of the early phases of paintings belong to the Upper Palaeolithic.

Conclusions

The Upper Palaeolithic lithic assemblages in India

can be tentatively grouped on the basis of typo-technological criterion into flake-blade, blade tool and blade and burin groups. These only suggest regional variations in patterning of blade tool complexes and do not indicate any subcultural sequential developments. The evidence from the Kurnool cave sites indicates the possibility that bone-tool technology might have been supplementary to the lithic in different regions, but the non-availability of bone artifactual and other organic remains at most of the open-air sites could be due to unfavourable conditions for preservation in open air settings.

The distribution of Upper Palaeolithic sites in different areas indicates that habitats as varied as desert areas, forested, hilly and cave regions, and riverine zones in the plateau country were inhabited by these hunter gatherers.

Table 1. Flake-blade Industry

STATE, District, Site(s)	*Mode of occurrence/features*
ASSAM. Garo Hill, Selbalgiri and Watri Abri.	Surface sites on the terrace of Rongram river. Flake and blade assemblage with a high frequency of blade-flakes at Watri Abri.
BIHAR. Palmau, Prattappur and Marvania (Sitaram Roy *et al.* 1959-60: 12 & 14, VIIB).	Surface sites in the north Koel valley. Upper Palaeolithic bladės.
BIHAR. Palmau, Dhekula. *IAR* (1965-66: 8).	Flake-blade assemblage in a stratigraphical context. Scrapers, points, blades, knives, burins, awls, cores and waste flakes. Porcilinite rock
BIHAR. Singhbhum. Fifteen sites in the Chandil, Sini, Ghatsila and Jamda areas. The sites of Saldih, Ukri and Nuia are shown in Fig. 1 (Ghosh 1970: 1-68).	In the upper clay deposits of the strarified river sections of the Subarnarekha (Chandil, Ghatsila and Sini areas) and the Sanjay (Sini area) valleys, succeeding a flake industry (Middle Palaeolithic). Flake-blade industry: choppers (11.91%), scrapers (53.32%), points (11.91%), blades (9.05%), knives (1.91%), borers (1.43%), burins (0.95%) and cores (9.52%). Agate, Jasper and other siliceous rocks.

Table 2. Blade-tool Industry

STATE, District, Site(s)	*Mode of occurrence/features*
ANDHRA PRADESH. Cuddapah, Vemula. (Reddy 1970: 227-34).	Surficial occurrence. Tools on flake and flake-blades, predominantly scraper variants, simple and retouched blades, a few tools with burin edge, flakes and prismatic and flake cores, Chert and chalcedony.
ANDHRA PRADESH. Kurnool, Betamcherla., (Murty and Reddy 1976).	Open-air findspots in the cave areas. Scrapers (7.33%), chisels on nodules (3.33%), perforators (0.70%), burins (2.00%), flakes (28.66%), blades (34.66%), nodules (10.66%), cores (9.33%) and chips (3.33%). Chert, quartzite, limestone and sandstone.

STATE, District, Site(s)	*Mode of occurrence/features*
ANDHRA PRADESH. Kurnool. Muchchatla Chintamanu Gavi, a cave site near Betamcharla. (Murty 1974: 196-230).	In stratified cave sediments along with a bone tool industry and Late Pleistocene fauna. Flakes (26.00%), blades (41.35%), cores (5.45%) and chips (27.20%). Lime-stone, cherty lime-stone and compact shale.
KARNATAKA. Bijapur and Gulbarga. Salvadgi, Meralbhavi, Gulbal, Benhatti and Hunsgi. (Paddayya 1970: 165-90).	Workshop sites on surface; at Salvadgi, the tools occur up to a depth of 60 cm in a matrix of black sticky clay. The artifact forms at Salvadgi and Meralbhavi comprise: finished tools—retouched blade tools (51.52%), backed blades (3.84%), burins (8.39%), simple points (14.12%), tanged points (2.29%), borers (6.11%); misc. types (13.73%) and simple artifacts—blades (62.02%), blade sections (15.89%), core flakes (6.91%), core rejuvenation flakes (3.16%) fluted cores (9.48%), flakes (0.53%) and rejects (1.61%). Chert.
KARNATAKA. Belgaum, Yadwad. (Pappu 1971-72: 37).	Surficial occurrence. Scrapers on flakes and blades, points, simple blades, a few backed blades, flakes, flake and blade cores. Chert.
MADHYA PRADESH. Mandla. Bamni. (Sen 1960-61: 60; Ghosh 1961: 209-15).	In a stratified context on the river Banjer, a tributary of the Narmada, preceding the Mesolithic. Predominantly scrapers, points and burins. Jasper, chert and flint.
MADHYA PRADESH. Raisen. Cave IIIF-23, Bhimbetka (Misra, Mathpal and Nagar: 1977).	In a stratified sequence ranging from Acheulian to Mesolithic succeeding Middle Palaeolithic and preceding Mesolithic. Scrapers (especially end scrapers being most typical) blades, burins, points and denticulate tools. Chiefly quartzite.
MADHYA PRADESH, Seoni, Alonia, Chhapara and Bandol (all close to Seoni). (Joshi 1966; 276-80).	Associated with the gravel II of the upper Wainganga valley, succeeding Middle Palaeolithic (gravel I). Wainganga B industry: scrapers, points (including tanged and shouldered), borers, thick blade, tranchets, and burins. Chert of varied colours.
MAHARASHTRA. Ahmednagar. Nevasa. (Sankalia 1956: 35-52).	Surficial occurrence that may correspond to gravel III (younger than Middle Palaeolithic). Blades, flake tools and burins. Chalcedony.
MAHARASHTRA. Ahmednagar. Dhavalpuri. (Sankalia 1974: 207-30).	Surficial occurrence of workshop centres. Scrapers, flake-blades, blades, a few backed blades, burins, borers, cores and debitage. Chalcedony, chert and agate.

STATE, District, Site(s)	*Mode of occurrence/features*
MAHARASHTRA. Chanda. Papamiya-Tekdi. (Srinivasan 1960-61: 22-24).	On the surface of the topmost gravel (yielding Middle Palaeolithic) of the Jharput nala, a tributary of the Wardha. Blades, scrapers, burins and awls. Carnelian, agate, chalcedony, jasper and vein quartz.
MAHARASHTRA. Greater Bombay. Khandivli and Marve. (Todd 1939: 257-72).	A blade industry on the top of middle clay comprising cores, blades and scrapers. On the top of the overlying upper gravel occur factory floors of blade and burin industry. This is succeeded by a brown clay which had yielded a developed blade and burin industry comprising polyhedrons, angle and parrot beak burins, scrapers, borers and blades. A microlithic industry occurs on the surface.
MAHARASHTRA. Nanded. Bhokar. (Joshi & Pappu 1979: 86-91).	Workshop centres on hill slopes. Scrapers, burins, blades, borers, points and knives. Chert, jasper, chalcedony and agate.
MAHARASHTRA. Pune. Inamgaon. (Sali 1974: 147-60).	In a gravel horizon on the river Ghod. Scrapers, blades, points and fluted cores. Chalcedony.
RAJASTHAN. Ajmer. Budh Pushkar lake. (Allchin, Hegde and Goudie 1974: 358-68).	Factory floors on surface I and II of the sand dunes overlooking the lake. Blades, flakes, burins, scrapers, composite points and barbs, awls, blade cores, flake cores and blade core tablets. Quartz, quartzite, and crypto-crystalline silica.
UTTAR PRADESH. Allahabad. Belan Valley. (Sharma 1967).	In stratified sections of the river Belan and in three contexts. Layer 5: Middle Palaeolithic type scrapers (43.00%) and Upper Palaeolithic blades (55.00%); Layer 4: exclusively blade industry; and Layer 3; Upper Palaeolithic type blades (27.00%) and non-geometric microliths (73.00%). Chert and other fine grained materials, and quartzite artifacts (6.00%) are also present in Layer 5.
UTTAR PRADESH. Banda. Bariyari. (Sharma 1955-56: 4).	In stratified sections of Terrace 2 of a tributary of the river Yamuna. Flakes and flake tools of the Levallois techniques and tools on larger blades showing Upper Palaeolithic traits. Quartzite.
UTTAR PRADESH. Allahabad, Banda and Mirjapur. Near Jogdah bridge and Khajuri dam on the river Son. Amilia Kachchha Ka Nullah and Khajuri Nullah of the Belan river, and Lohand Nullah of the Seoti river. (Sharma *et al.* 1968-69: 33-34).	Near Jogdah bridge in the uncemented younger gravels preceded and succeeded respectively by Middle Palaeolithic and Mesolithic tool bearing clay deposits. On surface as well as in the river sections at other places. Large number of broad blades distinct from the Middle Palaeolithic and Mesolithic. Chert.

Table 3. Blade and Burin Industry

ANDHRA PRADESH. Chittoor. Sites around Renigunta. (Murty 1970: 106-28).	On the ancient aggradational plane of the river Rallakalava, a tributary of the Swarnamukhi. Occupation scatters on red sandy silt up to a depth of 20 cm. and on creamy-white concretionary patches on the eroded surfaces. Finished forms (13.20% of the total collections): Choppers (3.20% among the finished forms): scrapers (7.5%), burins (16.34%), backed blade variants (67.30%), awls (3.70%) and points (2.00%); blades (19.30% of the total collectoin); and other categories (67.50% of the total collection): primary flakes (2.65% among other categories), flakes (5.45%), core flakes (9.57%), cores (4.70%) and chips (59.20%). Chiefly fine grained quartzite, a few on lydianite.
ANDRHA PRADESH. Guntur. Nagarjunakonda. (Soundara Rajan 1958: 49-113).	Surficial occurrence. Blade tools, scrapers, burins, flake-blades and blades. Flinty chert and jaspery quartzite.
ANDHRA PRADESH. Kurnool. Giddaluru. Gundla Brahmesvaram and Nandi Kanama Pass, all close to each other. (Soundara Rajan 1958: 49-113).	On surface in gravel III succeeding Middle Palaeolithic or on the top of red clay covered by red sandy soil at Nandi-Kanama Pass. Slender blades with blunted backs, a few burins, planning tools and scrapers. Flint like material resembling lydianite.
ANDHRA PRADESH. Kurnool. Thirty-six sites in the Nallamali area and eight sites in the Erramalai area. (Isaac 1960).	On surface; in the middle somewhat cemented gravels in association with the Middle Palaeolithic and exclusively in the upper thin loose gravels. Points (28.00%), scrapers (24.90%), axe types (4.00%), borers (2.90%), burins (6.30%), picks (0.91%), crecentic forms (1.5%), trapezoidal (3.00%), flake-blades (3.80%), blades (22.40%), awls (0.78%) and cores (1.44%). Chert and other fine grained material.
ANDHRA PRADESH. Cuddapah. Nandipalle. (Reddy 1978: 32-40).	Surface occurrence in the Sagilore basin. Scrapers, burins, backed blades, knife edged tools, points, blades, blade-flakes, blade cores and flake cores. Midium coarse to fine grained quartzite.
ANDHRA PRADESH. Cuddapah. Vodikalu, Beelu and Rallachenu near Pedda Raju Palli (Rachapalli). (Raju 1981: 184-297).	Extensive occupation scatters along the bank of Gunjana river. Total collection of 14,825 specimens 10,596 (71.47%) from Vodikalu, 2,183 (14.72%) from Beelu and 2,046 (13.80%) from Rallachenu; finished forms in the total collection are 1,926 (12.99%); choppers (0.73% among the finished forms), scrapers (25.29%), denticulates (1.09%), notches (0.63%), knives (8.20%), burins (0.47%), points (4.62%) and backed blade variants (58.98%), debitage constitute 12,982 (86.90%) specimens of the total collection:

complete blades (23.13% of the debitage), broken blades (10.69%), flakes (14.61%), core rejuvenation flakes (0.99%), chips (40.03%), flake cores (2.85%), blade cores (4.79%), worked nodules (1.30%) and miscellaneous (1.59%). Other categories are 5 bored stones, 1 hammer stone and 1 anvil. Trial excavation of an exclusive Upper Palaeolithic horizon yielded the above types plus 84 pieces of grinding stones.

MAHARASHTRA. Jalgaon. Patne (Sali 1974:154-58).

In the central Tapti Basin, in a deposit of fluvial and aeolian origin of 1.5 m thickness succeeding the Middle Palaeolithic (Phase I) and preceding the Mesolithic (Phase III); the Upper Palaeolithic occurs in five layers (Phases IIA to IIE). Phase IIA: end and side scrapers on blades, backed blades, blades; Phase IIB: backed blades, burins, blades and borers; Phase IIC: relative increase in the number of blades and burins and beginning of reduction in the size of tools; Phase IID: above types continue with further reduction in the size, typical burins and engraved ostrich egg shell fragments; and Phase IIE: along with above artifact types, triangles and trapezes make their first appearance; significant increase in the representation of lunates, points and borers; and engraved ostrich egg shell fragments. Phase IIE is transitional between the Upper Palaeolithic and Mesolithic. Jasper in Phase IIA and IIB and chalcedony in others.

REFERENCES

Agrawal, D.P. and A. Ghosh (eds.), 1973. *Radiocarbon and Indian Archaeology*, Bombay.

Allchin, B. & R. 1982. *The Rise of Civilization in India and Pakistan*, Cambridge.

Allchin, B. & Goudie A. 1971. Dunes, aridity and early man in Gujarat, *Man*. 6.

Allchin, B., Hegde, K.T.M. and Goudie, A. 1972. Prehistory and Environmental change in Western India: A note on the Budh Pushkar Basin, *Man*. 7, 4.

Indian Archaeology—A Review; 1962-63.

Indian Archaeology—A Review; 1963-64.

Indian Archaeology—A Review; 1968-69.

Bordes, F. 1968. *The Old Stone Age*, London: World University Library.

Brown, J.A. 1889. On some highly specialized form of stone implements found in Asia, North Africa and Europe. *Journal of the Royal Anthropological Institute*, 28:134-139.

Cammiade, L.A. and M.C. Burkitt. 1930. Fresh light on the Stone Age in Southeast India, *Antiquity*, 4: 327-39.

Foote, R.B. 1884a. Rough notes on Billa Surgum and other caves in the Kurnool District. *Records of the Geological Survey of India*. 27: 2.

Foote, R.B. 1884b. Mr. H.B. Foote's work at the Billa Surgum Caves. *Records of the Geological Survey of India*, 27: 4.

——1885. Notes on the results of Mr. H.B. Foote's further excavations in the Billa Surgum Caves. *Records of the Geological Survey of India*, 28: 4.

Ghosh, A.K. 1961. A new lithic site in Mandla District. *The Eastern Anthropologist*, 14: 3: 209-15.

Indian Archaeology—A Review. 1965-66.

Ghosh, A.K. 1970. The Palaeolithic Cultures of Singhbhum. *Transactions of the American Philosophical Society*. 60: 1: 1-68.

Gordon, D.H. 1950. The stone industries of the Holocene in India and Pakistan. *Ancient India*. 6: 64-90.

Isaac, N. 1960. *The Stone Age Cultures of Kurnool*. Unpublished Ph.D. Thesis, Poona University.

Joshi, R.V. 1966. Middle Stone Age in India. *Atti del VI Congresso Internationale dell Scienze Preistoriche e Protostoriche*. V-VII: 276-80.

Joshi, R.V. and Pappu, R.S. 1979. Bhokar: An Upper Palaeolithic factory site from Central Godavari Basin, Maharashtra. *Man and Environment*, 3.

Kajale, M.D., Badam G.L. and Rajaguru, S.N. 1976. Late

Quaternary history of the Ghod Valley, Maharashtra. *Geophytology*. 6: 1: 122-32.

Lydekkar, R. 1886. The Fauna of Kurnool Caves. *Palaeontologia Indica Series*. X: 4: 2.

Lal, B.B. 1958. Birbhanpur, a microlithic site in the Damodar Valley, West Bengal. *Ancient India* 14: 4-48.

Mathpal, Y. 1978. *Prehistoric Rock Paintings of Bhimbetka*. Unpublished Ph.D. thesis, Poona University.

Misra, V.N. 1982. Evolution of the blade elements in the stone industries of Rockshelter II F-23, Bhimbetka. In R.K. Sharma (ed.), *Indian Archaeology New Perspectives* Delhi: Agam Kala Prakashan.

Misra, V.N., Mathpal, Y. and Nagar, M. 1977. *Bhimbetka—Prehistoric Man and his Art in Central India*. Exhibition Sovenir, Poona.

Murty, M.L.K. 1966. *Stone Age Cultures of Chittoor District Andhra Pradesh*. Unpublished Ph.D. Thesis, Poona University.

Murty, M.L.K. 1970. Blade and Burin and Late Stone Age industries around Renigunta, Chittoor District. *Indian Antiquary* 4: 1-4: 106-28.

Murty, M.L.K. 1974. A Late Pleistocene Cave site in Southern India. *Proceedings of the American Philosophical Society*, 118: 2.

Murty, M.L.K., 1975. Late Pleistocene Fauna of Kurnool Caves, South India, in A.T. Classon (ed.) *Archaeozological Studies* (Amsterdam).

Murty, M.L.K. and Thimma Reddy K. 1976. The significance of Lithic Finds in the cave areas of Kurnool. *Asian Perspectives*. 18: 2: 214-26.

Nambi, K.V.S. and Murty M.L.K. 1981. Thermoluminiscence dating of burnt clay from an Upper Palaeolithic occupation level at a cave site in south India. *Current Science*, L: 21.

Paddayya, K. 1968. *Pre and Protohistoric investigations in Shorapur Doab*. Ph.D. Thesis, Poona University.

Paddayya, K. 1970. The Blade Tool industry of Shorapur Doab. *Indian Antiquary*, 4: 1-4: 165-90.

Pandey, R.P. 1982. *Archaeology of the Upper Mahanadi Valley, Madhya Pradesh* (India). Ph.D. Thesis, Poona University.

Raju, D.R. 1981. *Early Settlement Patterns in Cuddapah District, Andhra Pradesh*, Ph. D. Thesis, Poona University.

Ranov, V.A. and Davis, R.S. 1979. Towards a new outline of the Soviet Central Asian Palaeolithic. *Current Anthropology*, 20: 2: 249-70.

Sankalia, H.D. 1956. Animal Fossils and Palaeolithic industries from the Pravara Basin at Nevasa, District Ahmednagar. *Ancient India*, 12: 35-53.

Sankalia, H.D. 1974. *Prehistory and Protohistory of India and Pakistan*. 207-30.

Sali, S.A. 1980. *Stone Age Culture sequence at Patne, District Jalgaon*, Maharashtra. Ph.D. Thesis, Poona University.

Sen, D. 1960-61. *In Indian Archaeology—A review*, 60.

Seshadri, M. 1962. Stone Age Tools from Salvadgi, Bijapur District Mysore State. *Journal of the University of Mysore*, 25: 2: 1-5.

Sharma, G.R. n.d. *Explorations in Allahabad, Mirjapur and Sahajahanpur District* (Unpublished report, 1967).

Sharma, G.R. 1955-56. *In Indian Archaeology—A Review*, 4, Pl. IB.

Sharma, G.R. *et al*. 1968-69. *In Indian Archaeology—A Review*, 33-34.

Soundara Rajan, K.V. 1952. Stone Ageindustries near Giddalur, District Kurnool. *Ancient India*, 8: 64-92.

Soundara Rajan, K.V. 1958. Studies in the Stone Age of Nagarjunakonda and its neighbourhood. *Ancient India*, 14: 49-113.

Todd, K.R.U. 1939. Palaeolithic Industries of Bombay. *Journal of Royal Anthropological Institute*, 79: 1: 257-72.

Varma, R.K. and Pal, J.N. n.d. The Upper Palaeolithic Culture of the Vindhyan region. Paper presented at the *International Conference on Indian Prehistory* (1980). Allahabad.

Wakankar, V.S. and Brooks, R.R.R. 1976. *Stone Age Paintings in India*, Bombay.

The Mesolithic Cultures of India

RADHAKANT VARMA
Allahabad University

THE mesolithic period as we know, coincides with the onset of the milder climatic conditions after the last glaciations' pluvials. It marks a definite stage not only in the history of the formation of earth but also in the history of mankind. With the swing towards the milder climate the face of the earth changed. Gone were the ice-sheets that once had covered the surface of the earth in glaciated zones. Likewise the big marshy lands started drying up. Such places were replaced by grassy lands, scrub jungles and dense forests in suitable ecological zones. The fertility of the soil increased many folds with the result new types of grasses ancestor to the most of the modern grains sprouted at suitable places. The change in the climate and flora were of very great significance. The fauna—specially animals were greatly affected and the law of natural selection for survival played a very vital role. The great mammoths and their cousins that roamed majestically on the surface of the earth during the Pleistocene gradually vanished and were replaced by smaller animals such as cattles, deer, goat etc., who were fleeter of foot and were better suited for the changed conditions.

Man the crown of all creations, too, could not remain a mute spectator. It was a question of his survival too. In order to make adjustments for survival, with the fast changing ecology he reacted mainly in two ways:

(i) by the modification of his extra corporeal equipment,
(ii) by the modification of his living pattern or economy.

Both the above modifications were gradual and covered a very long span of time. The evolution of microlithic tools and the fabrication of composite tools therefrom was the result of the gradual modification of his extra corporeal equipment. The fabrication and use of composite tools which achieved their greatest perfection during the mesolithic period may be regarded as a technological revolution. It completely changed the life pattern of the men. It is an acknowledged fact that the man changes his tools or adopts a new way of life in conditions of extreme necessity. The popular use of bow and arrow, the sickle made by inserting a number of tiny microliths in a slotted hardened wood or bone, tiny scrapers etc. may be regarded as of revolutionary importance. The changes in the equipment further indicate the growing complexity of human brain and the capacity of conceptual thought of the man. The new inventions in technology made his weapons more effective because they enabled man to catch the games that were previously beyond his reach. They added to the striking power and the speed of man who was physically weaker than most of the other animals.

In order to supplement his economy which during the pleistocene largely depended upon game animals, he searched and experimented with vegetal food resources which were in comparative abundance during the period. His life now did not depend solely on the results of hunting but it was supplemented by gathering wild roots, nuts, grains of wild grasses etc. There is a popular misconception among some scholars that the microlithic tools are best suited for hunting purposes only. In fact a variety of them such as blunted back blades, lunates etc. are better suited for procuring and processing vegetal food, scrapers for processing barks and hides, points, triangle, trapeze etc., for hunting. In short the microliths can be used in the variety of ways by simply changing their position at the time of hafting.

The economy based on multiple food resources opened up new vistas of development the dimensions of which cannot be grasped easily. The invention of pottery, the evolving settlement pattern of incipient villages of semi-sedentary groups, specialisation and evolving system of barter all this may be traced from relatively an economically stable society.

The Back-Drop

Till recently the very existance of the mesolithic cultures in India was in doldrums because of the paucity of stratigraphic evidence. It was represented by a few scattered assemblages of microlithic tools from the surface on low hillocks, rock-shelters, banks of *nalas* or hilly rivers, open fields in hilly terrain etc. The one common factor in the assemblages from the different places was that they were all made on microlithic flake/blade and had unmistakable evidence of retouch or use or both. Working on the analogy of researches made in Europe, the father of Indian Prehistory Robert Bruce Foote (1916) postulated a theory of 'Hiatus' or a yawning gulf between the palaeolithic and the neolithic for India also. In Europe this gulf was soon filled up with the excavation at Mas d'Azil in France in 1895 but in India it continued. The situation here was more complicated because the developmental sequence of cultures preceding the mesolithic and succeeding the mesolithic was also not clear. The stratigraphic position of Lower Palaeolithic became clear only after the publication of the Yale Cambridge report of de Terra and T.T. Paterson in 1939. The position of Middle Palaeolithic was still hazy. The picture emerged with the discovery and publication of Nevasa section on the Pravara river by Sankalia (1956) where he found three different lithic industries in a stratified deposit in 1956. He divided the three lithic industries in series I, II, III. Series I consisted of handaxes, cleavers and scrapers of the Lower Palaeolithic and were obtained from the 1st or the basal gravel. The tools of the Series II—blades-flakes-scrapers—were recovered from the middle gravel. The tools of series III—microliths were obtained from the surface. On account of their mid-position the tools of series II were called Middle Palaeolithic (Sankalia *et al.* 1960: 140-163). Though the stratigraphic position with regard to the Lower Palaeolithic and Middle Palaeolithic was now almost clear but still nothing was known about the Upper Palaeolithic which is the precursor of the Mesolithic elsewhere. The very existence of the Upper Palaeolithic in India was doubted. A section of the Indian Prehistorians thought that probably the Indian Stone Age did not have the same sequence as Europe. On the analogy of the African terminology Subbarao proposed that the Lower and the Middle Palaeolithic should be known as Early Stone Age respectively and the Mesolithic period should be called Late Stone Age (Subbarao 1958: 39-40). It was also supposed that the microlithic Industries of the Mesolithic might have developed from the Levalloisian tradition of the Middle Stone Age. The suggestion of Subbarao though was accepted as a working hypothesis yet a large number of scholars pleaded against it (Misra, 1962: 113-124). Their disagreement was based on the fact that though stratigraphic evidence for Upper Palaeolithic industries was lacking, tools similar to those had been reported from time to time (Cammiade and Burkitt, 1930: 327-339; Isaac. 1960).

The entire controversy was resolved with the discovery of the Belan Section and its reporting in the International Symposium on Carbon 14 and Indian Archaeology organised by the TIFR in 1971 at Bombay.

In the meantime similar industries were reported from besides Allahabad and Mirzapur (Varma, 1970: 30), Chittoor district (Murty 1968: 83-101), Shorapur Doab in Gulbarga, district Mysore (Paddayya 1968), Singhbhum near Dhakulia, district Palamau, Bihar (Ghosh 1965) etc.

Genesis of the Microlithic Industries of the Mesolithic

When the position of the Upper Palaeolithic was not clear the scholars were inclined to think that after the Middle Palaeolithic the evolution of Stone Age Cultures might have followed the African pattern where the microlithic industries developed not from the Upper Palaeolithic but the Levalloisian itself had developed into the microlithic facies (Subbarao 1958: 39). The discovery of the Belan sections which run for miles and miles together without break and gap in the deposits, not only established the position of the Upper Palaeolithic but gave a firm base to the mesolithic industries also. A short review of the section will not be out of place here. The entire section from bottom upwards has been divided into ten deposits consisting of the three gravels and the intervening deposits. Cemented gravel II or the deposit marked (7) and overlying reddish silt deposit (6) have yielded middle Palaeolithic assemblage.

Over the reddish silt (6) rests a yellowish silt numbered as (5) has yielded an industry which can be called transitional between the Middle Palaeolithic and the Upper Palaeolithic.

Cemented gravel III or deposit number (4) is the true Upper Palaeolithic horizon followed by overlying layer (3) which has yielded Upper Palaeolithic blades along with microlithic blades and flakes. Layer (2) and (1) have yielded microliths associated with geometric shapes.

The top most three layers of the Belan Section have been correlated with the excavated layers of Chopani Mando excavation (Sharma 1980). The lower most deposit or that of period I can be correlated with the third deposit from the top. The middle deposit or that of period II is correlatable with the second layer of the Belan section. The topmost deposit or that of period III is comparable to the topmost deposit of the Belan section.

In the Lekhahia excavation also thick and broad blades were noticed in the bottom most layers (Sharma 1965). Cockburn (1894) had also noticed similar blade element in the bottom most layers in his diggings. Besides from 1963 onwards, a very large number of sites have been located by the author and his collegues in the districts of Varanasi, Mirzapur and Allahabad in Uttar Pradesh and Sidhi and Rewa in Madhya Pradesh which on the basis of typology should be placed between the Upper Palaeolithic and the Mesolithic industries. For the sake of convenience such sites have been grouped under the term epi-palaeolithic (Sharma *et al.* 1980). The characteristic feature of such tools are that they are made generally on thick irregular flake or blade with triangular cross-section on cherty or flinty material. The microlithic fluted cores and associated blades do appear but are not common. The lunates are comparatively very broad and thick on the arc side. The points are mostly crescentic in shape. Most of the tools are made on irregular flakes and not on true blades. On comparison the epi-palaeolithic shares many common features with the lithic material of the layer (4) at Baghaikhor, in the lowest stratum in the Lekhahia open air trenches and Chopani Mando excavation. Here it would not be out of place to mention that even the sites grouped under the epi-palaeolithic caption show variations if analysed critically.

The above discussion would suggest that the evolution of microlithic tool tradition was a long drawn process and we have sufficient grounds to believe that it developed from the Upper palaeolithic industries of the Indian sub-continent.

Evolution of the Mesolithic Industries

Till the fifties of the present century almost nothing was known about the Mesolithic industries and their associated cultural equipment. The important known sites during that period were Singrauli basin in Uttar Pradesh (Krishnaswami and Soundara Rajan 1951); Giddalur II near Nandikanama pass (Soundara Rajan 1958); Langhnaj in Gujarat (Sankalia 1956); Birbhanpur in Bengal (Lal, 1958: 4-48); Teri industries in Tamil Nadu (Zeuner, F.E. and Allchin, B. 1956: 4-20). The microlithic assemblages of the sites enumerated above were roughly placed within the Mesolithic though they differed from each other in their typology and associated material. On the basis of typology the above sites may be divided into two groups. In the first category are included only such sites which yielded only non-geometric microliths unassociated with pottery. They are singrauli basin, Giddalur II, Khandivli, Birbhanpur, and Megnanpuram of the Teri group. The second category includes sites which have yielded geometric microliths with or without pottery. Among the sites of this category mention may be made of Langhnaj and Teri. It should be made clear here that at Langhnaj three levels were demarcated. The microliths of the lowest levels were unassociated with pottery (Sankalia 1960: 40). Now only two main layers are recognised (Sankalia 1974: 252). The second layer is the main microlithic deposit and it yielded most of the human skeletons, animal bones, as well as microliths and a few pieces of pottery.

A critical study of the assemblages indicated that at least three categories could be distinguished in the then mesolithic assemblages:

1. Non-geometric microliths without pottery.
2. Geometric microliths without pottery.
3. Geometric microliths with pottery.

In the sixties of the present century a very large number of surface sites were located throughout India. My own explorations in the district of Mirzapur (Varma 1964) brought to light a large number of sites which presented a verigated picture. Some of the sites yielded non-geometric microliths quite a few of them yielded geometric patterns also associated with or without pottery. Besides, some of the sites of the geometrical microliths yielded markedly diminutive type of microliths. The other scholars, too, who were working in the field, observed similar facts. The question that immediately came to our mind was 'do these different assemblages of microliths represent various stages in the evolution of the mesolithic industry?'

In order to clarify the position small scale excavations were undertaken in and outside the rock-shelters of Morahana Pahar and Baghai Khor in the year 1963 (Varma 1964 and 1965). The very next year Lekhahia rock-shelter in the near vicinity of the village Bhainsore was excavated by V.D. Misra and Sharma (Sharma 1965). The results obtained in the excavations were very rewarding because they gave a clear evidence of the development of Mesolithic industries that was hitherto devoid of stratigraphic sequence. The above excavations in the area revealed that the mesolithic industries developed through at least four distinct phases:

- (i) The earliest phase is represented by non-geometric tools made purely of impure cherty-flinty material.
- (ii) In the second phase geometric shapes appear but they were still unassociated with pottery. Triangle precedes the emergence of Trapeze.
- (iii) In third phase pottery makes its appearance.
- (iv) In the fourth stage the microliths tend to become smaller and the geometric shapes are made with precision.

To cross-examine the results of the excavations on top of the Kaimurs further excavations were undertaken down into the Belan valley towards the north of the Vindhyas on an escarpment at the site of Chopani-Mando first in the year 1967 and then again in 1977. The following culture sequence was obtained at Chopani-Mando (Sharma *et al.* 1980: 36-37).

Phase I. *Epi-palaeolithic—*

The lithic artefacts of this stage show a transition from Upper-palaeolithic to Mesolithic. The lithic tools of this phase in comparison to those of the Upper-palaeolithic are reduced in length, width and thickness and are bigger and broader than those of the true mesolithic phase.

Phase IIA. *Early Mesolithic*—Non-geometric microliths

The lithic assemblage of this phase is represented by Non-geometric microliths un-associated with pottery.

Phase IIB. *Early Mesolithic—*

It is characterised by the occurrence of geometric microliths unassociated with pottery.

Phase III. *Advanced Mesolithic or Proto-Neolithic*

This phase is characterised by the emergence of fragile handmade pottery and the artefacts show reduction in size.

In a nutshell, the sequence of industries obtained in the excavations at Chopani-Mando only confirmed the results obtained earlier in the excavations on top of the Kaimurs in and outside the rock-shelters. The four stages of the development of the mesolithic industries help us in fixing the tentative relative chronology for the numerous sites which are scattered through out the length and breadth of the country.

Antiquity

The antiquity of the Mesolithic in India was a point of debate among the prehistorians. It was supposed to have flourished fairly late in the Holocene but now there is hardly any doubt that as in the other regions of the Old World, the Mesolithic industries developed immediately after the Pleistocene with the ushering of milder climate. Moreover we have now a fairly large number of dates from levels preceding the Mesolithic as well as from the Mesolithic settlements representing the different stages of development. This has made our task of fixing the time brackets of the mesolithic cultures of India easier. In the Belan Valley carbon dates from different levels are available at one place. The dates are as under—

Pre-Mesolithic Level

Gravel III. Upper-palaeolithic

- (i) 23,840 B.C. (PRL 86)
- (ii) 17,765 B.C. (TF 1245)

Gravel IV. Exposed at Mahagara. Represents the final stages of Belan Terrace formation. Equated with the last Terrace of Chopani-Mando.

- (i) 12,190±390 B.C. (PRL 603).
- (ii) 9,350±130 B.C. (PRL 602).
- (iii) 8,395±110 B.C. (SUA).
- (iv) 8,080±115 B.C. (SUA).

Mesolithic Sites

- (i) Non-Geometric Pre-Pottery—no dates.

(ii) Geometric Pre-Pottery
Sarai Nahar Rai
(i) 8,395±110 B.C. (TF 1104)
Bagore Phase I
(ii) 4,480±200 B.C. (TF 786)
(iii) 3,835±130 (TF 1007)
(iv) 3,285±90 B.C. (TF 1012)
(iii) Geometric with Pottery
Langhnaj 2,040±110 B.C. (TF 744)
Lekhahia (i) 2,410±115 (TF 419)
(ii) 1,710±110 B.C. (TF 417)

A casual glance at the dates given above would indicate the antiquity of each stage. Gravel IV that has got four dates from two different labs represents the stage of transition from the Upper-palaeolithic to Mesolithic. In other words it may be equated with the industries referred to as Epi-palaeolithic and can be given a time bracket of 12,000 B.C. to 8,000 B.C. with marginal overlaps.

The Non-geometric pre-pottery stage can be placed with marginal adjustments within the time bracket of 10,000 B.C. to 8,000 B.C.

Geometric Pre-pottery, stage may be fixed between 8,000 B.C. to 2,000 B.C. with marginal overlap.

Geometric with pottery stage may be fixed between 5,000 B.C. and 1,500 B.C. Pottery must have been introduced at an early date on account of contact with the pottery using neolithic people.

Thus we may place the mesolithic cultures of India in a time bracket of 12,000 B.C. to 1,500 B.C.

Life and Subsistance Pattern of the Mesolithic Folk

The Mesolithic folk are normally described as hunters and gatherers who led a nomadic life. Their tools are often described as hunting type or fishing type. It is also generally supposed that hunting for food was the major occupation of the mesolithic man. In quest of animals he roamed from place to place and depended heavily on meat diet. Recent researches have brought welcome light on the life pattern of the mesolithic man and have clarified some of the above misleading conventional interpretations.

Studies made into the food habits of the modern primitive groups show that meat forms not more than 35% of the diet. It may be the preferred food but it is generally not the stable one. David Clark who studied the food habits of the modern North Europeans and North Americans came to the conclusion that even though they esteem meet, it merely contributes 1/3 of the diet by weight. Hunting though played an important role in the lives of the mesolithic man his subsistance depended on gathering vegetal food. There is hardly any doubt in the fact that 'hunting is a high risk, low return subsistence activity whereas gathering is a low risk, high return subsistance activity.' Hence it was but natural that wherever the plant food occurred reliance on plant resources increased. The easy availability of vegetal food prompted the man to lead a semi-sedentry life. In this connection the example of the newly excavated mesolithic settlement of Mahadaha in the Ganga Valley is worth mentioning. Here it should be noted that a very large number of quern, muller, anvil, muller-cum-anvil and hammer etc. have been found which indicate that the people exploited fully the vegetal remains of the area. A glance at the inventory of stone tools, bone tools and stone objects indicating their actual number would indicate their dependence on vegetal food. The total number of stone tools is 87 (Sharma *et al.* 1980 : 104), bone tools is 45 (Sharma *et al.* 1980 : 107), stone objects (complete) 301 (Sharma *et al.* 1980 : 105). Querns, mullers etc. are such stone objects which are used for processing vegetal food and their production in large number is noteworthy. People do not normally invent new tools and implements until the need is there and as the preparation of these large querns and mullers fashioned out of hard stones involves a considerable amount of labour, the processing of cereal food must be presumed to have reached to a degree of paramount importance within the economy. I do not agree with the contention of Sharma *et al.* (1980: 112) that "All the implements (microlithic tools) recovered are connected with hunting." A mere look on the inventory of tools would indicate that blades constitutes 52.86% and Lunates 9.19%. Anyone will agree that both these can effectively be used for purposes other than hunting. The concentration of heavy stone tools in a very small area, at least four phases of burials together with four phases of hearths, depleted condition of lithic tools relatively high percentage of bone tools and a population of small children, adult and old people all this taken together indicates that the mesolithic folk there led a semi-sedentary life. The contention of Sharma *et al.* (1980 : 78) that these sites should be treated as camp-sites where these people settled for one season or were camping sites (in case of Mahadaha and Sarai Nahar Rai) which were visited time and again is not correct. The Mesolithic settlement of Mahadaha presents the picture of an incipient village settlement.

Chopani Mando in the Belan Valley is another such site where stone objects such as ring-stone, rubbers, mullers, querns etc., have been found. These people made pottery and also made pits for storage purposes. Here, too, vegetal food formed an essential element of their economy. Seeds of wild variety of rice have been found embeded in the lumps of burnt clay (Sharma *et al.* 1980). Chopani Mando presents an advanced stage from that of Mahadaha because these people knew pottery and had devised ways for storage.

Domestication of Animals

Animal bones have been reported from almost all the excavated sites of the mesolithic settlement but the evidence of domestication comes only from the sites of Bagor and Adamgarh. The faunal remains of Bagore were first studied by Dr. (Mrs.) D.D. Shah of Baroda University and she did not get any evidence of domestication. Dr. Alur who studied the collection recently is of the opinion that sheep/goat and some cattle bones were of domesticated variety (Misra 1973 : 63) (Sankalia 1974 : 271). Adamgarh is the only site where fifty per cent of the animal bones are said to be of the domesticated variety. The scanty evidence available at present does not present a clear picture of domestication of animals during the Mesolithic phase yet we may surmise that some headway had been made in this direction during the period under discussion.

Structural Activity

Evidence of structural activity in the form of hutments, paved floor or windscreen comes from a number of settlements. The earliest evidence of the construction of hutments comes from Chopani Mando (Sharma *et al.* 1980 : 37-40) Phase IIA which is Early Mesolithic yielding non-geometric microliths. Phases IIB and III have also revealed evidence of hutments with post holes. They are roughly circular or oval. One hut of Phase IIA (Sharma 1980 : 38) is partially paved with stones. There is evidence to prove that the floor of the huts were used as working floors.

Evidence of Stone Paved floors and wattle huts has been obtained from Bagor Phases I and II (Misra 1973 : 104 ; Sankalia 1974 : 261). The Mesolithic folk of Bhimbetka too made floors with flat stone slabs. In cave III F-23 a wall 6 m long and 1 m wide made of stone boulders was found (Misra *et. al.* 1977 : 16).

The evidence from sites reported above indicate clearly that during the Mesolithic period the people had started making shelters in the form of hutments for living.

Hearths or Evidence of Fire

Evidence of fire for roasting meat comes forth from Langhnaj (Sankalia 1974 : 257), Bagor (Misra 1973: 106), Sarai Nahar Rai (Sharma 1973), Bhimbetka (Misra 1977: 16), Mahadaha and Chopani Mando (Sharma *et al.* 1980). At Langhnaj and Bagor charred bones have been found but the evidence of any kind of hearth is lacking. Probably they roasted the meat in open fire.

At Chopani Mando four circular hearths (Sharma *et al* 1980: 40), at Mahadaha eight hearths—one circular and seven oval have been reported from the different phases. (Sharma *et al.* 1980: 98). At Sarai Nahar Rai eight small hearths and one community hearth which was later sealed by a floor were excavated. The smaller hearths were circular, oval or of indeterminate shape. At all places they are of the pit hearth type and only slightly vary in diameter and depth. At Chopani Mando only they contained charcoals also (Sharma *et al.* 1980: 40) but at Mahadaha and Sarai Nahar Rai charcoal was absent. The hearths contained loose blackish soil resembling ash, burnt clay-lumps and charred and semi charred bones.

It is evident from the above discussions that the Mesolithic folk roasted meat before eating.

Pottery

Pottery has been reported from a number of excavated sites such as Langhnaj, Bagor Phase II, Nagarjunakonda, Morahana Pahar, Baghai Khor, Lekhahia, Chopani Mando, Ghagharia rock shelter I in the Son Valley. We have already seen that pottery comes to be associated with the Mesolithic cultures after the introduction of geometric shapes on the sites located on top of the Kaimur and in the Belan Valley. At all these places they are unassociated with metal. At Bagor Phase II which yields pottery is associated with metal. The pottery of both the types—handmade and wheel turned—is reported. At most of the sites the sherds are very small and it is difficult normally to make out shapes. A closer look indicates that the pottery types are very simple and unstandardised. Shallow and deep bowls with featureless rim are the most popular types. Small sized vases with straight or concave neck are also available at the Vindhyan sites (Pal 1980) and Nagarjunakonda (Khare 1975: 113). At Langhnaj the sherds are very small and no recognizable shape can be made out (Sankalia 1974: 255).

The clay used for making the pots is not well levigated. It is coarse and mixed with plenty of sand particles and minute lateritic pallets. At the Vindhyan sites on the basis of surface colour the pottery may be divided into two categories—(1) ordinary red ware and (2) brownish grey or khaki ware. At Nagarjunakonda only reddish brown pots are found. At Langhnaj they are mainly of two types—(1) red ware, (2) black and red ware. Red ware has further been divided into two categories—burnished and coarse. Evidence of burnishing from the Mesolithic level comes from Langhnaj only.

Though the fabric of the mesolithic pottery is coarse, yet the mesolithic folk have artistically decorated them by incised or impressed designs. Incised decorated pottery has been found at Langhnaj and Bagor. Impressed pot sherds are reported from the Vindhyan sites they are divisible into two groups—(a) pottery impressed by engraved dabbers, (b) tortoise bone impressed designs resembling the cord impression. Impressed pottery of Group A is confined only to Chopani Mando and a few sherds have been found at Lekhahia also. The pottery of Group B have been obtained from Baghai Khor, Lekhahia and Ghagharia.

The absence of pottery on Ganga Valley sites looks strange at the first thought but it should be borne in mind that necessity is the mother of all inventions. It seems that food in all the seasons was readily available, and the practice of cooking in vessels had not started yet.

Burials

Burials have been excavated at a number of Mesolithic settlements—Dorthy Deep and Jambudvipa Rock shelters in the Mahadev hills in Madhya Pradesh, Langhnaj in Gujarat, Bagor in Rajasthan, Baghai Khor and Lekhahia rock-shelters in district Mirzapur, and Sarai Nahar Rai and Mahadaha in Pratapgarh, Uttar Pradesh. These present before us not only a clear picture of burial practices but at the same time new light is thrown on sociological aspects of the Mesolithic folk.

A review of the burial remains at different sites indicates that three types of burial practices were prevalent during the Mesolithic period.

1. Extended Burial.
2. Flexed Burial.
3. Fractional Burial.

1. The practice of extended burial in shallow graves was the most common one. In the extended type of burials, skeletons were placed either on their backs or in supine position. Extended burials have been reported from Dorothy Deep and Jambudvipa rock shelters (Hunter 1935: 28-57, 1936: 127-144), Baghai Khor (Varma 1965: 73-74), Lekhahia (Sharma 1965 : 77-78), Bagor Phase I (Misra 1972: 58-65), Sarai Nahar Rai (Sharma 1973: 129-144) and Mahadaha (Sharma *et al.* 1980: 80-98).

The orientation is either east-west or west-east. The head being either towards the east or west. The orientation west-east seems to have been more common at the sites of the Northern Vindhyas, in south Uttar Pradesh and Ganga Valley. At other places the East-West orientation has been followed. The skeleton of Bagor Phase I and skeleton number 14 at Langhnaj are exceptions because they have been buried in west-east direction.

2. The tradition of burying the dead in a flexed position was common at Langhnaj where almost all the skeletons excavated so far were buried in flexed condition. Similar evidence comes forth from Bagor Phase II where all the three skeletons were found buried in a flexed position. But here it should be remembered that Bagor Phase II is associated with metal objects. In Lekhahia skeleton number IV was laid in a flexed position.

3. Fractional burial, too was practised but does not seem to be as common as the other types of burials noted in the preceding lines. At Langhnaj some fractional burials were found. At Bhimbetka also two secondary burials have been reported.

Grave goods

It seems that the mesolithic folk had developed some belief in life beyond death because we find that in several cases grave goods have been found with the skeletons.

At Langhnaj microliths, animal bones and beads have been reported. At Lekhahia associated with skeleton V we found a buffalow rib, a mandible, horn of deer, molusc, shell and microliths. At Sarai Nahar Rai molusc, shell, some charred bones and microliths were found. At Bhimbetka was found a bone ornament and a pierced rib fragment of some animal. At Bagor with the skeleton of Phase II metal objects and earthen pots too were found. At Mahadaha ornaments made of another bone, bone arrowheads and animal bones, microliths were found.

Detailed osteological and racial studies of the skeletons is not available from most of the sites enumerated above. The best studied site in this connection is Langhnaj where a number of scholars have studied the skeletons. Anthropologically the Langhnaj skeletons betray mixed racial features—dolicocephalic head with fairly large cranial capacity, medium and long stature with their thin legs, pronounced supra-orbital ridges and a slight prognathism of the mouth and probably a snub-nose. Ehrhardt and Kennedy are of the opinion that these features are indicative of a mixture of Mediterranian and Veddid Traits (Sankalia 1974: 256-57).

Kennedy has recently studied the skeletal remains from the Vindhyan sites and the Ganga valley. Regarding the skeletons of the Ganga Valley Kennedy is of the opinion that these people were long headed (dolicocranic) and moderately broad nosed with deep nasal roots and not projecting face. Their large body size and distinctive cranial features remind physical anthropologists of some of the Upper Palaeolithic population of Europe and Western Asia.

Life Expectancy

The life expectancy of the mesolithic people of India does not seem to have been very high. The average age of the Vindhyan skeletons ranged between 20-21 years. The life expectancy at the Ganga valley site seems to be a little higher. At Sarai Nahar Rai the age of the maximum number of skeletons ranges between 16-30 years but at Mahadaha where the highest number of skeletons have so far been excavated in a mesolithic settlement in India the age expectancy is the highest. The age of the largest number of skeletons ranges between 18-40 years. In the case of one individual it is observed that he had attained the age of 50 years.

The higher age expectancy rate at Mahadaha may be due to the fact that the Mahadahans had a comparatively easy life existence.

Sociological Aspects

The mesolithic burials specially at Sarai Nahar Rai and Mahadaha throw some very valuable light on some sociological aspects which hitherto were unknown.

At Sarai Nahar Rai in one instance and Mahadaha in two instances evidence of multiple burials have been obtained. At Sarai Nahar Rai in grave number VII four individuals were entered at one time is indicated by the grave and the placement of the skeletons. Two pairs of a male and a female have been placed in two layers one above the other. The male was placed to the right of the female in both the cases. At Mahadaha grave numbers I and V contain two skeletons each. In case of grave number I skeleton number 1 is that of a female and skeleton number 2 that of a male. In grave number V skeleton number 11 is of female whereas the sex of the skeleton number 10 could not be determined. The above instances indicate that there was a practice of burying male and female together. Whatever might have been the circumstances of the multiple burials they do raise certain basic questions. The first question that comes to the mind is that was the placement of male and female side by side in a grave intentional? It does seem to be intentional because in all the graves of this type the skeletons have been arranged in a way to accommodate two persons. Moreover the fact of the placement of male to the right of the female in each case cannot escape our attention. This type of burial, it may be suggested, indicates some special relationship between the man and the woman. Did they form a unit? Are we not justified to think that the family unit of a male and female had evolved during the mesolithic period?

The idea of smaller units finds confirmation from the fact that a very large number of small pit hearths have been found both at Sarai Nahar Rai and Mahadaha. At Chopani Mando also small hearths have been reported. Large number of small hearths indicate that there may have been smaller units consisting of a few individuals or members of a family.

Ritual and Religious Belief

The large number of burials discovered at different mesolithic settlements of India indicate that the mesolithic men had developed concern for the welfare for the individual after death. The meticulous way in which burials have been made and the way in which the skeletons have been placed take the form of a ritual and the performance of ritual by a social group presupposes the development of eschatalogical concepts and group consciousness. Probably this concept, later on took the form of the beginning of religion. The flexed position in which the burials at Langhnaj have been made is not possible without deliberate action. The neat manner in which the skeletons have been folded up and laid [Sankalia 1974: Fig. 65a (ii)] is noteworthy. The meticulous way in which the graves have been prepared and the way in which the body was placed in side the grave deserves our attention. It takes the form of ritual carefully performed. The preparation of burial at all the different places looks to be so similar that it at once strikes at the question was it an accepted practice—a ritual?

The placement of grave goods in the form of microliths, meat—charred bones, moluscan, shell and bead etc. further confirm the hypothesis that the mesolithic people had developed ritual practices and believed in some sort of life after death.

The orientation of the graves towards west-east at Sarai Nahar Rai and Mahadaha is so perfect that it requires closer thinking. There is hardly any doubt in the fact that the direction must have been guided by the direction of the sun. The variation is only of a few degrees which may be on account of the variation in the position of the sun at different times of the year. The Sun must have attracted them and they must have been aware of the life giving qualities of the Sun. Will it be wrong to trace Sun worship from the Mesolithic period?

Aesthetic Activities

The people of the mesolithic period had a developed aesthetic sense is attested to by the discoveries of a very large number of painted rockshelters in the country. The detailed study of the paintings of the rockshelters in the district of Mirzapur and the adjoining regions have been made by the author. Some of the rockshelters has been excavated by him and his colleagues. The studies and the excavations indicate that though the paintings cover a very long duration of time yet the period of greatest painting activity coincides with the Mesolithic period. On the basis of superpositions of the paintings and style the paintings of the north Vindhyan region have been divided into four phases. Similarly, Wakankar, Misra and Mathpal have made intensive studies of the rock-paintings of the Bhimbetka group of shelters. Their studies, too, indicate that the largest painting activity during the prehistoric times in India took place during the Mesolithic. On the basis of superposition, subject-matter and style of paintings at Bhimbetka they have been divided into nine phases and the paintings of Phase I-V belong to the Mesolithic culture only (Misra *et al.* 1977: 19).

The mesolithic paintings all over show a remarkable homogeneity in the choice of subject, place and technique of painting. They deal primarily with animals. They are shown standing, moving, running, grazing etc. In the paintings of earlier phases individual animals are shown but in later ones large combinations showing herds of animals have been depicted. Men also figure in a number of scenes specially hunting scenes. The earlier paintings are remarkable for their naturalistic depiction, later on stylization in figures creeps in and in the third phase symbolic representations predominate and finally there is a swing back to naturalism.

The paintings have generally been executed in shades of red ochre but sometimes bluish green, yellowish or white colours have also been used. The colours were prepared by mixing juices of wild trees or animal fat etc. with mineral colours. Figures were painted both in outline and flat wash. Ground nodules of haemetite have been found in the excavations at several places which attest that they were used for making colours. The paintings were made on the natural surface of the rock.

The artistic activity of the mesolithic people did not confine to the painting activity only. Recently, a fluted core of the mesolithic period has been reported by Sonawane (Sonawane 1981: 2) from Chandravati. It is of very great significance. On the patinated cortex of the core is a rhomboid in fluted or spiralled formation in a pair of parallel lines going clock-wise beginning from the centre is engraved. Even though it is a solitary evidence yet we may postulate that probably mobiliary objects were also decorated. Unfortunately more evidence is wanting.

Ornaments

Like the men of any other age the mesolithic men too devised ways and means to decorate himself. Evidence of the use of ornaments comes from a number of sites such as Bagor, Mahadaha, Adamgarh, Bhimbetka etc. Beads of semi-precious stone and bones have been reported from Bagor, Adamgarh and Bhimbetka but evidence of a complete necklace and earrings comes only from Mahadaha. The stone-bone bead necklace reported from Bagor belongs to Phase II. At Mahadaha evidence of the use of necklace and earrings made of antler bone comes from three different graves (Sharma *et al.* 1980 : 108-109). From grave V were obtained both earrings and necklace. The earring (*kundala*) is open at one end probably for getting inserted in the lobe of the ear. Presumably as part of a necklace eleven small rings were also found around the neck of the same individual. Graves VII and IV yielded two and five small-sized rings respectively. All the rings were prepared by slicing antler bones. Some of the antler bones from which slices could not be removed show incisions and deep grooves. It gives a clear picture of the process in which the rings were removed.

I am deeply indebted to my colleague Sri Jagannath Pal and my research scholar Km. Tulika Banerji for helping me in various ways in the preparation of this paper.

REFERENCES

Bruce Foote, R.B. 1916. *The Foote Collection of Indian Prehistoric and Protohistoric Antiquities, Notes on their Ages and distribution*, Government museum, Madras.

Cockburn, J. 1894. On flint Implements from the Kon ravines of south Mirzapur, *JASB*, 63.

Commiade, L.A. and Burkitt, M.C. 1930. Fresh light on the Stone Ages of South-east India, *Antiquity*, 4.

Hunter, G.R. 1935. Interim Report on the excavation in the Mahadeo hills, *NUJ*, 1, 1936, Final Report on the Excavation in the Mahadeo hills, *NUJ*, 2.

Issac, N. 1960. The Stone Age Cultures of Kurnool, Ph.D. Thesis, Poona University, Pune.

Khare, M.D. 1975, in *Nagarjunadkonda (1954-60, I)*, MASI, 75.

Krishnaswami, V.D. and Soundara Rajan, K.V. 1951. The Lithic Tool Industries of the Singrauli basin, District Mirzapur, *AI*, 7.

Lal, B.B. 1958. Birbhanpur, A Microlithic site in the Damodar Valley, West Bengal, *AI*, 4.

Misra, V.N. 1962. Problems of Terminology in Indian Prehistory, *EA*, 15, 2, 1973, Bagor A Late Mesolithic settlement in North-West India, *WA*. 5, 1, 1973. Problems of Palaeoecology, Palaeoclimate and Chronology of Mesolithic Cultures of North-West India, *Radiocarbon and Indian Archaeology*, (ed.). D.P. Agrawal and A. Ghosh, 1977, Bhimbetka, Pune.

Murty, M.L.K. 1968, Blade and Burin Industry near Renigunta, *PPS*, 34.

Paddyya, K. 1968, Pre and Protohistoric Investigations in Shorapur Doab, Ph.D. Thesis, Poona University, Pune.

Sharma, G.R. 1965, in *Indian Prehistory: 1964*, (ed.) V.N. Misra & M.S. Mate, Pune, 1973 Mesolithic Lake Cultures in the Ganga Valley, *India*, DDS, 39.

Sharma, G.R. *et al* 1980. *Beginnings of Agriculture*, Allahabad.

Sankalia, H.D., 1956. The Microlithic Industry of Langhanaj, Gujarat, *JGRS*, 18, 1960, Houses and Habitations through the ages, *BDCRI*, *XX*, 1974, *Prehistory and Protohistory of India & Pakistan*, Pune.

Subbarao, B., 1958, *The Personality of India*, 2nd Edition, Baroda.

Varma, R.K., 1964. Stone Age Cultures of Mirzapur District, Ph.D. Thesis, University of Allahabad, 1970. *Bharatiya Pragitihas*, Pt. I, Allahabad.

Zeuner, F.E. & Allchin, B. 1956. Microlithic sites in Tinnevelley District, Madras State, *AI* 12, 4-10.

Fresh Light on the Neolithic Cultures of India

B.K. THAPAR
New Delhi

IN India up-to-date neolithic cultures have been recognized in six different geographical regions: (i) Northern, covering the Kashmir Valley; (ii) Belan Valley, covering the Vindhyan Plateau in Districts Allahabad, Mirzapur, Rewa and Sidhi; (iii) Northern, Bihar or Mid-eastern covering District Saran; (iv) North-eastern, covering Assam and the adjacent Sub-Himalayan regions; (v) Central-eastern, covering Chota Nagpur Plateau with its Peneplains extending in West Bengal and Orissa; and (vi) Southern, covering the Peninsular India. In each region at least two sites have been excavated to understand the charter of the culture, the Southern region, however, being more extensively investigated with over a dozen sites located in different parts (Karnataka, Andhra Pradesh and Tamil Nadu) having been excavated to a varying scale of work (Thapar, 1964, 1974, 1978). Among the neolithic cultures of these six regions, recent work in the first two, viz. Kashmir Valley and the Belan Valley, has added significantly to our existing knowledge, both in material equipment and the level of subsistence, which the present paper seeks to discuss.

The neolithic culture in the Kashmir Valley is represented by nearly three dozen sites, all located on the elevated flats of the Karewas, often overlooking streams and lakes. As regards depositional environment, SEM (Scanning Electron Microscopy) studies have indicated that the deposit preceding the neolithic occupation at different sites is a wind-borne silt called loess, the deposition of which ceased much before the advent of the neolithic culture in the valley (Pant, *et al.* 1978). Pollen diagrams constructed from the Haigam Lake (Singh, 1968), not very far from Srinagar, had furnished evidenced for a three-stage disturbance of natural vegetation as shown by the decline and appearance of pine forests. The clearance of pine forests at one stage is thought to have been related to the farming experiments of the neolithic settlers in the valley. Of these sites, only two, viz. Burzahom and Gufkral have been systematically excavated. The former, literally meaning the place of birth, and situated 16 km north-east of Srinagar, was initially excavated in 1935 by De Terra and Paterson (1939) and during 1960-71 by T.N. Khazanchi (1976-77). These excavations had yielded a three-fold sequence of cultures, beginning with the Neolithic followed by the Megalithic and the Historical. The current excavation at Gufkral, (Sharma 1981b), literally meaning the cave of the potter, and situated 41 km south-east of Srinagar, while confirming the same sequence has added new dimensions to the neolithic culture of the region which now shows three phases of evolution, labelled Periods IA, IB and IC, the earliest of which was aceramic, having been identified for the first time in India. The characteristics of these three phases are outlined below.

During period IA, which was aceramic, the subsistence economy of the people seems to have been both specialized food gathering and cereal farming, including stock-raising as evidenced by the finds at Gufkral of bones of both wild (ibex, bear, sheep, goat, cattle, wolf and Kashmir stag) and domesticated (sheep and goat) animals and the grains of wheat, barley lentils, peas and clover. So far as it goes confirmatory evidence in respect of domesticated animals is also available at Burzahom. As regards cereals no direct evidence of their find has so far come forth from that site but Palynological studies carried out near the site have revealed the existence of weeds, usually associated with the cultivation of wheat and barley. The analysis of the bones of domesticated goats reveals the absence of the very old animals and a pre-dominance of immature ones suggesting herd management. The inhabitants lived in underground pits, which on plan were mostly circular or rectangular and less frequently oval or squarish. The pits were cut into the natural loessic soil and had their floors often painted in red ochre. As protection against weather, the pits had a birch cover, supported on wooden posts, as indicated by the presence of post-holes along the periphery of the mouths. In close proximity to these pits were also found neatly plastered floors, hearth and shallower pits which were used by the dwellers as storage-bins. The floors of the storage pits at Gufkral were also found treated with a red ochre paint. Instance of a rubble wall and mud-platforms were also recorded at Gufkral. The platform was found to be surrounded by a number of post-holes of almost equal diameter. A post-hole with a bigger diameter was noticed in the centre of the platform indicative of the method of supporting the superstructure. For their daily occupation, they used both bone and stone tools, the former consisting of points needless, harpoons and scrapers and the latter of axes, adzes, drills, picks, points, pestles, pounders, querns and mace-heads or ringstones. Besides, some tools were also made of antler-horns. The stone tools were made of Himalayan trap while the bone ones were made of bones of various animals; including goat, sheep and stag when the bones were in green stage.

In the succeeding Period IB, pottery came to be used. Among animals, cattle and dog also began to be domesticated in addition to those already known in the previous period. During this period as also in the following, the percentage of the bones of the domesticated animals shows a progressive increase and those of the wild animals a corresponding decrease. It is interesting to note that all the animals hunted during the various phases of the neolithic culture belong to the herbivorous group. The other items of cultural equipment of the previous period continued during this period with greater variety of tool-kit-harpoons, needles with or without eye, awls, arrow-heads in bone and chisels, hoes and adzes, etc. in stone. It must, however, be realized that in view of the restricted extent of the excavation in the aceramic levels (period IA) no emphasis can at the present stage be laid on the presence or absence of a particular bone or stone tool in the deposits of periods IA and IB. The inhabitants continued living in the sub terranean pits and chambers. Of these, the latter were found mostly in the Central part of the settlement and the former in the peripheral (as recorded at Burzahom) suggesting perhaps a planned layout of kinship grouping. Some of the pit-chambers had depressions on all the four sides and storage-pits and hearths in the centre. Besides thick floors composed of compact clay mixed with chunam, post holes and circular hearths were also recorded. Coming to pottery three principal fabrics, all hand-made, were in use during this period: thick coarse grey ware, fine grey ware, and gritty dull red ware. Among these, the thick grey ware predominated over the rest. The main shapes represented in the ware are the globular jars, bowls and basins, both of which show disc bases, often bearing mat impressions, suggesting high level of the development of fabric and mat technology. At Gufkral, a potter's kiln, having a diameter of 1.7 m was also exposed.

The last phase of the neolithic culture in the valley, labelled as Period IC (Khazanchi's Period II), marks a distinct change from the previous phases. The underground dwelling-pits and chambers were no longer used, most of them being filled up and covered up with mud-plastered floors having a thin coat of ochre. The dwelling units began to be built overground either in mud or mud-bricks or adobe. The subsistence economy seems to have undergone progressive change. The entire herd of sheep, goat and cattle was domesticated. Two important new species viz., pig and fish made their appearance. The period saw a further diversification in material equipment, perhaps through contacts with other regional and extra regional contemporary cultures. Not only did the tools begin to be made to a better finish and in larger number, indicating craft specialization, but some new types were also added to the kit like small-sized bone points and needles with or without eye, double-edged picks, spindle whorls and the harvesters (rectangular or semi-lunar knife with holes) of stone. The latter was made both in stone and bone and probably fastened to the hand with strings through the holes for purposes of cutting, scraping and harvesting. Micro-wear studies of the tool however belie this use. Similar tools are often met within the early farming cultures of China, particularly the Yang-Shao Culture of the Huang Ho Valley (Chang 1977). Other finds from this period include terracotta bangles, courie shells, and a coma-shaped pendant of light green jade. In ceramic, another diagnostic fabric called the burnished grey ware was added to the already existing range. Principal shapes represented in this ware are high-necked globular jars, bowls, basins, etc. Noteworthy among the finds of pottery, however, is the occurrence in the lower levels of the Period (at Burzahom) of a wheel-made vase of orange-slipped ware, painted in black with a horned figure panelled between the neck and the shoulder bands. Both in shape and the painted design the pot resembles the pre-Harappan Kot Diji fabric (Khan 1965; Dani 1970-71) and obviously must have been an import from the nearest site of that genre, viz. Sarai Khola, situated in the Potwar plateau (Halim 1970-71). From the upper levels of the period at Burzahom was also found a wheel-made red ware pot containing as many as 950 beads of agate and carnelian, which again seems to be out of context with the existing assemblage. Metallurgy as such does not seem to have been practised by the early farming communities of the Kashmir Valley, but a few copper arrow-heads, a ring, bangles and a pin (with flattened coiled head) were found in the deposits of this period Their occurrence, however, seems to be as intrusive as the wheel-made painted pot and agate beads and as such did not alter the basic neolithic subsistence economy and technology of the Period.

Other finds of the Period which deserve special mention are the two engraved stone-slabs found fixed in a rectangular structure. Of these, one depicts a hunting scene, while the other shows an incomplete pattern identified as tactiform (Pande 1971-72). Evidence regarding the burial practices of this Period was provided by six human interments exposed at Burzahom (Sharma, 1967) which indicate that both primary and secondary interments were in vogue. Besides, examples of animal burials, showing in one case fragmentary bones of wild dogs with two antlers of *barasingha*, were also attested (Sharma, 1968).

As to the dates of this neolithic culture, the available C-14 dates indicate a time-bracket of 2400-1500 B.C (uncalibrated), to which a century or so could be added on the initial end of the bracket to provide for the newly discovered aceramic phase.

Coming to the Belan Valley and the Vindhyan Plateau, the findings at Chopani Mando, Koldihawa and Mahagara, indicate a continuous sequence of transition from the stage of intensified foodgathering and selective hunting (Epi-Palaeolithic) through incipient food producing (Advanced Mesolithic or Proto Neolithic) to settled village farming (Neolithic). This admittedly is the first evidence of its kind in India which seeks to dispel notions of diffusion of the neolithic way of life either from West Asia or South-east Asia, and to establish the primacy of the neolithic culture of the Belan Valley, particularly in the light of the proposed chronology (seventy-fifth millennium B.C) for the latter and the existence of antecedent stages thereof.

Chopani Mando is located within a former meander on the left bank of the Belan, 77 km east south-east of Allahabad. The excavation revealed a three-fold sequence of cultures, extending from the Epi-Palaeolithic, through Early Mesolithic to Advanced Mesolithic or proto Neolithic. The first two cultural periods are distinguished largely by the occurrence of particular tool types as blades, non-geometric and geometric microliths, their gradual reduction in size and the change in raw material. In the Proto Neolithic Period, significant additions to the repertory of tools and other cultural equipment were: (i) tranchet; (ii) groundstone tools like hammer-stones, anvils, querns, mullers and ring-stones; and (iii) use of hand-made pottery (red ware and Khaki or brownish grey ware), sometime decorated with impressed designs. Of special importance at this site was the discovery of a number of hut foundations and hearths, which began to appear from the Early Mesolithic Period onwards. Thirteen such huts belonging to the Proto Neolithic Period were exposed. These were either round or oval on plan with an average diameter ranging between 5.7 and 3.5 m. The floors of these huts were littered with a large number of microliths, anvils, hammerstones, sling balls, mullers, querns, etc., fragments of burnt clay, animal bones, pot-sherds, etc. These huts were closely situated to each other in a bee-hive fashion. The economy of the settlement was that of gathering and hunting. There is no evidence for the domestication of animals or plants. From the presence of querns and mullers, however, one may infer some sort of incipient cultivation, perhaps the people were on the very threshold of effective food-production. The excavation yielded remains of wild rice (carbonized, embedded in lumps of burnt clay) and bones of wild cattle and goat/sheep. The Mesolithic period at Chopani Mando is ascribed to *circa* ninth-eighth millennium B.C.

The other notable sites in the region which deserve our attention are Koldihawa and Mahagara, situated on the opposite banks of the river Belan, the former on the left bank and the latter on the right, only 3 km of Chopani Mando, and about 85 km south-east of Allahabad. The excavation at Koldihawa revealed a three-fold sequence of cultures covering the Neolithic, the Chalcolithic and Iron Age. The Neolithic Culture was distinguished by the occurrence of ground stone tools including celts, microliths and hand-made pottery represented by cord impressed rusticated and burnished wares. Palaeobotanical analysis of the rice-husks used in the paste of the pottery showed that the rice belongs to the domesticated variety, which on the basis of the C-14 dates obtained for the Neolithic deposit (seventh-fifth millennium B.C) provides the earliest so far known evidence for rice cultivation in the sub-continent (Sharma, G.R. *et al.* 1980).

Mahagara is a single culture (neolithic) site with a 2.60 m thick occupation-deposit, indicating six structural phases. As many as twenty huts, represented by floors and pos-tholes were exposed in the excavated area. Of these, eighteen belonged to the last structural Phase (VI). The sides of these huts were perhaps retained by wattle and daub screens as evidenced by the presence of burnt fragments of daub bearing impressions of reed or bamboo. These eighteen hut-floors are reported to constitute the remains of eight houses situated in a nucleated ring-like fashion rather along a line. On these hut-floors lay scattered neolithic blades and microliths, pottery, querns, mullers, sling balls, celts, bone arrow-heads, terracotta beads and bones of animals. An interesting feature of the excavation was the discovery of a cattle-pen, irregular rectangular on plan, measuring 12.5×7.5 with the longer axis oriented north-south. The cattle-pen seems to have been fenced by twenty post-holes with wider spaces left for the openings, of which three can be surmised, two on the eastern and one on the western side. Within the fenced area no pottery or other finds were found, instead a large number of hoof-impressions of cattle belonging to different age groups, occurring in clusters, were recorded. From the number of hoof-marks, it is estimated that the cattle-pen would accommodate about 40 to 60 animals. Outside the pen, near the hut clusters were found hoof-marks of sheep or goats, situated almost in a straight line, suggesting the moving stage of the animal. The neoltithic pottery is represented by four wares called cord-impressed, rusticated, burnished red and burnished black, all hand-made and ill-fired. Among these, the cord-impressed ware is the most distinctive. The subsistence economy of the people was both hunting and farming, as attested by the occurence of both wild (cattle), and domesticated (cattle, sheep, goat and horse) animals and rice. The simultaneous existence of skeletal remains of wild and domesticated cattle is indicative of the process of transition from the hunting to the food-producing economy.

Let us now address ourselves to the problems which these discoveries have posed. Coming to Gufkral and Burzahom we have noticed that an aceramic stage of the neolithic culture has been indentified in the valley which in an evolving cultural sequence is in consonance with findings in West Asia, including Turkey. But the transition or trsnsformation from the terminal hunter-forager stage to the farming economy and the adaptation to the post-Pleistocene environmental changes has not so far been recognized in this area. Current investigation into this admittedly complex problem have, however, revealed at Sombur a lithic industry based on jasper, silicious limestone and trap, and represented in such tool types as burins, points and borers (Pant *et al.* 1982). This industry, being the first find of its kind in the valley, may perhaps indicate a particular stage in this long-drawn process of transformation from the exploitive to productive economy. It may be recalled that De Terra and Paterson had also found some thin indeterminate flakes near Sombur in the lowest Jhelum terrace which they had postulated as presenting a late palaeolithic culture (De Terra and Paterson 1939). Our understanding of the origins and early spread of farming in the valley, therefore, is still very insecure and fragmentary.

Coming to inter and extra regional relationship, we find that the Kashmir Neolithic culture shares certain apparent traits with the neolithic cultures of Sarai Khola in the Potwar plateau (Halim 1972; Mughal 1972), Ghaligai and Loebanr in the Swat (Stacul 1969, 1976 and 1977) and Yang-shao of the Huang Ho Valley in China (Chang 1977) which call for an analytical study. As regards Sarai Khola, the neolithic levels have yielded a burnished red-slipped were with mat or basket-impression on the base, one celt, two microliths and eight bone objects. The similarity, therefore, extends only to the technique of potting to produce mat-impressions on the bases and straw scratchings on the body of the pots and to the use of celts and bone objects, irrespective of their small number. Admittedly, these are only rudimentary similarities. The distinctive elements of the Kashmir Neolithic culture, viz. the dwelling-pits (circular and rectangular), the entire range of ceramics, the variety of stone and bone tools and the conspicuous absence of microliths remains unparalleled. This is not to deny the existence of contacts, howsoever tenuous, between the two regions. The occurrence in the levels of Period IC at Burzahom, of typically Kot Dijian globular vase (Mughal 1972: Fig. 12) which is one of the dominant types of Period II at Sarai Khola is illustrative of such an intercommunication. The painted pots from Sarai Khola could have been brought to Burzahom any time during the life time of Period II at the former site, possibly in the latter half when their frequency rises to thirteen per cent (Mughal 1972: tables 9 and 10). At any rate the linkage invests the sequence at both sites with some measure of contemporaneity.

Considering Ghaligai and Loebanr, the reported similarities with the Neolithic Culture of Kashmir in the case of the former are principally the occurrence in strata 17, 16 and 15 of grey or grey brown drab ware and burnished black ware, sometimes with mat-impressions on the bases and bone implements, and in case of the latter, the presence at Loebanr III of underground dwelling pits and the use of black-grey burnished ware and gritty drab ware with basket—or mat-impressions, of stone (celts and mace-heads) and bone objects (points, awls, etc.) and of a jade bead or pendant. A closer analysis of the neolithic assemblages in each region would show that the similarities are only generic. At Ghaligai, the neolithic culture is associated with a flake-tool industry and at Loebanr with a wheel-made painted ware, terracotta human and animal figurines and objects of copper and iron. It may be stressed that the above-mentioned traits, but for the instrusive copper objects in Period IC at Burzahom, are conspicuously absent in the Neolithic Culture of the Kashmir Valley. Furthermore, the appearance in Swat region of the bowl-on-stand is probably connected with the influence originating from northern Iran. The C-14 dated obtained from the deposits of Loebanr III/Ghaligai III demonstrate a later manifestation than that of Kashmir.

For contacts with China, we find unmistakable examples of two items of material equipment of the Yang-shao Culture, viz. harvester and jade beads which were included in the inventory of the neolithic cultures, respectively of the Kashmir Vallay (*circa* 2400-1500 B.C.) and Swat (*circa* 1600-1200 B.C.). Besides, the occurrence of the semi-sub terranean dwellings and of mat or basket-impressions on the bases of some of the pots in common in all the three regions. For a proper appraisement of this inter-relationship of nexus we may take into consideration both the temporal horizon and form of the Yang-shao culture. The time-spread of the Yang-shao Culture in Chung Yuan region is ascribed to 6000-3000 B.C. and in the Kansu to 3000-1800 B.C. (Chang 1977). In respect of material equipment, the Yang-shao Culture in both regions presents a different cultural style than that of Kashmir as revealed by the range of ceramics and forms, especially tripods with solid legs, including the painted ware, terracotta human figurines, house-models and separately located cemeteries *vis-a-vis* the habitation area (Chang 1977). The mechanism of diffusion or borrowing of only two characteristic items of equipment of this culture by the Neolithic Cultures of the Kashmir and Swat valleys still remains inadequately understood. Meanwhile, a significant addition to our knowledge on the subject has been made by recent exploration undertaken in the north Sikkim, where typical harvesters have been found in association with other neolithic tools, like celts, some with single or double perforations, adzes, etc. from a number of locations in the Djangu area (Sharma 1981 a). It may be recalled that single perforated celts have also been reported from the neolithic assemblages of Honan province in northern China. Such close affinity in artifactual remains in these areas would suggest a southward penetration of the cultural influences from north China sometime in the early part of the third millennium B.C. or a little later through Lungshanoid cultures (Dikshit 1982) some of which were characterized by the use of burnished grey-black pottery. The possible route of this penetration into Kashmir and the Indus Valleys was through a series of passes which link the Gilgit Valley with Wakhan and Chinese Turkestan. In the absence of culturally identifiable sites located between north China and Kashmir, Potwar and Swat regions it would be premature to consider the manifestations of the neolithic cultures in these regions 'as separate extensions from one long cultural tradition of Yang-shao neolithic culture' as suggested by Mughal (1972). More field-work is, therefore, called for to understand the mechanism of diffusion. Meanwhile, on the basis of the available evidence one can argue that the Kashmir Neolithic Culture had a distinctiveness of its own; it no doubt borrowed certain elements from other regions but this borrowing was at a late stage of its life. We must, however, find more details of its antecedents stages.

As regards similarities of the neolithic culture of the Belan Valley with other neolithic regional and extra-regional cultures we find that cord-impressed ware alone provides some comparative basis. In India this ware has been reported from Daojali Hading, a neolithic site of the north-eastern region. But in surfice colour and the range of decoration pattern, the wares of the two regions differ from each other. Furthermore, the neolithic culture of the north-eastern region, besides being younger than that of the Vindhyan, shows complete absence of the stone blade industry which is an integral part of the Vindhyan Neolithic. Outside the sub-continent, cord-impressed ware has been found in neolithic contexts over a wide-ranging territory in East and South-east Asia, notably associated with the Jomon Culture in Japan and the Hoobinbian in South-east Asia ranging in time from seventh to the third millennium B.C. Here again the resemblance is confined to the technique of pottery, the remaining industries in the assemblages of each culture being different. In the absence of any mechanism of diffusion between such disparate regions, the significance of such analogies remains inadequately understood and as such can hardly be stressed.

We have noticed that current field-work in the area has furnished evidence of the transition from the wild species to the domesticated ones in respect of cattle sheep/goat and horse; similar evidence is also available in respect of rice. This is, therefore, the only neolithic region in India which shows transformation from foraging to farming economy. Significantly enough, in this process no aceramic stage of the neolithic has been met with. Instead pottery makes it appearance in the Proto-neolithic or Anvanced Mesolithic Period when both animals (cattle, sheep/goat) and plats (rice) were undomesticated, indicating thereby the primacy of the manufacture of pottery over the domestication of animals and plants. Considering the chronological bracket to which this period has been assigned, viz. *circa* ninth-eighth millennium B.C. it would appear that it is the earliest recorded evidence of the use of pottery. It is widely familiar that both in West Asia (Jarme, Jericho, Catal Huyuk, Hacilar, Cayonu, Tepe Sang-e-Cazmaq Yaria Tepc, Tepe Guran, Aq-Kupruk) and in East Asia (excepting perhaps the Jomon Culture), the manufacture of pottery started later than eighth millennium B.C. and followed the domestication of plants and animals. Consistent with this date of the Advanced Mesolithic Period of the Belan Valley, however, is the proposed date of the Neolithic Period, viz. seventh-fifth millennium B.C. (discounting all the younger dates obtained from Mahagara), which again indicates a far earlier time-bracket than that of the neolithic cultures in other regions of India (Thapar, 1978), discounting the recent conjuctures to place the North-eastern neolithic culture in *circa* 5000-2000 B.C. (Sharma, T.C. 1981). The neolithic occupation at Mahagara seems to have a long history and may have continued in subsequent millennium. It has, however, not been demonstrated whether the neolithic cultures in the region continued till the beginning of the chalcolithic period in the mid-second millennium B.C. At Kaldihawa a break in occupation after the neolithic culture has been hinted without a plausible explanation. This aberrant phenomenon of very early beginnings of agriculture in the Belan Valley requires to be confirmed by further field-work and more closely-observed sampling of the radio-carbon determinations. Meanwhile, the importance of the finds, particularly relating to the stages of transition from the food-gathering to food producing economy in the region must be fully appreciated.

Another possibility for the early beginning of 'primitive agriculture' in India is indicated by the palynological studies made at the Sambhar Lake in Rajasthan, whereby, based on the presence of a *cerelia* type of pollen in association with a large number of comminuted charcoal pieces, a pollen diagram has been made (Singh 1967 and 1974), showing disturbance of vegetation as early as *circa* 7000-6000 B.C. This has been interpreted as forest clearance and the beginning of some sort of primitive agriculture. Archaeological evidence, however, is so far found wanting to establish this postulate. At Adamgarh in the Mahadeo hills of Central India bones of domesticated animals have been found in association with a microlithic industry, indicating perhaps a stage of transition from the terminal foraging to farming. More intensive work is called for in this area.

REFERENCES

Agrawal, D.P. 1981. Multidisciplinary Investigations in Kashmir: 1979-80 A Report, *Man and Environment* (Pune), Vol. V, pp.87-90.

Basu, Arabinda and Pal, Anadi 1980. *Human Remains from Burzahom* (Calcutta).

Beaching, Captain 1868. Notes on some stone implements found in the District of Singhbhum, *Proceedings, of the Asiatic Society of Bengal.* p. 177.

Chang, Kwang Chih 1977. *The Archaeology of Ancient China* (Third Edition, New Haven).

Chang Kwang Chih 1960. Prehistory and Protohistory of Eastern India (Calcutta).

Dani, A.H. 1970-71. Excavation in the Gomal Valley, *Ancient Pakistan* (Peshawar), Vol. V, pp. 1-177.

De Terra, H. and Paterson, T.T. 1939. *Studies on the Ice Age in India and Associated Human Cultures* Washington D.C.

Dikshit, K.N. 1982. The Neolithic Cultural Frontiers of Kashmir, *Man and Environment* (Pune), Vol. VI, pp. 30-36.

Halim, Mohd. Abdul. 1970-71. Excavation at Sarai Khola, Part I, *Pakistan Archaeology* (Karachi), no. 7, pp. 23-89.

Halim, Mohd. Abdul 1972. Excavation at Sarai Khola, Part II *Pakistan Archaeology* (Karachi) no. 8.

Kaw, R.N. 1979. The neolithic cultures of Kashmir. In *Essays in Indian Prehistory*, Eds. D.P. Agrawal and D.K. Chakrabarti (Delhi), pp. 219-28.

Khan, F.A. 1965. Excavation at Kot Diji, *Pakistan Archaeology* (Karachi), no. 2.

Khazanchi, T.N. 1976. Pit-dwellers of Burzahom, *The Illustrated Weekly of India*, Sept. 5 (Bombay).

Khazanchi, T.N. 1977. North-western neolithic Cultures of India *News Letters* 7 and 8, Indian Institute of Advanced Study, Simla.

Lubbock, Sir John. 1867. The Stone tools of Assam, *Athenem* June 27.

Mughal, Mohd. Rafique and Halim, Mohd. Abdul. 1971. The Pottery, *Pakistan Archaeology* (Karachi) no. 8.

Pandey, B.M. 1971. Neolithic Hunting Scene in a stone-slab from Burzahom, District—Srinagar Kashmir. *Asian. Perspectives*, Vol. XIV, pp. 194-98.

Pandey, B.M. 1972. A Neolithic Tectiform from Burzahom, District Srinagar, Kashmir, *Journal of the Indian Anthropoligical Society*, Vol. 7(2), pp. 175-77.

Pant, R.K., Agrawal, D.P. and Krishnamurthy, R.V. 1978. Scanning Electron Microscope and other Studies on the Karewa beds of Kashmir. In, *Scanning Electron Microscopy in the study of Sediments* ed. Whalley, W.B., pp. 275-82.

Pant, R.K., Claire, Gaillard; Nautiyal, Vinod; Gaur, G.S. and Shali, S.L. 1982. Some new Lithic and ceramic industries from Kashmir, *Man and Environment* (Pune), Vol. VI, pp. 37-40.

Sharma, A.K. 1967. Neolithic Human Burials from Burzahom, Kashmir, *Journal of the Oriental Institute* (Baroda), Vol. XVI, no. 3, pp. 239-42.

Sharma, A.K. 1968. Animal Burials from Burzahom—A neolithic settlement in Kashmir, *Journal of the Oriental Institute* (Baroda), Vol. XVIII, nos. 1 and 2 pp. 40-44.

Sharma, A.K. 1981a. Prehistoric Exploration in Sikkim, *Puratattva* (New Delhi), no. 10, pp. 82-83.

Sharma, A.K. 1981b. Excavation at Gufkral: 1981, *Puratattva* (New Delhi), no. 11. pp. 19-25.

Sharma, G.R.; Mishra, V.D.; Mandal, D.; Mishra, B.B.; and Pal, J.N. 1980. *Beginning of Agriculture* (Allahabad).

Sharma, T.C. 1981. The Neolithic Pattern of Northeastern India. In Madhu. *Recent Researches in Indian Archaeology and Art History*: ed. Nagaraja Rao M.S. (Delhi), pp. 41-52.

Singh, Gurdip. 1967. A Preliminary approach towards the Resolution of some important problems in Rajasthan. *Indian Geohydrology*. Vol. 3(1).

Singh, Gurdip. 1968. A Preliminary Survey of the Post-glacial Vegetational History of Kashmir valley, *Palaeobotanist*, Vol. 12(1) pp. 73-108.

Singh, Gurdip; Joshi, R.D.; Chopra, S.K. and Singh, A.B. 1974. Late Quaternary History of Vegetation and Climate of the Rajasthan Desert, India, *Philosophical Transactions of the Royal Society of London*, Biological Science 267/889, pp. 467-501.

Stacul, Giorgio. 1969. Excavation near Ghaligai (1968) and Chronological sequence of protohistorical cultures in the Swat Valley, *East and West*, New Series (Rome), Vol. 19, nos. 1 and 2, pp. 41-91.

Stacul, Giorgio. 1976. Excavation at Loebanr III (Swat Pakistan) *East and West*, New Series (Rome) Vol. 26, nos. 1 and 2, DD. pp. 13-30.

Stacul, Giorgio. 1977. Dwelling and Storage pits and Loebanr III (Swat, Pakistan) 1976, Excavation Report, *East and West*, New Series (Rome), Vol. 27, nos. 1-4, pp. 227-53.

Thapar, B.K. 1964. Neolithic Problems in India, in *Indian Prehistory* (Poona), eds. Mishra, V.N. and Mate, M.S.

Thapar, B.K. 1974. Problems of the Neolithic Cultures in India, *Puratattva* (New Delhi), no. 7, pp. 61-65.

Thapar, B.K. 1978. Early Farming Communities in India, *Journal of Human Evolution* (London), Vol. 7, pp. 11-22.

Vishnu Mittre 1968. Protohistoric Records of Agriculture in India. *Transactions of the Bose Research Institute*, Vol. 31(3). pp. 87-106.

The Dynamics of Pre-Harappan Culture

SHASHI ASTHANA
National Museum, New Delhi

THE 'birth' of Indus Civilization is still a vital issue with us since opinions are widely divided on it. For some it is still shrouded in mystery and for others it has generically evolved out of the Rehman Dheri-Kot Diji-Sothi-Hakra complex. One thing, however, is, certain; the term birth is rather inapt, the better term is 'formation' since it implies the notion of 'process' over a long period of time involving various stages. It avoids 'suddenness', 'one time affair', 'definitive act' and 'predictability'—the meanings generally associated with the term 'birth'. Once we reject the terms 'birth' and 'death' in the context of Harappan Culture in favour of 'formation' and 'decay' then it becomes clear that we have to go to pre-Harappan cultures to locate the so-called 'birth' of the Harappan culture. Stratigraphical analyses of some sites show that the choice has to fall on a few of the indigenous cultures. It was not introduced from outside. All theories tracing its origin in West Asia have been more or less completely discarded. The archaeological discoveries now clearly show that the plains of the Indus system were not a *tabula rasa* before the Indus Civilization emerged, more than a millennium before the land was inhabited by human beings, although sparingly. Baluchistan was also not just a land of refuge for the fourth millennium Iranians as was earlier believed by Piggott (1950), Allchin (1968) and Sankalia (1974). People lived there with their indigenously developing cultures, continuosly from about the eighth millennium B.C., i.e. several millennia before the eastern plateau of Iran developed their village cultures using painted potteries some of which show common decorative motifs.

We have here chosen to deal with the early cultures of Baluchistan and the Indus. After the initial stage of the Neolithic folk, Baluchistan developed a number of chalcolithic cultures much before the Harappan Culture developed. The whole of Baluchistan has been found inhabited by these folks during the early fourth millennium B.C. Some of these cultures are Amri, Nal and Kulli in southern Baluchistan and some like Quetta and Zhob, are in northern Baluchistan. The plains of the Indus system, on the other hand, were inhabited mainly by two groups of people, commonly known as Hakra, Kot Dijian and Sothi people named, as usual, after their primary habitations.

To present a meaningful survey of these Pre-Harappan cultures, all of which appear to have contributed something or the other in the formation of the Indus Civilization is faced with a number of problems. The first and foremost of which is to establish their precise chronology and cultural interactions and connections amongst them. The second is to trace their original home : whether each one of them developed autochthonously or they were largely imports from West Asia. Thirdly, we also have to find out within a definite framework of time and space the migrations of the chalcolithic people who colonized the Indus plains. Lastly, we have to determine the exact nature of relationship of these cultures with the Harappan culture in terms of generic connections.

To begin with, it was in 1964 that for the first time A. Ghosh (1965: 113-124) discussed the 'Sothi Culture' in great depth and tried to show that the Sothi contributed substantially to the make-up of the mature Harappan culture. He also visualized that the Sothi culture may have originated in northern Baluchistan. Later on this theory was developed by Mughal in 1970, who wrote his Ph.D. thesis analysing these cultures in still greater details. Others simply followed the lead given by these two scholars.

We now know that Amri, Nal, Kulli, Rehman Dheri, Kot Diji, Hakra and Sothi cultures were more or less contemporary to each other generally flourishing into their individual culture-areas, but sometimes also penetrating into each others' territory. Significantly although the individuality of Amri, Nal and Kulli cultures has been established, the same cannot be said about the Rehman Dheri, Kot Diji and Hakra and Sothi; some take them as one and call it Kot Diji-Sothi complex while others take them as two or three separate complexes of intimately connected groups of people sharing many common items. Indeed, all of them have certain common characteristics in pottery but stone foundations of mud-brick architectures and leaf shaped chert arrow-heads are the features not encountered in the Sothi Culture so far. In pottery the use of white is very rare at Kot Diji while it forms a characteristic feature of the Sothi ware. The use of white in Baluchistan, at Mehargarh, Rehman Dheri, Lewan and also at Jalilpur in the Indus plains, has been attested. As the Sothi culture has some other significant parallels in northern Baluchistan in pottery motifs, it appears that originally these complexes belonged to some commonly shared traditions. However, in course of time when it expand in space, regional variations developed markedly. In southern Baluchistan also cultures like Amri, Nal and Kulli were closely related. A number of sites have yielded the Amri and the Nal potteries mixed in a single cultural level. Amrian concentrated in Sind, penetrated into southern Baluchistan at a number of places. However, the Kot Dijian cultures penetrated into the Amrian area in the south-west and also crossed the Indus and expanded in the Indo-Gangetic divide in the east.

During this period, in northern Baluchistan, Quetta region in particular, a Bronze Age culture was in full swing. Its remains could be seen at Mehargarh VII where some Kot Dijian pottery is also present (Jarrige & Lechevallier 1979: 509-532; Jarrige & Meadow 1980: 122-133). Earlier it was thought that during this period Turkmenians of Namazga III culture overpowered this area and it was their culture which was known as the Quetta Culture. But now we know how superfluous this view has been. At least advanced centres like Mehargarh are not at all found colonized by the Turkmenians although their elements were used by the Mehargarihans in forms completely Indianized. Significantly, the early Bronze Age sites of Baluchistan have been generally found deserted with the growth of the cities in the Indus Valley. Probably a large part of the population was absorbed in the Harappan towns, some of which appear to have been trading posts on major trade routes such as Nowsharow and Dabarkot.

It appears that though many of the pre-Harappan towns were in close contact amongst themselves in Baluchistan, Sind and the Indus plains as well as with the towns in Turkmenia and eastern Iran, they do not appear to have formed an organized trade net-work during the fourth millennium. Their requirements of luxury items like lapis lazuli and turquoise may have been met through irregular exchanges. The presence of such items may not always be interpreted in terms of regular imports as we have a lot of lapis and turquoise in the early neolithic times at Mehargarh when the question of 'organized' trade does not seem to arise.

With this general backdrop, we shall move to the specific problems and current views on pre-Harappan cultures.

To begin with, the classical wares in Baluchistan—wheel-turned bichrome, polychrome and grey ware—were considered by Piggott (1950) as the diffusionistic traits coming from Mesopotamia and Iran. Baluchistan was considered by Allchins (1968) as a corridor which transmitted cultural influences from the West to the East and *vice versa*. Baluchistan was also considered by Childe (1934), McCown (1942) and others as a refuge zone for the Iranian chalcolithic people who were defeated and uprooted by the Aryans coming from northern Iran and Soviet Central Asia.

However, the discovery of Mehargarh proved a turning point in this regard. These theories have now been openly questioned. The excavation conducted here by Jarrige (1979) demonstrated the developmental stages of various pre-Harappan cultures from the eighth through the third millennium B.C. It has thus proved that northern Baluchistan was the nuclear zone where man seems to have changed from the hunting-gathering stage to the food-producing-herding stage, independent of distant neolithic cultures in northern Iran, Palestine and Anatolia.

South Baluchi cultures, like Amri, Nal and Kulli have now been provided with not only longer chronologies but also being freed from many ill-founded views about them. Neither the Nal Polychrome Ware is now connected with the Jemdet Nasr Polychrome nor Kulli is obliged for its birth to the Scarlet Ware of Mesopotamia. However, the formative stages of these cultures still remains unexplored. But the probability of their being derived from northern Baluchistan cannot be ruled out; in fact that what has now been proposed by various scholars. May be some day we get the transitional phases of these cultures, possibly in Kalat region.

Thus these pre-Harappan cultures are autochthonous in spite of the fact that many of them had occasional contacts with West Asian and Central Asian cultures.

With this we move to the Indus system where at least three pre-Harappan culture-complexes have been recognized. We will call them three phases for they appear to belong to a single developing phenomenon of culture growth. Each phase has local cultural variations but in totality they share some dominant cultural features, hence grouped under one phase, particularly when they appear to be contemporary. Each one may not have been related with the other directly but chain relationship appears to be there. On this basis, the first phase is represented by the neolithic cultures of Sarai Khola I, Gumla I and Jalilpur I and possibly some more sites in dried up belt of the Ghaggar-Hakra which are as yet not known. The second is represented by a kind of mixed chalcolithic Baluchi cultures of Amri I, Balakot I, Kot Diji lower levels, Gumla II, Rehman Dheri I. The third is represented in the upper levels of Kot Diji, Rehman Dheri II, Gumla III, Kalibangan I, Jalilpur II, Banawali I, etc. in the Ravi-Ghaggar Valley and Sarai Khola II in the Potwar region near Taxila.

In this connection two observations may be made. First, that while Phase I is as represented at Jalilpur and Hakra sites, some 99 of them, known so far, have close contacts with each other in pottery. The second concerns two reasons for dividing the pre-Harappan Kot Diji-Sothi complex into two groups (Phases I & II): (a) Phase II sites, like Gumla and Rehman Dheri have predominance of Baluchi elements but in Phase III their number not only decreases considerably, they are found in highly naturalized forms which have shed their Baluchi character to a large extent, and (b) the phenomenal growth and expansion which could not be visualized exclusively in the context of the known dynamics of Baluchi cultures.

Phase I

It represents the first stage of movement of the Baluchi people generally in areas east of the Indus. The neolithic cultures of Phase I have been found at Gumla I in Bannu basin, Sarai Khola I in the Potwar, Jalilpur I in the Indus plains. The complex is represented by the abundance of bone points, chert blades and handmade red burnished pottery with basket impressions on their bases. A few examples of handmade pots with outer surface decorated with applique designs have also been found.

This evidence shows that the people who for the first time moved into the Indus system and nearby regions belonged to the developed ceramic neolithic faces. They established small pastoral settlements and lived in huts. They produced handmade pottery, largely crude and stone and bone tools. Although it is difficult to establish their ancestory at this stage, yet it is possible to make a few observations: Quetta in Northern Baluchistan appears to be their source, at least for Gumla it is likely to be the major, if not, the only source. For Sarai Khola and Jalilpur, however, northern Baluchistan might not have been the only source. Some neolithic sites in the Kashmir Valley which may be older than Burzahom (Khazanchi) and Gufkral (Sharma 1979-80) could provide another source for them since the pottery with basket impression at the bottom, as recorded at Jalilpur, has also been found at Burzahom and Gufkral and other neolithic sites in the Kashmir Valley. But admittedly, at the present state of our knowledge, it is only a conjecture since while Jalilpur may go back to the fourth millennium B.C. Burzahom and Gufkral do not appear to be older than 2500 B.C.

Mughal (1982) has noted ninety-nine sites of Hakra culture, oldest known culture in Cholistan. This has been designated as Hakra because of their first discovery and great concentration along the Hakra-Ghaggar flood plains. Its pottery repertoir is very distinctive although B.B. Lal and B.K. Thapar (personal communication) who have handled this pottery feel that it is practically the same as Kalibangan I (pre-Ḥarappan) Ware—an observation, if correct, will make the Hakra Ware an early phase of the Kalibangan Pre-Harappan Ware. In any case, it is characterized by handmade red ware with incised decoration. The major shapes include from large and thick walled vessels to small thin bodied pots. Applique pottery has also been found. The external surface is treated with thick coat of mud mixed with bits of pottery either all over the body or just below the neck. The neck below the rim is also painted in black. It recalls the pottery found at Jalilpur I. Significantly, it overlaps with Kot Dijian pottery in Jalilpur II levels. The incised Hakra Ware has no exact parallel in the Indus plains. But 'Periano A' Ware of northern Baluchistan provides some significant similarity for this pottery. The Hakra Ware also includes a small percentage of wheel-thrown buff ware with paintings in black whose exact parallels are yet to be located. The lithic artefacts of Hakra culture are, of course, similar to those found in Jalilpur I and II, Sarai Khola I, Gumla I and Rehman Dheri. This tool-kit consists of parallel sided blades, micro-blades, borers, leaf shaped arrow-heads, scrapers and cores. Animal figurines, shell and terracotta bangles and fragments of grinding stones are also found at Hakra culture sites.

Hakra sites are heavily concentrated around Derawar Fort, and also towards its south-west, although a few sites also occur east of Derawar.

Two observations may, however, be made in this context. One, more than fifty per cent sites belong to what is called 'camp sites'. It means they cannot be counted for the concept of 'concentration of sites which is applicable to the 'areas of attraction' with large sedentary population. In fact, 'camp site' stands for a social situation which is just the opposite of it—nomadism. It must also be borne in mind that the 'settled sites' of the Hakra are also very small, none is possibly more than two acres, a fact which will also show that they represent small communities of shifting nature.

On the whole, the Hakra sites, represent a pastoral people on their march from the west to the east. The second observation concerns its exact relationship with the Kot Diji-Sothi complex, about which we have already quoted the views of Lal and Thapar. The applique pottery is present at all the Sothi sites, including Kalibangan. The same observation applies to the incised ware. Obviously, the Hakra wares continue in the Sothi complex. But does it mean that the Hakra and Sothi represent one and the same culture-complex? It is difficult to give a categorical answer to this question at this stage. The only excavated site of this ware is Jalilpur (Period I) where it has been located below the Kot Diji levels (Period II). Thus, we have to wait and watch for the results of a few more excavated sites.

Phase II

It represents the second stage of colonization of the Indus system. It was initiated by the chalcolithic village communities living in the hilly tracts of Baluchistan, an attempt in which the Phase I people seem to have actively participated. Probably the pressure of growing population in a comparatively restricted land for agricultural pursuits pressed them in the last quarter of the fourth millennium B.C. to move out into the plains. If pottery is even a rough guide for cultural identification they came in the Indus basin in different waves, often intermingling in different proportions. Gumla II complex, for example, includes pottery of northern Baluchistan and south Turkmenian (Namazga III) type. At Sarai Khola II, the lower levels have yielded potsherds of Anjira I Ware, Siah Damb I Ware and Kile Gul Mohammad Ware. Kot Diji and Balakot also repeat the same story in their lower levels. It clearly shows that the population of this phase at most of the important sites was mixed, consisting of several groups, belonging to different regions of Baluchistan and beyond. It is significant to note that these mixed complexes at a later stage slowly tended to be homogeneous one. The movement of the Baluchi people primarily into the Indus basin and the Potwar region seems to have followed the Gomal Pass, Sanghar Pass and Bolan Pass, the three traditional routes.

Phase III

This phase marks the third stage of colonization of the Indus system. It is in fact an extension of the second. During this period one witnesses the spread of the Indus basin people into Ravi-Ghaggar plains. Obviously, the Baluchi elements which had come to stay in the pre-Harappan complexes, generally at the Indus basin sites, also found a place in the complexes of the Ravi-Ghaggar sites. This alone explains the presence of Periano Wet Ware, Khojak Parallel Striated Wares, vessels with black band at Jalilpur and other sites to the east of the Indus. All these traits originally belonged to Periano Ghundai or some other site in the Baluchi hills. Now in this phase we come across a sufficiently high stage of culture: pottery decorated with a number of painted and incised designs, terracotta cart-frames, wheels and triangular cakes, mud-brick houses, sometimes with stone foundation, etc. At Jalilpur, Kalibangan, Banawali, Siswal, etc. the pot-decorations included several new items, e.g. white bands and curves, deer and trident. It is called Sothi Ware which is a local development of the Ravi-Ghaggar plains. Mud-brick fortifications, mud-brick houses with several rooms, drains paved with burnt bricks, agricultural innovations of twin crop-system in well laid ploughed fields, etc. as evidenced at Kalibangan, represent a stage much more developed than that of Gumla II, Rehman Dheri I-II, Amri Ia-Ib, Kot Diji (lower levels), and Balakot I (lower levels), etc. The Kot Diji-Sothi sites throughout the Indus system are marked by characteristics which are typical of the river valley cultures, i.e.

hortizontally expanding towns with closely packed brick houses, duly fortified with walls of standardized mud-bricks laid in well-planned manner, such as alternate courses of headers and stretchers, wheeled conveyance and agricultural fields with animal drawn 'L' shaped ploughs whose terracotta models have been found by Mughal from Jalilpur, etc. These items exhibit the emergence of a process by which different communities in the Indus system progressed from the stage of First Village to the stage of First Cities with highly corporate life-style and a kind of regimented socio-politico-economic structure based upon professional specialization and a high degree of economic as well as social interdependence for which now our archaeologist friends in the United States with basic qualification in anthropology, use the term 'Complex Societies'.

With this we come to traditionally difficult questions of terminology, chronology, etc. It is absolutely clear from the excavations that all the cultures we have included in our present study are pre-Harappan cultures in the sense that the initially appeared earlier to what we now generally call mature Harappan Culture or the Indus Civilization. It is significant to note that although stratigraphically speaking all of them arose earlier to the Harappan Culture some of them overlapped with it and continued to live for quite sometime in that stage, some in fact out-lived the Harappan Culture, such as the Siswal Complex. Kulli was partly contemporary to Harappan culture as the evidence from Balakot shows. The MASCA corrected radio-carbon dates show that around 3500 B.C., due to certain unknown reasons, but most probably population growth and its socio-economic consequences, people started migrating from northern Baluchistan to the Indus basin. They came down from the hills in several waves. Mehargarh IV-V Gumla II-III, Nal, Amri, etc. belong to this period. The Ravi-Ghaggar pre-Harappan sites like Jalilpur II, pre-Defence Harappan, Kot Diji, Sothi, etc. belong to the last decades of the fourth and the beginning of the third millennium B.C. By the beginning of the second quarter of the third millennium emerges the Harappan Culture.

Coming to terminology, so far two terms have been in general use for some of the culture-complexes we are considering here: Pre-Harappan and Early Harappan. The term Pre-Harappan should in fact be a general term in which p should be small and not capital, denoting thereby the chronological position of certain cultures *vis-a-vis* the Harappan Culture. Its basis is stratigraphy although cultural consideration of items like script and, weights and measures are also there. Mughal (1970) has, however, been insisting on the term 'Early Harappan' for the Kot Dijian and Sothi complexes as he is of the firm opinion that they represent the formative stages of the Indus Civilization which he prefers to call Mature Harappa Culture for obvious reasons—the prefix 'Early' would otherwise hang in air. In other words, he believes that the Harappan culture evolved directly out of the Kot Dijian Complex. Indian, as well as some Pakistani archaeologists, however, provide these cultures a different status. According to them, the Harappan culture represents a distinct cultural identity which cannot at the present state of our knowledge be placed as firmly in the unilinear evolutionary model of culture-growth, as Mughal would like us to do, for example, the absence of writing and weights and measures in the Kot Diji-Sothi complex and rather developed form of script in the Harappan complex is enigmatic. To recapitulate, at least six years earlier to Mughal, A. Ghosh (1965) had considered the possibility of Harappan culture being evolved out of Sothi culture. At that time Y.D. Sharma (1965: 132) and later on Khan (1981: 21) pointed out the technological difference between the thick and sturdy Harappan pottery and light and thin Kot Dijian pottery. They feel that the thick black-on-red Indus Ware could not originate from the thin pinkish Kot Diji Ware. But at Kot Diji, the Kot Diji Complex includes the thick sturdy Indus Ware.

The term pre-Harappan is, of course, loose since it covers practically all chalcolithic cultures preceding the Harappan culture. It does not explain the special status that the Kot Diji and Sothi enjoyed in relation to the Harappan culture since out of all the known pre-Harappan cultures only these two (if we leave Bara complex for the moment for the early phase of which also this term is applied) overlap with each other in a big way. This is notwithstanding the fact that at the key sites like Kot Diji and Kalibangan the end of the Kot Diji-Sothi complex has been catastrophic which is projected as a serious snag to the 'Early Harappan' theory. Moreover, there are strong indications that at least in three fields the Kot Dijians were the forerunners of the Indus Civilization : the use of fortification walls, copper technology and some decorations on pottery, such as the fish-scale and intersecting circles. We, therefore, have to admit that the exact relationship between the two complexes is still far from clear. It is clear that all the pre-Harappan cultures were not transformed into the Harappan culture but certainly many of them contributed their own share to the long list of cultural items which are found in the mature Harappan deposits. Still, probably it is only the highly fertile land of Bahawalpur region, where a large concentration of pre-Harappan sites has now been located, which is likely to have witnessed the transformation of pre-Harappan culture complex into the Harappan. If this proposition, as was earlier proposed by Gupta (1975-76) is accepted then even the sites like Mohenjodaro will be younger to the Bahawalpur sites. Recent researches of Michel Jansen (personal communication) in fact give clear indications of this situation.

To sum up, the archaeological data have shown that the vast region, stretching from the present day eastern Iranian borders to the north-western India, had witnessed the growth of several cultures right from the neolithic times through the earliest times of the Harappan Culture. Northern Baluchistan, Quetta-Bolan area, in particular, was the most crucial area for the growth of early cultures and for some alien cultural impulses.

From the Mesolithic to the Neolithic, i.e. from the hunting stage to the herding stage, the change took place in this area. The evolutionary stages of various cultures from the pre-Ceramic Neolithic to the Chalcolithic are documented at the recently discovered sites at Mehargarh. From this area, the first cultural impulses travelled to southern Baluchistan and the Indus system. At a later stage, the intermingling of various cultural complexes gave birth to a somewhat homogeneous culture-complex in the Indus basin in the form of Kot Diji culture. The Sothi culture in the Ghaggar basin was perhaps a cognate complex. Ultimately, this Kot Diji-Sothi complex turned into Harappan culture at some selected places. How and where exactly it happened, we have as yet no idea.

The continuity in the basic character of these cultures is itself the proof that these cultures were indigenous to the area.

REFERENCES

Allchin, F.R. 1968. *The Birth of Indian Civilization*, Harmondsworth: Penguin.

Childe, V.G. 1934. *New Light on the Most Ancient East*, London.

Ghosh, A. 1965. The Indus Civilization: its origins, authors, extent and chronology. In *Indian Prehistory 1964*, edited by V.N. Mishra and M.S. Mate, Poona, pp. 113-156.

Gupta, S.P. 1975-76. Origin of the Form of Harappa Culture: A New Proposition. *Puratattva*, no. 8, pp. 141-146.

Jarrige, J.F. & M. Lechevallier. 1979. Excavations at Mehrgarh, Baluchistan: their significance in the Prehistoric context of the Indo-Pakistan Borderland. In *South Asian Archaeology*, 1977, edited by M. Taddei, Naples. pp. 463-536.

Jarrige, J.F. & R.H. Meadow. 1980. The Antecedents of Civilization in the Indus Valley. *Scientific American*, Vol. 243, no. 2, pp. 122-133.

Khan, F.A. 1981. Kot Diji Culture: Its Greatness. In *Indus Civilization New Perspectives*. Edited by A.H. Dani. Islamabad, pp. 15-24.

Khazanchi, 1962. Excavations at Burzahom. *Indian Archaeology—A Review* 1961-62, pp. 17-21.

Khazanchi, 1969. Excavations at Burzahom. *Indian Archaeology—A Review*. 1968-69. pp. 10.

McCown, D.E. 1942. *The Comparative Stratigraphy of Early Iran*. Studies in Ancient Oriental Civilization, no. 23, Oriental Institute, University of Chicago, Chicago.

Mughal, M.R. 1970. *The Early Harappan Period in the Greater Indus Valley and Northern Baluchistan* (c. 3000-2400 B.C.). Ann Arbor, University, Microfilms.

Mughal, M.R. 1982. Recent Archaeological Research in the Cholistan Desert. In *Harappan Civilization—A Contemporary Perspective*, edited by G.L. Possehl, New Delhi, pp. 85-95.

Piggott, S. 1950. *Prehistoric India*, Harmondsworth, Penguin.

Sankalia, H.D. 1974. *Prehistory and Protohistory of India and Pakistan*, Poona.

Sharma, A.K. 1982. Excavations at Gufkral. *Puratattva*. no. 11, New Delhi, pp. 19-25.

Sharma, Y.D. 1965. *Comments in Indian Prehistory 1964*, edited by V.N. Mishra and M.S. Mate, Poona.

Harappa Culture: Emergence of a New Picture

JAGAT PATI JOSHI
Archaeological Survey of India,
New Delhi

BEFORE the partition of India (1947), comparatively only a few sites of Harappan civilization, more popularly known as Indus Civilization, had been discovered. However, by that time the results of excavations at Mohenjo-Daro, Harappa and Chanhudaro were already published and the explorations carried out in Punjab, Sind and Baluchistan by Stein and Mazumdar were also available in the Memoirs of the Archaeological Survey of India. The civilization as such was understood as highly developed urban civilization confined more or less to the Indus basin and havirg 'stagnating' diagnostic cultural traits.

After Independence the entire position regarding the extent, culture-contents, regional variations, etc. of the Indus civilization has changed. During the last six decades, due to constant efforts of the archaeologists, more than 862 pre-Harappan, Harappan and the late Harappan sites have been discovered in India. In India the area of distribution of Harappan settlements runs broadly from Manda in southern Jammu (J & K) through Daimabad in southern Maharashtra and Mehagam and Bhagatrav in southern Gujarat, to Hulas in District Saharanpur in Western U.P. If sites in Pakistan are also included it covers an area 1.3 million square kilometres.

The excavated sites of Harappa culture have yielded a substantial number of radiocarbon dates. As a result a shorter chronology for the Harappan culture was once proposed which ranged from *circa* 2300 B.C. to 1750 B.C. However, when caliberated (MASCA), the dates for Harappan culture range between *circa* 2790 and 1900 B.C.

Distribution

By and large, the pre-Harappan and Harappan sites are located along the major rivers. Contrary to this, the late Harappan sites are found along tributaries, towards upper reaches of these rivers. For convenience sake, the area covered by Indus civilization can now be divided into six sectors:

Directional	*Geographical*
1. Northern	Punjab (type site: Harappa)
2. Eastern	Rajasthan, Haryana (type sites: Kalibangan)
3. Central	Bahawalpur (type site: Ganveriwala)
4. Southern	Sind (type site: Mohenjo-Daro)
5. South-western	Baluchistan (type site: Kulli Harappan)
6. South-eastern	Gujarat (type site: Lothal)

Of these, the first four domains have a number of sites where the Harappan culture is found stratigraphically later than a variety of chalcolithic cultures which are termed as 'Pre-Harappan'. Our experience has shown that practically in every region there are three kinds of situations: (a) Where there is a clear cut stratigraphic break through the Pre-Harappan and Harappan cultures, although the two complexes are found in mixed form through a number of layers subsequent to the layer marking break e.g. Kot Diji and Kalibangan; (b) Where the stratigraphic break is not clearly marked, e.g. Banawali; (c) Where the Harappan culture never reached the site of Pre-

Harappans, such as Jalilpur, Sarai Khola, etc.

Origin and Form

To some without any known beginnings the Harappan culture is available in a full-fledged form in the Indus valley, Rajasthan and Gujarat and Ghosh has said, 'This itself lend to it a peculiarly romantic charm while death from unidentified source is understandable, unnatural birth is an unnatural phenomenon'. Wheeler has postulated that 'opportunity' and 'genius' might be responsible for the origin of this civilization. One thing is certain it did not appear with a bang. Various theories have been propounded regarding the 'origin' and 'form' of the civilization and it would be clear that its origin cannot be explained by a single factor whether 'colonization' or 'acculturation'. Pattern of culture contacts between the Indus plain and the adjoining region on the west varied according to both time and space, with the result that we often have a spectrum of intermediary situations between the two opposite extremes viz. 'colonisation' and 'acculturation'.

Cardinal Traits

In spite of the fact that considerable regional variations within Harappa culture have been discovered, the following diagnostic traits of the culture can be postulated which give it an unified character throughout perhaps with a central authority.

(a) Citadel and Systematic town planning having chess board pattern and use of bricks with a ratio of 1 : 2 : 4,
(b) Red Ware pottery painted with black designs, well fired; paintings consisting of vegetal and geometric disigns, concentric circles, intersecting circles, *pipal* (*Ficus religiosa*) leaf, banana tree (*Musa sapientum*), landscapes, fish scale design, etc. and chapes including dish-on-stand, 'S' shaped jars, beakers, goblets, perforated jars, etc.,
(c) Steatite beads and long tubular beads of carnelian,
(d) Terracotta mother goddess,
(e) Terracotta cakes of triangular, circular, round and *mushtika* type,
(f) Bangles of terracotta and faience,
(g) Chert blades,
(h) Seals and sealings,
(i) Pictographic Inscriptions,
(j) Chert and agate weights,
(k) Burials, extended and pot burials,
(l) Copper and Bronze objects.

Settlement Pattern Movement and Distribution

So far as the layout plan of cities in different parts of the Indus culture domain is concerned, there appears to be regional variations. While Mohenjo-daro, Harappa and Kalibangan have basically the concept of a citadel and a chess board patterned lower city, at Lothal there is an acropolis and a lower city and at Surkotada the citadel and the lower township is made in a single fortification complex. At Lothal which is trapezoid in plan, the acropolis is at a higher level. Allahdino and Balakot (Pakistan) have a precisely laid grid plan. The position of the citadel in those settlements has already been discussed by Thapar. Thus regional variability is available in the settlement pattern. Environment has been a major factor for the growth, expansion and possibly for the decline of the civilization. To a considerable extent environment seems also to be responsible for 'Urbanization' and subsequent 'deurbanization' of the culture.

On the basis of explorations carried out by the author from 1965 to 1980 considerable light has been thrown on the movements of the Harappans in the third-second millennium B.C. in Kutch and patterns of settlement in southern Punjab.

Between 1975 and 1980 we also explored parts of Punjab and Haryana, as well as Jammu, since we expected to locate sites in the eastern regions, which are still devoid of any significant number of Harappan sites. The area now covered by the districts of Ropar and Patiala have yielded Harappan and pre-Harappan sites. But districts of Amritsar, Gurdaspur and Jullundur, have yielded only Late Harappan sites. In Mansa Tehsil of District Bhatinda (Punjab), along the dried up tributaries of the Ghaggar, twenty-one pre-Harappan and Harappan sites were located, some of which are indeed very large, comparing in extent Harappa. The explorations carried out earlier by the Archaeological Survey along the Ravi, Beas and Sutlej rivers did not yield any Harappan site. Since the explorations have yielded Harappan sites in southern parts of Bhatinda, adjoining Sriganganagar District of Rajasthan, it appears that the established route for the movement of the people passed directly between northern and southern Punjab. A large number of pre-Harappan and Harappan sites were explored earlier in District Patiala in Punjab and District Hissar in Haryana. They neatly connect our newly discovered sites. Significantly except for the mature Harappan site of Manda, District Jammu, on the Chenab, no Harappan site has so far been located on the Chenab as well as the Beas.

Leaving northern India, when we reach lower Sind and Gujarat, the sites locationally behaved slightly differently. In 1967, the author explored a large number of sites in Kutch and postulated that there is a case for movement of the Harappans by land routes from Sind to Kutch, for Kutch is easily accessible from Allahadino (Karachi) which is only about 400 km from Kotara, a Harappan site in Khavada, District Kutch. From Allahadino and other sites in lower Sind one could reach this place by crossing the Biar Bet, Gainda Bet and Kuver-Bet, and then travelling through the narrow valley between Kala Dungar and Gora Dungar could cross a strip of Rann at Amarpur, about 6 km in width, and reach Kotadi (in the neighbourhood of the village Dhola-Vira), a large Harappan fortified establishment. If one had to go still further, one crossed the Rann, reached the present day Rapar Taluk where besides Surketada, a cluster of Harappan sites is now available. Incidentally, the route from Rahim-ki-Bazar to Luna and then to Desalpur in Kutch may also have been in use; besides a few other less popular land-routes which passed through the Rann. Recent explorations have brought to light some Harappan sites in District Mehsana, Gujarat, viz. Dudkha, Lorala, Subpur Kuwar and Firojpur which evidently attests that the Harappans came to north Gujarat through the Little Rann of Kutch.

The picture that emerges from the above-mentioned data shows that in the Punjab the pre-Harappans were closely followed by the Harappans and significantly enough on the same sites; a fact which might show that if the change in culture from the pre-Harappans to Harappan took place locally, it was at sites where the pre-Harappan (or Sothi or Kalibangan) and Harappan sites have been found together. The cluster of twenty-one sites in an area of approximately 50 km × 25 km (i.e. 1250 sq km) in Mansa Taluk of District Bhatinda may indicate that this was a very important region in the Harappan times. The pre-Harappans and Harappans preferred the Ghaggar and a few of its selected tributaries, like the Chautang and Sirhind, as this was a more static river system than the Beas, Sutlej and Ravi which were erratic in their behaviour, changing their courses very often. In fact, Sirhind provided the most important line of communication between the Punjab and Rajasthan sites. The raw materials like timber, especially *deodar cedrus* (*deodara*), used in house-building activities. Significantly, the settlements in Mansa Taluk fall in three categories: (1) 'cities' of about 1500 × 1500 m area, such as Dhalewan, Gurnikalan, Beglian Da Theh, Lakimirwala, and Hasanpur; these are generally situated at a distance of 3 to 5 km from each other; (2) in between, there were six 'towns' ranging in area between 900 × 900 m and 500 × 500 m at Karampura, Dallewala I, Sannewali, Hirka, Dellewala II and Bare II, (it has been observed that all the 'cities' and 'towns' were situated on the eastern side of the river where inundation by floods was less); and (3) a series of 'village', numbering 14, each covering approximately an area of 200 × 200 m to 400 × 400 m Denewala I, Denewala II, Chhoti Mansa, Lallianwali, Bhikhi, Gurni Kalan II, Nahriwala, Naiwala I to V are, however, situated on the western side of the river which was subjected to occasional floods. At present also, big cities on the Yamuna are situated on the southern side of the river where the thrust of floods is not much. This area, therefore, gives the best evidence of all the three types of settlements placed near each other, creating an ideal situation of an urban complex. Their commercial interaction was the pre-requisite for a developed civilization.

In other words it seems that Sirhind was an important 'economic pocket' which mobilized the resources of the northern region of the lower Himalayas and transported them to Bhawalpur area via Kalibangan, and also to Harappan sites in Haryana and Punjab. The situation is almost the same which exists in Kutch which was a half-way house with a concentration of as many as 25 sites between Sind and Gujarat. It may be pertinent to mention that there was yet another 'economic pocket' on the same Ghaggar in the Bahawalpur region where M.R. Moghul has located about 250 sites in an area of 1000 sq km from Yazman to Derawar Fort.

The availability of three 'economic pockets' e.g. in Mansa area in Punjab, Bahawalpur area in Pakistan and Kutch area all falling on the Sarasvati-Hakra system and comprised of 931 pre-Harappan, Harappan and late Harappan sites.[1] Out of these 721 sites belong to mature Harappa and late Harappa cultures. The availability of such a large number of Harappan sites on Sarasvati Hakra-system postulate that the Harappa civilization was flourishing more in this river system than in the Indus basin itself. At the moment Kalibangan is the only site which has been excavated and many more sites await the archaeologist's spade. The idea regarding 'nuclear' area once again needs reassessment. Perhaps that day is not far off when the entire civilization may have to be relabelled as Sarasvati (Hakra) civilization. The environmental factor, regional variability, patterns of settlement lead one to reassess the entire emerging picture in 1982, after a fruitful discussion on the major issues indicated above.

REFERENCES

1. Based on the up-to-date data compilation of Pre-Harappan, Harappan and late settlements and their distributional patterns done by Miss Madhu Bala, Dy. Superintending Archaeologist, and maps prepared by Shri J.R. Batra, Sr. Draftsman, Archaeological Survey of India, New Delhi.

Late Harappan Cultures–A Reappraisal

K.N. DIKSHIT
Archaeological Survey of India,
New Delhi

THE later phase of the Indus civilization was reflective of changes. It marked the end of writing, use of weights and measures, construction of monumental buildings and idea of town-planning. This phase has been placed at the moment somewhere in a bracket between 1800 B.C. and 1200 B.C.

Definition

The term late Harappan culture has been variously described. Literally the term could mean the end or the diffusion of a civilization at the climax period. Precisely the late Harappan cultures could be identified with the archaeological assemblages which follow the cultural continuity of mature Harappan and its associated miscellany. Wheeler proposed the specific name for the late and developing branch of the Indus civilization in Saurashtra (Kathiawad) and even further south as 'Saurashtrian Indus' (Wheeler 1966: 87). He also called it provincial or late varieties of Indus civilization with a caution on the use of the term 'Indus'. The transformation of Harappan culture in Gujarat and Saurashtra is an accepted phenomenon but in Haryana, Punjab and Western Uttar Pradesh this picture has emerged only in the last decade.

The homogeneity of Harappa culture which existed throughout its mature phase was broken and the diversity became the significant factor of the late Harappan cultures. It may also be mentioned that different pottery types and other cultural traits revealed the regional dynamics of the Harappa Culture. However, for labelling any assemblage as 'Late Harappan Culture', the presence of a few of the cultural traits of mature Harappans are must as revealed from the excavations at Mohenjo-daro, Chanhudarao, Harappa, Lothal and Kalibangan.

The Late Harappan Culture represented a devolutionary stage of the Indus civilization. In fact the devolution of a civilization would involve in its practical application, the reversal of a few abstract criteria of urbanization as laid down by Childe and discussed by Adams (Childe 1950: Adam; 1966). According to Ghosh, Indus de-urbanization involved: decrease in settlement size and population, in surplus food production, cessation of construction of monumental buildings, in use of writing and in long distance trade. All these suggest weakening of central authority (Ghosh 1979). Ghosh identified Late Harappan cultures with those which are later than the mature Harappan but still have affinities with it in a degenerate form. To be more concrete, the cultures represented at Rangpur IIB (possibly also IIC) and allied sites in Gujarat and sites in Punjab, Haryana and Western Uttar Pradesh are Late Harappans (Ghosh 1977 pers. com.). Possehl in Gujarat context called these sites as post-Urban Harappan. The pattern of change in Indus Civilization was the progressive modification of the distinctly urban form, a shift in the level of socio-cultural attainments which existed throughout its mature phase but slowed down in later stage. It was centrally less organised less differentiated and less specialised than in the urban phase (Possehl 1980: 20). Lal is of the opinion that a civilization may devolve or deteriorate but its bearers are not normally expected to wipe out. And, this is precisely what seems to have happened in the case of the Indus Civilization as well (Lal 1979). Wheeler suggested that the Indus empire was followed by a long phase of cultural fragmentation, not altogether unlike from which it sprang but including perhaps remoter exotic elements (Wheeler 1977: 84). The material culture also becomes poor when the urban fabric of a culture disintegrates (Gupta 1979). With the decline of this civilization the sophisticated Harappan traits were watered down by a mingling with impoverished local cultures until what was once distinctively Harappan was diluted to the point of non-existence (Dales 1966). In fact the devolution of culture appears to be the outcome of economic decline which produces cultural transformation and changes the internal interaction of the society (Dikshit 1979, 1981).

Field Data

A survey of some of the excavated sites and other exploratory field data in north India namely Manda in Jammu and Kashmir, Kotla Nihang Khan, Ropar, Chandigarh. Bara. Dher Majra, Sanghol, Katpalon, Nagar and Dadheri in Punjab, Mitathal, Banawali, Balu, Mirzapur, Daulatpur and Bhagwanpura in Haryana and Alamgirpur, Bargaon and Hulas in Uttar Pradesh, have provided sufficient material for understanding the settlement pattern and other social and cultural aspects including the chronological framework of the Harappan *vis-a-vis* Late Harappan Cultures (See Comparative Charts I and II for the survival of characteristic traits from the mature to the Late Harappan phase and also new traits which emerged exclusively in the later phase in north India). In Gujarat and further south, excavations at Lothal and Rangpur in north Gujarat plain, Surkotada and Desalpur in Kutch, Rojdi and Somnath in Saurashtra, Bhagatrav and Malwan in south Gujarat plain and Daimabad in north Maharashtra have provided sufficient comparative data. In north India the migration took place along the river system but in Gujarat and Saurashtra it was possibly also along the coastal belt. The expansion of Indus settlements depended upon the nature of soil and easy availability of water for irrigation and domestic use. The annual floods also helped in irrigation and this may be the reasoning that even the banks of the smallest streams in Punjab, Haryana and western Uttar Pradesh were directly occupied. The migratory pressure of Harappans to Gujarat and further south and to Punjab, Haryana and western U.P. did not appear to be only for agricultural produce but must be coupled with some other weighty reasons such as exploitation of timber from the forest hills of Himalayas (Joshi 1982), copper from Khetri area and production of cotton from clayey alluvial plains.

Outside India in Pakistan the renewed excavations at Jhukar provided evidence to substantiate the theory that the so-called Jhukar was in fact, a representative of the late decadent Harappan civilization in Sind and should not be considered a different class of people as thought earlier (Mughal 1979). At Amri IIC, a transformation was noticed in Harappan pottery. The pot-forms with the thicker and more stylized decoration are termed as forerunners of the Jhukar ware which also continued in next phase (Casal 1964, 88-89). Cemetry-H people succeeded the Harappans in Punjab at Harappa and a number of sites in old Bahawalpur region. Even at Mohenjo-daro in the upper levels, a late squatter type of occupation was noticed (Dales 1966: 93-98). For these seemingly post-Harappan cultures, the term late Harappan is being increasingly used, suggesting perhaps that Harappan traditions continued both in Jhukar and Cemetry-H.

In Afghanistan, Mundigak (Casal 1961) provided an early chronological sequence of the Indus civilization, whereas Shortughai, a site north of Hindukush furnished a sequence starting from mature Harappan to a late phase of mature Harappan. Statistically, the relative importance of mature Harappan elements decreased and some of the ceramic shapes changed. At the same time, new shapes appeared that could be related to Central Asiatic materials. The architecture did not change in a significant manner but the working of lapis-lazuli stopped (Francfort 1981: 93).

The undivided Punjab and western U.P. to some extent from ecologically a continuous unit, whereas northern Rajasthan and Haryana go with lower Indus or Sind. The mature Harappans occupied the banks of the major rivers: Sutlej in Punjab and Saraswati and Drishadwati in Haryana. But in later phase of this civilization, even smaller perennial streams were preferred. In western U.P. the tributaries of Yamuna such as Maskara, Nagdeo, Katha Nala, Krishni and Hindon were the focal points of site location. However, between the Sutlej and the Yamuna only smaller settlements were noticed. The larger settlements are absent. But the same cannot be said about Haryana which is an extension of Kalibangan culture-complex. The growing population also led to new settlements but it must be within a certain arrangement of towns and villages.

The economic and ecological factors also affected the size of the population of the settlement. In Punjab, Harappan settlements are located at a distance of 8 to 12 km from each other. This included also the mature as well as late Harappan sites. This spacing conforms well with Gujarat or further east with Haryana or western U.P. In Punjab area the mature Harappan site of Kotla Nihang Khan measures approximately 26 m east-west and 100 m north-south (2.60 hectare), Dher Majra—105 m by 90 m (0.95 hectares) and Bara—550 m north-south and 300 m east-west (16.50 hectare) etc. The mounds at Ropar, Sanghol, Nagar and Katpalon are superimposed by later deposits and the Harappan deposits were confined only in a limited area, as such their exact extensions of Period I are not known. However, if the site of Kotla Nihang Khan be taken as a case study, it can be said with certainty that most of the settlements must be of average size and smaller in area and population in comparision to their counterparts in the proper Indus valley. The duration of these settlements must be reasonably long as is evident from the occupational thickness at Kotla Nihang Khan which is about 2 m.

Indus people came to Kotla Nihang Khan during the hey-day of Indus Civilization. The cultural retardation which took place due to economic upheaval in the nuclear region was a later event. Ropar and Chandigarh survived as urban-centres but on a very small scale. Sanghol, Dadheri, Nagar and Katpalon were their satellite villages. Bara also never achieved urban character and continued only on cultural borrowings.

In Haryana the excavations at Siswal, Banawali, Balu and Mitathal revealed a culture-sequence starting from pre-Harappan to mature Harappan and late Harappan times. Mirzapur, Daulatpur, Mitathal IIB and Bhagwanpura IA indicated a general decandence in fabric, potting and treatment of surface. At Bhagwanpura IB, the interlocking of Late Harappan culture with PGW was seen (Suraj Bhan 1975, Singh 1977, Joshi 1977, Suraj Bhan and Singh 1981).

In the Gangetic doab, the Harappan culture complex at Alamgirpur and Bargaon were found more influenced by the material remains of Sutlej valley, whereas Hulas appears to have its mooring in the Sraswati-Drishadvati complex of Haryana.

The settlement pattern at Hulas, divisible into three phases, revealed three successive living usages. The rectangular and mud brick houses were confined to the lowest phase, whereas circular huts and rectangular mud walled houses with and without furnaces were in the middle and upper phases of occupation. However, circular huts are not found continued in upper phase. The extensive or large sites are absent in western U.P. Only medium and small-sized sites are present. More than 75 member of sites were noticed, but on an average they are not more than 200 metres in length and 150 metres in breadth, suggesting that the habitations belonged to small cluster of families. These sizes suggest a linear planning or a nucleated one as worked out by Chitalwala in Saurashtra is difficult to say (Chitalwala 1979). However, one can notice at present in upper doab the linear settlements along the Burhi Jamuna and circular pattern of settlement in Solani-Ratmau divide. Most of these sites which are located along the edge of the alluvial strips flanking the tributaries of Yamuna proper, are relatively on higher grounds ensuring safety against the recurring floods and generally follow the drainage lines and the nature and degree of slope. In the districts of Muzaffarnagar and Meerut these sites are uniformly spaced at distance of 8 to 12 km. But in Saharanpur area, the spacing is less, between 5 to 8 km.

In Haryana, Harappans have closely connected net works of towns and villages around them but in Punjab and western Uttar Pradesh in the absence of large settlements, the situation cannot be viewed from the point of urban net-work. As already pointed out environmental and economic factors are very important in determining the form of the settlement pattern including the emergence of urban centres. The pattern of settlement of central Indus valley of twin mounds—citadel area and lower town is absent in Sutlej and Yamuna, whereas in Saraswati and Drishadwati riverine valleys this pattern continued. Assuming that economic development in Doab was quite restricted, it appears from the availability of the cultural items found in excavations in this region, the absence of large Harappan settlements is self-explanatory. The structure of settlement pattern has close correspondence with the type of economy they serve. The layout of Harappan settlements undergone changes and quality of structures demonstrate a gradual process of degeneration and decay.

The sites in Gujarat were also not extensive. Lothal including dock-yard was 7.5 hectares in area, whereas Rojdi and Somnath which appear of the same size required further work for knowing as to whether or not the entire area was ever occupied at one time. Other later sites in Ghelo and Kalubhar valleys ranged between 5.3 and 2.00 hectares (Possehl 1980: 64-65). Rangpur IIA was less urbane in comparison to Lothal. The quality of structure was very poor. Lothal A port town revealed typical mature Harappan assemblage, whereas in Lothal B a gradual transformation was noticed which could be equated with Rangpur IIB (Rao 1963). The excavations at Surkotda, Desalpur, Rajdi, Prabhas Patan, Somnath, Awra and Lakhabhawal also indicated a gradual transformation. At Prabhas Patan late Harappan microlithic blade industry and segmented faience beads were noticed in the earliest levels, whereas in Period IIA Lustrous Red Ware made its appearance which declined in IIB and a plain slipped ware emerged.

The Indus civilization did not die a sudden death with the destruction of towns in Central Indus valley and Rajasthan, but survived for many centuries in Saurashtra and Gujarat, north Maharashtra, Haryana, Punjab and western Uttar Pradesh including Sind and Bahawalpur area. In Gujarat and Saurashtra Late Harappans established their settlements near the sources of raw material. So was the case in northern India. At Sanghol and Dher Majra in Punjab, the major industry was the production of beads in different materials including gold, whereas in Haryana the late Harappans thrust was in south possibly for the exploitation of copper from Khetri or other adjoining areas and transporting them to other contemporary urban centres. This also gives an idea that the exploitation of traditional mines used by classical Harappans remained no more a lucrative proposition for them, partly because of the deteriorating economic condition in the Indus valley and other due to far off distances.

According to some scholars as no significant climatic change occurred in the last three thousand years in northern India, the plains of Sutlej and Yamuna must have opened vista to Indus people for agriculture and other commercial produce. The area of west Punjab and Sind now in Pakistan are the main cotton producing regions. At present, Ferozepur, Hissar and Bhatinda south of the Sutlej, are the chief cotton producing districts. Others are Amritsar, Patiala and Ludhiana. In western U.P. cotton has recently been replaced by sugarcane (Singh 1972: 104, 165). The cloth impression on the Harappan pottery found at Alamgirpur is a pointer in this direction. The Harappan migration to Gujarat and further south in Maharashtra was also possibly for the exploitation of cotton. From soils' point of view alluvial loam soil and calcareous clayey alluvium of north India and black clayey soil of south were quite appropriate for the production of cotton.

The site at Kotla Nihang Khan on the Sutlej, Mitathal (IA) on the Drishadvati and Hulas on the tributary of Yamuna, are the excavated type sites in Punjab, Haryana and western U.P. The characteristic traits of Kotla Nihang Khan possibly influenced from Harappa continued at Ropar, Alamgirpur and Bargaon but in a diminished manner, whereas the cultural gamut of Banawali, Balu and Mitathal IA was an extension of central Indus-Kalibangan complex and extending to Mirzapur, Hulas and Daulatpur. In Ganga valley both these cultural waves are present, thereby opening a new area of discussion. In Sutlej valley the stylistic parallels conform to Harappa and it was the late mature Harappan phase which survived longer, whereas in Haryana early mature phase survived much longer. In western Uttar Pradesh only late mature phase entered and survived.

Food Economy

During the late Harappan period, the earlier food economy, i.e. the use of wheat and barley, was in vogue. A few potsherds and carbonized grains from Hulas revealed (on investigation by the Birbal Sahani Institute of Palaeobotony, Lucknow), barley, wheat, horse gram, peas, green gram, black gram, finger millet (ragi) grass pea and also rice. Rice was possibly adopted by the late Harappans when they came and settled at Hulas. The ornamentation pattern of the rice husk revealed characters common between the cultivated rice *O sativa* and the wild perennial *O rufipogan*. From Daulatpur in Haryana, the charred lump revealed rice seeds and rice husks both of wild and cultivated variety. Un in western U.P. yielded only wild rice which are believed to be the immediate ancestors of the cultivated species *O sativa*. The other wild seeds are of the seeds which occur in paddy fields. The finger millet (ragi) has so far not been reported from any Harappan site in north India.

Pot forms

The devolution of gradual transformation of the Indus civilization from mature to late is very clear in pottery forms from Manda in Jammu, Dher Majra, Chandigarh and Sanghol in Punjab, Mitathal IIB, Mirzapur and Daulatpur in Haryana and Alamgirpur, Bargaon and Hulas in western Uttar Pradesh. The Painted Harappan pottery in late stage is replaced by less intricate designs and unpainted plain ware with new pot-forms. It appears that in the later phase different types of wares such as pre-Harappan survivals, Harappan and also some non-Harappan wares like Cemetry-H and Jhukar coalesced and continued. The famous metallic ring of the pottery was replaced by a feeble echo. The plain black-and-red, Painted Grey Ware and Grey Wares were, no doubt, the new elements but found only at a limited number of sites. It appears Harappan survived longer in certain pockets as at Bhagwanpura etc., and diluted to a point when there was nothing Harappan in it and it was at this stage that survived late Harappan pot-forms interlocked with PGW complex.

In the later phase the pottery such as goblets, beakers, perforated and certain other types of jars and vases which derived the forms and designs often from mature phase indicated a general decandence in fabric, potting and treatment of surface. From Chenab to Sutlej and Yamuna including Saraswati and Drishadwati, characteristic classical forms like dish with projected rim and carinated shoulder, globular vessels with a flange round the neck, shallow dish with incurved rim, perforated pot and jar-stand with a concave profile were noticed but in a limited number, whereas a few new forms such as dish-on-stand with drooping rim, jar with horizontally splayed out rim, medium sized jar with everted rim, bowl-like-lid with central knob and a few miniature pots with a ring or pedestalled base were in profusion. The classical tall storage jar with 'S' twist found at Mohenjo-daro, Harappa, Lothal and Kalibangan etc. is completely absent. The type sites are Ropar, Sanghol, Mitathal, Alamgirpur and Hulas. In the grey ware the types are limited. Only basin with out-turned rim, thick jars with under-cut rim and bowls with everted rim were found. The painted motifs confined to less sophisticated designs from simple bands to tringles and mat designs to intricate once including peacock or crane. The classical designs like pipal leaf, intersecting circles etc. are present but rare. The incised decorations which are confined on the exterior conform to Bara pattern, whereas the internally incised designs are totally absent from this late phase.

In Gujarat also perforated jars, Indus goblet etc. were absent at Rangpur IIB and IIC. In the last phase it was associated with Lustrous Red ware and at places also with the painted black-and-red ware of Ahar tradition. The Harappan fabric became coarser in texture and execution.

Minor Antiquities

The Indus Civilization is well known for its minor antiquities. With all round deterioration in the late phase a set back also occurred in this field. The seals of Indus civilization in northern India were found at Ropar, Banawali and Rakhigarhi. At Rangpur, no square steatite seal was found although many of the typical seal and sealings were present at Lothal. Except a terracotta sealing found at Hulas, no steatite seal was reported from western U.P. At Ropar, a small steatite seal with script symbols and sealing with impression of three different seals carrying the bull and legend were noticed. The seal has no perforated boss on the reverse. In the later phase of this Civilization for example at Ropar or for that purpose at Hulas where Harappan layout of cities is absent, the seals gradually lost their importance and went out of use. Even at Mohenjo-daro in later phase the deftly executed animal figurines were replaced by cruder effigies. Other items like saddle-querns, mortars and hammer-stone continued in later stage but other objects like mace-heads, chert-weights and burnisher were rare. No object for measuring the length was noticed in later stage. In Gujarat, cubical stone weight and terracotta cakes were absent in later period. The graffiti on the pottery was replaced by indistinguishable scratching and chert by local jespar and chalcedony. Human figurines and characteristic painted designs were no more in vogue. In Gujarat use of faience and steatite vanish but in north India steatite stopped but faience was freely used.

The Harappans used a variety of metals for making a long range of articles. Copper was one of them but arsenic, tin and nickel were added to alloy copper for better fusibility and for obtaining more strength and hardness. In the late phase objects requiring complicated casting were not found. The metal objects comprised of chisels, spearheads, axes, knives, curved razors, bangles and fish-hooks.

Burial Customs

The Indus civilization is well known for its cemetries like R-37 at Harappa, Lothal and Kalibangan. The cemetries found at Ropar and Chandigarh, slightly away from habitational areas became smaller in dimensions possibly hinting on the size of the settlements. These burials revealed typical mature Harappan pots and personal ornaments. The evidence of burials, both ordinary and crematory was also noticed along with pots at Dher Majra but details are not clear. At Bhagwanpura, two skeletons lying in north-south direction with heads towards the north were found from the habitational area of sub-period IB. There was no funerary good in the graves.

The presence of skeletons without funerary objects at Bhagwanpura in habitational area give rise to new theories. At Ropar and Chandigarh diagnostic Harappan traits survived and so was the custom of separate cemetary away from habitational area. It appears at Bhagwanpura IB, Harappans were supplanted by 'Sub-Indus' cultures.

Trade Contacts

In recent years the discovery of a number of Indus artefacts from sites in Persian Gulf, south and south-east Iran, Afghanistan and south Turkmania showing economic interaction shed valuable light on the trading net-work prevailing in these regions, although for understanding it, one must know the resources and mechanism of exchange to each of smaller geographical units from the Indus to the Gulf, Messopotamia and Oxus (Chakrabarti 1977). The alluvial plains of Indus lacked mineral materials like copper, gold, lapis-lazuli, turquoise, carnelian and even building timber. All these items including the essential as well as luxury one, were often imported from very considerable distance into the cities. The extent of the state control on the trade in Indus civilization is less clear (Lamberg-Karlovsky and Sabloff 1979). The import of rare commodities from distance area required settlement survey analysis before one can appreciate trade mechanism.

The Indus trade in its later phase with the west Asian centres came to halt. The absence or scarcity of certain trade items like lapis-lazuli, chert, barrel type of carnelian beads, alabaster cups and copper and bronze vessels bear testimony to this fact. This must have resulted due to the rise of insecurity on the trade-routes thereby suggesting the weakening of central authority or a process of gradual restrictions on the routes which must have served as a check in the development of commercial enterprise. The exploitation and export of timber, copper and cotton may not have posed any problem being a commonly available material as was the case with semi-precious materials. Sind no more remained in this phase a port of commercial intercourse with Gujarat. However, one point of caution has also to be added here. Most of the late Harappan sites excavated are rural settlements and have got their own limitations.

CHART I

Comparative Chart—Survival of Characteristic Traits from Mature to Late Harappan Complex in North India

Sr. No.	*Characteristic Traits*	*Harappa*	*Late Harappa*
1.	Dish-on-stand	√	√
2.	Goblet	√	√
3.	Perforated Jar	√	√
4.	Beaker	√	√
5.	Typical painted design Pipal leaf and Intersecting circles	√	√
6.	Graffiti	√	√
7.	Burnt-brick (4 : 2 : 1)	√	√
8.	Cart Frame & wheel	√	√
9.	Triangular cakes	√	√
10.	Chert blade	√	√
11.	Carnelian beads barrel type	√	√
12.	Faience	√	√
13.	Steatite beads	√	√
14.	Steatite Seals & sealings	√	√
15.	Lapis-Lazuli beads	√	√
16.	Copper and bronze vessels	√	√
17.	Shell	√	√
18.	Cemeteries	√	√

CHART II

Emergence of New Traits in Late Harappan Complex in Northern India

Sr. No.	*New Traits*	*Late Harappan Horizon*
1.	Dish-on-stand with drooping rim	√
2.	Prominent drum of dish-on-stand	√
3.	Jar with horizontally splayed out rim	√
4.	Bowl-like-lid with Central knob	√
5.	Exterior Incised decoration on jars	√
6.	Mat and bold curves in painted designs	√
7.	Stylization of birds in Painted design	√
8.	Animal head-handled pots	√
9.	Terracotta beads—Short barrel bicone type	√

Sr. No.	*New Traits*	*Late Harappan Harizon*
10.	Oblong terracotta cakes with finger impressions	√
11.	Burnt bricks (unusual ratio) with finger marks	√
12.	Indeterminate terracotta object ending with two curves	√
13.	Terracotta animal figurine with elongated thin body	√
14.	Burials in habitational area	√
15.	Long-necked flask	√

Chalcolithic Cultures: A Socio-Economic Perspective

M.K. DHAVALIKAR
Deccan College, Pune

SINCE the accidental discovery of Jorwe (Dt. Ahmednagar, Maharashtra) in 1950, many chalcolithic cultures have been discovered during the last three decades in different parts of the country in general and in the central and western India in particular. These post-Harappan cultures, which flourished during the second millennium B.C., share certain common features. They are all characterised by a painted ceramic, usually black-on-red, a specialised blade/flake industry of the silicious material like chalcedony and copper which, being scarce, was used on a restricted scale. Their economy was based on subsistence-agriculture, stock-raising and hunting-fishing. But our knowledge of these first farmers is as yet sketchy save that of the Jorwe culture, notwithstanding the fact that scores of chalcolithic sites have so far been excavated. This, in the main, is due to the fact that almost all the excavations except those at Ahar, Navada Toli and Inamgaon were just vertical digs. The present paper is an overview of the lifestyles of the pioneering colonizers of central and western India. Since all of them share certain common features, I have attempted a different approach in dealing with them for the simple reason that the evidence is well known; and secondly, I would like to emphasize how much we are lagging behind in the application of new methodology. Therefore, instead of describing the cultures in a chronological order, I have divided the study into settlement patterns, subsistence strategies, socio-political organization, technology, exchange networks and religious beliefs. When we analyse our evidence from this angle, we become keenly aware of our shortcomings and that perhaps, more than anything else, is my aim.

Cultures and Chronology

In the present study only the following cultures have been taken into consideration :

1. Kayatha Culture (c. 2000-1800 B.C.)
2. Ahar or Banas Culture (c. 2000-1400 B.C.)
3. Malwa Culture (c. 1700-1200 B.C.)
4. Prabhas Culture (c. 1800-1200 B.C.)
5. Rangpur Culture (c. 1500-1200 B.C.)
6. Jorwe Culture (c. 1400-700 B.C.)

The most important distinguishing feature of these chalcolithic cultures is their distinct painted pottery. The Kayatha culture is characterised by a sturdy red-slipped were painted with designs in chocolate, a red painted buff ware and a combed ware bearing incised patterns. The Ahar people made a distinctive black-and-red ware decorated with white designs. The Malwa ware is rather coarse in fabric, but has a thick buff slip over which designs were executed in dark brown or black. The Prabhas and the Rangpur wares are both derived from the Harappan, but the latter is distinguished by a gloss, hence its appellation, Lustrous Red Ware. The Jorwe ware too is painted black-on-red, but has a matt surface treated with a wash. Each ware has its own characteristic forms which are too well known and need not be discussed. The associated ceramics are non-descript coarse, handmade red/grey wares.

I have not included in the present study the chalcolithic cultures of Bihar and Bengal for the simple reason that not much is known about them except pottery. It may also be made clear at the outset that I have not discussed the characteristic ceramics, their forms, and other associated artifacts such as beads and metal tools and ornaments for they are too well known. Besides, my main aim is not to enumerate the trait lists of these cultures, but to deal with those aspects which have hitherto received scant attention. To many, this essay may appear rather speculative, but it may be emphasized that we can arrive at far reaching conclusions by adopting new paradigms from sister disciplines such as anthropology and geography.

Environment

Although the chalcolithic cultures of western India flourished in a semi-arid region, there are differences in the micro-environments of each zone. Starting from south-east Rajasthan, the focus of the Ahar culture, the region is drained by the Banas and its tributaries. It is a genissic plain, about 475 m above the sea levels, and forms a part of the Mewar plateau. On the west it is delimited by the Aravalli range which decreases in elevation towards the south. In the south-east lies the famous Malwa plateau, known for its fertile land and in the east is the Vindhyan plateau of central India. It is through this corridor that the Ahar culture reached Malwa. In the southern part, where the soil cover is thick the land is quite fertile. The annual rainfall is about 650 mm. The Mewar plateau is in fact the northward extension of the Malwa plateau.

Malwa is known since antiquity for its rich black cotton soil. It is the western part of the present state of Madhya Pradesh with the Vindhyas in the north and the Satpura in the south and in between lies the vast fertile basin of the Narmada. The Chambal also drains it in the north but forms a part of the Ganga system. The annual precipitation ranges around 1000 mm and, therefore, the region has good vegetation cover and game too.

Gujarat resembles Malwa in several respects and so also does the Tapi valley, but further down south, in the Godavari and the Bhima valleys of Maharashtra, the rainfall pattern decreases, and soil cover also becomes thin. It will thus be clear that the environment in western India from south-eastern Rajasthan to Maharashtra is characterised by black soil, and the rainfall ranging between 375 to 1000 mm. The entire region comes under the influence of the southwesterly monsoons. The only variables are the availability of natural resources e.g., copper in south-eastern Rajasthan, the abundance of chalcedony and carnelian in Malwa, Gujarat and Maharashtra and the dolerite for polished stone axes in the Deccan. But for minor climatic changes, the region can be broadly said to form one ecological unit; it supports the hypothesis that "like environment evokes like cultural responses".

Settlement Patterns

The close of the third millennium was the heyday of the Harappans, but as is well known, the decline also starts from the pinnacle of glory, and the beginning of the second millennium marks the emergence of chalcolithic cultures. The authors of these cultures obviously had to locate their settlements in the areas outside the pale of the Harappans. The earliest among them, the Kayatha culture, selected the western parts of Malwa for their habitation. Over forty sites of this culture have so far been located on the Chambal and its tributaries (Wakankar 1967). The black cotton soil of Malwa had attracted the evil eye of the invader throughout its chequered history and the Kayathans were the first among them. All the Kayatha settlements were considerably small, extending not over 2 ha. in extent. They are usually located more on the tributaries than on the main river possibly because of the danger of floods of the Chambal.

In contrast to the small Kayatha settlements, those of the Ahar culture, at least two of them, are quite large. Ahar itself, the type site, is quite extensive (500×270 m); and so also is Gilund (400×200 m); whereas most of the sites range between 0.5 to 2 ha. Of all the sites, the most remarkable is the location of Ahar which is situated on the outskirts of Udaipur city in a picturesque setting. It is very well protected by hills all round with only one opening on the north-west. The hills form a basin which has good soil and adequate rainfall besides plenty of game. The people of the Malwa culture also selected a scenic spot for locating their largest settlement at Navda Toli which has hills on north and south with the vast expanse of the Narmada in between. "Such a picturesque area would naturally catch the imagination of a people who were artistic by nature or inheritance" (Sankalia *et al.* 1971: 7). The site extends over 10 ha. and is one of the largest chalcolithic settlements in the country. Navda Toli, Eran and Nagda are three known centres of the Malwa culture. Although the first mentioned site is the largest, the other two also appear to be important centres as they are said to have been fortified. It is suggested that Nagda probably had a rampart with a mud-brick bastion (IAR 1955-56: 14). Eran similarly had a fortification wall and a moat on the northern side (Singh 1962). Although the chalcolithic date of the fortification has been suspect, it is clear from the location of the site in the sharp meander of the river, that it could have been fortified with little extra effort. Perhaps because of its strategic location it became a city state in the Early Historic period and maintained its position till the Gupta epoch. But most of the remaining sites of the Malwa culture are quite small ranging from 1 ha. to 4 ha. in extent. It is likely that some people had also occupied rock-shelters and caves in the Vindhyas (Joshi 1978: 84); they may perhaps be camps for hunting or for collecting forest produce. We, however, cannot hazard any guess about the Prabhas settlement pattern for not even half a dozen sites of this culture are known, and except Prabhas, the remaining are randomly dispersed. Of the Rangpur culture, 15 of the 31 sites are located on the Ghelo and Kalubhar rivers demonstrating a linear pattern (Possehl 1980: Fig. 11) whereas the remaining are widely scattered. Possehl (1980: 61-63) has postulated a sharp decrease in population during the Rangpur period on the basis of the diminishing number of sites and their extent as well. But Rangpur itself seems to have been a very large centre (Rao 1962-63).

Our knowledge of the Jorwe settlement pattern is somewhat better than that of the preceding cultures. Although over two hundred Jorwe sites have been discovered so far, the precise occupational area in each is hard to estimate in a multi-culture site. A notable feature of the Jorwe settlement organisation is that there was a large centre in each region, e.g. Prakash in the Tapi valley (Thapar 1967), Daimabad in the Godavari valley and Inamgaon in the Bhima valley. The largest of these was Daimabad, about 20 ha. in extent whereas Prakash and Inamgaon would be around 5 ha. each. If we accept the modest estimate of 200 persons per hectare, the population of the regional centres would have been around 4,000 and 1,000 respectively. Daimabad, therefore, appears to be the primary regional centre which is also corroborated by the find of a unique hoard of bronzes having religious affiliation (Dhavalikar, 1982a). As regional centres, Prakash and Inamgaon were probably of equal importance. Prakash was a vertical dig and we do not know much about it, but Inamgaon was probably well fortified with a mud wall having stone rubble bastions. A similar feature has been noted at Daimabad also (IAR 1959-60: 18). In addition, the diversionary channel and the embankment on the western periphery at Inamgaon also may have afforded a measure of protection to the settlement.

A vast majority of the Jorwe settlements can be classified as villages. They are usually from 1 to 3 ha. in extent with their population ranging from 200 to 600. A few of these villages such as Sonegaon, Chandoli and Apegaon have been excavated. Nevasa and Bahal, however, were somewhat larger, with population from 500-1,000. Besides, there are some sites which are very small, 0.5 to 1 ha. in extent, and consisting of a few households. An excellent representation of this class is Pimpaldar (Dt. Nasik) which is situated in the historic Baghlan Pass linking the Tapi and the Godavari valleys. It may have served as a trading outpost considering the number of complete vessels it has yielded (IAR 1957-78: 66). All these belong to the category of hamlets whereas there are many others, especially in the Tapi valley, which can be identified as farmsteads. These are quite small, 0.5 to 1 ha. in area, but are situated close to a village, about 2 to 3 km from it. They are like the present *wadis* of Maharashtra and may have facilitated the conduct of agricultural operations. They may have been occupied by a single extended family or perhaps by a few more. A representative of this class is a small site, about 3 km south of the ancient site at Inamgaon, which is about 0.5 ha. in extent and may have been occupied by two or more families of agriculturists who may have lived there during the agricultural seasons while spending the summer in the main settlement. An example of a camp is furnished by the Pachad cave at the foot of the Raisad fort which may have served as a meeting place for the people of the plateau and those of the coastal region.

A casual glance at the distribution of chalcolithic sites in Maharashtra is enough to give a fair idea of the site spacing. There is a heavy concentration of sites in the Tapi valley, less in the Pravara-Godavari and sporadic in the Bhima valley. This gradual decrease in habitations from north to south is certainly due to the ecology of the respective river valleys and is governed by the principle of resource maximization and effort minimization. The Tapi valley is the most fertile topographic unit in Maharashtra; it has large tracts of rich black cotton soil with plentiful water supply from the Tapi. But a curious feature is that most of the Chalcolithic settlements here are located not on the Tapi itself but on its tributaries as is the case at present. According to C.D. Deshpande (1948: 148-49) : "The richest half is not the immediate banks of the Tapi, but the immediate plain—in the danger of suffering rapid erosion—developed on the Black Cotton soil. Quite contrary to the general pattern of rivers, the Tapi discourages population concentration on its banks. Erosion and 'bad lands' topography prevent irrigation and intensive cultivation". This also explains the prehistoric situation.

The Pravara-Godavari valley, in sharp contrast to the Tapi valley, is characterised by undulating surfaces, at least in its upper reaches, where the early farming settlements are sparsely located. But in the lower reaches with rich black cotton soil, the number of settlements increases. The sparse habitation in the Bhima valley was probably due to the fact that the entire basin is dry with annual precipitation around 400-700 mm and although the low-lying areas have black soil, the upland zones have very thin soil cover. The first farmers, therefore, selected only those pockets where arable land was available as at Chandoli, Songaon, Walki and Inamgaon.

From a careful analysis of the distribution of chalcolithic sites a somewhat distinct pattern emerges. The Kayatha sites indicate a random pattern whereas the Ahar ones, situated only along river banks, are characterised by a linear pattern. This obviously is due to the scarcity of rainfall and the habitation therefore took place along the water courses where good soil was available. The Malwa sites appear to be somewhat clustered around such regional centres as Nagda, Eran and Navda Toli, whereas the Jorwe sites are dispersed. These observations are bound to be tentative in the absence of requisite published data not only in the respect of excavated sites but even in the case of the explored ones.

Can we derive any systems, i.e. rules that generated the chalcolithic settlement patterns ? Even the settlement pattern studies have yet to make any headway in Indian archaeology, let alone the settlement system. We can at the best say that most of the sites are located on or near the point where the river is crossable and that a site hierarchy existed.

Micro-settlement Pattern

We cannot say anything about the micro-settlement or the community pattern of the Kayatha culture as the excavation at Kayatha was a small scale dig. But we know precious little about Ahar culture. The people built rectangular houses, some of which were quite large (10×4 m) and others ranging between 7×5 m—3.5×3 m. The largest house had a partition wall, about 50 cm wide, in the middle. The houses were built with foundation and plinth of schist slabs which are plentifully available in the surrounding areas. Over these, mud walls were built but mud bricks and even burnt bricks are attested at Gilund (IAR 1959-60: 41-44). The house floor was made of gravel and clay rammed well, and sometimes even burnt clay from earlier structures was also used. The walls were decorated with quartz nodules betraying a weakness of the people for designs of white spots as on their pottery and its survival today on the Bandhani fabrics. At Gilund the house walls were plastered with clay and white-washed (IAR 1959-60: 41-44). The houses contained large *chulhas* with two, three or four arms, and having knob-like projections on the inside for supporting a cooking vessel. Some of these, the excavators suggest, might have been used for smelting copper ore (Sankalia *et al.* 1969: 216).

Like Ahar, Navda Toli was also a large scale excavation, but still we do not know anything about the layout of the settlement. It appears that the houses were mostly circular on plan, their diameter varying from 2 to 3 m but a few were also rectangular. Circular houses probably formed clusters of two or more (Sankalia *et al.* 1971: 61-63, Fig. 20 & 24). They had low mud walls while above probably was wattle-and-daub, and the roof may have been conical. As against this, the rectangular structures were roomy (3-5 m × 2 m), and had large enclosures. In one such rectangular structure, which was burnt most of the contents were intact; there were several jars with stands and containing grains. The wooden posts were of *babul* (*Acacia arbica*), a hardy plant which abounds in the whole of western India. At Nagda, the use of mud bricks in house building is attested (IAR 1955-56: 14). The *chulahs* with arms are identical with those from Ahar. The floor was made of rammed clay. The circular huts of Navda Toli are said to have been used for storing fodder etc., but their well made floor suggests that they were in all probability, used for residential purposes. The Prabhas houses were rectangular structures built of miliolite stone rubble set in mud masonry whereas those at Rangpur are of mud brick and are rectangular on plan. It is likely that the houses were multi-roomed.

For the Jorwe settlement pattern at macro-level, we have interesting evidence from Inamgaon where over hundred and thirty houses belonging to different periods have been unearthed. The Jorwe (i.e. Early Jorwe, Period II) houses were large rectangular structures with low mud walls (about 30 cm high) over which was the wattle-and-daub construction Fig. 9.1 The thatched roof may have been conical. There appears to

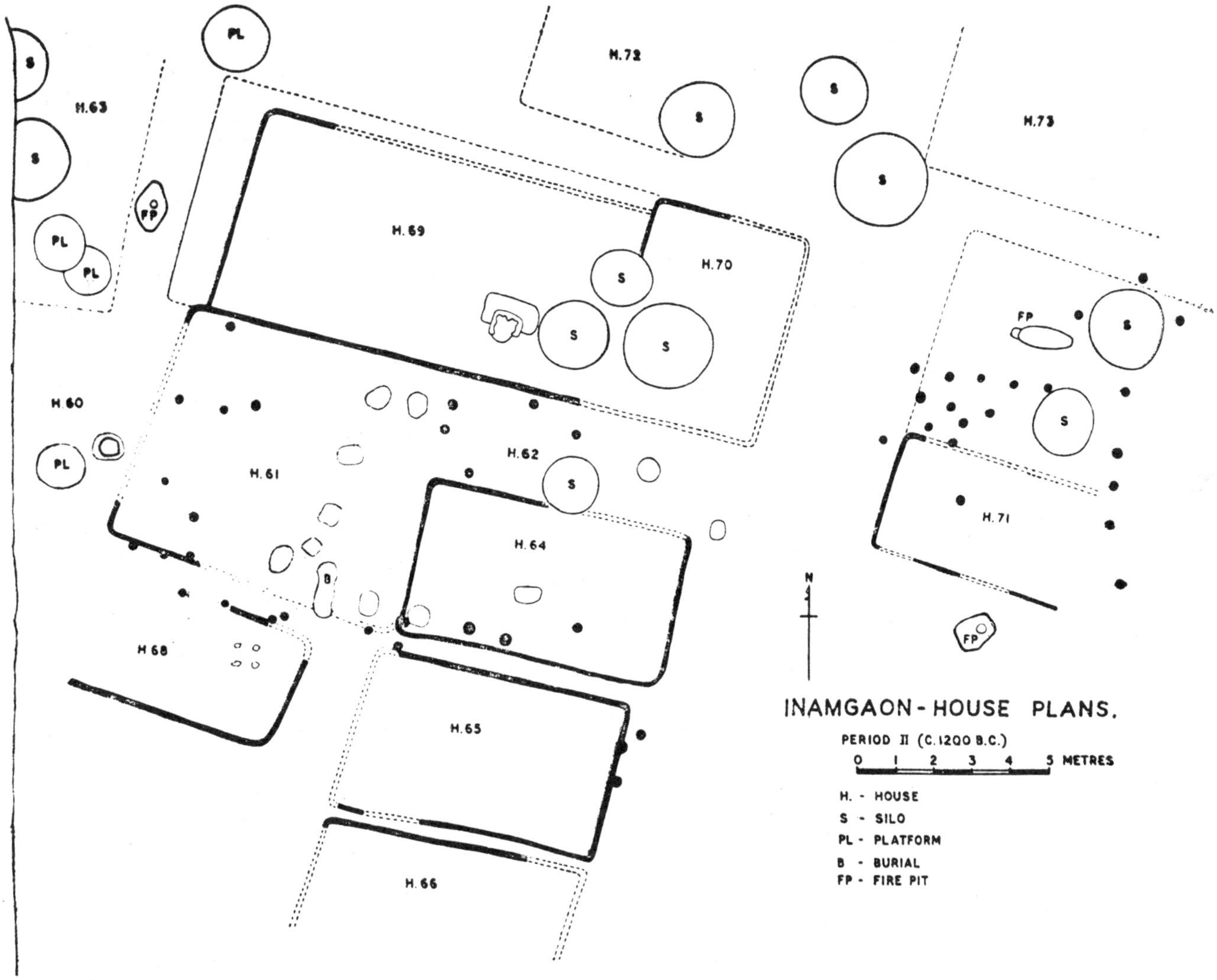
INAMGAON - HOUSE PLANS.
PERIOD II (C.1200 B.C.)
0 1 2 3 4 5 METRES
H. - HOUSE
S - SILO
PL - PLATFORM
B - BURIAL
FP - FIRE PIT
N
H.63
H.72
H.73
H.69
H.70
H.60
H.61
H.62
H.64
H.71
H 68
H.65
H.66

Fig. 9.1.

be some modicum of planning the settlement, for the houses were laid out almost in rows with an open space (about 1.5 m wide) in between which may have served as a road or lane. The settlement reminds us of the planned *Padas* of the Kolams in the Deccan. The Inamgaon houses vary in size, 5×3 m to 7×5 m; the larger ones were very often divided into two rooms by a partition wall in between. Inside the house would be a small oval firepit, sometimes with high clay walls to serve as a protection from wind, whereas outside in the courtyard invariably we come across a large oval fire pit (1 × 0.5 m) which was probably used for roasting hunted animals. Almost every fire pit has a flat stone in the centre at the bottom, which was daubed with mud to serve as a stand for the cooking vessel. Very often inside, but rarely outside also, there was a pit silo, 1 to 2 m in diameter and equally deep, and lined with lime for storing grain. In addition, there was a round mud platform, with 1.5 m dia. and 10 cm high, which served to support a storage bin. The house floor was made of rammed clay with silt and fine sand spread in layers and even the courtyard was well made. The domesticated animals, sheep/goat and cattle, were tethered in the courtyard as indicated by the nitrogen content of the soil.

All this undergoes sudden change in the Late Jorwe period from 1000 B.C. The drop in rainfall pattern led to the decline of agriculture and the resulting poverty is reflected in the house type and coarse pottery. Instead of large rectangular houses, we see small round huts in clusters of three or four or more. Inside there is a small circular firepit and outside also, and the pit silos are replaced by a four-legged storage jar supported on four flat stones. The round hut had a very low mud wall, hardly 10 to 15 cm high and its function was to prevent the rainwater from entering into the hut. The roof and walls above were thatched. In the closing phase of the Late Jorwe in the 8th cent. B.C., the huts become extremely flimsy, with an irregular plan and without any well made floor. There was no wattle and daub construction above the low mud wall, but only the thatched roof which was very low (Pl. I).

A remarkable feature of the Jorwe (both Early and Late) settlement is that the houses of the artisans such as the potter, the goldsmith, the limemaker, the lapidary, the ivorycarver etc., were located on the western periphery of the principal habitational area (INM-I) whereas those of well-to-do farmers were in the central part. The house of the ruling chief in Early Jorwe was in the central part whereas in the Late Jorwe it was located in the eastern part, on the river front. This recalls to the mind the present day villages in Maharashtra in which the houses of craftsmen are generally found near the entrance gate to the village, whereas the village chief—the Patil—lives in the central part. Of the five different localities at Inamgaon, the largest one (INM-I) was occupied by artisans and well-to-do people and the ruling chief whereas the others (INM-III & IV) were probably occupied by poor farmers and in the westernmost area (INM-V) lived the labour looking after the upkeep of the embankment and the irrigation channel. This arrangement suggests that it was a ranked society.

Subsistence Strategies

These early farming communities subsisted on farming and hunting-fishing. They reared cattle, sheep-goat, buffalo and pig, which were also slaughtered for food. Their subsistence agriculture was mainly dry farming since the entire western India is a semi-arid zone, with the annual rainfall ranging between 400-1000 mm. They also enjoyed the facility of artificial irrigation which is attested at Inamgaon. The soil, except in Rajasthan, was the black cotton soil, which is known for its fertility and the moisture retention capacity. In south-east Rajasthan, the home of the Ahar culture, the soil is rather loamy and quite fertile. But the monsoon being erratic, then as now, agriculture must have been a gamble with nature, for even today every third year is a bad year and every fourth a famine.

A variety of crops were grown, and although a single crop per year may have been the rule, the Jorwe farmers practised even crop rotation, *Kharif* and *Rabi*, as of today. The evidence from Inamgaon gives us a fair idea of the early agriculture, but that from other regions is quite poor. The principal cereal was barely (*Hordeam vulgare*), but wheat (*Triticum vulgare compactum*) too was cultivated in areas which receive winter rains as in Malwa. Rice is reported from Inamgaon and the long seeded variety (*Oryza sativa* Lin.) from Ahar. Bajra (*Pennisetum typhoides*) occurs at Rangpur, but more interesting is Jowar (*Sorghum vulgare*) in Ahar and Jorwe cultures, the millets are supposed to have been introduced into Saurashtra from East Africa in the beginning of the second millennium. Mention should also be made of *Kulith* (*Dolichos lablab*) and *Ragi* (*Eleucine corocana*). Besides there were the green pea, grass pea (*Lathyrus sativae* Linn), lentil and green gram, black gram. A most interesting cultigen is the hyacinth bean (*Dolichos biflorus*) from Inamgaon; it requires a higher rainfall, over 800 mm and is grown today only in the upper reaches of Ghod and in the Konkan area.

All these chalcolithic cultures flourished in the black cotton soil zone. This, according to Leshnik (1968: 295), "clearly represents an ecological adaptation dictated by available technology, knowledge and means. An analogy with the present day agricultural methods in these regions leads to the supposition on that we are dealing here with a system of dry-farming, dependent on moisture retentive soils".

It has been presumed that these early farmers could not have cultivated the black cotton soil in the absence of iron plough (Kosambi 1963: 315-16) and may have confined their agriculture to the alluvial strips along the river banks (Agrawal 1982: 218). Both the presumptions are totally unfounded for there is evidence to show that the early farmers did not cultivate the alluvial strips only but the black soil also. The agricultural history of Europe shows that "Pollen studies and other archaeological research point to the worldwide use in the neolithic period of a system of cultivation of forest plots, probably veiy much resembling the type of cultivation that is now found in many primitive communities. This contrasts with an earlier theory according to which intensive cultivation in river valleys would have preceded the cultivation of forest land. The older theory seems to have been based upon the view that forest land was too difficult to cope with for very primitive people. This, however, ignored the fact that not felling but fire was the method of clearing forest land, and it seems that experts in the field now tend to think that river shore cultivation may have been taken by the descendants of tribes who had lost the forest land they had cultivated owing to dessication or exhaustion and aided by crowding along the rivers" (Boserup 1965: 17).

That the forest land, and not alluvial strips along the river banks, was cultivated by the early farming communities is indirectly corroborated by the type of agricultural tools used by them. Neither plough nor hoe has been attested at chalcolithic sites, but perforated stone discs, which were used as weights for the digging stocks, abound. The digging stick can be useful only in the slash-and-burn or zoom cultivation. Plots of forest land are easy to clear by buring the trees, after which the clumps of the trees remain, and no plough or hoe can be used. Sowing and planting can be done directly in the ashes, without land preparation and without the use of any other tool than perhaps a digging stick to scratch the ashes or punch the holes in which to plant the roots or sow the seeds. It is not possible to use a plough on land cleared by this method. But under the zoom cultivation, the land has to be kept fallow after one or two years. It takes about 25 years for the forest to grow again, but by constant use the forest will give place to small bush for sometime and finally the land will be completely cleared for annual cropping. The plough can be effectively employed only on such type of land.

The problem of plough has also to be explained satisfactorily. The famous adage that "the black cotton soil ploughs itself" is not without significance. During summer it develops large, deep fissures which help in the circulation of air, thus fulfilling the function of plough. We have shown elsewhere that the black soil may have been cultivated by means of a wooden plough as is done even today in Malwa (Dhavalikar and Possehl 1974).

Our knowledge of the chalcolithic agriculture is still sketchy owing to the fact that sufficient attention was not paid in the earlier excavations for the recovery of grains. Inamgaon is the sole exception for here a vast quantity of charred seeds was collected by floatation as a result of which we can now reconstruct the history of agriculture in the Deccan. The Early Jorwe (c. 1400-1000 B.C.) was a period of great prosperity. The farmers cultivated four cereals (wheat, barley, rice and jowar) and four pulses (horse gram, hyacinth bean, lentil and field pea) which is not done even today. They seem to have used their scarce resources, especially water, very economically and intelligently or else they would not have been able to raise such a large variety of crops. The problem, however, is that the region is semi-arid with hardly 450 mm of rainfall and is a perpetually draught affected area and hence the cultivation of so many crops is enigmatic. What they did was to divert the flood waters through a channel (extant length 118 m, 3.50 m deep, 4 m wide) and a sort of guidebund or an embankment was built parallel to it. Its basal courses were of stone rubble set in mud mortar and the upper portion was earthen. The channel was deep in the middle (3.50 m) and thus served also as a narrow tank for storing water which was probably used for pot irrigation. The traces of the channel suggest that the water could have been diverted to the adjoining fields by gravity flow. There may not have been much loss of water by way of seepage as the channel has been dug into the rock bottom and its sides into the pulverised rock (*murrum*). Probably because of this facility of artificial irrigation the Early Jorwe farmers could cultivate wheat and hyacinth bean. Rice may have been grown in small carefully tended plots wherein rain water was ponded as is the case today. The irrigation channel fell into disuse after 1000 B.C. A similar ditch and an embankment has also been laid bare at Malwan, a coastal site near Surat in Gujarat (Allchin and Joshi 1972).

There is no doubt that fishing formed an important part of the diet of the chalcolithic people as is evident from fish bones, fish hooks and the fish motif on pottery. Especially noteworthy is the acquifauna so exquisitely depicted on the Savalda ware (Sali 1963). But the most curious is the presence of marine species at Inamgaon which may have come either from Kalyan or Mahad, the nearest creek ports about 200 km west of Inamgaon. Hunting also was equally important. The people had developed a weakness for venison. Wild pig too occurs. The domesticated animals were slaughtered for food, but whether their milk was consumed or not is problematic for it has been observed on the basis of ethnographic analogues, that the early farming communities may not have milked their cattle and sheep/goat (Sherratt 1981: 275-77). Even the Gonds of Bastar think that the milk is only for the young animals and do not milk their cattle.

Socio-Political Organization

No attempt has so far been made in this country to infer about the socio-political aspect of prehistoric cultures. However, the evidence at our disposal enables us to form some idea about the social and political organization of the chalcolithic cultures. The evidence consists of site hierarchies, certain structures and burials.

We have seen that there are basically two sites categories of the chalcolithic viz., regional centres and villages which reflect a two level settlement hierarchy. It has been suggested that a settlement hierarchy implies some sort of an administrative organization for there is some evidence to show that large sites could control smaller ones by virtue of their location; and trade has also been cited as a factor in state formation (Wright & Johnson 1975: 270-74). It may be stated that a single level hierarchy indicates a tribal society whereas a two-level one suggests the emergence of chiefdom, because in such a society some settlements dominate over the entire society as they are the loci of regional socio-political authority. Their number is always quite small as compared to the dependent settlements.

The two level site hierarchy of the chalcolithic settlements would thus indicate that they were ranked societies. On the basis of ethnographic parallels it has been shown that the most important criterion of a chiefdom society is the existence of public structures such as fortification, a temple, a granary, etc. (Peebles & Kus 1977). Of the cultures falling within the purview of this study, we have so far no evidence of any public architecture at Kayatha, the only site of the culture excavated so far. Ahar too has not yielded any evidence of this kind but at Gilund, which can be identified as a regional centre of the Ahar culture, a curious structure was encountered. It is too complex and has not unfortunately been exposed fully. It consists of a series of parallel walls of mud brick, the space in between being filled with sand (IAR 1959-60: 41-44). They probably represent the concentric fortification walls recalling those at Dimini in Neolithic Greece. The structure is no doubt enigmatic, but is certainly an example of public architecture.

Of the Malwa sites, only Eran has yielded evidence of a rampart and a moat (Singh 1962) but doubts have been expressed about its chalcolithic date (Ghosh 1973: 62-63). It may, however, be stated that Eran in fact is one site which is most strategically located. Here the chalcolithic habitation took place in the sharp meander of the river affording natural protection on three sides, and only with little effort people could dig a moat and use the same mud for constructing the rampart. The excavator of Nagda has hazarded a guess that the chalcolithic settlement at the site also had fortification (IAR 1955-56: 14). Similar guesses have been offered for Navda Toli (Sankalia 1974: 438) and Daimabad (IAR 1958-59: 18) while at Inamgaon there are traces of a rampart wall of mud with bastions built of stone rubble. Daimabad has also yielded a terracotta seal which is betoken of administrative hierarchy. A public structure, altogether of a different kind has been laid bare at Prabhas Patan which belongs to the Late Prabhas period (c. 1500-1200). It has been identified as a warehouse (Dhavalikar 1977-78) which yielded one seal amulet of steatite carved with seven and five deer on front and back respectively. It is in the Harappan tradition. From the same area was picked up an obsidian flake, obviously an import from West Asia. This evidence of public architecture assumes greater importance because trade is taken to be an important factor in the primary state development.

Another important example of public architecture is furnished by the granary at Inamgaon. It is a mud walled structure about 10 m sq. divided into two parts by a low mud wall. It yielded no evidence of human habitation but contained many pit silos and round mud platforms for storage bins, besides two large fire pits. It was located in the central part of the principal habitation area (INM-I) by the side of the largest house so far discovered at the site. The latter was a five roomed structure, in sharp contrast to the single roomed houses of the common people. In fact, it was the only multi-roomed structure of that phase and can therefore be identified as the residence of the most important person in the settlement, perhaps the ruling chief because of the location of the granary by the side of his house. He might be collecting taxes in the form of grain from the people which was stored in the granary as an insurance against drought which must have been as common then as at present.

Yet another evidence of public works comes from Inamgaon itself. We have already described the diversionary channel and the massive embankment at Inamgaon and the irrigation ditch at Malvan in Gujarat. It has been observed that the construction of such hydraulic works implies a central administrative authority (Wittfogel 1959) not only for mustering the communal effort but also for controlling the distribution of water, and it only strengthens our surmise of the existence of a ruling chief at Inamgaon, at least during the Early Jorwe period.

The most important evidence for a ranked society is furnished by burials. An individual's treatment at the death is a reflection of the position occupied in a status system in life and an elaborate burial would indicate what Binford (1972: 225) calls the *social persona* of the deceased. But unfortunately all the chalcolithic cultures save Jorwe, have not yielded any evidence of burials. A few burials, however, have been reported from the Malwa levels in Maharashtra although they are totally absent in Malwa itself.

Although human burials occur at every Jorwe site, it is only at Inamgaon that we have come across evidence bearing on the ranked society. Usually, the children were buried in two grey ware urns, placed mouth-to-mouth horizontally in a pit specially dug for the purpose inside the house or outside also. The body of the child was placed inside with head towards north and feet towards south. Small pots, probably containing food and water, were also placed in the burial pit. The adults were buried in a pit with the body placed in a supine position, but the portion below the ankles was chopped off. This was the normal mode of burial but there are only three examples, which belong to a different category. All these three are of the same type, occurring in the same house complex which we have identified as that of the ruling chief, thus providing additional support for the proposed identification. The first of these occurred in the courtyard of the house where in a high cylindrical pit was found a four-legged clay jar which contained the skeleton of an adult male, placed in a sitting, cross-legged posture, with the feet intact. This differential treatment is certainly betoken of the person being different from the rest of the community. His feet were not chopped off probably because the normal rules of the community were not applicabe to him. Inside the jar were two painted vessels, a bowl and a spouted jar which bore the design of a boat with oars.

Yet another burial of this class was located at the same place but in the preceding level. Here there were two four legged clay jars, one full and the other half, placed by its side. Both the jars, however, did not contain any skeletal remains; there was only a painted globular jar containing an animal bone and covered with a knobbed lid. It was obviously a symbolic burial probably because the dead body could not be recovered, but the status of the person was such that a ceremonious burial was thought to be necessary.

In the third example there were two clay jars, fitted one into the other, and containing the skeleton of a child about 8 years old. This lay in a very large rectangular house, quite close to the house of the ruling chief and may in fact have formed a part of the same complex. All these three burials, of the same variety and from the same area, suggest that the persons were related to each other. The person represented by the symbolic burial was probably the father or the grandfather of that in the clay jar, whereas the child in the double jars may have been the progeny of the ruling chief. Reference should also be made to yet one more burial—a twin-urn child burial—which was found just by the side of that in the four-legged jar described above. The child in it wore a necklace composed of large, barrel copper and a red jasper beads, indicating its high birth. In the case of a similar child burial found in the house adjoining that of the ruling chief, there was a necklace of marine shells. This occurrence of non-local material perhaps indicates the wealth of the person and his status in the society.

The house of the ruling chief of Late Jorwe was located in the eastern margin of the main settlement (INM-I) on the river front. Most of the Late Jorwe houses were round huts occurring in clusters, but that of the chief consisted of four rectangular rooms. In one of the rooms on the south there was a burial containing two adult skeletons, that of a male below and the other of a woman over him. The legs of both were intact. Besides, there were 14 pottery vessels in the burial pit. The house also yielded a crucible and a copper arrow-head with barbs and two holes for fastening. The arrow-head is certainly non-local, resembling the Harappan type, and indicates the status of the person. It is highly likely that in the Late Jorwe the chiefdom passed on to some other family.

The chiefdom in the Early Jorwe society appears to have been hereditary as is suggested by the two identical burials, occurring at the same place, one in an earlier level and the other in the later. It also shows that it was a male-dominated patriarchal society. Some idea of the rules of inheritance can also be had from the artifacts and houses. Thus, there were quite a few cases at Inamgaon where the same house was enlarged in the later period, or also sometimes shortened, suggesting inheritance.

Some observations regarding the social organization are pertinent at this stage. It has been shown that rectangular houses are betoken of a fully settled life whereas round huts suggest a seasonally settled existence (Flannery 1972). This is also corroborated by the ethnographic evidence furnished by the seasonal labour working in the sugar factory in the neighbourhood of Inamgaon. It enables us to conclude that the people of the Malwa culture no doubt enjoyed the luxury of a settled life but at the same time there was some element of transhumance if the round huts at Navda Toli and Inamgaon are is any indication. The Jorwe people, however, lived a settled life, but their successors in the Late Jorwe could not afford it, save a few lucky souls who lived in rectangular houses.

There is some evidence to show that the Early Jorwe society consisted of extended families. A large house belonging to the mid-levels of Early Jorwe contained three big pit silos and nearby was a *chulah* on mud platform. But with the increase in the members of the family, several rooms were added attached as and when required. They were all independent structures which would have been wrongly identified as houses, but none of them had a *chulah* and a storage facility. The house complex can therefore be said to have been occupied by an extended family, with father, mother, grand parents and grown up children for whom as and when they were married different rooms were added. This observation has been based on a study of artifacts recovered from the different rooms.

Our contextual—or conjuctive—approach has enabled us to identify the activity areas on the basis of which we could devide the Late Jorwe round huts into various clusters, each consisting of two or more huts. An analysis of the artifacts shows that in these clusters there was usually one hut containing a *chulah* and a storage facility whereas most of the other rooms save one could be associated with women's activity. It is, therefore, likely that the Late Jorwe was a polygamous society in which every time the person acquired a new wife, a new hut was built for her. This is precisely what the Kohalis of Vidarbha do today. It may also be stated that in other parts of the world the round huts are generally taken to indicate a polygamous society (Flannery 1972).

Technology

The early farming cultures had made considerable progress in ceramic technology. The painted pottery was wheel-made and well fired. Only two pottery kilns have so far come to light, both from Inamgaon, of which one belongs to the Malwa Period (Pl. II) and other to the Early Jorwe. Both are similar in construction, the only difference is in their size. The Jorwe kiln, which is bigger, is built on stone foundation and consists of a huge clay basin (dia. 1.75 m) with flues at its base, below which is the fire chamber. The opening at the base was spanned by oblong clay cushions which have holes in the middle and grooves on sides; through which the hot gas passed upwards. The Malwa kiln is almost identical in construction, but is smaller (dia. 1.55 m). An open kiln, in the form of a shallow pit, is also reported from Inamgaon detable to the late Jorwe period (c. 1000-700 B.C.); it resembles the open kilns in use today.

The black-on-red painted pottery along with its varieties was baked under oxidizing conditions. The Jorwe ware was fired at 700°F whereas for Malwa the temperature ranged between 500°-600°F. The white painted black-and-red ware probably involved double firing to achieve the double colour effect (Majumdar 1969). The painted pottery forms roughly half of the ceramic yield while the remaining pottery was coarse and handmade; it was more utilitarian.

Metal technology was also to some extent advanced. The two copper axes from Kayatha are excellent examples of casting and are the finest of their class. But most of the copper objects such as axes, chisels, beads, fish hooks etc., were made by heating and beating. It has been suggested that there was probably a single source of copper ore, Khetri in Rajasthan, which supplied ore to all the chalcolithic centres. It is, however, highly likely that local ores, wherever available, as in the Amreli District of Gujarat, may have been utilized. Native copper occures at several places in the Banas valley which may have been exploited by the Ahar people. It may be recalled that the ancient name of Ahar was Tambavati, a town for copper smelting. Some of the large *chulahs* at Ahar, as the excavators suggest, may have been used for smelting copper (Sankalia *et al.* 1969: 216). A small fire pit of the Early Jorwe level at Inamgaon also may have been similarly used (Dhavalikar 1975-76: 52, Fig. 4). It is likely that the two crucibles from Inamgaon were used for melting copper also. The Kayatha hoard of copper bangles, 28 in number, of different sizes, which were found deposited in pots, may not have been intended for actual use, but probably represented only the metal as in Bronze Age in Europe. They all belong to the Kayatha culture.

Gold ornaments, though extremely rare, occur in Jorwe levels, and one specimen of an ear ornament comes from Prabhas. The nearest source of gold for the Jorwe people was the Hatti (Dist. Gulbarga, Karnatak), but placer gold may have been exploited in each region. The find of crucibles and pairs of tongs of copper from Inamgaon show the working of the goldsmith. Chalcedony drills were used for perforating beads of semi-precious stones, and copper drills for ivory beads, both of which occur at Inamgaon (Ansari 1978-79).

Lime making was a very flourishing industry of the Early and Late Jorwe periods as testified by the Inamgaon evidence. Kankar, which abounds in Maharashtra, was used for lime making. A lime kiln, constructed of undressed stones was encountered in the Late Jorwe levels at Inamgaon along with large quantities of lime balls. Shell lime was also probably made. Lime was used for plastering pit silos, walls and floors of houses, but the ethnographic analogous suggest that it is required more in preparing hides.

Exchange Network

There is evidence to show that the chalcolithic communities exchanged materials with their contemporaries, but very little work has been done in this direction. We have a few excavated sites and non-local materials at many centres. This, however, cannot rightly be called trade which is associated with state societies, but rather reciprocal exchange which is characteristic of a chiefdom society (Service 1962: 136). There are several sites and materials which were exchanged between them and hence they seem to have formed a network (Plog 1977). The network model therefore, seems to be quite appropriate for the inter-regional and intra-regional exchange systems of the chalcolithic societies. In these networks in different cultural zones the regional centres such as Ahar, Gilund, Nagda, Navda Toli, Eran, Prabhas, Rangpur, Prakash, Daimabad and Inamgaon may have served as focal points for regional exchange and as redistributive centres as well for it has been shown that "chiefdoms are *redistributional societies* with a permanent agency for co-ordination." (Service 1962: 144).

The first and the foremost is the Kayatha culture which, as we have seen, was a junior contemporary of the Harappan. All the sites of this culture including Kayatha are quite small, whereas the excavated evidence displays a very high technological achievement as is evident from the copper axes, two necklaces composed of 173 and 160 beads respectively, besides over 40,000 micro-beads of steatite of unmistakable Harappan affinity. This would suggest some exchange between the Kayathans and the Harappans of Rajasthan, but what the rural folk of Kayatha gave in exchange to the urbanized Harappans cannot be ascertained. Copper may have come from the neighbouring Mewar plateau where the Aharians were already exploiting it.

The Aharians also probably supplied copper to the Malwas; we may, however, never know whether they supplied the ore or the finished tools. The latter is more likely on two counts: in the first place most of the copper axes from chalcolithic sites bear some indentation marks, which are almost identical, suggesting that they may be the trade marks of the smiths, who made them; and secondly, in spite of the large scale excavations at Navda Toli no evidence of copper smelting has come to light. The itinerant smiths, like the present day blacksmiths of Rajasthan, may have been supplying these artifacts in western India. Rajasthan had a long tradition of copper technology going back to the early third millennium as is testified by the recent discoveries in the Ganeshwar region (Agrawal 1981) and it appears to have continued in the second.

The people of Malwa had trading contacts with Rajasthan and Maharashtra. They may have obtained copper from south-eastern Rajasthan and couch shells for bangles from Saurashtra but again the question is what they offered in exchange. They had no doubt

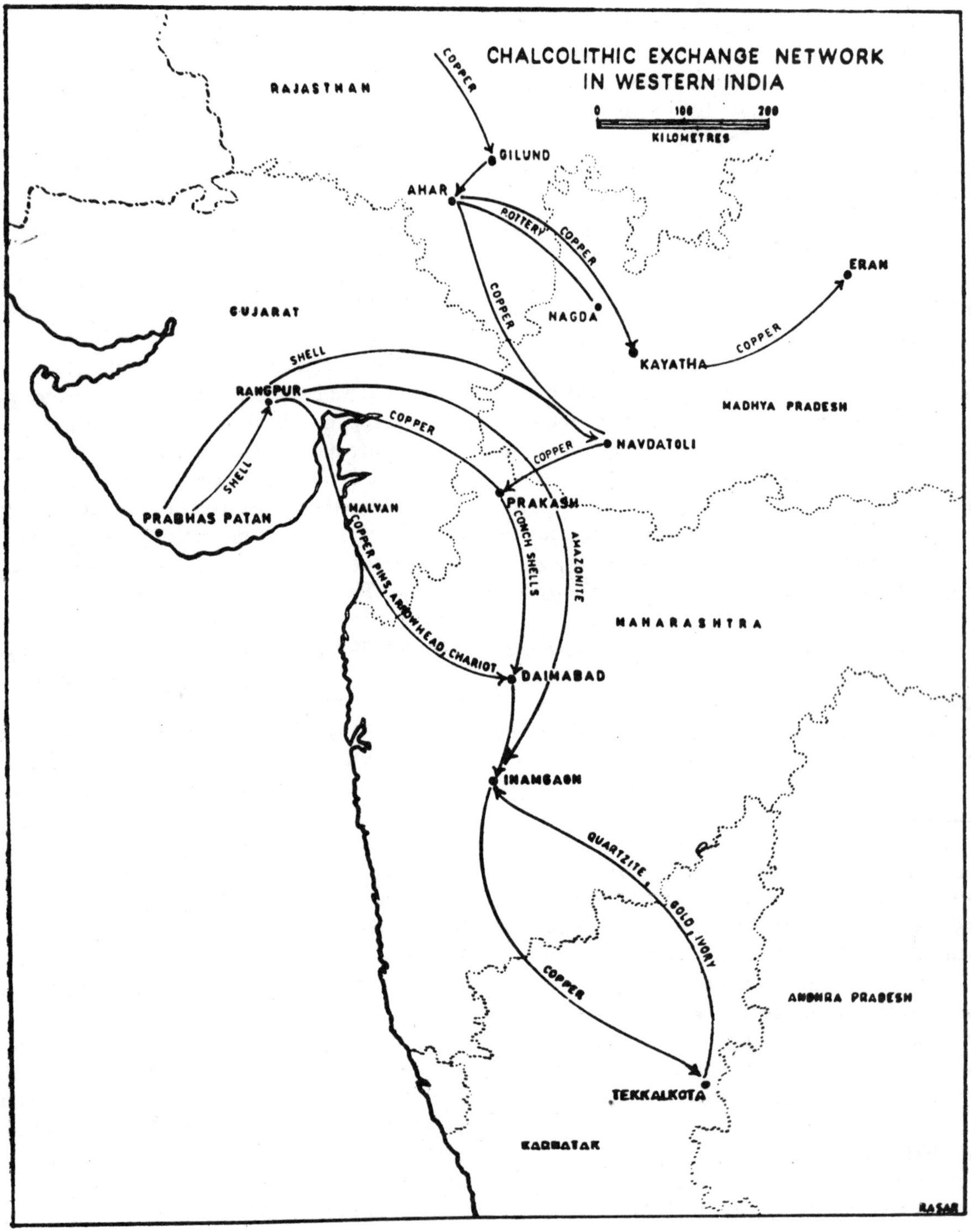
CHALCOLITHIC EXCHANGE NETWORK
IN WESTERN INDIA
0 100 200
KILOMETRES
RAJASTHAN
GUJARAT
MADHYA PRADESH
MAHARASHTRA
ANDHRA PRADESH
GILUND
AHAR
NAGDA
KAYATHA
ERAN
RANGPUR
PRABHAS PATAN
NAVDATOLI
PRAKASH
MALVAN
DAIMABAD
INAMGAON
TEKKALKOTA
COPPER
POTTERY
SHELL
CONCH SHELLS
AMAZONITE
COPPER PINS, ARROWHEAD, CHARIOT
QUARTZITE, GOLD, IVORY

Fig. 9.2

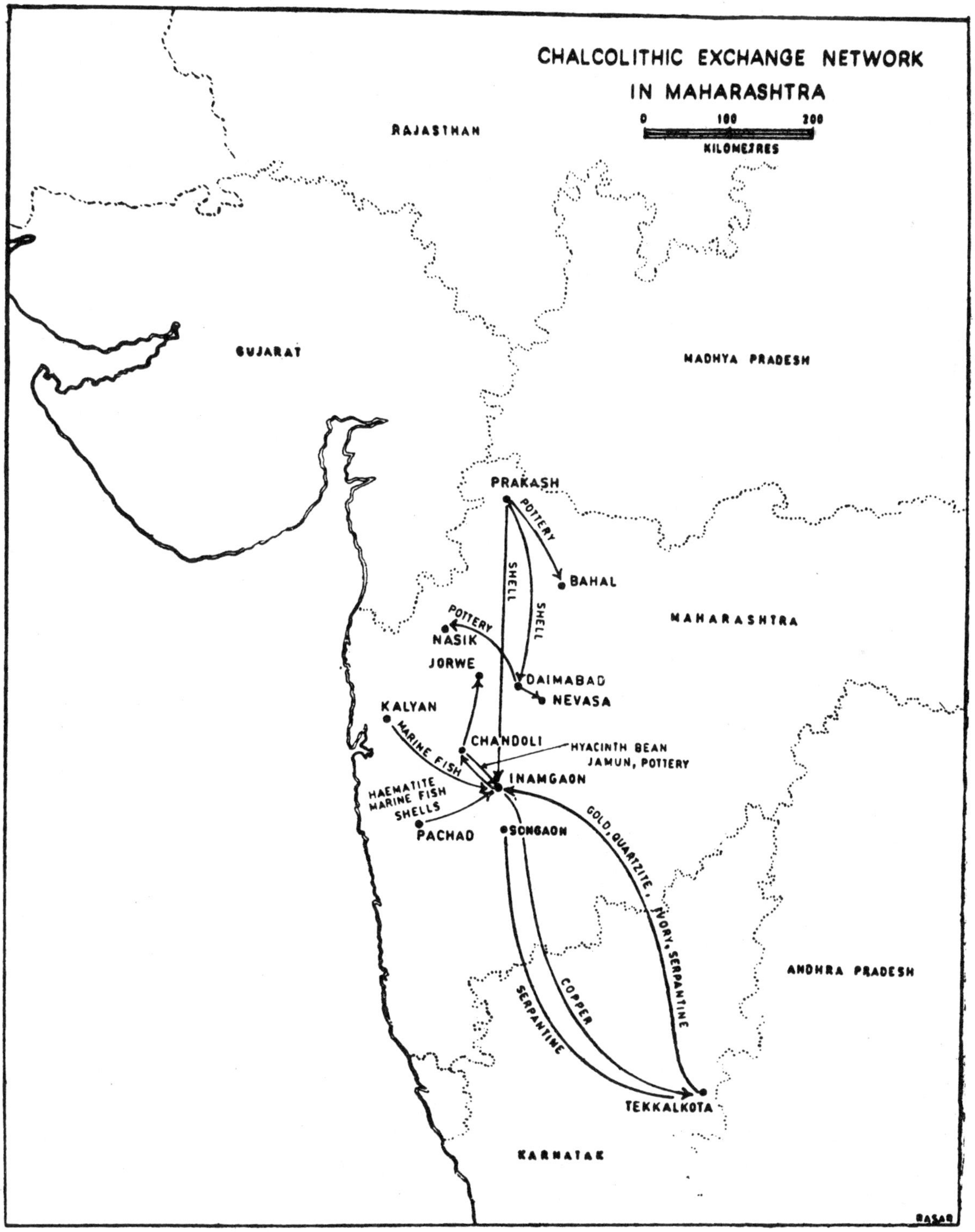
CHALCOLITHIC EXCHANGE NETWORK
IN MAHARASHTRA
0
100
200
KILOMETRES
RAJASTHAN
GUJARAT
MADHYA PRADESH
MAHARASHTRA
ANDHRA PRADESH
KARNATAK
PRAKASH
POTTERY
BAHAL
SHELL
SHELL
POTTERY
NASIK
JORWE
DAIMABAD
NEVASA
KALYAN
MARINE FISH
CHANDOLI
HYACINTH BEAN
JAMUN, POTTERY
INAMGAON
HAEMATITE
MARINE FISH
SHELLS
PACHAD
SONGAON
GOLD, QUARTZITE, IVORY, SERPANTINE
COPPER
SERPANTINE
TEKKALKOTA

Fig. 9.3

spread far and deep into Maharashtra, but not much is known about their exchange system.

The people of the Prabhas culture had inherited the trade of the Harappans, but perhaps by the middle of the second millennium, the overseas trade with West Asia had almost become nonexistent. But it may have continued on a very small scale or else, there was no need to construct a huge warehouse at the port settlement at Prabhas. This apart, the evidence of a seal amulet and an obsidian flake point to some trading contact with West Asia or with the Persian Gulf region in the latter half of the second millennium. Vavri of the *Rigveda* may not be Babylon as is supposed, but may be Bahrain.

The Jorwe people too traded with many of their contemporaries including the hunter-gatherers. They obtained gold and ivory and serpantine from Karnatak, copper ore from the Aharians through the intermediary Malwans, conch shells for bangles from the Saurashtra coast which was occupied by the Prabhas people and amazonite from Rajapipla in Gujarat. Copper may also have come from the Amreli District in Gujarat (Lamberg-Karlovsky 1967). Within Maharashtra, they brought haematite marine fish and shells for necklaces from the Konkan coast and hyacinth been (*Dolichos biflorus*) from the upper reaches of Ghod. Both these regions were not colonized by farming communities, but were occupied by hunter-gatherers whom they might have given in exchange beads and pottery. Within the Jorwe culture zone itself, large centres such as Inamgaon and Daimabad may have been supplying pottery on the intra-regional level. Our statistical study indicates that the Inamgaon potters may have been supplying pottery to the inhabitants of Chandoli which is situated on the same river, about 70 km upstream (Dhavalikar and Marathe 1978-79).

Just as the Ahar smith may have supplied copper artifacts to their contemporaries in central India, the Late Harappan smiths may have supplied them to the Jorwe people in Maharashtra. They had already established their settlements in the Tapi valley and had also reached the heart of Maharashtra around 1800 B.C. as is clear from the Daimabad evidence (Sali 1982). The bronze hoard from the site has certain Harappan affinities (Dhavalikar 1982a) and the barbed arrow-head from Inamgaon is unmistakably Harappan. Similarly the two spiral headed copper pins from Inamgaon recall Harappan specimens.

What did the Jorwe people give in exchange ? To the Neolithic Karnatak, they might have supplied copper and even pottery, for the Jorwe ware occurs as far south as T. Narsingpur. The gold ornaments—spiralled like the latter day sarpa-kundalas—from Daimabad and Tekkalkota are so identical that they were perhaps made by the same goldsmith. With their contemporary hunter-gatherers, from whom they may have obtained the forest produce, they may have exchanged copper tools and ornaments. But what they gave to the people of Malwa and Gujarat cannot be ascertained in the absence of concrete evidence. The only possibility is that they might have made the payment to the traders in the form of grain.

For the inter-regional exchange, the river valleys may have served as routes of communication. The present railway routes through the Gambhiri valley, between the Mewar plateau and Malwa-Khandwa-Ajmer section, is the only route and the same must have been used by the chalcolithic people. Similarly the Burhanpur gap was probably the route for the migration of the Malwa culture into Maharashtra. But there does not seem to be any interaction between Malwa and Gujarat. Obviously due to the fact that Narmada runs into a deep gorge on the Gujarat border, and this proved an insurmountable obstacle, as it is today. But for communication between Gujarat and Maharashtra, the Songadh Pass is the excellent route. The location of Jorwe sites in the Bhima valley mark the route to Karnatak. Small boats with oars, which are painted on Jorwe vessels, were used for river transport, but carts with solid wheels, one of which is incised on a Jorwe pot from Inamgaon, may not have been useful for long distances.

Religious Beliefs

Religion was one aspect which interlinked western India into a single sphere of interaction; the worship of mother goddess and the bull was in vogue. Although the evidence for the Kayatha culture is almost non-existent the Aharians seem to have worshipped a mother goddess (Sankalia *et al.* 1969: 194). Their bull worship is attested by the bull figurines in the Ahar levels at Kayatha. They have been reported in good numbers, and the naturalistic among them may have served as votive offerings, but the stylized ones may have been hung around the neck as the Lingayats do today. We can trace the evolution of the stylized figurines from those with block legs to a pair of horns on a pedestal. This bull cult, however, appears to have been predominant in Malwa during the Ahar period, but not totally absent in the original home of the culture

(Ansari and Dhavalikar 1975: 129-30).

The mother goddess of Malwa is depicted on a huge storage jar in applique design. She is flanked by a woman on the right and a crocodile on the left, by the side of which is represented a shrine (Dhavalikar 1976: 78). Considering the association of crocodile with Durga in the historical period, the mother goddess can be taken to be proto-Sakti. Small, half baked, terracotta female figurines were perhaps associated with prosperity; they are similar to those from the Jorwe levels at Inamgaon the significance of which will be discussed later. The fiddle shaped figurines also probably represent a mother goddess for they resemble the *śrivatsa*, the symbol of Laxmi, the goddess of wealth in the historical period (Dhavalikar 1976: 74). The evidence of an *agnikunda* from Navda Toli suggests the existence of fire worship.

The gods of Malwa are noteworthy. One of them, with dishevelled hair recalling the Rudra of the later period, is painted on a pot. The other too is painted on a globular jar of the Malwa fabric from Daimabad; he is surrounded by animals and birds such as tigers and peacocks. The god has a muscular body and wears a sort of lower garment. Probably an identical representation occurs at Prakash too. It is highly likely that the Malwa people adopted this 'Lord of Beasts' after colonizing Maharashtra where the divinity was already being worshipped by the Late Harappans at Daimabad. The bronze hoard from the site consists of a bull chariot being driven by the god, and an elephant, a rhino and a buffalo, recalling the famous 'Pasupati' on a seal from Mohenjo-daro. He reminds us of the god Tvastr of *Rigveda* who is described as the 'Lord of Beasts'. That apart, it is certain that the chariot and the animals were taken into a procession on a fixed day for such a procession occurs on a Harappan seal (Dhavalikar 1982a). This suggests the organised nature of the religion during the chalcolithic period. This is also to some extent corroborated by the evidence of a fire altar (agni-kunda) at Navda Toli.

The Jorwe people too worshipped male divinities (Pl. III). Two clay figurines from Late Jorwe levels were probably made on a certain occasion, if the present ethnographic parallel is any indication. He is a sort of proto-Ganesha who was worshipped before embarking on an undertaking for success (Dhavalikar 1970). But in the Jorwe period, the mother goddess was predominent considering the number of figurines from Inamgaon. They can be grouped into four categories. The all powerful Mother who was worshipped is represented by well fired figurines, whereas the unbaked ones may have been worshipped on certain occasions only. Small plaque-like specimens were probably connected with vegetative fertility. One such figurine was found in the centre of three pit silos. Similar figurines are made even today by farmers in Andhra Pradesh who place them in silos before storing grain into them. One Inamgaon figurine has punched marks on the body; they may be tattoo marks or even ornamentation, but they look like pustules and the figurine may represent a divnity connected with small-pox which was endemic in the country till very recently. Finally, there were figurines without head recalling the goddess Visira of the *Mahabharata* and may be connected with the well being of children. They were unbaked, indicating their occasional use. In one case, we found in the corner of an Early Jorwe house, a small pit, a clay box containing a mother goddess, and another without head over the lid of the box and a bull, all unbaked. Their careful deposition suggests that some ritual connected with childbirth was performed in the house. The association of bull is to betoken of animism. The plaque-like flat bull figurine may have been used as offerings.

Of all the chalcolithic farmers only the Malwa and the Jorwe people seem to have had belief in life after death as is evident from their burials. The Malwa adult inhumations occur at Daimabad and the twin-urn child burials at Inamgaon. The Jorwe people also buried the children in two urns, one large and the other small, in which the body of the child was placed. The twin urn symbolism recalls the sky and earth the father-mother-symbolism—the larger urn seems to represent the father and the smaller one the mother, and their union representing regeneration. The idea probably was that after death, the child goes back to mother's womb and perhaps that explains why the front of the legged burial urn was shaped like that of a female. This is precisely what Sankaracharya says :

Punarapi janmam punarapi maraṇam
punarapi janani jaṭhare śayanam

In the case of adults, the portion below the ankle was chopped off. The same is presently done in Goa for women who die in pregnancy, so that they should not run away and then turn into ghosts. The same superstition may have been prevalent in chalcolithic times.

Origins and Authors

Of the chalcolithic cultures, the Kayatha has some

Harappan and even pre-Harappan elements but their precise contribution in its make up cannot be ascertained. Similarly, the black-and-red ware, the distinguishing feature of the Ahar culture, may also be the contribution of the Gujarat Harappan. It is likely that some of the mesolithic hunter-gatherers in these areas: forced by the increase in population, may have resorted to food production by adopting the agricultural techniques from their civilized neighbours, the Harappans. In the case of the Prabhas and the Rangpur cultures, there was no problem of borrowing since they were the direct descendants of the Harappans (Dhavalikar 1982b).

The Malwa and the Jorwe do not seem to owe anything directly to the Harappans. But the Malwa ware, to some extent, recalls to the mind the red-painted buff ware of the Kayatha culture. This is only a guess and has to be corroborated by more evidence. At Kayatha itself, the Ahar culture intervenes between the Kayatha and the Malwa. The Jorwe culture, however, seems to have been derived from the Malwa, as is clear from the Inamgaon evidence. The Malwa ware in Maharashtra developed some new traits in form and fabric; it is of finer fabric and the forms include the spouted jar and the carinated bowl, the guide shapes in the Jorwe ware. Besides, the pottery kiln of the Malwa period and that of the Jorwe are identical in design and function but for their size. The Jorwe house plan also follows that of Malwa. The Jorwe can therefore be said to have derived from the Malwa.

All these painted pottery cultures are also characterised by a coarse, handmade red/grey ware which was the utilitarian pottery. In the Jorwe area, it can clearly be identified as the contribution of the southern neolithic but as we go north, its percentage decreases. The ceramic is also associated with the Malwa and the Kayatha cultures, but has only a superficial similarity with the neolithic grey ware. Can we hypothesize a movement of the pre-Harappans and Harappans and the southern neolithic farmers in opposite direction ?

The most vexing problem, however, is the authorship of the chalcolithic cultures. The problem is almost insoluble because of the absence of skeletal evidence, save that from the Jorwe culture. West Asian origin has been postulated on the basis of the designs on spindle whorls from Ahar and certain pottery forms from Navda Toli (Sankalia 1963). Although the West Asian origin has been vehemently criticised) (Chakrabarti 1977), it can hardly be denied that the footed goblets and the pedestalled cups from Navda Toli, including their decorative motifs, are un-Indian. There is nothing West Asian in the Ahar culture except the spindle whorls, whereas the origin of the Malwa may ultimately be traced into the Kayatha. What is therefore likely is that people and ideas were perhaps moving from West Asia into India in the second millennium B.C.; this was nothing new but was only a continuation of the earlier intercourse of the Harappan times. This would explain the West Asian influence on the chalcolithic cultures.

The Prabhas and the Rangpur population may reasonably be assumed to be the successors of the Harappans, who are said to resemble the present day population of Gujarat (Sarkar 1964). It is, however, surprising that they did not practice burial as their predecessors did. The Jorwe people buried the dead, and the few skeletons which have so far been found and studied are said to be of the Mediterranean type with some mixture of Proto-Australoid elements. The Inamgaon skeletons, though few in number, are also of the Mediterranean type. The recent study of the Late Jorwe skeletons reveals that the people, though of the Mediterranean type, were taller and well built than their predecessors in the Early Jorwe period (Lukacs & Badam 1981). Their dentition too was strong. This may perhaps be due to their subsistence on animal foods more, for the Late Jorwe marks a sharp decline in agriculture.

End

The chalcolithic cultures, flourished during the second millennium except the Late Jorwe which survived till *c.* 700 B.C. But Ahar, Malwa, Prabhas and Rangpur (Possehl 1980: 40-47) died out in the closing centuries of the second millennium. By the end of the second millennium the whole chalcolithic activity comes, as it were, to a grinding halt. At Nagda, a Malwa site, an overlap has been suggested. But our own observation at Kayatha, Prabhas, Prakash, Nasik and Nevasa shows that there was a hiatus of about four to six centuries between the chalcolithic and the early historic which is stratigraphically represented by a sterile layer betraying soil characteristics. The chemical analysis of soil profile from Nevasa suggests a decline in the rainfall pattern, and this holds good in the case of Kayatha, Prabhas and Prakash. It is further corroborated by the pollen analysis of lake deposits in Rajasthan carried out by Gurdeep Singh (1971) who has inferred a dry period starting from about 1200 B.C. It is also supported by the evidence of an intensely cold period in Europe from *c.* 1000 B.C. onwards (Butzer 1976: 195).[1] The decrease in the rainfall pattern and the consequent drought periods probably led to the desertion of settlements by these early farming communities of western India. At Inamgaon the people continued to leave a precarious existence but shortly thereafter, around 800 B.C., they had to resort to a semi-nomadic life by practising sheep/goat pastoralisms. They were soon uprooted by the Iron Age Megalith builders. This may have happened in other areas too.

1. Recent investigations carried out on deep sea sediments in the Bay of Bengal and Arabian sea and also on continental sediments in the Indian sub-continent have shown that the south-west monsoons were weak during the peak of the last glaciation (*c.* 18000 B.C.). This, perhaps, would suggest a correlation between glaciation in Europe and aridity in India (Rajaguru 1983).

REFERENCES

Agrawal, D.P. 1982. *The Archaeology of India*, London, Curzon Press, Scandinavian Inst. of Asian Studies, Monograph Series No. 46.

Agrawala, R.C. 1981. Recent Explorations in Rajasthan, *Man and Environment*, Vol. V, pp. 59-63.

Allchin, F.R. and Joshi, J.P. 1972. Malvan, In S.B. Deo (ed.), *Archaeological Congress and Seminar Papers*, Nagpur, pp. 36-42.

Ansari, Z.D. 1978-79. Lithic drill-heads from Inamgaon, *Bull of the Deccan College Research Inst.*, Vol. 38, pp. 9-12.

Ansari, Z.D. and Dhavalikar. M.K. 1975. *Excavations at Kayatha* (1968). Poona, Deccan College Res. Inst.

Binford, Lewis, R. 1972. Mortuary Practices.—Their study and their Potential. In Binford, Lewis R., *An Archaeological Perspective*, New York, pp. 208-239.

Boserup, Ester, 1965. *The Conditions of Agricultural Growth*, London, Allen & Unwin.

Chakrabarti, D.K. 1977. India and West Asia, An alternative approach, *Man & Environment*, No. 1, pp. 25-38.

Butzer, Karl W. 1976. *Geomorphology from the Earth*, London, Harper Row.

Deshpande, C.D. 1948. *Western India—A Regional Geography*, Dharwar, Students Own Book Depot.

Dhavalikar, M.K. 1970. A Prehistoric Deity of Western India. *Man*, 5: pp. 131-33.

——1975-76. Settlement Archaeology of Inamgaon, *Puratattva*, No. 8, pp. 44-54.

——1976. Chalcolithic Religion. In U.V. Singh (ed.), *Archaeological Congress and Seminar* 1972, Kurukshetra University, pp. 74-84.

——1977-78. An Early Warehouse on the Western Coast, *Puratattva*, No. 9, pp. 100-103.

——1982a. Daimabad Bronzes. In Gregory L. Possehl (ed.), *Harappan Civilization—A Contemporary Perspective*, pp. 361-66, New Delhi, Oxford-IBH.

——1982b. Sub-Indus Cultures of Central and Western India. In B.B. Lal & S.P. Gupta, (eds.), *Sir Mortimer Wheeler Volume*, Delhi.

Dhavalikar, M.K. and Marathe, Ashok, 1978-79. Jorwe Pottery: A Statistical Study, *Bulletin of the Deccan College Research Inst.* Vol. 38, pp. 17-22.

Dhavalikar, M.K. and Possehl, Gregory L. 1974. Subsistence Pattern of Early Farming Community of Western India. *Puratattva*, No. 7, pp. 39-46.

Flannery, Kent V. 1972. The origin of the village as a settlement type in Meso-America and the Near East. In Peter Ucko, Ruth Tringham and G.W. Dimbley (eds.) *Man, Settlement and Urbanism*, pp. 23-54, London, Duckworth.

Ghosh, A. 1973. *The City in Early Historical India*, Simla, Indian Inst. of Advanced Study.

IAR—*Indian Archaeology—A Review.*

Joshi, R.V. 1978. *Stone Age Cultures of Central India.* Poona, Deccan College Post-Graduate & Research Inst.

Kosambi, D.D. 1963. The Beginning of Iron Age in India. *Jr. of the Econ. and Social History of the Orient*, Vol. VI, pp.309-18.

Lamberg-Karlovsky, C.C. 1967. Archaeology and Metallurgical Technology in Prehistoric Afghanistan, India and Pakistan, *American Anthropologist*, Vol. 69, pp. 145-62.

Leshnik, Lawrence S. 1968. Prehistoric Exploration in North Gujarat and Parts of Rajasthan, *East and West*, Vol. 18. pp. 295-310.

Lukacs, John R. and Badam, G.L. 1981. Palaeodemography of Post-Harappan Inamgaon: A Preliminary Report, *Jr. of Indian Anthro. Soc.*, Vol. 16, pp. 59-74.

Mujumdar, G.G. 1969. Problem of Black-and-Red Ware: A Technological Approach. In A.K. Narain (ed.), *Seminar Papers on the Problem of Megaliths in India*. Varanasi.

Peebles, Christopher S. and Kus, Susan M. 1977. Some Archaeological Correlates of Ranked Societies, *Amer. Antiquity*, Vol. 42, pp. 421-48.

Plog, Fred. 1977. Modelling Economic Exchange. In Early, Timothy K. and Ericson, Jonathone, E. (eds.), *Exchange Systems in Prehistory*, New York, Academic Press.

Rajaguru, S.N. 1983. On the Problem of Late Pleistocene Aridity in India. *Man and Environment*, Vol. VII in Press.

Rao, S.R. 1962-63. Excavations at Rangpur and other explorations in Gujarat, *Ancient India*, Nos. 18-19, pp. 5-207.

Sali, S.A. 1963. A new ceramic of the chalcolithic from Dhule District Maharashtra. *Jr. of the Asiatic Society of Bombay*, Vol. 38, p. 207.

—— 1982. The Harappans of Daimabad. In Gregory L. Possehl (ed.) *Harappan Civilization—A Contemporary Perspective*, pp. 175-184, New Delhi Oxford-IBH.

Sankalia, H.D. 1963. New Light on the Indo-Iranian or Western Asiatic Relations between 1700 B.C. —1200 B.C.,

Artibus Asiae, Vol. 26, pp. 312-32.

Sankalia, H.D. 1974. *The Prehistory and Protohistory of India and Pakistan*, Poona, Deccan College Post-Graduate Res. Instt. Revised Edition.

Sankalia, H.D. *et al.* 1969. *Excavations at Ahar*, Poona.

——1971. *Chalcolithic Navdatoli*, Poona.

Sarkar, S. 1964. *Ancient Races of Baluchistan, Panjab and Sind.* Calcutta.

Service, Elman R. 1972. *Primitive Social Organization*, New York, Random House, 2nd ed.

Sherratt, Andrew. 1981. Plough and pastoralism: aspects of the secondary products revolution. In Ian Hodder (ed.), *Pattern of the Past-Studies in honour of David Clarke.* Cambridge Univ. Press.

Singh, Gurdeep. 1971. The Indus Valley culture seen in the context of post-glacial climatic and ecological studies in northwest India. *Archaeology & Physical Anthropology in Oceania*, Vol. 6, pp. 177-189.

Singh, U.V. 1962. Excavations at Eran, *Jr. of the M.P. Itihas Parishad*, No. 4, pp. 41-44.

Thapar, B.K. 1967. Prakash 1955: a chalcolithic site in the Tapti valley, *Ancient India*, Nos. 20-21, pp. 5-167.

Wakankar, V.S. 1967. *Kayatha Excavations, Jr. of Vikram Univ.* spl. no.

Wittfogel, Karl A. 1959. *Oriental Despotism—A Comparative Study of Total Power*. New Haven, Yale University Press, 3rd Printing.

Wright, Henry, T. and Johnson, Greg A. 1975. Population, exchange and early state formation in southwestern Iran. *American Anthropologist*, Vol. 77, pp. 267-289.

Study of the Iron Age in India

DILIP K. CHAKRABARTI
Delhi University

WHILE the concept of an Indian "Iron Age" is recent and dates from N.R. Banerjee's publications on the subject in 1965 (Banerjee 1965a, 1965b), the academic interest in Indian iron goes back to the eighteenth century and possesses a much broader dimension than a narrowly archaeological one. Both these issues are, however, interrelated and cannot be studied in mutual isolation.

I. Review of Research till 1982

Since its beginning in the eighteenth century the research on Indian iron has undergone a number of phases. The first phase which lasted from 1795 to about the middle of the nineteenth century shows three types of writings. The first related to the direct scientific analyses of pre-industrial south Indian steel known as *wootz* (derived from the Canarese word *ukku* meaning steel) in Europe. *Wootz* was considered in many respects superior to anything that the western steel-makers had till then produced, and in view of the beginning of Industrial Revolution in England in the latter part of the eighteenth century this scientific interest in the manufacturing process and composition of *wootz* is understandable. Secondly, there was an interest to determine the causes of the external pattern of the Damascus sword-blades which were manufactured in India as well. Thirdly, there were travellers' records and different investigative reports on the distribution and processes of pre-industrial iron-smelting which could then be observed extensively in different parts of India. During this period an independent origin of Indian iron-metallurgy was taken for granted.

The second phase lasted from the middle of the nineteenth century to about 1930. First, the data on pre-industrial Indian iron was systematically incorporated in the contemporary geological and metallurgical literature. Secondly, there was an interest in the composition of ancient Indian iron artifacts. Some megalithic iron objects from near Kamptee, the Delhi and Dhar iron pillars, an iron wedge recovered from the foundation of the Heliodorus pillar and the iron beams of the Konarak temple were the subjects of technical studies. Thirdly, there was an increasing speculation on the origin and antiquity of Indian iron. Phoenicia and Babylon were looked upon as the centres of its origin but at least one scholar argued that there could be no objection to the multiple origin of iron-smelting and that India could be considered an independent centre of iron metallurgy. The fourth feature of this phase is limited to the work of a single scholar, Panchanan Neogi, who published his *Iron in Ancient India* in 1914. Neogi was a teacher of chemistry in Bengal and he synthesised in this book the relevant literary, archaeological, geological and metallurgical data. Although his assumptions are outmoded today, his work is of a great pioneering significance. He was an ardent nationalist who found solace in championing the cause of ancient Indian metallurgy:

"Whilst studying the history of Indian metallurgy of any one of the metals the student or the reader will have to divorce himself from the existing circumstances and transport himself to a remote past, rich in memories of ancient greatness. . ." (Neogi 1918).

The third phase is from about 1930 to 1950, and if this brief period has been supposed to constitute a separate phase of research that is because this marks the beginning of interest in literary and/or archaeological data divested of the geological and metallurgical dimensions. In 1927-31 M.N. Banerjee's interest was entirely literary and in 1950 D.H. Gordon's preoccupation was entirely archaeological. (For a detailed review of research up to 1950, complete with references, see

Chakrabarti 1977a).

The fourth phase was initially dominated by Mortimer Wheeler (1959) who refused to take the beginning of Indian iron beyond the Achaemenids. The most significant feature of this phase was the publication of N.R. Banerjee's *The Iron Age in India* in 1965. Although this book was much criticised both on account of its totally diffusionist framework and the details of interpretation of some archaeological data, it must be acknowledged in retrospect that this was the first attempt to define the scope of Iron Age studies in India and deserves as such full recognition as a pioneering work in the context of modern Indian archaeology.

The diffusionist approach is evident in a number of writings after Banerjee (cf. Tripathi 1973) but in 1974 the present author tentatively tried to visualize the evidence of early Indian iron in terms of a few centres and argue that there was no logical basis to connect its beginning with any diffusion from the west, from Iran and beyond. In the same year M.D.N. Sahi (unpublished) read a paper to the annual session of the Indian History Congress suggesting that a reconsideration of the problem of the origin of Indian iron was perhaps necessary in view of the occurrence of iron objects and slag in an apparently chalcolithic context at Ahar.

The fifth phase possibly began with the present author's definitive study of the problem in 1976. According to this study the present archaeological evidence indicates six early iron-using centres in the subcontinent : Baluchistan, the northwest Indo-Gangetic Divide and the upper Gangetic valley, eastern India, Malwa and Berar in central India and the megalithic South. The archaeological evidence was put in the background of the history of research, the distribution of iron ores suitable for preindustrial smelting, the data on preindustrial iron, the literary data and some recent observations on the history of iron outside India. The conclusions arrived at were the following :

"...(1) the iron in central and south India is, on present showing, earlier than the iron in the north-western periphery of India. The central Indian centre seems to be the earliest of the six early Indian centres. (2) Iron seems to have entered the Indian productive system by *c.* 800 B.C. The literary data alone seems to suggest *c.* 700 B.C. (3) A look at the list of iron ore areas will show that all these early centres are either in or near the ore areas. The evidence of preindustrial smelting also comes from almost all these areas. (4) The evidence of preindustrial smelting and rich ore deposits is very impressive in central and southern India which also seem to show the first evidence of Indian iron. (5) The first Indian iron tool-types do not significantly correspond to the iron tool-types known in west Asia. There is no other demonstrable proof of diffusion during that period from west Asia to the Peninsular block of India. (6) There is an apparent continuity between the early and the contemporary (preindustrial) traditions of the iron metallurgy in India. These points suggest to us that India was a separate and possibly independent centre of the manufacture of early iron. The existing data are admittedly inadequate but the broad indications of this possibility should be clear enough" (Chakrabarti 1976:, 121-122).

Some details of this argument have also been published elsewhere (Chakrabarti 1977b, 1979a, 1979b).

In 1978, J.C. Shaffer (unpublished) pointed out the existence of iron artifacts and nodules in the "Bronze Age" contexts at Mundigak, Deh Morasi Ghundai and Said Qala Tepe in south Afghanistan. He also drew attention to the presence of lollingite nodules in Mohenjo-daro and the location of a mature Harappan pot in a deposit at Pirak, which also contained iron artifacts. The data had been brought forward to emphasize a continuum of "iron awareness" in south Asia. Shaffer further reviews the Indian Iron Age data and finds the present author's dating of the first iron in Malwa (*c.* 1100 B.C.) to be on the conservative side. He firmly supports the idea of an indigenous development of South Asian iron technology, an idea which was also endorsed in J. Jacobson's survey of recent developments in South Asian prehistory and protohistory (Jacobson 1979).

In 1979, Sahi published his analysis of the occurrence of iron objects in Phases Ib and Ic of the chalcolithic Ahar on the basis of data presented by the Ahar excavation report. Phase Ic yielded 4 arrow-heads, 2 chisels, 1 nail, 1 peg and 1 socket and Phase Ib showed 1 arrow-head, 1 ring and slag. There is a C-14 date from Trench X, layer 5, which yields an iron arrow-head—1270±110 B.C. There is no published evidence to suggest that the deposits in which these artifacts occurred were disturbed. On the contrary, their occurrence in 5 trenches (X, C, D, L and E) and in different layers supports their proper stratified locations. It is, in fact, a tribute to the integrity of the Deccan College workers at the site that they duly reported these finds, although the finds did not fit in with their general interpretation of the site.

It may be observed that the idea of different early

iron-using centres with an indigenously evolving base of iron technology has been accepted with some modifications in two recent interpretations of Indian prehistory and protohistory (Agrawal 1982, Allchin and Allchin 1982). B and F.R. Allchin (1982: 345) now put the first period of iron in the subcontinent between 1300 and 1000 B.C. but they prefer to correlate the spread of iron in the subcontinent with "the secondary spread of the Indo-Aryans". According to them "this need in no way conflict with the indigenous population's beginning to exploit local sources of ore to smelt their own ore" (Allchin and Allchin 1982: 356)..

II. The Idea of Polycentric Origin of Iron

On the basis of J.A. Charles' work (Charles 1979), cited in Posnansky 1982 "from copper to iron—the origin of metallic materials", Merrick Posnansky (1982) has argued that the possibility of iron-working developing independently in Africa (first quarter of the first millennium B.C.), perhaps as a by-product of copper technology, certainly seems strong. A similar metallurgical opinion has recently been expressed in the Indian context by K.T.M. Hegde (1981) who believes that the Indian iron-working developed indigenously. He gives his reasons:

"First of all, we have noted the evidence of a long tradition of advanced copper technology in the country. This technology will have provided the most essential infrastructure for smelting iron ore, that is, the furnace. Secondly, the earliest levels of the Iron Age sites have yielded only a few small fragmentary unidentifiable iron objects." This evidence suggests that at this stage the Indian iron industry was in an uncertain experimental stage. There is a reason for that.

"The technique required for smelting iron is a little more difficult than that is required for smelting copper. Iron melts at a much higher temperature (1534°C) than copper (1083°C). Also affinity of iron to oxygen is much stronger than that of copper to oxygen. Iron ore is associated with more impurities than copper ore. Iron, therefore, requires more critical conditions for its successful smelting. A temperature of 1250°C is necessary in the furnace to achieve separation of the unwanted gangue materials from the smelting charge. To obtain this high temperature the furnace will need a good supply of oxygen. With such a supply of oxygen it is difficult to maintain reducing condition in the furnace. The smelter has to know how to balance these conflicting demands. He has to maintain a strong blast of air through the furnace. To offset its oxidising effect it is necessary to feed the furnace with an excess of fuel at regular intervals, so that the reducing gas, carbon monoxide, produced in the furnace, dominates over carbon dioxide. All such technical prerequisites appear to have been gradually understood by the early Indian iron smelters. We have evidence of their experiments in the form of small quantities of poor quality iron occurring at the earliest levels of the Iron Age sites. It is, therefore, clear that we did not receive the technical know-how of iron smelting and smithery from an outside source" (Hegde 1981: 196).

In this context one may draw attention to Sahi's communication to the annual conference of the Indian History Congress in 1980. He points out that the iron contents of the three samples of the copper metallurgical slag from the chalcolithic Ahar, which have been analysed by Hegde, are 43.89%, 45.32% and 48.26%. Sahi depends on Hegde's observations to suggest that the Ahar coppersmiths could tackle the problem of alienating iron from copper ore and thus must have been conversant with the properties of iron ore. Moreover, Sahi argues, following Hegde, that one of the conditions for the removal of iron from copper is the high temperature of the smelting furnace, over 1200°C. The Ahar chalcolithic furnaces could obviously raise this temperature and in such furnaces iron could be expected to form a semi-fluid mass that can be forged and worked. Sahi concludes that "iron metallurgy was invented independently as an offshoot of copper metallurgy in India, particularly in the regions of Malwa and Banas cultures" (Sahi 1980 unpublished).

At a megalithic site in central India (Naikund ?) a Deccan College team recently excavated the remains of a furnace the model of which could be reconstructed. In this type of furnace the slag was tapped through an opening in the front. This type of furnace has a wide occurrence among the preindustrial iron-smelters of India. On the authority of R.C. Agrawal and V. Kumar D.P. Agrawal (1982: 255) refers to the discovery of a "crucible-shaped furnace used for direct reduction of ore", where the bloom was heated in an open furnace and forged on an adjacent platform. This type of furnace is a bowl-shaped cavity in the ground and among the most primitive types of furnaces.

III. Some Recent Archaeological Data

The overlap of the neolithic and megalithic periods, first observed at Hallur, has been traced at two sites at least in Andhra—Hullikalu (Anantapur district, IAR

1978-79: 62) and Pagidigutta (Mahbubnagar district, IAR 1978-79: 65). The most important break-through in the context of the south Indian megaliths seems to be four thermoluminiscent dates of the megalithic black, red and black-and-red pottery of a site called Kumarnahalli. These dates are 1320 B.C. (PRL-TL-46), 1380/1200 B.C. (PRL-TL-47), 1130/930 B.C. (PRL-TL-49) and 1440/1100 B.C. (PRL-TL-50). No other data are yet available but needless to say, this development needs careful attention.

It is now somewhat doubtful if the Painted Grey Ware level in the Doab can be credited with the first use of iron in this region. First, there is a apparently plentiful occurrence of iron in this level. At Jakhera (Sahi 1978), for instance, iron objects associated with Period IIB, supposedly representing "the mature PGW culture" include hoe, sickle, spearhead, arrowhead, dagger/chopper, chisel, axe, nails, rods, etc. Hulas has a large deposit of iron slag in the Painted Grey Ware level (personal information from K.N. Dikshit). The wide nature of finds casts doubt on the possibility that iron was introduced in the Doab only during this period. Secondly, at Noh "shapeless" iron fragments have been found in the black-and-red ware deposit (IAR 71-72: 42). Similarly, in Period IIA of Jakhera, which has only "a few pieces of PGW" from the upper deposits, there are reports of iron slag and bloom.

The situation further east is not quite clear, and as far as the present author understands it, the black-slipped ware phase may denote the earliest iron-using phase in the central section of the Gangetic plain (cf. the black-slipped ware level at Ganwaria in Basti district, U.P.). The evidence from two sites, both in Allahabad district, appears to be of considerable interest. At Koldihwa the Iron Age level includes iron axes and arrow-heads, besides crucibles and slag. This level is said to be a continuation of the earlier chalcolithic level. "Except for iron, other material equipment of this period is same as that of preceding cultures" IAR 1973-74: 27). The second site is Panchoh, reported in IAR 1975-76: 47. Apparently a single culture site this showed three layers from the top: a 20 cm thick whitish layer, a 25 cm thick blackish layer with small stone pieces and iron nodules and a 15 cm thick yellowish layer with iron nodules and *kankar*. The pottery was represented by handmade and ill-fired corded and plain red wares. The other items comprise, among other things, small neolithic celts and microliths.

An interesting situation has also emerged at a black-and-red ware site called Bahiri in Birbhum district, West Bengal (Chakrabarti and Hasan 1982). First, in the upper level of the black-and-red ware phase there is an extensive deposit of iron ore and slag. In one area this deposit could be traced for about 20 m The fact that an area 20 m across is full of iron slag and ore is perhaps worth pondering over. The site is on an edge of the Ajay flood-plain but about 1 km away there is an extensive lateritic spread locally known as *Muluker Danga*. There is no doubt that the iron ore utilized by the ancient settlers of Behiri came from this lateritic spread. The use of lateritic ore is a widely documented practice . among the preindustrial iron smelters of India. the wide occurrence of iron ore and slag in the upper levels of the black-and-red ware phase of the other excavated black-and-red ware sites in the western part of West Bengal, which is a continuation of the Chhotanagpur plateau, is a fact, as far as the present author is aware, although none of these other sites is as fully documented as Bahiri.

But what gives the evidence from Bahiri its special interest is not the rich deposit of iron ore and slag in the upper level of its black-and-red ware phase but the occurrence of a limited number of pieces of iron slag above the natural soil in three exposed sections. The material is properly stratified. There is no confusion about that. Moreover, it is not at all true in the case of Bahiri that the black-and-red ware becomes coarser in its upper, profusely iron-bearing level. At the moment Bahiri stands isolated but the possibility that small pieces of iron slag in the "chalcolithic" level were ignored in the excavated black-and-red ware sites in this region cannot be denied.

IV. Iron and "Second Urbanization"

The present author made his position clear on this issue as early as 1973 (Chakrabarti 1973). The beginning of iron was a low process and unlikely to have directly led to what has been called the "second urbanization" in the Gangetic valley. This conclusion was also independently arrived at by A. Ghosh (1973: 10). More recently, Shaffer (1978, unpublished) has strongly questioned "the assumed vital techno-economic role played by iron tools in the settlement of the Gangetic plain".

To sum up, the emerging trend of data on the Iron Age in India is decidedly significant and worth careful consideration. It is doubtful if anybody can now seriously suppose that iron technology was introduced in India from outside. However, much regarding the transition to iron technology remains uncertain and it is to this end that our archaeological and metallurgical researches should be directed in this context. The present paper has only tried to highlight some of these issues in the background of the earlier phases of research.

REFERENCES

Agrawal, D.P. 1982. *The Archaeology of India*, London : Curzon Press.

Allchin, B. and F.R. 1982. *The Rise of Civilization in India and Pakistan*, Cambridge University Press.

Banerjee, N.R. 1965a. *The Iron Age in India*, New Delhi : Munshiram Manoharlal.

Banerjee, N.R. 1965b. The Iron Age in India, In *Indian Prehistory : 1964* (eds. V.N. Misra and M.S. Nate) : 177-199, Pune : Deccan College.

Chakrabarti, Dilip K. 1973. Beginning of iron and social change in India, *Indian Studies : Past and Present* 14 : 329-338.

Chakrabarti, Dilip K. 1974. Beginning of iron in India : problem reconsidered. In *Perspectives in Palaeoanthropology : D. Sen Festschrift* (ed. A.K. Ghosh) : 345-356. Calcutta : Firma K.L. Mukhopadhyay.

Chakrabarti, Dilip K. 1976. The beginning of iron in India, *Antiquity* 50 : 114-124.

Chakrabarti, Dilip K. 1977a. Research on early Indian iron, 1795-1950. *The Indian Historical Review*, 4 : 96-105.

Chakrabarti, Dilip K. 1977b. Distribution of iron ores and the archaeological evidence of early iron in India, *Journal of the Economic and Social History of the Orient*, 20: 166-184.

Chakrabarti, Dilip K. 1979a. Iron in early Indian literature, *Journal of the Royal Asiatic Society* : 22-30.

Chakrabarti, Dilip K. 1979b. Early Iron Age in the Indian northwest. In *Essays in Indian Protohistory* (eds. D.P. Agrawal and D.K. Chakrabarti) : 347-364, New Delhi : B.R. Publishing Corporation.

Chakrabarti, Dilip K. and S. Jamal Hasan, 1982. The sequence at Bahiri (Chandra Hazrar Danga), District Birbhum, West Bengal. *Man and Environment*, 6 : 101-149.

Charles J.A. 1979. From copper to iron—the origin of metalic materials, *Journal of Metals*, 30 : 8-13.

Hegde, K.T.M. 1981. Scientific basis and technology of ancient Indian copper and iron metallurgy. *Indian Journal of History of Science*, 16 : 189-201.

Indian Archaeology—a Review. 1973-74, 1975-76, 1978-79.

Jacobson, J. 1979. Recent developments in South Asian prehistory and protohistory. *Annual Review of Anthropology* 8 : 467-502.

Neogi, P. 1914. *Iron in Ancient India*, Calcutta : Association for the Cultivation of Science.

Neogi, P. 1918. *Copper in Ancient India*, Calcutta : Association for the Cultivation of Science.

Posnansky, M. 1982. African archaeology comes of age. *World Archaeology*, 13 : 345-358.

Sahi, M.D.N. 1974. Antiquity of iron in India—a reappraisal. Unpublished paper.

Sahi, M.D.N. 1978. New light on the life of the painted grey ware people as revealed from excavations at Jakhera (District Etah). *Man and Environment*, 2 : 101-103.

Sahi, M.D.N. 1979. Iron at Ahar. In *Essays in Indian Protohistory* (eds. D.P. Agrawal and D.K. Chakrabarti) : 365-366, New Delhi : B.R. Publishing Corporation.

Sahi, M.D.N. 1980. Origin of iron metallurgy in India, Unpublished.

Shaffer, J.G. 1978. Bronze Age iron from Afghanistan : its implications for South Asian protohistory, Mimeographed paper.

Tripathi, Vibha, 1973. Introduction of iron in India. In *Radiocarbon and Indian Archaeology* (eds. D.P. Agrawal and A. Ghosh) : Bombay: TIFR

Wheeler, M. 1959. *Early India and Pakistan*. London : Thames and Hudson.

Historical Archaeology: Review and Perspective

S.B. DEO
Deccan College, Pune

IN India the number of excavated historical sites, are quite impressive. This is due to the entry of universities and research institutes in the field of archaeological investigations, both through explorations and excavations. This is the culmination of the wheelerian practice of inducting the universities in archaeological research. However, in the post-wheelerian era several of the universities and research institutions, besides the Archaeological Survey of India and State Departments have established their credentials for independent, planned and scientific excavations.

It may be stated here that problem-oriented excavations were first thought of and executed by Wheeler. Subsequently, this trend continued. However, even a casual perusal of the issues of *Indian Archaeology—A Review*, brings home one aspect which is not much in favour of historical archaeology. This is that during the last three decades the emphasis of investigations shows a predeliction more for protohistoric investigations, rather than to the historical. This has resulted in emphasising individual sites rather than co-ordinated problems of historical sites or larger issues like those of the process of urbanisation, the concordance between literary and archaeological sources, the settlement pattern, trade and economy and the level of technology of the different periods in a historical framework. It is proposed to focus attention of scholars to these issues, no less important as they are even in comparison to the period preceding the historical one. It is indeed a misconception that the social and economic dynamics of the historical period is relatively more explicit because of abundant contemporary literary and other data. Material culture still remains the most convincing source for building up the picture of contemporary economy and technology.

It may be stated here that in this review minor tappings and sites without much of significant data have not been taken into account. It is proposed to take a review of the significant excavations and through them to pose certain problems for the consideration of the scholars as also to outline the future planning.

It has often been stated that in India there were two urbanisations, one with the Indus Civilisation and the other around the sixth century B.C., when the Mahajanapadas and the various cities came into existence. However, in spite of several sites in different parts of India having been excavated so far, no integrated picture of the stages in the evolution of this second urbanization have been brought forth or emphasised. This has resulted in the data telling only the culture sequence at a particular site but not its role, if any, in the larger perspective of urbanisation or technological evolution. It would, therefore, be necessary to state the evidence as it has emerged and then to make general observations in respect of socio-economic framework of the early historic period.

The explorations and excavations in peninsular India have yielded an enormous data which has piled up and yet awaits co-ordination. It is indeed a pity that in spite of the region being exceptionally rich in historical data, what is available is a maze of unrelated evidence emphasising the individuality of each site. However, unless the evidence of the major sites—ignoring the less importance—is stated, it would be difficult to generalise.

Maharashtra, Andhra Pradesh, Tamil Nadu, Karnataka and Kerala constitute the area which may be termed generally as south India or Dakshinapatha which even in ancient Indian literature comprised of the region south of the Narmada.

Andhra Pradesh

Andhra Pradesh has proved to be the richest area so far as early historical sites are concerned. These normally range between the time span of *circa* 3rd cent. B.C. to the early medieval period. Amongst these, the most noteworthy feature has been the profusion of early Bhudhist sites with stupa complexes and sometimes also giving evidence of monasteries. No other state in south India, has given so many Buddhist sites as Andhra Pradesh.

So far as the sites with Buddhist establishments are concerned, the place of pride of course goes to *Nagarjunakonda* followed by *Yelleswaram.* Huge stupa mounds have also been reported from *Kalingapatnam* (*IAR* 1976-77: 10), *Dhulikatta* in Dist. Karimnagar (*IAR* 1975-76: 2-3), *Kondapur,* Dist. Medak (*IAR* 1973-74: 6), *Dupadu,* Dist. Guntur, *Chandavarman,* Dist. Prakasham (*IAR* 1976-77: 3) and *Viratraj Gudda,* or Erradibba in Dist. Khammam. All these Buddhist sites belong to the early centuries of the Christian era and speak of the spread of Buddhism and the large following it had enlisted among the people of this region. Apart from the stupas, amongst which the one from Chandavaram has been designated as 'Mahastupa', follow the pattern of construction and layout typical of the Satavahana-Ikshvaku times with gateways and ayaka platforms and *pradakshinapatha.* However, only the excavations at Nagarjunakonda have been carried out on such a magnitude as to give an idea of the layout of this capital of the Ikshvaku rulers who designated it as the Vijayapuri. Apart from religious structures like the stupas and viharas of the Buddhists and the temple of Pushabhadraswamin of Brahmanical affinities, a number of secular structures like an open theatre or arena for wrestling and elephant fight have been brought to light. Similar to Nagarjunakonda, the site of Chandavaram has evidenced a huge Buddhist settlement with a Mahastupa, monastic complexes, votive stupas, an apsidal chaitya and quite a range of sculptures which bespeak of the large scale religious settlement here. The site of Sannati in Gulbarga Dist., has also given evidence of a large scale Buddhist establishment of 1st-2nd century A.D.

Apart from these religious centres, remains of fortified towns have been recovered at *Dhulikatta* in Karimnagar Dist., Satanikota in Kurnool Dist., *Keesaragutta* in Hyderabad Dist. (*IAR* 1976-77: 3-4), *Peddabankur* (*IAR* 1973-75), Dist. Karimnagar and *Motupalli* (*IAR* 1973-74: 7) Prakasam Dist. Of these, the remains at Dhulikatta have been impressive in as much as the excavations here have exposed the remains of a fortified town with gateways, a palace complex and a stupa in a typically Andhra style with sculptured limestone slabs donated by the lay follower of Buddhism. The find of the coins of Satavahana kings places the township to the later Satavahana phase. This could as well have been one of the thirty walled towns of the Satavahanas.

The epigraphical and other data points to the fact that the economically affluent laity followed Buddhism. The expansion and relative political stability under the Satavahanas and the Ikshvakus and the economic prosperity resultant out of political peace, internal and external trade contributed to the rise of several township. The quicker means of communications brought closer contacts, helped the mobiliy of artisans and brought about a broad uniformity of religious architecture. This is evidenced by the rise of several well planned townships as evidenced also at Satanikotta in Dist. Kurnool. (*IAR* 1977-78: 3-11), again of the Satavahana period and following the plan of a fortified town as at Dhulikatta. It is significant to note that the regions of Andhra and Maharashtra were the key areas of Satavahanas empire in the initial centuries of the christian era and it is in these two regions that a number of fortified towns, emporia and ports have been evidenced.

Maharashtra

The feature of a number of townships, fortified establishments, prosperous emporia and busy ports has been evidenced in the region of Maharashtra close to the west of Andhra Pradesh. Prakash, Nasik, Nevasa, Junnar, Kolhapur, Bhokardhan, Ter, Paunar, Kaundinyapur and Pauni have given evidence of the nature of townships, arts and crafts, religious complexes, trade and economy of the early centuries of the Christian era. The find of the Red Polished pottery showing affinities with the Roman wares, clay bullae in imitation of Roman coins, bronzes of Roman deities, motifs of 'Yavana' idioms evidenced in the caves at Nasik and Junnar and the large number of rock-cut caves discovered at Panhale Kaji, hardly six kilometres as the crow flies from the port of Dabhol on the western coast, speak of the economic prosperity resulting from the political stability under the Satavahanas. This gave rise to the growth of ports like Kalyan, sopara and Chaul, trade centres like Ter ancient Tagarapura, rise of Buddhist centres following the trade routes, centres of art like Bhokardhan and large scale Buddhist centres as at Pauni in Vidarbha. The impact of this economy has been evidenced as far south as at Kolhapur (Hippokura of Ptolemy) where a number of Roman antiquities like the bronze statue of Poseidon have been recovered.

Prakash (Thapar 1964-65:5-167) situated on the Tapi in Khandesh flowered into a settlement of consequence only in the couple of centuries prior to and after the Christian era. Located as it is on a strategic point, the township seems to have grown up in the Satavahana-Kshatrapa period and one gets evidence of structures of baked bricks, coins of the Satavahanas and the Kshatrapas as also Red Polished ware. Nasik to its south, though first habitated in the Chalcolithic period, developed only in the early historical period i.e. periods II and III of the excavated sequence. This period witnessed the use of baked bricks for houses, elaborate drainage system evidenced by soakage wells, Roman wares, clay bullae in imitation of Roman coins and arts and crafts like bead-making and terracotta figurines. The nearby caves at Nasik stand testimony to the generosity of the 'Yavanas' who donated to the creation of rock-cut chaityas and viharas. Some of the caves show distinctive foreign features as for instance the Roman-like human faces decorating the beam-ends, the distinctive feature of making the surface smooth and well-marked before carving the record, the depiction of Atlants and decorative motifs of certain meshes and floral designs as also the names of the Yavanas who donated to these Buddhist establishments. These are so unmistakable evidences that tempt one to wonder whether Nasik was a Yavana centre in the early historic period. Side by side the local guilds were also generous to these Buddhist establishments. It is also significant to note that after the fall of the Satavahanas and the Kshatrapas, Nasik lost its affluence and this is reflected in the poverty of finds in the period after the third century A.D. The story is repeated in the excavations at Nevasa where again the economic affluence is attested in the early and late phases of the Satavahanas. The political chaos resulted in economic depression and the towns like Nasik, Nevasa, Junnar, Ter, Kolhapur and Bhokardan lost their previleged position.

The evidence is repeated at Kolhapur, Ter and Bhokardan. The early historic Kolhapur (Brahmapuri) (Sankalia & Dikshit 1952) had well planned brick-built houses with soak-pits for drainage and a separate kitchen room. Such houses with firm foundation of boulders of stone which replaced the earlier houses of clay, attest to the prosperity of the settlement. The rich could afford the import of Roman wine in amphorae as also items of luxury like bronzes, bronze utensils, special table ware and Roman coins. It is clear that Kolhapur was well-connected with the other trade centres. The find of the remains of a Buddhist stupa earlier again repeat the story of the well-to-do merchant class patronising Buddhism out of the affluence accrued due to at boost in internal and maritime trade.

The excavations at Ter and Bhokardan (Deo & Gupte 1974), Tagarapura and Bhogavardhana of ancient times stand testimony to the same social and economic conditions. The former which finds mention both in Pliny and Ptolemy has, in addition to giving evidence of a stupa complex of Hinayana tradition, brought to light practically a school of art excelling in the art of terracotta and Kaolin figurines of the Satavahana period. The excavations also gave evidence of wooden palisade of the early Satavahana times which might indicate that Ter was one of the thirty fortified towns of the Satavahanas. The stupa, like a *cakra* on plan and with *ayaka* platform and *pradakshina-patha* follows the traditional pattern as evidenced at several stupa sites in Andhra Pradesh, the latter being under the hegemony of the same dynasty. This is further strengthened by epigraphical data which helps to date the stupa complex to the initial centuries of the Christian era. Ter (*IAR* 1967-68) is also known for the structural temple, apsidal on plan and assigned to the same period. Ter thus appears to have been a town of consequence because of religious and commercial importance. Bhokardan, not for away from Aurangabad, Paithan and Ter, seems to have been essentially an establishment of the artisans of the Satavahana period. It has been mentioned in the records at Sanchi. The excavations gave evidence of the local ivory industry in the late Satavahana-Kshatrapa period in the form of a pair of ivory female figurines reminiscent of the one reported from Pompeii. The same levels gave sherds of the amphorae, bullae and beads of semi-precious stones in various stages of manufacture. It thus proved that Bhokarduan was a centre of ivory carvers and bead makers. It was also evidenced that with the fall of the Satavahanas and the eventual degradation of the importance of metropolitan towns like Paithan and emporium like Ter, the industry at Bhokardhan suffered a set back. The economic decadence is reflected in the archaeological evidence of the post-Gupta. levels

Pauni (Deo & Joshi 1972) in the Vidarbha region of

Maharashtra has brought to light an extensive Hinayana Buddhist establishment going back to the period of the NBP and subsequent times. The stupa was found to have been encased and enlarged in the initial centuries of the Christian era with the dome built up in boxes filled with rubble and brickbats. It had an elaborate lime concrete *pradakshina-patha*, inner and outer railing with beautiful sculptures and majestic gateways recalling those at Sanchi. It also gave evidence of a simpler stupa constructed to the south belonging to a later phase. The areas in between was full of brickbats possibly suggesting ruins of the monastery. Since strategically located on the perenial river Wainaganga, it has for the first time opened up the possibilities of the spread of Buddhism to the south through Vidarbha. This is further strengthened by the find of an extensive stupa and monastery complex along with Ashokan records in District Sehore in Madhya Pradesh, not far away from Pauni.

That there were extensive Buddhist establishments on the western coast has been evidenced by the *Panhale Kaji* and *Devaranwadi* both in Dist. Ratnagiri. Apart from Buddhism these places have also given evidence of Brahmanical and Jaina inroads at these places. Not only that, in the medieval period, Panhale Kaji also became a centre of the Nath Panthis which indeed is a new piece of information important from the point of religious and cultural history of this region.

Important finds of the Vakataka period have recently been brought to light at Mandhal in Nagpur District (*IAR* 1975-76 : 36) and Ramtek. The former, apart from evidencing habitations from the Satavahana period, has given brick structures, remarkable sculptures of the same period and belonging to Brahmanical faith and copper plates of Prithvisena II and Pravarasena II, both of the Vakataka dynasty. The recent find of the inscription of queen Prabhavati Gupta in one of the temples at Ramtek has supported the view of Mirashi that Ramtek could be Ramagiri mentioned by the poet Kalidasa in Meghaduta. Paunar, in Dist. Wardha, well-known for the series of Vakataka sculptures of Ganga, Ramayana panels, panels of Siva and the Seshasayin Vishnu, gave evidence of brick-built structures indicating that it was an important centre in the 5th-6th century A.D. (Deo & Dhavalikar 1967).

The region of Maharashtra, therefore, has given evidence of the dominance of Buddhism, the donations by the affluent merchant class, a prospering phase of internal and maritime trade contributing to the emergence of urban centres and giving rise to diversification of arts, crafts and professions organised in guilds.

Karnatak

Further south, in Karnatak, *Vadgaon-Madhavapur* in Dist. Belgaum has proved to be most promising site where extensive structural remains of the Satavahana period have been unearthed. The settlement shows well built houses of two rooms and verandah unit, circular wells, a large scale industry of beads and terracotta figurines and a large collection of coins of the Satavahanas and Kshatrapas. It thus indicates that it was an important urban centre in early historic period. Another similar centre, has been evidenced at Chandravalli, Dist. Chitradurga (*IAR* 1977-78: 27-29) where well built structures, coins and a range of sophisticated antiquities like beads, terracottas and metal objects have been found. Besides these two notable sites, a number of places have given Brahmanical sculptures and remains of structural temples.

Tamilnadu

The excavations at *Kanchipuram* and *Kaveripattinam* in Dists. Chingleput and Thanjavur respectively have given more significant evidence, though a number of ancient sites have been located in this region. The former, i.e. Kanchipuram (*IAR* 1974-75: 37-38) has shown that right from the second century B.C. onwards, the township seems to have had prosperous times indicated by brick structures and a range of objects like beads, coin-moulds, metal artifacts and imported wares like the Arretine. It thus seems to have been an emporium. Even now it is famous as a religious centre and an emporium. Literary sources give a picture of a very prosperous township in the early centuries of the Christian era and subsequently. Kaveripattinam (*IAR* 1973-74 : 25; *IAR* 1977-78 : 50) exposed viharas and shrines along with structures of moulded bricks and decorative stucco figurines.

The evidence, therefore, in peninsular India shows that in the early Satavahana period the process of urbanisation received a tremendous impetus with diversification of industries and the introduction of luxury articles in the life of the richer classes. The backbone to this prosperity was equally provided by agricultural production enhanced by the introduction and use of iron artifacts on a large scale.

Western India

The Gujarat, Kutch and Rajasthan areas have given

a number of early historic and subsequent period sites. However, several of these sites have been tapped on a small scale with the result that a comprehensive and integrated picture is yet to emerge. Though the Baroda University has tapped several iron-age sites, these have given a brief outline of the sequence of cultures rather than a reasonably detailed picture of different phases.

However, Somnath, Dwarka, Devni Mori and Karwan have brought to light noteworthy evidence. Prabhas Patan gave evidence of the massive fortification of stones assignable to c. 4th cent. B.C. — lst cent B.C. whereas Dwarka on the sea-coast evidenced its occupation in the initial centuries of the Christian era. However, Karwan, the ancient Kayavarohana in Dist. Vadodara gave evidence of an elaborate temple complex of the Saiva faith along with coins of the Kshatrapas and Maitrakas, Red polished Ware and terracotta bullae. It thus seems to have been a religious place (*IAR* 1974-78.)

Devni Mori (Mehta *et al.* 1966) has, on the other hand, evidenced a large scale Buddhist establishment with quite a range of terracotta and stucco statuary. The latter betrays the influence of the Gandhara idiom. It shows that Gujarat had a good number of followers of Budhism even in the initial three-four centuries of the Christian era.

Central India

Central India comprising the state of Madhya Pradesh has given evidence of numerous early historical sites, right from Mauryan times onwards. Several urbanised religious and trade centres like Maheshwar, Ujain, Eran, Tripuri, Vidisha and Malhar and scores of early Buddhist establishments have been brought to light. The location of the region being significant, it served as the link between the north and the south and seems to have received the impact of urbanisation from urbanised centres of Uttarapatha and a channel of transmitting Buddhism further south.

The earliest evidence of a fortified settlement of iron age has come from Ujjain which has played a significant role as commercial and the capital of Avanti because of its strategic location religious and political importance right till the medieval times. (*IAR* 1956-57). The picture of Ujjain in the 750-500 B.C. period is of a habitation protected by a mud rampart of 75 m. width and 13 m height with a moat 24 m wide. The riverside was protected with a caging having a massive gateway on the north-west. The plan of this fortified city was parallelogramatic. In the subsequent Maurya-Sunga period, it came further into limelight because of significant construction of a large tank and canal as also for its bead-making industry. For about a thousand years from 200 B.C. it continued to flourish not only politically and economically but also as a centre of learning under the Paramaras. Because of its strategic position it was well-connected with other centres like Mathura, Kausambi, Bharukaccha and Pataliputra, though a complete idea of the layout of the township in different periods is not available.

Another equally important centre was *Mahishmati*, the present day Maheshwar on the Narmada. A lot of legendary stories are associated with Mahishmati. It was supposed to have been founded by king Muchukunda and for sometime enjoyed the status of the capital of Avanti. Chronologically, subsequent to the first habitations at Ujjain, Maheshwar prospered around 4th cent. B.C. and subsequently for about three or four centuries as the well-made brick structures, use of iron artefacts and the find of the NBP attest. That Buddhism had a hold in the region is attested by the exposure of a Buddhist stupa at Navdatoli situated on opposite bank. The town continued to flourish till the late medieval period.

Eran and Tripuri were the other two centres which were of some consequence in the historical period. The former, the Airikina of ancient times, had better times from the Mauryan period onwards till the end of the Gupta. A number of punch-marked, tribal and Gupta coins and beads of a variety of semi-precious stones bespeak of the prosperity of the town. Coins of Ramagupta and inscriptions of his times indicate that Eran was an important centre in the initial centuries of the Christian era.

Like Maheshwar, *Tripuri* has the association of several legendary and historical accounts. In the early medieval period, it was a well-known Saiva centre with a large establishment of monastic complex (Dikshit 1952; *IAR* 1965-66.)

However, in recent years a very extensive early Buddhist monastery and stupa complex has been brought to light in the Bayan, Pangorgria and Talpura region of the Sehore Dist. (*IAR* 1975-76: 28-30). The most important evidence is the find of two Ashokan inscriptions one of which is a version of Minor Rock Edict I and the other records the visit of Piyadasi as Maharajakumara to the site. There was also found a *maha-stupa*, 76 m in diameter besides several others with scores of monastic cells. The site must have been of some consequence as to evoke the visit of Piyadasi. Not far away from this complex are a series of mounds which might contain the remains of ancient Nemavati Nagari, the present day Ninore.

Similar is the case of *Malhar* in Dist. Bilaspur and Vidisha and Besnagar in Dist. Vidisha. The former (*IAR* 1974-77) flourishing with well constructed brick and dressed stone structures and fortified by a mud wall prospered as a bead making and terracotta centre to develop around the 7th-9th centuries A.D. and as a Vajrayana Buddhist Centre with monastic establishment. *Besnagar* (*IAR* 1977-78) came up in Pre-Mauryan and Mauryan times as a settlement with stone drains and ring wells. During the subsequent period, it was a fortified town with the fortification wall having a width of 35 m and showing a novel constructional pattern in having brick constructed boxes filled with small rubble, pebbles and brick-bats. A large number of stone balls indicated their use as missiles. Perhaps it had a strategic value as it continued to be a town of some consequence in the subsequent Naga-Kushana and Kshatrapa-Gupta times as well. Even in the second century B.C. it had a rubble masonry fortification in criss-cross pattern with wooden palisades. It was further protected by a moat. The most noteworthy feature of Besnagar is the temple complex assignable to the Naga-Kushana period characterised by an apsidal shrine with a four pillared mandapa in front (*IAR* 1976-77: 33).

The evidence from Central India points to a speedy growth of urban centres with fortification, right from the Mauryan-Sunga times and the influence of Buddhism as well as Bhagavatism and Saivism. The strategic importance of the area connected the towns of the region with other parts of India resulting in the growth of trade and commerce. The epigraphical records from Sanchi, Bharhut, Vidisha etc., speak of the generosity of practically all classes of the society, from the labourer to the traders which was the result of prospering economy.

Northern India

It will be difficult to take stock of the archaeological data from the numerous ancient sites that have been tapped so far. The fertility of the soil, the undisturbed plain terrain, the perenial rivers, and easier communications made the plains of Punjab, Uttar Pradesh and Bihar fit for colonisation, growth and urbanisation backed by agricultural surplus. It is mostly in this region, therefore, that the Mahajanapadas and subsequently big empires like those of the Nandas, Mauryas, Kushanas and Guptas arose. Easy terrain made political consolidation easy and political stability led to the thriving trade, commerce and industries.

The noteworthy excavations giving important information of the early historical period are those at Kaushambi, Rajghat, Ahichchhatra, Rajgir, Kumrahar, Vaishali, Rupar, Purana Qila, Jagatgram, Mathura, Piprahwa, Ganwaria, Antichak, Sringaverapura, Champa, Ayodhya to name only a few.

Kaushambi (Sharma 1960 and 1969) the capital of Vatsa and present day Kosam, has given some remarkable evidence. For instance, the antiquity of iron here goes back to a period dated between 1165 and 885 B.C., the earliest known so far in the Yamuna valley. In the field of architecture, Kaushambi has given evidence of find of Ghoshitarama monastery confirmed by epigraphical evidence. The merchant, as the tradition goes, was contemporary of Buddha for whom the monastery was built.

Important sites like *Rajghat* which is a part of Varanasi and Ahichchhatra have unfortunately been dug on a small scale. It would be profitable to excavate these two on a horizontal scale with a view to know the layout of these ancient sites, as the excavations have so far pushed back their antiquity to the NBP and pre-NBP periods and the introduction of iron at an early period in their history. Equally important has been the site of *Rajgir*, ancient Rajagriha, the capital of Magadha. It is one of the most extensive sites and has in sporadic excavations (*IAR* 1953-54) evidenced mud rampart built by king Ajatasatru (5th cent. B.C.). Subsequently, the area known as Kumrahar was excavated which gave a sequence of habitations from c. 600 B.C. to 600 A.D. and continued till the late medieval. Yet another important site from Bihar is Vaishali (Deva & Mishra 1950) the birth place of Mahavira, the 24th Tirthankara of the Jainas. It is equally important in the history of Buddhism as it was the place where the Second Council was held. Further excavations (Sinha & Roy 1962) in 1962 brought out two important relics. The first is the evidence of defences originally built around 500 B.C. and subsequently renovated and strengthened in the Sunga, Kushana and Gupta periods. The second is the discovery of the mud stupa built by the Lichhavis to deposit the relics of the Buddha.

Bihar

In recent years important historical data has been obtained from Champa and Antichak, Dist. Bhagalpur, Nalanda and Balirajgarh in Dist. Madhubani in Bihar.

Antichak which has been excavated since 1973, has given reasonable idea of the nature of the Vikramshila establishment. Here the Buddhist monastery 330 m square in plan is equipped with a spacious courtyard with central shrine and 120 monastic cells (*IAR* 1973-78) besides several other structures of bricks and carefully planned drainage system. Dated between 9th and 12th centuries A.D. it has given a plethora of Buddhist icons as also those of the Brahmanical pantheon. However, the nature and purpose of different structures remains to be worked out with a view to have an idea of the integrated pattern of life of the monastic community.

The excavations at Champa (*IAR* 1974-77) for several seasons, though attesting habitation from pre-NBP period, seem to indicate a prosperous phase only in the Maurya-Sunga times culminating in the Gupta period when the town became a jewellery-manufacturing centre. Similar seems to have been the case with Balirajgarh (*IAR* 1972-75) which became a centre of terracotta and bead production. Katragarh on the other hand seems to have been a well-fortified town in the Sunga period with an earlier phase of mud fortification later on strengthened with bricks laid in English bond pattern and having a semi-circular watch tower. The site gave all the varieties of the NBP besides a large number of terracotta figurines and plaques as well as finished and unfinished beads indicating its role as an art and trade centre (*IAR* 1975-76: 8-9).

Remains of a slightly later period were exposed at Nalanda (*IAR* 1975-76: 8-9) where a brick-built temple, rectangular on plan, with moulded decoration, niches for images, votive stupas and corbelled drains were uncovered giving an idea of the religious establishment of 7th-8th cent. and later.

Uttar Pradesh

Some important excavations during the last decade deserve notice. They are Piprahwa, Mathura and Ganwaria besides a few others. Piprahwa in Dist. Basti has given remains of an extensive monastic and stupa complex besides secular structures. Besides the stupa built in three phases and having *pradakshina-patha* and a casket enshrined in the stupa, and large monasteries quadrangular on plan with a central courtyard, the site has given several seals. The excavator identifies Piprahwa (*IAR* 1973-74: 27-28) with ancient Kapilavastu which played an important role in Buddhism. Salargarh about 300 kilometres east of Piprahwa has also given remains of a Buddhist complex comprising a stupa and monastery of the Kushana period (*IAR* 1975-76: 50).

Similarly Mathura and Ganwaria, the latter in Basti Dist., have given important evidence. Ganwaria, adjacent to Piprahwa, has given extensive and majestic remains of structures including some identified as a school building, a shrine, residential complex with several rooms and bastion-like structures around it. It has been pointed out that the structures at Ganwaria (*IAR* 1974-75: 39-41) may represent the residential complex of king Suddhodana and his predecessors, and that one of the buildings identified as shool reminds one of the reference given by Hiuen Tsang who states that the place was famous for educational institutions. Bakraur in Dist. Gaya (*IAR* 1973-74; 9-10) which is associated with Sujata who offering the *payasa* to the Buddha has exposed the remains of a massive stupa which ultimately had a diameter of 65.50 m, *pradakshina patha*, railings and gateways. It thus seems to have been an important Buddhist establishment and the stupa might have been raised to commemorate the memory of Sujata.

Mathura, the famous sacred city and having a chequered career in the history of India has been tapped by several archaeologists so far and yet remains inexhaustible. In the excavations of 1956-57, evidence of habitation could be had from c. 6th cent. B.C. onwards. The excavations from 1973-76 onwards, have confirmed the antiquity of the site to the pre-NBP period but has attested to the fortified nature of the city in the Saka-Kushana period, even though earlier also it was fortified, with the fortifications having a basal width of 17 m. The plan of the fortifications was irregular crescentic with pronounced southern horn and with the Yamuna protecting the eastern sector. The enclosed area was 3 square m and the crescentic plan of fortifications has been confirmed by Puranic references. The township seems to have prospered in the early centuries of the Christian era, like Sonkh. The centre was also known as an art centre as the recovery of terracottas, beads and elaborate toys attest. Being a seat of political power and of prominent religious faiths, and well connected with other towns by trade routes, Mathura seems to have enjoyed material prosperity for a pretty long period.

It would thus appear that the regions of present day Uttar Pradesh and Bihar, by virtue of their possessing most of the factors inviting human colonisation, gave rise to a number of settlements which in due course became urban centres.

Eastern India

As compared to central and north India, eastern India have a limited number of urban centres. Throughout literature, one finds the mention of misgivings about the nature and people of the region. However, a few remarkable discoveries have been made recently. They are mostly of the early historical period.

Orissa

Sisupalgarh, Jaugada and Ratnagiri are the most noteworthy. Sisupalgarh in close proximity with Bhubaneshwar, has been identified with Tosali of the Ashokan records and Kalinganagara referred to in the inscription of Kharavela. Though the settlement here goes back to Mauryan period, subsequently it developed into a well fortified town, one square kilometer on plan with each side of the fortification having majestic gateways. Within the fortified area were the habitations of brick-built houses (Lal 1949: 62-105). Yet another site having fortifications was Jaugada in Dist. Ganjam (*IAR* 1956-57: 30-31).

Buddhist contacts with Orissa go back to the times of Mauryas, especially Ashoka who has left an edict as Dhauli. It appears that Buddhism appears to have survived in Orissa for several centuries as the remains of an extensive Buddhist settlement at Ratnagiri, Dist. Cuttack have evidenced. The site has given excellent sculptures and architectural remains datable to the 9th-10th cent. A.D. (*IAR* 1956-57).

Bengal

Bangarh, Bharatpur, Chandraketugarh and Tamluk are some of the notable historical sites in Bengal. Of these, Tamluk identified with ancient Tamralipti has given evidence of human occupation right from the Mauryan period till the medieval Pala times. It has given a remarkable range of terracottas, especially noteworthy being those of the Sunga and Gupta periods (*IAR* 1954-55: 19-20). Recent explorations there have given a varied collection of coins of different periods, seals of semi-precious stones and beads of different materials and shapes (*IAR* 1975-76: 51-52). Bangarh in Dist. Dinajpur repeats the same sequence, but in addition has brought to light distinctive constructions like a lotus-shaped tank with probably a pillared canopy. Such distinctive constructions have also been reported from Bharatpur, Dist. Burdwan (*IAR* 1973-74: 32-33; 1974-75: 51) where the remains of a stupa of square plan of pancharatha type and datable to *circa* 8th-9th cent. A.D., have been exposed. Similarly Chandraketugarh in Dist. 24 Parghanas, has given two votive stupas and a polygonal temple with Sarvatobhadra plan of the Gupta times (*IAR* 1956-57: 29-30).

Assam

This region has not yet been properly explored with the result that very few historical sites have been tapped so far. Ambari, a suburb of Gauhati gave evidence of habitation which might go back to the initial centuries of the Christian era (Ansari & Dhavalikar 1971: 79-87). Brick structures with Sivalingas, datable to 8th-10th centuries, could have been according to the excavators, the shrines of the Devas or gods mentioned by Yuan Chwang. Recently, at Gauhati, in an area called Dumar Jhar, excavations gave a terracotta boat-shaped object, 2.50 m in length, 0.65 m. in width and 0.33 m in depth with both its sides connected internally by a bridge (*IAR* 1974-75: 7). In several cases it has been found that boat-like objects served as funerary offering.

A review of the sites of early historical period excavated so far in different parts of India shows that save for a few exceptions, most of the sites have been tapped vertically and not horizontally with the result that a broad sequence of habitations and cultural periods at most of the individual sites is well-known. However, the integration of evidence has not been done so far, nor any attempt to know the total picture of the habitations of a particular period. This has resulted in the accumulation of a vast data without any full significance for the socio-economic and technological assessment. Different types of structures are known without their significance within the framework of the then social and economic organisation of the inhabitants, their economic division, the layout of the habitation with reference to the affluent and less affluent classes, the variety of professions without their technological level of efficiency and the economy of the relevant period, whether agricultural or otherwise and the pattern of subsistence. The classic case in instance could be that of the Painted Grey Ware or the NBP. In all excavations of the sites associated with these wares, the associated data has never been properly analysed and emphasised with the result that even in historic archaeology, there is a plethora of "ceramic cultures". No complete plan of any ancient city has so far been exposed anywhere. Yet another difficulty in historical archaeology is dynastic periodization or too broad a periodization. For instance, except the terracotta and sculptural styles, there is hardly any difference in the material culture of the Maurya and Sunga periods. Sometimes the periodization is so unwieldy as to include sometimes four to six centuries. For such a vast period, it does not become possible to study in depth other aspects like social organisation, economic set up and technological level.

Inspite of the handicaps referred to above, it is still possible to arrive at certain general observations based on the excavated data obviously with the handicap that one has to depend on the archaeological data collected by others in their own way. Our work at Inamgaon will bring home the point that one has to look up for archaeological data by One's own methodology and in totality only then analysis in depth and extent is possible.

The points that emerge out of the data far bringforth the following facts:

1. That in the period under review, there was growth in urban centres due to a large scale use of iron, especially in agricultural operations leading to deep ploughing, and the resultant agricultural surplus.

2. The agricultural surplus led to diversification of arts and crafts, not connected with agriculture, as for instance, bead making, ivory carving, smithy, terracotta making etc. To bring out qualitative standards as also to perpetuate the knowledge of certain crafts, guilds came into existence as the epigraphs attest, as also the relative stylistic uniformity.

3. That the motives leading to urbanisation and growth of certain centres were not necesarily economic for instance, certain township emerged because of strategic location (Junnar), some due to commercial importance (Kalyan, Bharukachha), some because of religious sanctity (Vaishali, Devnimoir), some purely because of flourishing art traditions (Ter, Bhokardan) and some sheerly due to extensive religious complexes (Antichak, Ratnagiri).

4. That organisation of arts and crafts in guilds gave a relative prosperity to the artist as an individual. This is reflected in the gifts and donations by the most humble craftsman like a mālākāra as a performer to religious establishments.

Inspite of the growth and prosperity the general pattern of a town seems to have been that of a habitation with fortifications and moat, as the various account of the towns excavated so far, show. This pattern, however, implied the scanty availability of a technical personal like the masons, smiths and surveyors.

6. Thorough means of communications are stated to have improved making it possible for large caravans, essentially of bullock carts, move the merchandise iuternally as well from the port-towns to the hinterland. These imported luxury Roman items were always within the reach of the affluent.

7. Because of the increase in trade, the diversification of arts and crafts monetary economy became popular as the large number of coins from different sites show.

However, with a view to have a better picture of the economy, technology and social organization, it would be helpful to plan excavations of the sites of specific period or periods so that we have better understanding of the time of Mauryas or Kushanas or Guptas. This will provide not only the stages in the process of expansion or otherwise of different urban centres but also help in regional distinction if any, and the possible causes that might have been responsible for them.

RFERENCES

Ansari, Z.D. and Dhavalikar M.K. 1977. *Journal of Poona University*, *35*.

Deva, K. and Mishra V.K. 1950. *Vaishali Excavation*, Vaishali.

Deo, S.B. and Dhavalikar M.K. 1967. *Paunar Excavations*, Nagpur.

Deo, S.B. and Joshi J.P. 1972. *Pauni Excavations*, Nagpur.

Deo, S.B. and Gupte R.S. 1974. *Excavations at Bhokardan*, Nagpur.

Dikshit, M.G. 1952. *Tripuri*, Nagpur.

Indian Archaeology—A Review 1953-54; 1954-55; 1955-56; 1956-57; 1957-58; 1964-65; 1967-68; 1973-74; 1974-75; 1975-76; 1977-78.

Lal, B.B. Sisupalgarh 1948: an Early Historical Fort in Eastern India, *Ancient India*, 5, New Delhi.

Mehta, R.N. *et al.* 1966. *Excavations at Devonimori*, Baroda.

Sankalia, H.D. and Dikshit, M.G. 1952. *Excavations at Brahmpuri* (*Kolhapur*).

Sharma, G.R. 1960. *Excavations at Kausambi*, Allahabad.

——1969. *Excavations at Kausambi*, Delhi.

Sinha, B.P. and Roy, S.R. 1962. *Vaishali Excavations*, Patna.

Thapar, B.K. 1964-65, Prakash—1955 A, Chalcolithic site in the Tapti Valley, *Ancient India*, 20-21, New Delhi.

Mediaeval Archaeology

R.N. MEHTA

NO sooner do we try to understand the past actions of Man of any period, we realise that the understanding comes to us from three different channels. These take the form of a dialogue, reading, and investigation of the material remains. The last is the specialised field of an archaeologist.

The study of archaeology is based on the idea that in the life process man modifies his environment in many ways. This modification in natural environment takes numerous forms of processes of cutting, flaking, burning, heating, burnishing, constructing etc., in which he mixes, measures, and uses many natural or modified materials. These materials lie scattered in the area of human activity and follow the rules of natural survival.

But the main theory and practice of archaeology differentiates itself to fall in line with the classificatory systems of time, area, and monuments and then it gets the adjectives of Prehistoric, Ancient Historic, Mediaeval, Puranic, Industrial etc., to indicate the interests and periods that are archaeologically examined.

Here I would like to examine the so-called Mediaeval Period from the angle of an archaeologist to indicate the wealth of information and interpretation that it can provide. My examples are drawn from Western Indian towns and villages where I have worked, but I hope they would indicate that similar phenomena exist in all parts of our country. Its main aim is to study what happened in the past on the basis of the material remains in their natural settings. While doing this, it takes in its purview the traditions and writings about them. These conditions set their own limitations to the study which has developed by stages.

The first stage in this study is the natural curiosity to know something about the standing structures amidst the habitation or outside it. A superficial look at our country is enough to point out that a lovely mosque becomes a place or a school, and inverted hollow tomb stone is identified as a water hole (ह्बाडा) and unused chimney becomes an entrance to an underground passage. An inscription that cannot be read becomes a record of the hidden treasures. An underground structure is a haunt of ghost, goblin or saint. An analysis of these explanations often indicates that they do not give historically a correct picture of what might have actually happened in the Mediaeval period, but they only try to give satisfactory explanations that are acceptable to the living generation. They survive as local traditions. These local traditions acting as satisfactory explanations of the phenomenon confront an inquirer. Change of explanation on a more satisfactory basis is often a formidable task because religious traditions and the prestige given by the educational process confront the inquirer who tries to search for the true picture.

The other tantalising phenomenon that faces a curious mind, is the occurrence of man-made materials that one comes across in the digging operations for foundation trenches of building, laying roads, digging canals etc. The explanations are not always easy or forthcoming. The discovery of a Vishnu image led to the identification of underground water as Yamunaji in Baroda. The discovery of a hoard of Jain images from the digging operations for brick laying were ascribed to the grace of the divinity. Such explanations form another part of the story of the material remains of early and late Mediaeval Period that one often comes across. A more satisfactory explanation of these phenomena is always essential. Such explanation is devoid of any supernatural phenomenon, and relies on human and natural agencies to arrive at the necessary exaplanations.

This explanation becomes available, when the

miateralls are studied in their natural settings. The methods that are called for in these studies are those of exploration, excavation, laboratory studies, interpretation and their correlation with known data. These are universal methods of archaeology for all the periods and areas.

In our country, these methods are extensively used to understand and interpret the phenomenon of what actually happened in the past. But, this past is the remote past, of the Prehistoric, Protohistoric and Ancient Periods on the classificatory scale of Indian history. They take care to use archaeology to understand the human phenomenon.

But in the more recent past that is vaguely and so far as our historical experience is concerned inaccurately classified as the period of Mediaeval India, archaeological study was not and is not used to any great extent, in spite of its availability and capacity for useful work. The reasons for this are obvious enough. The primary reason is the supposed availability of the written documents in the form of chronicles, travellers' accounts, Kavyas, Raso and other literature etc. These evidences refer to cities like Delhi, Agra, Ranthambhore, Benaras, Champaner, Surat, Golconda, Vijaynagar and others that were flourishing. Many stories of the marches of conquests and heroic deeds are detailed in work like Tarikh-e-Firozshahi, Akbar Nama, etc. Sensitive authors like Babur or Jehangir give interesting details of their experiences. The poems use traditions mixed with contemporary events and use poetic licence that has no restrictions of historical discipline. The influence of these sources is so powerful that the tendency to neglect the epigraphical sources is glaring. This has been commented on by Z.A. Desai in his thought-provoking paper in Gujarati, "Abhilekh Vidya no Vikas. Arabi, Farsi Abhilekho p. 39 in Visami Sadi nu Bharat."

तेंनु एक कारण इतिहास संशोधको अने इतिहास विदोनी उदासीनता गणी शकाय

"One of the reasons is the indifference of research scholars and Historians".

But a closer look at all these sources reveals that, though, they are important in their own right, they leave many stories untold and twist many others to suit their needs. The untold stories require to be narrated and the twists have to be straightened out to give a fair picture and clearer understanding. No amount of collation of texts, study of the different recorded versions and meditation on all the meanings that the sentences are capable of yielding by the inherent word power of *Abhidha*, *Vyanjana* and *Lakshana* would help us in these matters. A better picture however is likely to emerge if archaeological methods with their conjoint tools of topography and toponymy are used for the purpose. This was clearly demonstrated in many works in Western India where the author had the opportunity to investigate. His discussions with colleagues indicate that similarity of phenomenon exists, so that the theory and practice of archaeology in mediaeval period could be effectively used in all parts of our country.

As noted earlier, a curious mind tries to seek these sources when other methods fail. This became obvious to the present author when he asked questions like "How old is my own city? How has it developed? What type of people lived there? What are its socio-political and religious parameters?" A series of such questions remained unanswered, and hence the search of the data on new lines. The experiments for these investigations began at Baroda. They were successfully used at Vadnagar. (Subbarao and Mehta 1955) Nagara, (Mehta 1968), Karvan, Shamlaji, and other towns. As one's experience matured and methods were refined it was felt that more sites require to be studied by their application. As an experiment, archaeological investigation was undertaken to understand the viability of this method at Champaner, a mediaeval capital of Gujarat.

As result of these operations, the author was convinced that in India the more recent past, that is termed as 'mediaeval' could be effectively studied by applying the interpretative and experimental tools or the theory and practice of archaeology. Surat, (Mehta 1973-74: 81-92) another mediaeval town was also studied by using this method.

The method used at Surat was explorations of several areas. Plotting the results of these explorations on the map procured from the Surat Municipal Corporation, and correlation of these data with topography, toponymy and written documents. It may be mentioned that toponymy especially is a very useful tool in the hands of an archaeologist to understand the habitat, its divisions, use, expansion, changes and other aspects. In close association with archaeological field work toponymy clearly bring out the changing and the steady elements of the locality.

This was an essay both in urban archaeology and mediaeval archaeology. The essay was in urban archaeology because the unit of examination was an urban settlement. It was in mediaeval archaeology because the theory and practice of archaeology were applied on a site of the Mediaeval Period. As a preliminary study, the published works bearing on Surat were studied. The next step was procuring a blue print of the Map of Surat Municipal Corporation and transferring it on paper. This map indicated a mixture of the modern and the mediaeval materials in a close-knit palimpset that was difficult to be cleared by any amount of library study or discussion. Therefore, field studies were organised.

The field studies started giving rise to problems on one side and clues to solve them on another. While exploring, it was evident from the Municipal map that parts of the fort line built in A.D. 1715 were marked. This fort eulogistically termed as Alampanah was surveyed. Its fort-line and gateways were plotted on the map. Surat was reputed to have suffered from many floods and it is not free from them even now. Parts of the fort line had a thick deposit of mud, in which only the upper part of the fort and its merlons were visible. A large track of this mud flat was barren and remains unoccupied to this day. This flood story was archaeologically too obvious, and one has to imagine the damage it must have caused.

The Alampanah fort was easily marked. But the fort line of Shahar Panah built at the orders of Aurangzeb was a more difficult one for search. Its record on the map was almost non-existant. However, two aspects of the topography of Surat were helpful. One of them was the river front and another, the consequent streams that had developed bad land features at this town.

The meandering Tapi had not changed its bad as Yamuna has done at Shahjahanabad, Kotla Firozshah and Purana Qila front in Delhi, so it was comparatively easy to know that the river front that connected Surat with international fronitier was very much the same, with some change in the pattern of the meandering river. On the south western side, however, was a deep nala, coming from inland. It was named Makai Pul. A survey of this nala revealed that it drained the water from the Sagarampura, Navasari Bhagol and other localities. It was used for the construction of Gopi Talav by building a check dam.

On the right bank of the nala in the Ruderpura area of Surat a grave was seen above the road line on one side. It stood on a wall. The examination of this wall revealed that it was a thick fort wall. It was turning on the east, and crossed a road near Navasari Bhagol. This is a significant place name that suggest that when the fort line that was examined existed, the Navasari Bhagol was situated in its alignment. A circular road with marked low level on the outer side with the embankment of Gopi Talav, connected this unit with another area known as Kot Safil. The indications of the fort line that was destroyed were clearly observable. The features were very clear in the Kot Safil area. It was Kot Safil or the fort line that moved straight to Baranpuri Bhagol, and then towards the north of the town. This feature indicated the eastern fort line. This situation had its parallels at Baroda Kote Kot area and at Cambay on the eastern side. On the North near Idrus Wadi area the fortification walls were intact. From there they could be easily connected to the line on the river. Topographically here also a nala similar to that of Makai Pul controlled the area. These features indicated that Surat like Benaras grew up between two consequent streams to the main river.

This identification of the inner fort line, indicated two things, one of it was the demarcation of the Surat of the Period of Aurangzeb; and the other that after the attack of Shivaji, Surat continued to grow at least up to the first quarter of the 18th century.

If the Surat of 17th century was to be known two steps were necessary to identify the early aspects of this habitation. The 16th century military out-post at Surat and archaeological deposits to clear these problems. Historical references indicated that during the reign of Mahmud Sahid, Khvaja Safar Salmani (Mehta 1973-74) built the military out-post on the down stream of Surat, to protect it against the Portuguese depredations. The piratical activities of the Portuguese had caused much trouble to the ports of Malabar, Konkan and Gujarat. India had to be on its guard against this European piracy that began after A.D. 1498. Gujarat Sultans were directly affected by their activity. So they took steps to control them. A similar phenomenon in Malabar also requires close examination. Significantly this fort protected old Surat on the river bank and its new suburb of Gopipura. If this hypothesis had any validity, the Surat of the earlier period should lie on the river bank, and hence a survey of this area was essential.

Fortunately the survey indicated that it was the highest area where Furja, Mugal Sarai, the Mosque of the Tughluq period were scattered. The Mosque in particular indicated that 14th century Surat was in this area. A few images in the Chaintamani Parsvanath temple in Shahpore indicated the probability of the earlier Surat in this locality. A marble memorial stone of 13th century and Kichaka figures pointed to Surat of at least the Pre-Sultanate period. The Surat of 12th/13th century was confirmed by further discovery of a Tirthankara image of marble from this area. The checking of the data from the Municipal Engineer and the residents of this area added strength to the evidence obtained in the field.

This evidence pointed out that Surat was a small linear village settlement in the pre-Sultanate period. This settlement of the Rajput period had Jain and Shaiva population. It was conquered in the 14th century by the Khaljis, and during the period of the Tughluqs' it occupied the same area. Around it markets developed. During the period of the Gujarat Sultans, at least in the early part of the 16th century its suburbs started to grow. From the middle of the 16th century it steadily grew to the size of a big radial city. In the 17th century it engulfed the other areas. In the 18th century it continued its expansion by throwing a ring of suburbs. These suburbs were covered up by Alampanah. This was a larger radial town.

Surat suffered a set-back in the 18th century. The internal conflicts of the Marathas and Mughals on one side and a policy of the British to divert trade and commerce to Bombay seem to be responsible for this set back. But it steadily recovered. In the present century it is a much bigger town.

This essay on Surat indicated the potential strength of Mediaeval Archaeology. In our country Mediaeval Archaeology is directed to the study of the human activity of the last one thousand years through material remains in their natural setting in the living and dead habitations and other places. The most important problems that face one is of correlation of literature of folk tales that are current in a given region or areas. These are definite explanations of the local phenomenon as noted above. The mediaeval archaeologist has to squarely face these explanations and support, modify or reject them by their thorough examination from archaeological evidences.

This is a challenging and fascinating task that requires intimate knowledge of local language and the languages used in the area in this period. Unfortunately this equipment is weak in many field archaeologist as well as mediaeval historians. Due to this weakness the explanations current in the society are neglected as historical, legendary and mythical. This neglect costs dear to the subject, because it develops prejudices and dichotomy of explanations. It is not conducive to correct understanding of the mediaeval phenomenon. Besides, it leads to the loss of rapport with the local gentry, and hence the microstudies of towns and villages suffer.

When an overall view is taken of the perspectives of the human past, each action has its own local theatre. It is either confined to it or from the locality the action expands over a region or the whole country or across its borders, depending upon the will and the socio-economic and other favourable conditions of the time. If the basic elements of this human phenomenon i.e. the villages and towns, are neglected in the study, it will remain only of superfluous quality, in spite of some praise that it might receive.

However where local history is studied in the light of archaeological work as was done at Cambay, (Subbarao and Mehta) Vadnagara Bhinnamal (Parmar 1969), Modhera, Delmal, Dholka (Mehta u-d:59-69) and other sites in Gujarat and Rajasthan a phenomenon was observed that Indian traditions have a mixture c absolute historical phenomenon presented in the garb of transference of myths, growth of local traditions both historical and mythical on one side and explaining away certain phenomena on the other. Often these phenomena fall in the last thousand years which constitue the loose time span of the so-called Mediaeval Indian experience.

As rich historical phenomena two experiences could be cited one from, Baroda and the other from Dholka. The experience from Baroda is a small myth of migration of Goddess Kalika from Pavagadh. Baroda was captured by the Maratha power in 1732 and it became the capital of the Gaekwads from A.D. 1766. After the capture of Baroda, the earliest place occupied by the rulers was known as Juni gadhi. This was an area in which the Sultans and possibly the Mugals used to stay. Once the area was occupied by the Marathas, they closed the old gate by a screen wall and turned it into a palace temple. The family deity of the Gaekwads is Kalika. Her installation at this place seems to have led to the growth of the beautiful legend that the goddess came from Pavagadh behind Pilaji, on his request and stopped in the palace gate as he broke his promise of not looking back.

Archaeological examination, however, gives a clue to understand this legend in its religio-historical context, and adds significant details to the changing patterns of the habitation. A study of Mallapurana, Kaumarika Khanda, (Mehta 1965) Nagarkhanda, (Mehta 1968) Dharmaranya, (Mehta 1975) Prabhasakhanda (Mehta and Kantawala 1975) and such so called late puranas, on the basis of archaeological work have given very interesting historical and culture data for the town and the period for which they were written. To neglect these documentray aspects of Indian traditions as insignificant simply demonstrates our lack of understanding of what happened to the Indian tradition in the socalled mediaeval period.

Indian historical experience indicates that it has already preserved its ancient traditions of culture throughout its historical periods. It is a strong trend with us in the present age. During its existence this vast stream has met with different cross currents from other countries. In this process in the mediaeval period four distinct streams are discernible.

The most important stream is Indian. It has absorbed or eliminated the other currents by careful thought and action. The other important stream emanated from Arabia as Islam, and mingled in the Indian tradition on one side and tried to enforce its will under political pressure on the other. But these political pressures went on shifting from strength to weakness and destruction. But the commingling processes of the saints and sufis and people were long lived. They have produced a socio-religious phenomenon that demonstrates the impact of India on Islam and vice versa. Many of the socio-economic works of this phenomenon have been absorbed by local traditions of a variety of types. One such tradition that has absorbed its elements and its change is noted here.

Dholka was a large town and a capital of the Vaghela branch of the Chaulukyas. It has its local tank known as Malav Talav (Mehta u.d.). In Gujarat as elsewhere water scarcity is a marked phenomenon. As a result, conservation of water is always an important task. The Malav Talav indicates archaeologically a tank with its silting chamber and many sided flight of steps and a bridge running to the centre where there was a platform on which a temple of a deity existed. This tank was brought to this condition probably in the Vaghela period.

After the conquest of Dholka in the 14th century, the new rulers felt that the tank needed enlargement. It was done by raising the earth work and consequent rise of the water level. At this time a platform was built for sitting, on the south of the bridge. The stone revetment and the platform had *uruhsrungas* and images fixed in them in such a way that they were not visible. The phenomenon of the platform is explained as a work of queen Minal Devi, the mother of Siddhraja Jayasimha, the Chaulukya ruler (A.D. 1093-1143). It is narrated that when she built the tank she changed the design of the tank because one ganika refused to part with her house on the bank. This feature indicated the sense of Justice of the princess. This particular story with a full fledged historical narrative is not supported by archaeological investigation of the earth work, the stone work, the water level, design and other relevant factors, as well as the surrounding monuments. On the other hand, archaeological investigation of this mediaeval tank, traces the efforts of the local citizens and the political powers to maintain the tank in excellent repair for a period of more than a thousand years.

Mediaeval archaeology indicates the Western Asiatic and Central Asiatic relations in the use of language and materials like ceramics, and other features and explains many aspects of this trend, by its continuous search.

The third trend of the mediaeval period is the European one. Its initial destructive effects were felt in many towns of western coast of India. But the strong political states of India kept it in check in the 15th, 16th and 17th centuries. Only after the middle of the 18th century this trend, specially under the British began to exert its pressure. It struggled for about a century for establishing its supremacy and by the middle of the 19th century became very strong. The Indian struggle to eradicate its political power was equally glorious. Now we are trying to assess its strength and reorient our cultural needs in the present day.

Archaeologically this trend is both interesting and important. The early graves of the Europeans use semi-western design and Indian workmanship. This colonial trend set by them and for them in the 17th century is a marked element of European policy that they try to follow to this day.

When these forms were being practised in India, Indian architecture and material culture flourished as a strong current which supplied the required raw materials and skills to the needy Europeans in their endeavour.

The last current was a rather weak oriental one from China and South East Asia. It sent its merchandise both by land and by sea. The Chinese and probably Thai and Vietnamese porcelains, celadons, constitute the material relics on Indian habitats. They play an important role for isolating many of our traditional ceramics as mediaeval. The Ming period was very active in this trade, and the Ming blue and white Chinese ceramics is a rich Indian archaeological heritage. If Khvaja Nizamuddin is to be believed, India imported enormous material from China.

It must be indicated that the material wealth that lies scattered on our mediaeval sites not only clear these main trends but help in understanding trade routes, some materials that moved up and down, local manufacture of caramics, metals, lime concrete, bone and ivory material, and with a careful analysis, their food habits, division of property, religious practices, war fare and many other aspects of life, and provide a broad vista for better understanding and appreciation of the life, of the last one thousand years. It is time that we rise to the occasion and study and preserve this wealth before it disappears in the reckless craze of expansion and so-called modernisation.

REFERENCES

Mehta, R.N., u.d. Dholkanu Malav Talav, *Swadhyaya* (Gujarati), III, 1.

———1965. Kumarikakhaud, *Journal of the M.S. University of Baroda*, XVI, 1.

———1968. *Excavations at Nagara*, M.S. University of Baroda.

———1968. Nagarkhanda—A study, *Journal of the M.S. University of Baroda*, XVII, 1.

———1971-72. Puranic Archaeology, *Journal of the M.S. University of Baroda*, XX-XXI. Also see Prapannadvidya, Chirapat, Dharmaranya Purana—A Cultural study, A thesis submitted to M.S. University of Baroda, 1975.

———1973-74. Urban Surat, "An Archaeological topographical and toponymical perspective," *Journal of the M.S. University of Baroda*, XXII-XXIII (Combined issue).

Mehta, R.N. & S.G., Kantawala 1975. Patala Vivara myth in the Prabhaskhanda—A study, *Journal of the Oriental Institute*, Baroda, XXV, 2.

Parmar, Bhutimal M. 1969. Cultural and critical study of Srimalla Purana Ph.D. Thesis submitted to the M.S. university of Baroda.

Subbarao, B. & Mehta, R.N. 1955. Excavations of Vadnagara, *Journal* of the M.S. University, of Baroda, IV, 1.

Indian Tradition and Archaeology

B.P. SINHA
University of Patna, Patna

THE Indian traditions are stored in the Puranas and the Epics; some corroborations and additional informations are available from the vast Vedic literature. And scholars like Pargiter, Rajchaudhuri and Bhargava have devoted considerable time and labour to reconstruct a working sequencial history of the Pre-Mahabharata or even Pre-Buddha times. But the crux of the problem has been the chronology and it is not relevant here to speak about the various schemes of chronology for ancient pre-Bharata and pre—Buddha dynasties worked out by Indian and foreign scholars. The problem appeared insoluble because as no contemporary or even near contemporary absolute date was available. Often in sheer despair, and confused by the inconsistencies, and mythical accounts in the ancient traditional literature, it was held by some like D.C. Sircar that the entire accounts are imaginary and certainly provide no base for sober history.

But some other scholars continued to hold that the traditions contain some real truths, and that they refer to genuine historical traditions and events about men and material culture gleaned through a maze of labyrinthic myths and chronological absurdities contained in them. Puratattva No. 8 is very largely devoted to the discussion of the theme "Archaeology and Tradition" by eminent archaeologist and historians, who have tried to identify the various chalcolithic and PGW cultures with one or the other early and later pauranic dynasties. I do not here propose to cover the same ground again except by pointing out that in view of uncertainty about the chronology and sequence both in the vedic and puranic literature, and the incomplete reconstruction of the material cultures on the basis of archaeology from the end of the Harappan to the beginning of the historical period, any attempt to identify any particular archaeologically exposed cultures with one or the other of the vedic and puranic dynasties or peoples would still remain more or less speculative. Sankalia's (1975-76: 83) observation 'we surely miss the identity of the authors of (these) regional and subregional culture' is sad but apt. Here we are concerned with the impact of archaeology on the truth or otherwise on the most popular and living traditions about Rama's story and about Krishna and the Mahabharata. The problem whether they are merely myths or are even partly *Real* is exercising our mind. 'Mahabharata, Myth and Reality' (Gupta 1976), Ramayana 'Myth or Reality' (Sankalia 1973) are two serious exercises in the line.

Here I am only to examine the impact of archaeological activities on the varacity of the traditions. Schilemann's (1878) was probably the first attempt to seek corroboration of the Iliad's story by archaeology, and he proceeded with complete faith in Homers' account, and following it doggedly and devotedly in spite of physical, financial obstacles and scholastic jeers, he struck at the real site Troy. Then we all are aware that excavations in Lebanon, Palestine and Syria with a view to corroborate the Bible cities or sites have led to appreciable good results (Albright, 1966).

It was therefore, rather late in this country that scholars turned to archaeology for the verification of the Epic stories. This was partly because the earlier archaeologists from Cunningham onwards were very much concerned with Buddhist sites about which there were Chinese accounts and datable Buddhist and Jain literary texts. As a matter of fact it was in the wake of the excavation of the Buddhist stupa that the Indus Valley Civilization was struck at in the twenties of the 20th century, and since then archaeologists remained busy in enlarging their knowledge about the Indus Valley Civilization—Chanhudaro, Further excavations at Harappa, and Mohanjodaro and work in Kalibangan took practically all the time of archaeologists except for Arikamedu, Brahmagiri and Maski.

It was left to B.B. Lal on the morrow of Indian independence to embark on the adventure of testing Indian traditions on the crucible of archaeology. He started with the Mahabharata sites—sites with place-names and geographical location as described or nearly described in the Mahabharata. And the first site selected was Hastinapur, the capital of the Kurus, which was excavated. (Lal 1954-55: 4-151). Lal found in Period II Painted Grey Ware. This is found at the lowest levels in all the traditional Mahabharata sites as stated by B.B. Lal (1976: 52). In the top layers of Period II iron was found. Lal believes that the PGW is the Mahabharata pottery and the Mahabharata was an event when iron was already in use. He dated the PGW ware 1100—800 B.C., and fixed the date of the Mahabharata war in cir 836 B.C. (Lal 1976: 58). This date he arrives on the basis of average of the successive generations that passed between Udayana and Parikshit. His date for the war is not much far from Pargiter who had on the same basis-average of reigns—had suggested 950 B.C. for the event, Lal's average being 14, and Pargiters 18.[1] Lal found corroboration of his archaeological finding at Hastinapur which showed that the city was flooded and abandoned and after a gap of flood deposits intervening, NBP settlement arose at Hastinapur. The Puranas refer to floods at Hastinapur, which led Nicakshu to abandon Hastinapur and shift to Kausambi as his new capital, and at Kausambi late PGW sherds were found. Nicakshu is 6th in line from Parikshit, including the former. If Lal's average is taken, Nicaskhu should be separated from Parikshit by 70 years. Now if we include a few years of the reign of Yudhisthira after the Mahabharata war dated in 836 B.C., Nicakshu should be deemed to have come to the throne 836-70(—reign of Yudhisthira)=766 B.C.× (or still a few years later). Now as the common denominator of the pottery culture in all the Mahabharata sites is PGW, the conclusion seems irresistible that the PGW is the pottery of the Mahabharata times, unless the time bracket proposed by Lal for the PGW is found to be too late for the Mahabharata. Agarwal (1974: 130-132) and Dikshit (1973: 152) believe that PGW can't be dated earlier than 800 B.C. and the Atranjikhera date 1025±110 B.C. for the PGW is erratic and should not be taken into account. Sankalia (1975-76: 83) appears to agree with the view that the PGW has to be dated between 800-400 B.C. Lal (1975-76: 130) has countered the argument, and the calibration taken into account, brings the PGW date even nearer to the proposed date for the War, more dates for PGW are certainly desirable to settle the issue beyond dispute. To me it appears that Lal is right in proposing the time bracket, specially when we have a pre-iron PGW complex at Bhagawanpura and the PGW lower levels at Hastinapura are also free from iron.

When traditional sites of the Mahabharata were being tested by archaeology, Ramayanic tradition could not be left out. B.H.U. team struck at Ayodhya, the capital city of Rama and found nothing earlier than NBP. As the probings were on small scale, Lal with greater expertise and resources took up Ayodhya again. As many as 14 different sites in the Ayodhya city were taken, and everywhere the earliest habitation did not go beyond the NBP, or Early NBP Phase as Lal would now christen it (Lal 1981: 30-33). This was rather intriguing if not astaunding as Rama is consistently put much earlier than the Mahabharata heroes, according to persistent Indian literary and religions traditions. Sankalia who refers to PGW sherds found on surface in Ayodhya, (1975-76: 80, had hoped, 'Any way Ayodhya when excavated should give us thick deposits and earliest should go back to atleast 2500 B.C.' But as Lal observed (1975-76: 131) 'let the spade speak, not me!''. And the spade has spoken. The common denominator at all Ramayana sites excavated is NBP (in its early phase), and so younger than PGW, the sites of the Mahabharata traditions. Lal and Dikshit also investigated Nandigrama, Bharadvaja Ashrama and Sringaverapura sites closely associated with Ramas story and everywhere they noticed the lowest common denominater to be the early NBP. At Sringaverapura two earlier cultures, like OCP, and Black-slipped ware, were encountered, but as these are not found in any other Ramayanic sites, none of these can be considered as Ramayanic pottery. So the evidence of archaeological investigations to date is that the Ramayanic sites are younger than the Mahabharata sites. At Sringaverapura the earlist occupation of a

1. It is interesting to note that long ago Fergussion also concluded that the average of reigns of west Asiatic Kings was 14 James Fargussion—The Palaces of riot readable.

nomadic tribe using red ware (may be related to OCP) has been noticed. It has been dated c. 1050-1000 B.C. This is followed by Period II (*circa* 950-700 B.C.), with Black-slipped ware and plain grey-ware as the diagnostic ceramic, some PGW, sherds were also found. Then is the early NBP (Period III) with some PGW sherds continuing. This is put to 700 B.C., as IIB is said to end in *circa* 700 B.C. (Lal and Dikshit 1978-79: 6). And early NBP is common to all the Ramayanic sites and so according to Lal and Dikshit may represent the time of Rama's story.

Apparently the conclusion is that Rama is later by more than a century to Krishna, the wire—puller of the Great War. This is a big jolt to cherished beliefs, and is contrary to almost all literary traditions. I have used the phrase 'almost', because Lal has shown that there is a literary tradition in support of his theory that Ramayana-story is later than that of the Mahabharata War. He quotes the Brhdaranyaka Upanisad (III. 3, 1) where Yajnavalkya in the court of Janaka is asked, where have the Parikshitas gone'? This shows that in the time of Yajnavalkya and Janaka of Mithila, the dynasty of Parikshit son of Abhimanyu and grandson of Arjuna, the hero of the Mahabharat had already passed away sometime before and was a living problem of enquiry. This Janaka has been referred to as Siradhvaja Janaka, the father-in-law of Rama, by Bhavabhuti (Mahavira carita (I, V. 14). So Rama, younger contemporary of Janaka, lived much later than Parikshit (II) of the Puranic list. How much later? Janamejaya's priest was Tura Kavasheya, and Uddnlaka Aruni and his pupil Yajnavalkya were 5th or 6th step below Tura Kavasheya. So the gap between Janamejaya and Janaka of Videha whose contemporaries were Uddalaka Aruni and Yajnavelkya should be five generations, and 30 years is the average length between two generations of Patriarchs. So they are (Raychaudhuri, 1972: 46 47), 150 years. Now if Janamejaya, son of Parikshit, is placed in *circa* 822 B.C. (836.14) and then Janaka being separated by 5, generations of Patriachs (*gurus*), should be placed in 822—150= 672 B.C. The archaeological dating of early NBP would also coincide with that. The archaeological period and the period of Janaka on the basis of Brhadaranayaka Upanishad thus synchronise.

In support of Lal's hypothesis I may suggest another synchronism. According to vedic sources, Uddalaka Aruni was the younger contemporary of Asvapati king of Kekaya, who also instructed Aruna Alepavasi belonging to an older generation from Uddalaha Aruni. So he was an elder contemporary of Uddalaka Aruni. (Raychaudhuri 1972: 58). Now Asvapati king of Kekaya was maternal uncle of Bharata. Now Raychaudhuri and Y. Mishra believing that Rama was much earlier than the Mahabharata, could not think that this Asvapati could be contemporary of Janaka and Dasaratha, and so they thought of a later Asvapati. While there could be more than one Asvapati as king of Kekayas, some king of Kekaya is not referred to as Asvapati. If what archaeology is trying to show, then this contemporaniety of Janaka with Asvapati may suggest that Bharata's grand-uncle or maternal uncle could have flourished towards the end of the 8th century B.C. Another Pauranic statement may be referred to as indirectly suggesting an ancient tradition about the precedence in time of Krishna over Rama. Mucukunda was son of Mandhatr a great king. Harivamsa says that he slept in a cave for a long time where Kalayavana name persuing Krishna, and the awakened Mucukunda killed Kalayavana. (Pargiter, 1972: 43). Stripped of the mythical; long sleep, the story suggests a tradition that Mucukunda, an early ancestor of Rama was a contemporary of Krishna.

It may be of some value to note that some Mahabharata heroes like Dhratarashtra Vicivratirya are refered to in the Vedic literature. Even Devakiputra Krishna is referred to in the Chandogya Upanishad as a pupil of Ghora Angirasa (Vedic Index Vol I. p 184). Winternitz 1927: 447) finds it difficult to separate this old sage of the time of Upanishads with the Bhagavat-gita. But Rama or Dasaratha is not mentioned at all even in the later Vedic literature; he does not appear even in old Upanishads (Winternitz 1927: 515) and even Ayodhya is not mentioned in the later Vedic literature, as M.C. Joshi (1975-76: 98) would think (Lal 1978-79: 45-49). Could not this negative evidence strengthen the view that Rama was later then the end of the Vedic literature. Rama is not even alluded to by Panini who mentions Vasudeva, Arjuna and Yudhisthira. Panini may be placed in the early 5th-4th Century B.C. and by then Rama's story had not become well known, it appears.

Now the question is whether the archaeological data up-to-date and stray references or absence of references in the literary traditions mentioned above prove to the hilt that Krishna and the Mahabharata War preceded Rama.

To me there is no escape from such a conclusion. The archaeological evidence as exposed-to date and brilliantly analysed by Lal (1981 : 31) leaves little scope for doubt. Lal himself admits 'No body can say what lies buried in the areas not excavated'. It is possible to speculate that in some other trenches if taken in Ayodhya and Sringaverapura, the two sites comparatively well excavated, some earlier cultures than of early NBP may be struck at, and it has been the experience of archaeologist that the lowest cultural level at a site is not encountered in every trench. It may also be speculated that Ayodhya of Rama could have been washed away entirely in the wake of the Saryu floods (tradition is that Rama took with him all the citizens of Ayodhya through the deep waters of the Saryu to the Saketa and no trace was left). As the Saryu has been changing courses, the Ayodhya of Rama could be buried in the mid Saryu. But all this speculation is weakened when we find that as many as 14 sites in Ayodhya city and Nandigrama were taken. No flood deposits or earlier culture were contacted. So while possibility may be there, *probability* is very little that any earlier culture would be found in Ayodhya. But this evidence raises a tearing controversy as it runs counter to the almost unanimous traditional and religious literature. Lal (1981: 33) himself hinted at one such tradition. Traditionally Rama is of 12 kalas, and Krishna of 16 kalas, and followings the law of evolution Krishna, the complete God (Krishnastu Bhagavana Swayam) should follow Rama, who is only 3/4 God. This problem may be skirted by pointing out that Rama belonged to solar (Sun-Aditya's) race and Krishna to lunar (Moon= Candra) race and there are 12 Adityas while the Moon has sixteen phases. So both Rama of solar descent and Krishna of lunar descent were complete in themselves. On this ground to argue precedence of one over the other should be irrelevant.

But more serious objections may be raised. One is of methodology. The archaeological evidence (to date) brought up by Lal goes against the consistent literary traditions and the Puranic genealogies according to which Krishna is 28th generation later than Rama (Pargiter 1972: 147-48). Now Lal literally turns the table upside down and appears to reject the Puranic geneological accounts completely in the reconstruction of Rama's chronology.

But Lal himself in his reconstruction of the Mahabharata chronology, in the light of his archaeological findings, leading to identification of PGW culture with the Mahabharata times, relics on the Pauranic-geneological accounts from Udayana to Parikshit for even the flood of Hastinapura, he inflect, rejects completely the pre-Parikshit royal dynasties in the Puranas, because it seems counter to his proposed thesis. His identification of Siradhvaja of Janaka with Janaka contemporary of Yajnavalkya is also not unchallenged. There have been many Janakas and more than one Yajnavalkya (Pargiter 1972: 145, 331). Yogendra Mishra, the latest authority on history of Videha, gives no credence to the testimony of Bhavabhuti, and observes and late reference of a dramatist (not a historian or an epigraphist) cannot undo that in any way "(Misnra 1981: 79-80). Raychoudhuri 1972 : 44-54) is sure that Janaka, the great philosopher king was later than the Parikshitas, 'admits of no doubt,' and he finds it very difficult to identify any one of the many kings bearing Janaka-names in the Epic and Puranic literature with the 'great Janaka of the Vedic texts'. After quoting the relevant verses in the Mahaviracarita (Act I verse 14) and the Uttara-Ramacarita (Act II, verse 9) of Bhavabhuti, making Siradhvaja Janaka and Yajnavalkya contemporary. Raychaudhuri observes, the identification of Siradhvaja with Vedic Janaka appears to have been accepted by Bhavabhuti'. But Raychaudhuri does not appear to accept Bhavabhuti unhesitatingly, as Lal does, and says 'it is impossible to say how far the identification of the Vedic Janaka with the father of Sita is correct' Raychaudhuri (1972 : 44-52) Winternitz (1927: 515) observes, 'Whether that king Janaka of Videha who is frequently mentioned in the Upanishads is the same as father of Sita must remain an open question.' It may be pointed out regarding the proposed identification by B.B. Lal that Janaka, even in the Balakanda (wherein he is only mentioned) and which is a late addition and not composed by Valmiki, is refered to as Satyavikramam, nishthitam Savasastreshe tatha Vedeshu nishthitam (I.12.18) and dharmavatsalam, dharmikam (1.69.7.) no where even distantly he is referred to as philosopher-king or patron of philosophars as the Vedic Janaka definitely was. So down to the 2nd century A.D., if not later, Janaka the father of Sita, was not considered identical with Janaka the Vedic king. I would very much like to know the several other sources where in Janaka the father-in-law of Rama is described as a philosopher king as Lal (1975-76: 131,) would lead us to believe. The internal evidences from the Ramayana and the Mahabharata also multiply difficulties in the way of proposed identification. Rama's story is included in the Mahabharata as an Upakhyana, an old legend, while on Mahabharata hero is referred to in the Ramayana. It is quite clear that even done to me the 4th century A.D., when the Mahabharata is believed to have acquired the present critical test the tradition of

Rama story happening long before the Mahabharata was persisting. Winternitz puts the time bracket 4th century B.C. to the 4th century A.D. for the transformation of the Epic Mahabharata into the present compilation (on the whole, even later interpolations p. 474 were made), he further says that 'It is probable that the original Ramayana was composed in 3rd century B.C. by Valmiki on the basis of ancient ballads, and received its present extent and contents as early as towards the close of the 2nd century A.D. (Winternitz 1927: 474, 516-517). As the Ramopakhyana in the Mahabharata clearly takes Rama as an incarnation of Vishnu, (not at all discernible in the original Ramayana-II-VI by Valmiki), it can certainly be said that the akhyana in the present form could not be included in the Mahabharata before the end of 2nd century A.D. rather in 3rd or 4th century A.D. So it is clear till then it was believed that Rama was earlier than Krishna. "It is therefore, permissible to conclude that the original Ramayana in which Rama was a human being was composed by Valmiki in the 3rd or more probably in the 4th century B.C. and that with the addition of Book I and VII and with some passages in the other books it assumed its present form at the end of the 2nd century A.D. when Rama was definitely dicfied as an incarnation of Vishnu (Majumdar 1968: 254). Incidental references in the Ramayana and the Mahabharata about south India and the Deccan may also be used to support the long lived tradition. While in the Ramayana, Deccan and south India is in mere tribal state, a Janasthana with the non-food producing Vanaras and the Rakshasas, in the Mahabharata there are organised kingdoms in south India with a fair degree of civilization. Chanan in his work "Spread of Agriculture in Ancient India" shows that Ramayanic society had two distinct cultures, agrarian in Kosala and tribal in the land of the Vanaras and Rakshasas. While it is true that both the Epics were composed long after the events, if we believe them to be rooted in history (Lal has no doubt that they refer to historical events). We have to admit that incidental references in them about regions and socio-economic conditions should betray some resemblance of the times they are supposed to describe, and a comparative study of these would show that the time of the Rama's story is earlier than that of the Mahabharata. Attention may be drawn to the fact that in the Mahabharata references to cavalry encounters (horsemen fighting horsemen) are many, though no Mahabharata hero fights on horseback. This shows that cavalry as a limb of war was known though was not so significant as later. Cavalry is not known in the Ramayana at all. Desaratha and Ravana fight from horse-drum chariots but no horsemen as soldier is known. Does it not show that the Ramayana times were earlier than the Mahabharata. Again, we should not ignore the testimony of the Gita incorporated in the Mahabharata. The Gita is certainly not a work of the time of the great war, but it is cretainly not as late as the 5th century A.D. when the Mahabharata is said to have reached its final stage of compilation, the facts that the Gita does not even remotely allude to the foreigners, even to the Mahayana Buddhism indirectly, and that its zeal to place bhaktiyoga on the same if not higher pedastal than gyana and Karmayoga would show that Bhagavatism had not till then attained its supreme position as it did certainly by 3rd-4th centuries A.D., and was quite entrenchd as early as 2nd century B.C. as to attract the Greek Heliodorus to it. I would place Gita not later than 2nd century A.D. Winternitz (1927: 437-438) thinks it not to be too bold to assume that the old Bhagvadgita was written at about this time (the time of Heliodorus-pillar-inscription beginning of 2nd century B.C.). The form in which appears the Mahabharata today was fixed in the early A.D. (Majumdar: 1968 249) And in the Gita, Krishna is placed later than Rama. We should note that while the theory of avataravada is clearly enunciated in the Gita, (IV, vs. 6-8) no where any actual incarnation is refered to, no allusion even to Fish, Tortoise, Boar, Narasimha, not even of Rama as his incarnation. Where Krishna is saying that he is Ramas the warrior (Ramah Sastrabhrtamanam) he is not referring to his previous incarnation as Rama. In the relevant verses in the Gita, Krishna claims to be Himalaya, Sagara, Asvatha tree, etc. (Gita X, vs. 21-31). What he is saying is that best of every kind is He, the ultimate God. So in our view except for the theortical exposition of the principle of incarnation no actual list of incarnations was drawn up when the Gita was composed. This would further show the antiquity of Gita vis-a-vis the development of the theory of incarnation. It is in the Narayaniya section (definitely a much later addition) that the theory of incarnation is held and ten avataras including that of Rama-Dasarath is mentioned (Chattopadhyaya 1962: 88-89). In the same section number of avataras is six or four, showing the theory still in a fluid state. In the background of the archaeological evidence-to-date, the question to answer is when was the actual order of events (Krishna preceding Rama), was turned upside down by the Brahmanical authors who must have then very effectively and on a large scale, overhauled the entire earlier kshatriya traditions to make Rama earlier than Krishna.

And the other more important query is, if so, why? What was the compelling motive for them making Rama earlier than Krishna and overturning the historical sequence in the light of the present archaeological evidence ? We may have to look into the comparative antiquity of Krishna and Rama cults. In view of the uncertainty about the date of the principal religious and Epic works, let us take inscriptional and sculptural evidence. While Krishna is refered to in the inscriptions from 2nd century B.C. onwards, (Chattopadhyaya 1962: 25), epigraphic notices of Rama are much later. Even Megasthenes Maccrindle, 1960: 206) in the 3rd century B.C. refers to Heracles cult (Vasudeva cult) among the Soursenis (in Mathura region, the playground of Krisnna). He does not mention Ayodhya at all, nor Rama. Sculptures describing scenes from Krishnas life found in Mathura may be dated from 1st-2nd century A.D. at the latest. V.S. Agarawal refers to a statue of Balarama (Samkarshana of Vasudeva Krishna cult) as belonging to 2nd century B.C. (quoted by Chattopadhyaya 1962: 35). But Rama's statue is not available before 5th century A.D., sculptured Ramayanic scenes from Devagarh in Madhya Pradesh and Aphsad in Bihar are dated in 6th and 7th centuries respectively. We may say that Rama as God, an incarnation of Vishnu is quite a late phenomenon. Rama son of Dasaratha in the Ramayana is dercribed as a human hero but in a later passage, near the end of the original work, occurs a chapter describing how Sita entered the fire when the Gods appeared and Brahma declared Rama to be Narayana (Chattopadhyaya 1962: 90) relying on the Encyclopeadia of Religion and Ethics, (VII: 194). At the end of the Balakanda the washing away of all sins by hearing Rama's noble deeds is certainly mentioned but Winterniz rightly points out that the first canto was not composed by Valmiki (Winternitz 1937: 478). Winternitz succintly points out that in the genuine books (II-VI), Rama is only a human hero and that it is only in books I and VII and (in a few interpolated passages of the other books) that he appears as an incarnation of the God Vishnu (Winternitz 1927: 501); Winternitz (1927: 496) explicitly refers to the statement (496) quoted by Chattopadhyaya and regards it as interpolation. And in later history also the cult of Krishna is more dominant and popular. Then why should have the more popular and dominant Krishna-cult at least down to the 4th-5th centuries, (allegedly) acquiesed (If Lal's view is accepted) the overhauling, rather, turning upside-down the genealogies as revealed from the extant Epics and the Puranas which made their Hero God later in time to Rama ? It needs some explanation at least. It appears to assume to much planned conspiracy and craftiness on the part of the Rama's bhaktas to temper so effectively with the sacred literature. Then it is usual for later bhaktas or discendants to attribute more and more antiquity to their ancestors or cult-hero. If Lal is to be believed the Krishnas powerful adherents are an exception.

Then another difficulty in accepting Lal's hypothesis also crops up. According to Lal the lowest denominator of all the Ramayanic sites is early NBP which could not begin earlier then 700 B.C. I donot think that Lal's case is that Rama founded the city of Ayodhya. If there were earlier generations of kings of Ayodhya (Rama is 64 steps down from Ikshavaku (Pargiter 1922: 145-147) then he should have settled it first in *circa* 700 B.C., would not Rama then come too close to the Buddha ?

Thus the archaelogy of the Ramayana has thrown up a veriable challenge to archaelogists and historians. Lal cannot but truthfully record the evidence unearthed and explain accordingly and that he has done admirably. If modern Ayodhya, and Sringaverapura are the place-names of Ayodhya and Sringaverapura of Ramas time then the excavations show that Rama could not be earlier than 700 B.C. This is a clear archaeological finding. If literature, historical and religious traditions, go counter to this, Lal may retort that this is a problem demanding attention of historians believing in the truth of the traditions to reconcile the archaelogical evidence. Pargiter, a great proponant of the value of historical traditions himself had asserted "the general trustworthiness of the tradition is the fact demonstrated, whenever it has been possible to test tradition by results of '*discoveries and excavations*' (italics mine) (Pargiter 1972: 6) Lal. has tested the trustworthiness of the traditions by 'discoveries and excavations' and has found the traditions working. Lal himself is a believer in historicity of Rama's story. His work so far has shown that if present Ayodhya and Sringaverapura are the ancient sites of the Ramayana times and not mythical or in different geographical setting (I completely agree), his conclusion about the sequence vis-a-vis Rama's and Krishna's times has to be accepted. But what I am pleading for is to make the proposed conclusion unavailable, doubts expressed about its correctness could be removed if excavations and explorations were continued at the sites more extensively and thereby 'continue to discover (the grains of truth of the Vedic and Puranic accounts) by long and continuous sieving' (Sankalia 1975-76: 85). One has to admit that today the archaeology and literary traditions '(about mutual chronological position of Rama and Krishna)' appear to be 'twain' that 'do not meet'. But as East and West have met falsifying Kipling, I am sure in near future we will strive and strive with success to make Archaeology and Tradition about Rama and Krishna meet on the same plane of time. I am encouraged by one fact that the Mahabharata and Archaeology have very much concurred. Archaeology and traditions, in case of the Ramayana, may not play hide and seek for long.

REFERENCES

Agarwal, D.P. and Kusumagar Sheela 1974. *Prehistoric Chronology and Radio-Carbon Dating in India.*

Albright, W.F. 1966. *Archaeology and Historical Analogy and Early Biblical Tradition* 1966, U.S.A.

Chattopadhyaya, S. 1962. *The Evolution of Theistic Sects in Ancient India*, Culcutta 1962.

Chanan, D.R. 1963. *Beginning of Agriculture in Ancient India*, New Delhi.

Dikshit, K.N. 1973. In *Radio Carbon and Indian Archaeology* (ed.) by D.P. Agarwal and A. Ghosh, Bombay.

Lal, B.B. 1954-55 Excavations at Hastinapura and other Explorations in the upper Ganga and Sutlej Basin. *Ancient India*, 10-11.
Puratattva, 1975-76, 8.

Lal, B.B. 1981, *Antiquity* LV.

Lal, B.B. 1976. In *Mahabharata-Myth and Reality* (ed.) S.P. Gupta, Delhi.

Lal, B.B. 1973. *Annals of Bhandarker Oriental Research Institute*, IV p. 1-4, pp 1-8).

Lal, B.B. and K.N. Dikshit, 1978. *Sringaverapura : A Key site for the Prehistoyr and Early History of the Central Ganga Valley, Puratattva*, 10.

Macdonnel and Keith 1912. *Vedic Index*, Two volumes. Third reprints 1967.

McCrindle J.W. 1976-77, 1960. Ancient India as discribed by Megasthenes and Arisu, The Age of Imperial Unity.

Mishra, Yogendra 1981. *History of Videha*, Patna 1981.

Pargiter, F.E. 1922. *Ancient Indian Historical Tradition*, Oxford, 1922. Reprint 1972.

Raychaudhury H.C. 1972. *Political History of India*, 7th Edition, Calcutta.

Sankalia, H.D. 1973. Ramayana Myth or Reality, Delhi.

Sankalia, H.D. 1975-76. *Puratatva*, 8.

Sankalia, H.D. 1977. *Aspects of Indian History and Archaeology*, Delhi.

Winternitz, M. 1927. *A History of Indian Literature*, Vol. I.

Archaeological Chemistry in India– Some Aspects

R.V. JOSHI
Deccan College, Pune

THE archaeological research in India is now becoming more and more multidisciplinary employing the methodology of physical and natural sciences. In them chemistry with its several branches has been playing important role in enhancing the value of the research for meaningful results. In this short paper it is proposed to take the stock of various areas of such investigations so far covered in India. Some of these experiments and their results have already been published. Only a brief mention of such attempts has been made while those which are under investigation have been dealt with in some detail.

Conservation of Monuments and Antiquities

From the beginning of cultural studies simple chemical methods are being used in cleaning the antiquities made of stone and metal. In the recent years we achieve these results by elaborate methods by employing advanced scientific appliances. Experiments are also being carried out on some selected monuments to study the effects of environment and air polution.

Chemical Studies of Metal Objects, Ores, Slags and Ancient Glass

Chemical analysis of metal objects, ores and slags are being carried out for investigating ancient metallurgical processes involved in obtaining the metal used in the manufacture of various antiquities like weapons of war, agricultural implements and various art objects. Such studies throw considerable light on the socio-cultural and economic activities of the ancient times.

In stratigraphical studies and palaeoclimatic investigations particularly in prehistoric investigations in sedimentological determinations of the deposits some chemical tests are made though generally these experiments fall under geological discipline.

Studies of Ancient Ceramic

Another field of investigation is the study of ceramics the objects of which are abundantly obtained from the archaeological sites. Useful information is now available about the manufacturing processes of the pottery like Black-and-Red, Painted Grey ware and N.B.P. pottery. Some of them are however still in the experimental stage.

Considerable literature on the above mentioned investigation has been published and has been reviewed in the publications by D.P. Agrawal, H.C. Bharadwaj, B.B. Lal, K.T.M. Hegde and others.

Chemical Analysis of Archaeological Deposits (Anthrosols)

It has been established by experiments that human occupation of the land and several activities connected with the habitation considerably affect the concentration of elements such as phosphorus, nitrogen, carbon etc. in the resulting achaeological debris. The proportions of these elements in the occupational deposits varies according to the size and life (or duration) of a particular settlement. Large population and longer period of occupation naturally increase the amounts of these elements. Their preservation in the archaeological deposit is however to some extent controlled by the environment or geographical location of a settlement. If large number of samples belonging to different regions are chemically analysed it is interesting to see the behaviorial pattern of these elements. If the samples are from well dated horizons and supported by the evidence of several other antiquities it is possible to attempt the intensity of habitation at a particular period. It is necessary to emphasise here that unless such experiments are attempted on some living settlement under controlled conditions, for example, at a tribal site with known human and animal population, no absolute or quantitative estimates of the ancient habitation could be made. Even in estimating the climatic changes in the past we do studies on the samples of soils or sediments. If the sample size is large enough and where other controlling (environmental) factors are known the inferences made of the intensity of habitation by chemical studies of the anthrosols need not be considered hypothetical.

In the experiments carried out at the Deccan College under the U.G.C. Project about 400 samples of habitational deposits collected from 26 sites situated in different climatic zones and covering cultures from palaeolithic (prehistoric) to historic periods were analysed. In addition over 100 samples of the modern soils and the deposits underlying the archaeological sediments (archaeologically sterile or virgin soils) were tested for determining the change in percentage of these elements.

Of the three elements C and N are susceptible to rapid destruction due to oxidation and only under special conditions they are preserved in the ancient deposits. The phosphorus is comparatively very stable element. Due to its specific property of becoming practically inert and immovable except by physical process of erosion of the deposit it is by far the best indicator of ancient human occupation of the area.

The organic carbon content at Kalibangan (Rajasthan) is very low, on an average 0.24% mostly because of the high temperature as in the hot climate oxidation loss is more. On the contrary at Burzahom (J.K.) its percentage is very high, average 1% due to cooler climate. Chronologically both sites are more or less of the same age but the climate has played a major role at these sites. In Peninsular India the preservation of organic matter is generally poor due to strong oxidising environment.

At some sites in a few cultural levels relatively high proportion of these three elements (C, N, P) has been recorded, viz., at Daimabad (Savalda culture), Apegaon (Ramtirth culture), Inamgaon (E. Jorwe) and Burzahom (Neolithic). Excepting these at other localities the organic carbon and nitrogen have not shown any notable difference in 'on-site' and 'off-site' samples.

As per the frequency distribution polygon the distribution of organic carbon and nitrogen is somewhat erratic. Organic carbon clusters around 0.2 in majority of the samples from non-habitational areas, while it varies from 0.3 to 0.8 in the samples from habitational deposits. Nitrogen shows exactly similar trends as organic carbon. In the graphical distribution the organic carbon shows unimodality in samples from non-habitational areas indicating homogenity, and trimodality in habitational deposits suggesting heterogenity.

The most reliable and indicative element from archaeological point of view is phosphorus. The accumulation of P is more in areas covered by human settlements than that present in non-occupational areas. The mean value of all P percentage falls within the range of 0.14 to 0.66. While the mean of non-habitational or archaeologically sterile soil is 0.06. It is thus two and half to eleven times more in on-site samples than off-site samples.

In the graph of P distribution the maximum number of samples fall at 0.4% P level and the range of maximum distribution is 0.2 to 0.1. Not a single sample from non-habitatational area crosses the limit of 0.1. Most of them are within the range of 0.05 to 0.09. It can be said that the P content of 0.2 or more than that is an indication of archaeological site. The bones do not necessarily increase the P of the archaeological deposits. In cemetary burial pit at Kalibangan P is 0·05—0.07% and Lothal it is 0.08%. At Mahurzari it ranges from 0.04 to 0·06 and Naikund it is in traces. If we consider all samples from burials the range will be 0.04 to 0.08.

Fluorine Content and Fossilization Process of Ancient Bones

Animal and human bones are often found at the archaeological sites. The former are being systematically studied for understanding not only the nature of the ancient fauna but also for knowing human food habits and to some extent the nature of palaeoclimates. It is needless to mention the importance of the study of human remains as they are the most valuable objects for understanding the ancient man and his evolution through the ages.

The chemical analysis of animal and human bones obtained in archaeological deposits throw considerable light on the degree of fossilization at every stage and also the possible effect of environment on this process. The fluorine content and sometimes even nitrogen content of the fossil is often used for the purpose of relative dating, for establishing contemporaneity or otherwise of bones occurring in the same deposit. As we already know Oakley and several others have successfully employed the fluorine dating method in solving some intricate problems of archaeology. There are however certain limitations in the application of this method. It is said that this method cannot be applied to material that had been buried under conditions of tropical weathering or where there is an unusually high concentration of fluoride in the region as in some volcanic areas or to fossil material buried under travertine or recovered from situations where exceptional conditions persisted.

As all the above conditions apply to the Indian region we tried to test these hypotheses. We selected two sites situated in the same region and having identical environment and more or less the same cultural sequence and carried out chemical tests on the bones obtained in the excavation. These two sites are Daimabad (19°31′ N, 74°42′ E) situated on the left bank of the Pravara river and Inamgaon (18°35′, 74°31′ E) laying on the right bank of the Ghod river. Both are the chalcolithic sites and belong to Malwa-Jorwe cultures.

The results of the analysis are as under :

Table 1

Site	*Culture*	*Period (B.P.)*	*F%*	*P%*	*N%*	*$100F/P_2O_5$*	*$CaCO_3$*
Fresh bone	—	—	0.035	10.62	4.39	0.123	9.56
Inamgaon	Jorwe	2700-3400	0.0355	12.51	0.056	0.120	22.10
Daimabad	Jorwe		0.0313	11.14	0.0475	0.125	24.40
Inamgaon	Malwa	3440-3700	0.0370	13.64	0.0904	0.119	20.11
Daimabad	Malwa		0.0432	12.37	0.0464	0.148	21.52
Inamgaon	Up Pleistocene (c. 20,000 yrs.)		0.9828	7.68	0.0112	5.88	48.08

It is interesting to note that the values of bone fluorine from Inamgaon and Daimabad are comparable. The flourine content of the soils is 60 ppm. Thus there is only slight increase of fluorine during the last about 4000 years. There is however marked increase in the F-content in the bone which is about 20,000 years old. In the chalcolithic bone the contents of phosphorus do not show much change from the initial value of the fresh bone. The nitrogen has been lost considerably while P has been added marginally. But calcium-carbonate shows definite increase.

-Several samples from other sites and cultures were studied from which it is observed that the values of F and particularly those of the ratio $100F/P_2O_5$ are constantly high with the greater antiquity of the fossil bones.

When the results of fossil analysis from India and western countries (see Table 2) are compared there appears to be considerable similarities in ratio $100F/P_2O_5$. In the Indian specimens the percentage of calcium carbonate is, however generally higher and this may be the effect of tropical environment. The nature of this material is being studied petrologically and SEM. On the whole there appears to be great potential in these studies and in course of time the pattern of behaviour of F, P, and other constituents of fossils from India i.e. Tropical or monsoonal region will become more clear.

Table 2

INDIA

Site	*Culture/Period*	*%F*	*%P*	*$100F/P_2O_5$*	*%C*	*%N*	*$\%CuCO_3$*
Tarsang	Microlithic	1.073	13.50	3.471	0.472	0.053	14.12
Betamcherla	E. Holocene	0.954	11.56	3.604	0.24	0.026	33.47
Deyakachar	Up. Palaeolithic	1.259	10.31	5.332	0.283	0.024	37.60
Narmada	Up. Pleistocene	2.280	12.19	8.169	0.199	0.022	15.84
Siwalik	Pleistocene	2.470	12.75	8.450	0.189	0.022	15.84
		%F		$100F/P_2O_5$			$\%CaCO_3$

BRITISH ISLES			
Mid Plesitocene	1.7–2.8	5.2—8	9—17
Late Up. Pleistocene			
Holocene	0.07—0.48	0.26–2.28	3–6
(Gouh cave Samples Contain	10—60%$CaCO_3$		

FRANCE			
Mid Pleistocene	0.9–1.7	3.7—5.1	9
Early Up. Pleistocene	0.3–1.2	1.0–3.4	
Late Up. Pleistocene	0.05–0.7	0.2—2.3	5—10

GERMANY			
Early Mid-Pleistocene	1.13–4.2	10—13	upto 48
Late Mid-Pleistocene	1.2—2.2	10–7	12
HUNGARY			
Mid.-Pleistocene	1.33—2.0	3.9—6.6	About 15
ITALY			
Early Up. Pleistocene	0.5—1.7	4—8	<5
SPAIN			
Up. Pleistocene	0.04—0.17	0.2—0.6	About 20

REFERENCES

Agrawal, D.P. 1976. *The Copper Bronze Age in India*, New Delhi.

Bhardwaj, H.C. 1979. *Aspects of ancient Indian Aechnology*, Delhi.

Deotare, B.C. 1981. Chemical analysis of archaeological sites in India, unpublished Ph. D. thesis, Poona University.

Deotare, B.C. and Joshi R.V. 1981. Behaviour of carbon, nitrogen and phosphorus in archaeological deposits from India, *Bulletin Deccan College*, Pune, 40:95-112.

Eidt, R.C. 1977. Detection and examination of anthrosols by phosphate analysis, *Science*, 197: 1327-1333.

Cook, S.F. and Heizer R.P. 1965. *Studies on chemical analysis of archaeological sites*, Los Angeles.

Oakley, K.P. 1980. *Relative dating of the fossil hominids of Europe*, Geology Series, 34 (1), London.

Hegde, K.T.M. 1962. Technical studies in N.B.P. ware, *J.M.S. University*, Baroda. XI (1): 159-161.

——1965. Technical studies in chalcolithic period copper metallurgy, Ph. D. thesis, M.S. Universtity, Baroda.

Pollen Stratigraphy of India

VISHNU MITTRE, CHHAYA SHARMA, A.K. SAXENA, KAMLA PRASAD, A. BHATTACHARYA AND M.S. CHAUHAN
Birbal Sahni Institute of Palaeobotany, Lucknow

IMPARTIALLY speaking it must be stated that, inspite of progress over the last two decades, we are still far from building up a complete Pollen Stratigraphy for the Quaternary Period in India. The lack or insufficiency of essential data-base (information concerning pollen production and sedimentation and the precise ecological requirements of modern taxa) for the diversity of vegetational and climatic regimes; the utter lack of polliniferous sediments in certain potential regions such as the continuous sections exposed along the Belan River near Allahabad in Uttar Pradesh, the Son river in district Sidhi, Madhya Pradesh and along the Mahi and other rivers and their tributaries in Gujarat; the absence of seeds and fruits in polliniferous sediments which could provide more dependable identity of former taxa; and parochialism on the part of researchers, etc. are some reasons to account for this. Time has indeed been expanded in building up the data-base, for the regions pollen analytically investigated though much needs to be accomplished. The publication of three dozen pollen diagrams and the construction of over a dozen unpublished ones is no mean achievement in the last two decades for such a vast country, howsoever sketchy the data is for building up the Pollen Stratigraphy of India.

A conventional and routine feature of Quaternary Pollen Stratigraphy is to recognise events of vegetational alterations in Pollen diagrams, which are designated as local and regional Pollen Zones. These are then correlated with Pollen Zones in other regions. The pollen stratigraphy thus built up is used as a time scale, the absolute time scale for which is provided by isotopic dates. The small number of pollen diagrams in each region investigated in India has disallowed the regional pollen zonation except for the northern part of western Rajasthan (Singh *et al.* 1974: 465-501), even though the pollen diagrams are supported by radiocarbon dates.

The use of radiocarbon dates is perhaps the only means to build up pollen stratigraphy of this vast country with diversity of vegetation and climate, as these help in tying up contemporary events of vegetational change even in distant regions with entirely different vegetation and climate.

Lately attempts have been directed to use parameters from other sister disciplines such as palaeontology, geomorphology, archaeology, etc., for independent evidence, even though not free from limitations and intricacies of individual disciplines, as a check against which inference from palynological data can be examined to overcome limitations in the palynological parameter. Such an approach can minimise parochialsm on the part of palynologists and consumers of this discipline.

The attempts at a much wider synthesis of contemporary events in vegetational developments from the isotopically dated pollen diagrams from various part of the country, howsoever, small their number is, has resulted in a skeletal model of pollen stratigraphy. This is presented here. Included in this model are also the major contemporary events as known from geomorphology such as the sea and land-level alterations, the polaeosols, etc. The future progress in Quaternary Palynology in India would indeed modify, improve upon or reject this model and replace it by another.

Synopsis of Pollen-Analytical Work In India

The salient features of the pollen-analytical work

crrried out in India and utilised in building up the skeletal model of pollen stratigraphy are briefly discussed below.

The beginning of the Pleistocene

It may not be out of place to mention that the exclusive palynological evidence employed universally to indicate the beginning of Pleistocene rests on the change from Tertiary floristics to the Quaternary, the extinction of Teritiary elements and the commencement of cooling. It may further be mentioned that it has been dated from 2.5 m years (Zagwijn and Doppert, 1978: 577-588; Michaux *et al.* 1979: 185-191).

According to Ghenea (1981: 49-54), the Matuyama Gauss boundary dated at 2.48 m. years might constitute/ Neogene/Quaternary boundary for global correlations. It has been discovered that the boundary at 2.48 m. years agrees with data from Mollusca, Ostracoda, Vertebates and pollen.

The palynological evidence together with other evidences from terrestrial sections is tending to suggest the lower limit of the Pleistocene at 2.5 m. years though evidences from oceanic cores seem to suggest the lower limit at 1.8 m. years—the Olduvai event. Thus the recent evidences continue to be indecisive. However, the accummulated palynological evidence dating its beginning at 2.5m. years is presently accepted here for the Indian Quaternary also. It is hoped that the palaeomagnetic dating of good palynological sequence satisfying the palynological criteria for its delimitation would support it. There is nothing of the kind at the present.

The palynological evidence in the stratigraphical background of de Terra & Paterson's Lithostratigraphical scheme for the Lower Karewas published in 1973 (Vishnu-Mittre 1973: 160-167) had suggested the beginning of glacial epoch on top of Lithozone I followed by the gradul immigration of temperate blue pine *Pinus wallichiana* into the steppic conditions at this time and its subsequent expansion in Lithozone II in response to gradual warming following the cool fluctuation. The entire pollen sequence revealed a succession of six cool and warm oscillations which in the absence of floristic elements of arctic-alpine nature or of any physical evidence of permafrost in the deposits, are indicative of a nonglacial Pleistocene. The massive glacial stuff overlying the Lower Karewa and considered of II Glaciation by de Terra & Paterson should on the above evidence be accorded the status of I Glaciation.

The recent pollen-analytical work in the background of new lithostratigraphic scheme for the Lower Karewas and dated by palaeomagnetism in the Hirpur region to predate 2.47 m years (Dodia *et al.* 1982: 21-26 Gupta *et al.* 1982a, 1982c) should as discussed above be considered of pliocene age. It therefore, does not merit discussion here. However, a cool phase is reported from Wapzan believed to be from the upper part of the Lower Karewas (Gupta *et al.* 1982b). The precise dating of de Terra and paterson's sections pollen analysed and referred to in the preceding paragraph needs to be done to support or otherwise the palynological parameter which dates it to the early Quaternary.

The Mid-Pleistocene (700,000-1,30,000 years)

The Middle Pleistocene now largely believed to date from 700,000 years to 1,30,000 years is truly glacial Pleistocene in the temperate regions in which glacial/ interglacial stages more or less as visualised by Penck and Brückner are recognizable (Butzer 1974). More or less corresponding series of pluvial and dry phases have been recognised in the tropical countries. The beginning of this is linked to the Brunhes/Matuyama geomagnetic reversal, and the palynological criteria suggested are the eradication of the last Pliocene elements (Butzer 1974 : 143).

The extensive sections exposed along the Mahi, the Narmada, the Belan and the Son rivers and believed to be of mid-Pleistocene age have been found without pollen grains by us. Likewise the Middle Pleistocene deposits in the Himalaya too have so far been found without pollen.

The Late Pleistocene (1,30,000-10,000 years)

The pollen evidence dating from before 40,000 years to the end of the Late Pleistocene is available from Ladakh and partly from Toshmaidan in the Kashmir Valley, from the Kathmandu valley in Nepal and from Ootacamund in the Nilgiris (Tamil Nadu) (Vishnu-Mittre, 1979a: 20-66; 1979b: 167-181 Vishnu-Mittre and Bhattacharyya, 1980 Bhattacharyya 1982; Singh and Agrawal, 1976: 232; Vishnu-Mittre and Sharma, Ms; Vishnu-Mittre and prasad, Ms).

A large part of the Tsokar Yake profile in Ladakh and of a profile from Sankhu in the Kathmandu Valley predate 40,000 years. Both the regions belong to entirely different climatic regimes and latitude. Ladakh plateau is 5000 m. above sea level and much above the tree limit whereas the Kathmandu Valley in Nepal is in the subtropical/temperate belt at 1300 m above sea level. The pollen sequences from both the regions cover a period of time from before 40,000 radiocarbon years to the beginning of Holocene.

The Ladakh pollen sequence shows successions between Steppe and Juniper expansion indicating successions between stadials and interstadials within a prevalent glacial climate. A prominent interstadial is dated here between 28,000-34,000 radiocarbon years and the subsequent ones, through extrapolation of dates and calculation of rate of sedimentation, between 21,000-18,375, and before 15,800 years ago. The event of deglaciation is dated between 18,000-19,000 years ago.

In the Kathmandu Valley, a brief phase of oak woods had occurred in the pre-40,000 radiocarbon years period of time followed by a long period of Steppe until 17,000 years and interrupted around 25,000 years ago by the expansion of oak woods. Thus, two warm oscillations occurred between pre-40,000 to 17,000 years B.P. and the third between 17,000-10,000 years ago when the valley was forested with open or oak-mixed pine woods indicating prevalence of warm and humid climate.

Within the Sedge-Chenopods-*Artemisia* Steppe in the pollen, sequence preceding 15,000 radiocarbon years at Toshmaidan, a brief episode of forest expansion indicates an interstadial possibly contemporary with a pre-15,800 years interstadial at Ladakh. From 15,000 years ago the Sedges-Chenopod-Grass-*Artemisia* Steppe had continued at Toshmaidan, and pines and *Cedrus* with small proportion of oaks had occurred in the vicinity. Chenopods declined thereafter and the Steppe now characterised by *Artemisia*-Sedge-Grass was invaded by brich by 14,000 years ago. small proportions of *Quercus*, elm, *Alnus* continued to occur in the vicinity. By 11,600 years ago, birch had expanded and the elm among others continued in the vicinity which too vanished prior to the beginning of Holocene.

In the Nilgiris, where the Kakathope pollen sequence at Ootacamund is estimated to date from 38,000 years ago, a warm fluctuation occurred between 32,000-25,000 years ago as indicated by increase in shrubs in the grassland Savannah. The initiation of forest began about 21,000 years ago culminating into forest between 14,000-15,000 years ago. The decline of forest commenced about 11,400 years ago earlier than beginning of the Holocene period. In the Ninjanad region, the grassland Savannah continued to occur from 20,000 radiocarbon years to Mid-Holocene.

The meagre evidence of *Terminalia arjuna* around 31,000 years ago in the vicinity of Mula Dam, Poona, and the evidence of *Holoptelea-Acacia* deciduous forest near Inamgaon in Maharashtra subsequent to 19-20,000 years ago suggest the occurrence during the late Pleistocene of dry deciduous riverain seral forests in this region of Maharashtra under dry climate with about 500-600 mm precipitation (Vishnu-Mittre, 1979a, 1979b).

***The Holocene** (10,000 years—Recent)

Even though some pollen diagrams viz., from Tsokar lake in Ladakh, Toshmaidan in Kashmir Valley and Kakathope in Nilgiris, discussed under the late Pleistocene extend, to the recent times, the criteria distinguishing the Holcene from the late Pleistocene (Pleistocene/Holocene boundary) have not been recognised.

Among the various bio- and litho-stratigraphical criteria for its delimitation such as the biogenic deposit, a change in climate and floristic change indicating warming are employed universally to limit this boundary. Based upon these, researchers elsewhere have dated this boundary from 8000-12,000 years ago. Nevertheless, the generalised opinion for its beginning at 10,000 years has continued. This is presently accepted for India too until more decisive information becomes available from future work.

Wholly or partly the vegetational development for the Holocene is represented by the top 1.2 m of Tsokar lake profile from Ladakh; the top one metre of the Toshmaidan pollen diagram and the middle part of the Haigam pollen diagram from the Kashmir Valley (the latter shows ± similar vegetational pattern as observed in Toshmaidan pollen diagram but for some local floristic features due to low altitude and for 14-C dates which must be redone); the Kumaon and Himachal Pradesh pollen diagrams in the Himalaya; the Ganga Plains, Rajasthan and Gujarat pollen diagrams from western India; the Bengal pollen diagrams from eastern India; and the extreme top part of the Kakathope pollen diagram and the others from Nilgiris in south India.

From above the tree limit in Ladakh, rise in Juniper and decline in Steppe in the pollen spectra in top 1.2 m deposit of Tsokar lake profile dated to 10,000 average radiocarbon years, indicating warm climate suggests the commencement of the early Holocene (Vishnu-Mittre and Bhattacharyya, Ms, 1980; Bhattacharyya 1982).

*Some Quaternary researchers (West, 1968, p. 225) have suggested the discarding of the term Holocene which according to them should be considered as the most recent stage of the Pleistocene.

The small Holocene sequence from Mari, 3313 m, above tree limit, in Himachal Pradesh reveals *Betula*-sedge stage dated 7500 radiocarbon years followed by *Betula-Quercus-Abies* stage and Sedge-*Betula* mixed wood stage. Another small profile from Betal 4200 m, above tree limit in Himachal Pradesh and dated from between 15000-1400 years ago shows Juniper-*Ephedra* Stage followed by *Ephedra* Stage, Juniper-*Ephedra* Stage and the *Ephedra* Steppe stage respectively, the last is dated to 500 radiocarbon years (Vishnu-Mittre and Bhattacharyya Ms, 1980; Bhattacharyya 1982).

The Holocene at Toshmaidan, Kashmir Valley from 10,000-95,000 years ago was characterised by declining trend in Steppe in which *Artemisia* declined substantially and Chenopods were already poor but sedges predominated along with Pine-birch woods, and some *Abies* and *Picea* occurred in the vicinity. The stratigraphical hiatus between 9500-3000 radiocarbon years observed at this site has destroyed evidence of vegetation for this period of time. From 3000 years to the present, the *Abies*-Birch-Pine community with much reduced Steppe represented by sedges only occurred in the vicinity of the site (Singh and Agrawal 1976; Vishnu-Mittre, Ms. in press).

The Haigam pollen diagram from the valley proper although has ± similar pattern of vegetational development but for some floristic elements owing to low altitude and non-tallying 14C dates prohibits its discussion here (Vishnu-Mittre 1974: 16-51; 1979b and Ms. in press).

From extrapolation of 14C dates from another unworked profile at Naukuchiya Tal and from dated pollen sequences in the adjoining Himachal Pradesh, the oak-Pine mixed woods in the published pollen sequence from here (Vishnu-Mittre *et al.* 1967: 539-40) seem to have continued here since about 5000 years ago, and the transition between the Chirpine oak woods and oak-Chirpine woods occurred here between 8000-7000 years ago or about 6000 years ago. However, in the Himachal Pradesh the oak woods were replaced by Chirpine about 500-600 years ago in the vicinities of Rewalsar and Parasram and by *Cedrus deodara* about 1250 years ago in the Khajiar vicinity (Vishnu-Mittre 1974, 1979; Sharma, Ms. unpublished).

In the northern Rjasthan desert, the thorn forest about 10,000-9,000 years ago consisted of *Calligonum Ephedra-Capparis* in the west and of *Mimosa-Ephedra-Maytenus-Acacia* commuinities in the East. By 500 years ago, this thorn forest was dominated by *Maytenus* (Singh *et al.* 1974). The progressively drying and warming climate with increasing aeolian activity and moderate and graded advance of sand dune activity climaxed during 5000-3000 years ago when the desert thorn forest increased under maximum dry and high summer temperatures and intense sand dune formation activity (Vishnu-Mittre 1978: 549-558; believed to be wet climate by Singh *et al.*) The *Calligonum* dominated *Capparis-Aerva* society continued thereafter in the extreme west of this region (Singh *et al*). The precipitation estimates indicate a graded pattern of 150-400 mm from west to east of the desert and the climate continued to be predominantly dry as indicated by predominance of *Artemisia.* Sedges and grasses, although *Artemisia* was comparatively less predominant in the extreme west. This may be due to differential biotic effect: sheep are known to eat *Artemisia* plants in harsher climate of Ladakh which are spared under congenial climate (Vishnu-Mittre, 1978: 549-558; 1979a, 1979b).

In the SW of the Rajasthan desert in the Jaisalmer region (Kanod Plays), the Sedge-Grassland Steppe occurred here during the early Holocene, from 9,500-8,700 years ago, when sedges predominated over the grasses thereafter the grasses predominated. *Artemisia* was the least represented, and the thorn forest tree genera *Calligonum*, *Ephedra*, *Prosopis*, *Capparis* occurred rarely—a great contrast from what has been observed in the north of the Rajasthan desert (Vishnu-Mittre and Saxena, Ms. unpublished).

In the dry/moist deciduous forest region of Gujarat, the vegetational development in early Holocene prior to 7000 years ago commenced with Chenopod-Grassland stage, into which *Holoptelea*, one of the seral elements for the deciduous forest invaded the Chenopod-Grassland by about 7,000 years ago and constituted the riverain forest which declined by about 5,000-4,000 years ago. Thereafter, the over-all predominance of Savannah had continued (Vishnu-Mittre, 1979a, 1979b).

In the vicinity of Pratapgarh, U.P., the Chenopod-grassland Savannah preceded as in Gujarat, but the forest here was comprised of *Tecomella* and *Anogeissus*, a dry deciduous forest constituted about 5,000-4,000 years ago. It declined about 2,000-4,000 years ago. The over-all predominance of grasses characterises the sequence significantly which was preceded before about 4000 years ago by Chenopod-grassland stage (Gupta 1978: 109-119).

The vegetational fluctuations in the dry deciduous *Anogeissus* forest in the vicinity of Ajmer, Rajasthan desert and believed to date from 3,000 to 4,000 years ago show the occurrence of *Anogeissus* forest within predominant grassland stage. Its invasion commenced more or less at this time by sand forming *Calligonum* species which after brief episode of predominance perhaps around 2,000-1,500 years ago declined and the *Anogeissus* forest recovered by or after 1,000 years ago. The open forests of *Prosopis-Capparis-Zizyphus* series developed into the *Acacia-Capparis* forests during the last 500 years. (Singh *et al.* 1974; Vishnu-Mittre 1978, 1979a, 1979b; Vishnu-Mittre and Saxena, Ms).

In the tropical montane region of Ootacamund in the Nilgiris, the vegetational development in the Holocene period as observed in the top 1.50 m of the Kakathope pollen diagram shows decline and degradation of the Shola forest *Peperomia* and the trailing *Gordonia* disappeared by about 7000 years ago, and both *Euymus* and *Eleocarpus* until 2,000 years ago. This decline in forest is followed by gradual increase in grasslands with herbs and shrubs. In the Pykara and Pearson's Valley of the Nilgiris the grassland Savannah had continued since 3,000-4,000 years ago (Blasco and Thanikaimoni 1974: 632-643). In the Upper Bhawani region of the Nilgiris, grasslands had occurred in this region until about 5600 years ago when scanty tree elements appeared in the Savannah. The re-immigration of forest in this region took place during the last 2,000 years (Rajagopalan *et al.* 1980: 56). At Nanajanad in the Nilgiris, the forest (Shola) was constituted about 5000 years ago and it has continued here until recent times (*BSIP, Annual Report 1979-80*: 26; Vishnu-Mittre and Prasad, unpublished), whereas at Colgrain in the Nilgiris, the Shola forest had immigrated about 8000 years ago in the Savannah (*BSIP, Annual Report, 1977-78*: 28).

The Holocene vegetational development in the Bengal Basin as built up from quite a few pollen diagrams about 30-35 km east and west of Calcutta, about 40 km north of Calcutta from sites near the Hooghley River and about 20 km island from sea shore are dated within6, 840±260 to 1,710±110 B.P. In the vicinity of Calcutta, the fresh water bils had been influenced by the back flow of tidal waters creating moderately salt water conditions whereas the sites upto twenty km inland from sea were directly affected by them. Marine inundations during this period of time were evidently due to sea and land level changes as evidenced by buried wood of *Heritiera* and *Sonneratia* found 2-3 or more metres below present sea-level. *Heritiera-Sonneratia* forests extended in the vicinity of Calcutta which are non-existent there today. These brackish water forests, which occur poorly in the western part of the Sunderbans in the deltaic region of the Ganga-Brahmaputra, had during mid-Holocene occurred much north of the Sunderbans. The vicinity of the present Calcutta was during mid-Holocene the deltaic region which now occurs about 60-70 km south of Calcutta.

Major Events in Pollen Stratigraphy and Contemporary Geomorphological Events

Among the salient features of vegetational development in various parts of the country briefly mentioned above, there are quite a few changes in vegetational development in entirely different vegetational and climatic regimes which occurred at the same date or within a small range of dates. The synchroniety in these major pollen events across the length and breadth of the country cannot be without significance. The floristic changes have largely been believed and interpreted to have been caused by changes in climate, geomorphology, or by biotic/anthropic interferences. The synchronous floristic changes have been believed to be due to secular changes in climate of which geomorphological changes are the other manifestations. For instance, high sea level is attributed to melting of glaciers, thus, both are manifestations of warm climate. To this may be added the emergence and submergence of land owing to sea level flnctuations, if these are not caused by tectonism. Likewise the evidence of coral reefs is correlatable with subtropical and tropical water phases, and the times of ocean surface warming corresponding with times of transgressions and the minor oscillations of sea level since 6,000 years B.P have been found correlatable with glacial events in East Asia (Taira, 1979: 194-204).

Palaeosols usually believed to have been formed under warm climate are the other manifestations of climate. Changes in the dominant pedogenic processes from pedological examination of past and recent soils can only be interpreted properly in terms of climatic environment. Such studies by Folster *et al.* (1977: 245-264) have revealed that the palaeosols in Western and Central Cordillera of Colombia were deposited under cold humid, cold dry or warm climate. No such studies in India on palaeosols have been carried out.

As floristic alterations, sea and land-level fluctuations and the formation of palaeosols are largely speaking manifestations of climate, the contemporary information on these events as far known from the country (Agrawal *et al.* 1973: 1981: 5-8, Gupta 1972: Cullen 1981) is also included in the model on All India Pollen Stratigraphy primarily based upon major pollen events. Indeed more work needs to be done in India to translate the geomorphological events in terms of climate.

Pollen stratigraphy alone brings about alterations in the kind and nature of botanical environment—the forested and forestless conditions and the kinds of forests that existed in the past all upon botanical residuals in sediments. The precise information on the status (seral and climax) of these forests and on the causative factors for the floristic alterations have lead to speculations reasonable and unreasonable, and such speculations permeat the literature published on pollen stratigraphy. These now considered on all India basis, as in the present synthesis of the available data, bring out metachronous situations, more particularly in the climatic inferences even though the floristic changes are synchronous. This may look strange to a believer in universal secularism of climates. Recent attempts at global synthesis of pollen-analytical data and climatic deductions therefrom reveal that many climatic events dated by radiocarbon in the northern and southern Hemispheres are not secular (Burrows 1979: 287-347). However, in the light of atmospheric circulation patterns, variations in position and strength of the subtropical anticyclones and the related changes in the position and wave amplitude of the subtropical westerly jet strems, the understanding of apparently non-secular climatic changes between Australia and North Africa, has been made clear by Regnon & William (1977: 285-327). The experience of Peterson *et al.* (1979: 47-82) in the synthesis of data available for 18,000 years B.P. is no different.

We have yet to gather this useful meteorological data and to apply it to understand environmental changes in the past from pollen and geomorphological data. Our knowledge of the control of plant communities by temperature, precipitation, humidity and nature of soils is already inadequate. Equally inadequate is our knowledge of the impact of biotic factor upon vegetation. Our inferences of the latter from pollen data are based upon circular arguments centred around large-sized grass pollen believed to be that of cultivated grasses which in fact cannot be distinguished from the wild grass pollen in the Indian subcontinent. Specially computed subsidiary pollen diagrams have also been prepared to depict phases of origin and progressive development of agriculture. Stretching such an evidence long enough to become convincing, the limitations of palynology should not be overlooked. Farming has been practised since millennia but limitations of palynology do not bring it out beyond. The evidence of charcoal for burning forest, grasslands falls in the same category. Where reasonably adjudged, in the background of local environment, it may appear acceptable. Then there are fires caused by a biotic factor too.

Viewed in the above light, the radiocarbon dated phases of pollen stratigraphy across the country together with geomorphological data present some events of the environments of the past, the understanding of the precise nature of which remains to be determined. This aspect for the reasons stated above is not stressed in the model for pollen stratigraphy of India constructed and presented here.

ALL INDIA POLLEN STRATIGRAPHY

As stated elsewhere in the text, this skeletal model for All India Pollen Stratigraphy for the Quaternary Period in India is based upon pollen events, sea- and land-level changes and palaeosol formation within a range of radiocarbon dates. Quite a few events are synchronous whereas the others are not. The analysis of this feature of the model is set aside for the present till more information has been gathered on the understanding of this feature. Nevertheless, the model will provide information on the environmental background of the human cultures that existed in various parts of the country.

Prior to 700,000 years (I Glaciation)

Cool and warm oscillations of climate : precipitation during warm oscillations around 1500-1000 mm, the cool period dry with comparatively less precipitation when Steppe vegetation occurred and temperature much lower.

Pre-40,000 years (60,000-40,000 years)

Succession between Steppe (stadial) and *Juniper* communities (interstadial) in Ladakh and a phase of oak wood followed by Steppe in Kathmandu Valley. An event of submergence in Sri Lanka dated beyond the limit of 14 C.

40,000-25,000 years

A prominent interstadial between 34,000-28,000 average radiocarbon years (Juniper rise, bigenic deposit) in Ladakh, and at 25,000 years (oak woods) in Kathmandu Valley: a cold phase between 38,000-32,000 years (*Rhododendron* Savannah) and a warm fluctuation (shrub rise) between 32,000-25,000 years in Nilgiris, and dry deciduous forest at 31,000 years in Maharashtra.

Sea level much higher than Mean High Tide Level (MHT) between 35,000-15,000 years in Saurashtra coast: at 38,400 years an event of submergence to—15 to-20 m. in Willington Island, Kerala coast.

Palaeosols predating 31,000 years ago at Burzahom, Saki Paparian and predating 35,000 years ago at Tsrar Sherif and between 25,000-28,000 years at Puthkhoh, Garhi and Pakharpur in the Kashmir Valley.

21,000-16,000 years

Two interstadials, between 21,000-18,000 years and between 16-17,000 years, in Ladakh; forest formation about 16,000-17,000 years at Toshmaidan and at 17,000 years in Kathmandu Valley; initiation of forest at 21,000 years in Nilgiris and Grassland Savannah at Nanajanad in Nilgiris from 20,000 years, and dry deciduous forest after about 19,000 years in Maharashtra.

Palaeosols between 18,000-19,000 years ago at Burzahom and Puthkhoh in the Kashmir Valley.

Decreased salinity in northern Bay of Bengal and the western Arabian Ocean at 18,000 radiocarbon years attributed to change in the pattern or intensity of circulation during southwest monsoon resulting in decreased precipitation and decreased run-off of the river systems (Cullen 1981: 315-356).

15,000-10,000 years

Continuation of forest in the Kathmandu Valley; Steppe at Toshmaidan with Pine and *Cedrus*, later (14,000) followed by birch with poor oak, elms, *Alnus* possibly in the vicinity, increase of birch by 11,600 years along with some elms, Forest in Nilgiris between 14,000-15,000 years and its decline by 11,400 years ago, but continuation of grassland Savannah at Nanjanad.

Sea level in Saurashtra coast higher at 15,000 years, a much lower level (upto —160 m) at 10,500 years ago.

A palaeosol between 12,000-13,000 years in the Kashmir Valley. Between 12,500-10,500 years ago increased upwelling (decreased salinity) attributed to increased precipitation and increased run-off of the river systems in the northern Bay of Bengal.

10,000-7,500 years

The Pine-birch Steppe at Toshmaidan between 10,000-9,500 years; the Sedge-Grass-*Artemisia* Steppe with thorn forest elements in northern part, and only sedge-grass Steppe in southwest part of the Rajasthan desert; Savannah in parts of Nilgiris but declining forest in the vicinity of Kakathope; between 8,000-7,500 years *Betula*-sedge community above tree limit at Mari, H.P.; and at 8,000 years forest at Colgrain in the Nilgiris.

Sea level between 10,400-9,100 much lower (upto-160 m) than High water level (HWL). An event of submergence of forest at 8,000 years ago.

7,500-5,000 years

Between about 7,000-6,000 years the invasion of oaks into the Chirpine woods in Kumaon;*Maytenus* dominated thorn forest *Artemisia*-Gramineae-Sedge Steppe in northern Rajasthan: Chenopod-Grassland Savannah in Gujarat and Ganga Plains and initiation of seral stages for the dry deciduous forest and its formation towards 5,000 years ago; Grasslands in Upper Bhawani and further decline of forest in Kakathope vicinity in Nilgiris; fluctuations in *Heritiera* forest in the vicinity of Calcutta.

The 2-3 m rise of sea level between 7,000-4,500 years ago.

5,000-3,000 years

Abies-Birch-Pine forest in Toshmaidan at 3,000 years Oak-Chirpine woods in Kumaon and H.P.; dry deciduous *Anogeissus* forest in Gujarat, Ganga Plains and possibly later in Ajmer region in western Rajasthan; simultaneous increase in Steppe, thorn forest elements and exotic pollen in northern Rajasthan: Savannah in the Nilgiris; fluctuations in *Heritiera* forest continued in Bengal Basin.

The 2-3 m rise of sea level until 4,500 years ago fluctuating 1 to 3 m above or below present after 3,000 years ago.

3,000-1,500 years

Continued *Abies*-Birch-Pine forest at Toshmaidan; continuation of Chenopod-Grass-Sedge-*Colligonum* Savannah in northwest part of Rajasthan desert; invasion and expansion of *Calligonum* in the *Anogeissus* forest in the vicinity of Pushkar in Rajasthan; Savannah or Grasslands in the *Ephedra* stage at Batal, H.P. between 1,500-1,400 years and continued fluctuations in *Heritiera* forest in Bengal Basin until 1,700 years ago.

Between 3,000-2,000 years sea levels fluctuating between 1-3 m but generally higher than present are reported but higher again 1,765 years ago.

1,500-500 years

Replacement of oaks by pine or deodar at 1,250, 900 and 500 years in subtropical Himachal Pradesh and *Ephedra*-Steppe at Batal in H.P. at 500 years; recovery of *Anogeissus* forest at 1,000 years and spread of *Acacia*-*Capparis* by 500 years in the Ajmer region.

REFERENCES

Agrawal, D.P., Avasia, P.K., and Guzder, S.R., 1973. A multi-disciplinary approach to the Quaternary Problems in Maharashtra. In *Radiocarbon and Indian Archaeology*, (eds.) D.P. Agrawal and A. Ghosh. Bombay.

Agrawal, D.P., Krishnamurthy, R.V., Kusumgar, Sheela, Nautiyal, V. and Radhakrishnamurthy, C., 1981. Chrono-stratigraphy and Neogene Quaternary Boundary in the Kashmir Valley. *Proc. Neogene/Quaternary Boundary Field Conference, India, 1979.*

Bhattacharyya, A., 1982. Studies in the vegetational history of the alpine region of north-west Himalaya. Ph. D. Thesis Lucknow University. *Birbal Sahni Institute of Palaeobotany, Annual Report, 1977-78, 1979-80.*

Blasco, F., and Thanikaimoni, G., 1974. Late Quaternary Vegetational history of Southern region. In *Aspects and Appraisals of Indian Palaeobotany*, Ed. K.R. Surange *et al.* Lucknow: Birbal Sahni Institute of Palaeobotany.

Burrows, C.J., 1979. A chronology of cool climate episode in the Southern Hemisphere from 12,000-1,000 years B.P., *Palaeogeogr, Palaeoclimatol, Palaeoecol*, 27.

Butzer, Karl, W., 1974. Geological and ecological perspectives on the Middle Pleistocene, *Quat. Res.*

Cullen, C.J., 1981. Microfossil evidence for changing salinity pattern in the Bay of Bengal over the last 20,000 years. *Palaeogeogr. Palaeoclimatol. Palaeoecol.*, 35 (2-4).

Dodia, R., Gupta, H.P., Mandavia, Chetna, Sharma, C., and Vora, A.B., 1982. Palynological investigations on the Lower Karewas. *Man and Environment*, VI.

Folster, H., Hetsch, W. and Schrimpff, E., 1977. Late Quaternary palaeosols in the western and central cordillers of Colombia. *Palaeogeogr, Palaeoclimatol, Palaeoecol*, 29.

Ghanea, Constantin, 1981. Remarks on the Plio-Pleistocene Stratigraphy in Romania. *Proc. Neogene Quaternary Boundary Field Conf. India, 1979.*

Gupta, H.P., 1978. Holocene Palynology from meander lake in the Ganga Valley, District Pratapgarh, U.P., *Palaeobot*, 25.

Gupta, H.P., Sharma, Chhaya, Dodia, Rekha, and Mandavia, Chetna. 1982a. Palynostratigraphy and Palaeoenvironments, Dubjan, Lower Karewa, Kashmir. Abstract. *Proc. Int. Workshop on the Late Cenozoic Palaeoclimatic changes in Kashmir and Central Asia*, Ahmedabad.

Gupta, H.P., Sharma, Chhaya, Dodia, Rekha, Agrawal, D.P. and Pant, R.K., 1982b. Pollen analytical results from Wapjan, Kashmir, Abstract. *Ibid.*

Gupta, H.P., Sharma, Chhaya, Dodia, Rekha, Mandavia, Chetna and Vora, A.B., 1982b. Palynostratigraphy and Palaeoenvironments of Kashmir. Hirpur Loc. III. Lower Karewas. Abstract. *Ibid.*

Gupta, S.K., 1972. Chronology of the Raised Beaches and Island Coral Reefs of the Saurashtra Coast. *Jour. Geol.*

Michaux, J. Suc., J.P. and Vernet, J.L., 1979. Climatic inference from the history of Taxodiaceae during the Pliocene and Early Pleistocene in Western Europe. *Rev. Palaeobot. Palynol.* 27.

Peterson, G.M., Webb, III, T., Kutzbach, J.E., Vander Hammen, T., Wijmetra, T.A. and Street, F.A., 1979. The Continental record of environmental Conditions at 18,000 years B.P. : An initial evaluation. *Quat. Res.* 12 1979.

Rajagopalan, G., Sekar, B., and Vishnu-Mittre, 1980. Birbal Sahni Inst. Radiocarbon Measurements-II. *Radiocarbon*, 22(1).

Ragnon, P. and Williams, M.A.J., 1977. Late Quaternary Changes in Australia and North Africa: A preliminary interpretation. *Palaeogeogr. Palaeoclimatol. Palaeoecol.* 21.

Ronai, A. 1981. Neogene/Quaternary boundary in the Hungarian Great Plain. *Proc. Neogene/Quaternary Boundary Field Conf. India, 1979.*

Sharma, C., Ms. Pollen analysis of a profile from Parasram Tal in Himachal Pradesh.

Singh, G., Joshi, R.D., Chopra, S.K., and Singh, A.B., 1974. Late Quaternary history of vegetation and climate of the Rajasthan desert. *Phil. Trans. Roy. Soc,; London*, B.267.

Singh, G., and Agrawal, D.P., 1976. Radiocarbon evidence for deglaciation in north-western Himalaya. *Nature, London*, 260.

Taira, Kazuhiro 1976. Holocene migrations of the warm water front and sea level fluctuations in the north-western Pacific. *Palaeogeogr. Palaeoclimatol. Palaeoecol*, 28.

Vishnu-Mittre 1973. The Lower Karewas. In *Palynology of Pleistocene and Holocene Proc. III. Int. Palynol. Conf. Novosibirsk, USSR, 1971.*

——1974. Late Quaternary Palaeobotany and Palynology in India—An Appraisement. In *Late Quat. Vegetational, Developments in Extra-european Areas.* Ed. Vishnu-Mittre Birbal Sahni Inst. of Palaeobotany, Lucknow, Publ. 5.

——1978. Palaeoecology of the Rajasthan desert during the last 10,000 years, *Palaeobot.* 25.

——1979a. Environment of Early Man in North-west India. Palaeobotanical Evidence. In *Early man in NW India* (ed.) SRK Chopra, Delhi: Allied Publishers.

——1979b. Environment of Early Men in Western and North-western India, *Grana*, 18.

——Ms. Quaternary Palaeobotany and Palynology in India—An overview. *Palaeobotanist*, (in press).

Vishnu-Mittre and Bhattacharyya, A. 1980. Vegetational and climate during the last Glaciation in Ladakh, Western Himalaya, Abstract. V., *Int. Palynol. Conf. Cambridge, England.*

——Ms. Unpublished work on Project on Quat. Vegetation and climate in the High altitude Himalaya above tree limit.

Vishnu-Mittre & Prasad, Kamla Ms. Unpublished work on Project on Quat. Vegetation and Climate of the Nilgiris.

Vishnu-Mittre and Saxena, A.K., Ms. Unpublished work on Project on Quaternary Vegetation and climate of the Rajasthan desert.

Vishnu-Mittre, and Sharma, Chhaya Ms. History of Vegetation and climate in the Kathmandu Valley, Nepal. *Pollen et Spores* (in press).

Vishnu-Mittre, Gupta, H.P. and Robert, R. 1967. Studies of the late Quaternary Vegetational history of Kumaon Himalaya. *Curr. Sci.* 36(20).

Zagwijn, W.H., Doppert, J.W. Ch. 1978. Upper Cenozoic of the Southern North Sea Basin: Palaeoclimatic and Palaeogeographic Evolution. *Geologic en Mi inbouw* 57(4).

West, R.G. 1968. *Pleistocene Geology and Biology*, London: Longmans, Green & Co.

Pleistocene Fossil Vertebrates in India

G.L. BADAM
Deccan College, Pune

THE Pleistocene period, as is well known, was a time of rapid evolutionary and ecological change culminating in the present pattern and diversity of ecosystems. The Pleistocene deposits of India, extend over an area of about 500,000 sq. km. and have yielded a diverse variety of animal remains of species which inhabited India in the past. However, in the present paper only a summary review of studies on some of the more important fauna especially the mammals and reptiles has been included.

The present paper is arranged chronologically and divided into three parts, the first deals with the faunal material from the Lower Pleistocene fossiliferous deposits of India, while the second part summarises the faunal remains collected from various Middle Pleistocene fossil sites. The third part gives an account of the important fauna belonging to the Upper Pleistocene period. Sufficient remarks have been added on the chronology, correlations, environments and routes of migration of animals in the Pleistocene period.

Since most of the fossils from the Peninsular localities have been collected either in association with or in close proximity to Stone Age tools, it has become imperative to make a passing reference to various cultures which have a direct bearing on the chronology of the faunal material.

The Pleistocene fossil localities in India have been brought to light as a result of researches carried out by palaeontologists more than a century ago. Large collections of fossils have been made from the Karewas of Kashmir, the Siwalik formations of the Punjab and Himachal Pradesh, the alluvial deposits of the Narmada basin, the Deccan river valleys and the Kurnool caves. A few localities in Assam, Bengal, Gujarat and Tamil Nadu have also yielded some faunal material. However, it is only during the last forty years or so that pre-historic archaeologists and anthropologists have developed an interest in these deposits and started an intensive research for the remains of Early Man, his tools and the contemporary fauna.

In the Indian sub-continent, the various subdivisions of the Pleistocene period viz., Lower, Middle and Upper, are based mainly on vertebrate palaeontology and Palaeolithic archaeology. The Lower Pleistocene deposits of north-west India are generally characterised by the presence of *Equus*, *Rhinoceros*, *Elephas* and *Bos*. The late Upper Pleistocene is well dated by a score of C-14 dates especially in western India. But the Middle and Early Upper Pleistocene are not precisely dated due to lack of proper index fossil assemblages and non-availability of the radio-metric dates.

Plio-Pleistocene Boundary in NW India

There are different schools of thought regarding the placement of the Plio-Pleistocene boundary in NW India. These are mostly based on interpretations o mammalian fauna and climate and are as follows:

1. At the base of the Tatrot-on palaeontologic and palaeoclimatic considerations (eg. Matthew, 1929; Lewis, 1937; de Terra and Paterson 1939; Colbert 1951).
2. Between the Tatrot and the Pinjoron palaeontologic considerations (eg. Sahni and Khan, 1964; Badam, 1977a).
3. The Pinjor as a transitional horizon between the Pliocene and the Pleistoceneon sedimentary, stratigraphic and tectonic considerations (eg. Wadia, 1951).
4. Between the Pinjor and the Boulder Conglome-

rate on palaeoniologic, stratigraphic, tectonic and palaeoclimatic considerations (eg. Pilgrim, 1944; Gill, 1951; Balasundaram and Sastry, 1972).

Thus there is at present no concensus regarding the problem of the Plio-Pleistocene boundary since the selection of the basic criteria necessary for placing this boundary are still in a fluid stage. According to Sastry and Dutta (1977) the recognition of this boundary is based on the precise correlation of the Siwalik faunal zones with those of European stratotypes where the boundary is much better defined and chronologically established.

A number of international colloquia on this problem have been held in various parts of the world and a clearer picture of the basic criteria on which this boundary should be based is gradually beginning to emerge. In fact it is not a single method but a number of combined disciplines which are necessary for establishing the lower boundary of the Quaternary in India. Until then it would continue to be one of the most debatable problems in Indian stratigraphy. The application of the palaeomagnetic dating technique could provide a firm basis for the correlation of the Siwalik beds with the dated standard palaeo-magnetic sequence. Recently Keller *et al.* (1977) have tentatively placed the Plio/Pleistocene boundary in the Pabbi Hills (Pakistan) as contemporary with the Olduvai Normal event, at 1.8 m. years ago.

Wtth the recently formed "International Union of Quaternary Studies" and co-ordinated efforts put by scientists from various disciplines, new and valuable information on the problem of the Plio-Pleistocene boundary is expected to emerge.

FAUNAL EVIDENCES

1. Lower Pleistocene:

(*a*) *Karewas Kashmir*: Though a great deal of work has been done on palynology, palaeobotany and palaeoclimatology of the Karewas, extensive areas of these bads, remained relatively unexplored. Consequently, there was a paucity of any interesting palaeontological data for a long time. Hora (1937) reported fish remains of *Orienus* and *Schizothorax* while de Terra and paterson (1939) referred to the occurrence of mammals, *Bos*, *Elephas*, *Equus*, *Cervus*, *Felis*, *Sus*, *Sivatherium* and *Rhinoceros* from various localities in the Karewas specially at Sombur, Magam and Ningal Nala. Subsequently, Badam (1968, 1972) described *Rhinoceros palaeindicus*, *Sivatherium giganteum*, *Equus sivalensis*, *Elephas hysudricus*, *Cervus* sp.. *Bos* sp., *Sus* sp. and *Giraffa* from some hitherto unknown localities (eg. Baramula, Zangam, Gandarbal etc.). More recently Tewari and Kachroo (1977) and Sahni (1981) have reported the occurrence of *Equus sivalensis* and *Elephas hysudvicus* from Shopian and Wapzan respectively. All the fossils collected so far leave no doubt that the base of the Karewas starts with the Lower Pleistocene.

(b) *The Siwaliks of the Punjab and Himachal Pradesh*: (The Pinjor formation): The Siwalik beds (one of the best known mammalian fossiliferous horizons in the world) have been the subject of research for a century and a half. Their studies have thrown considerable light on the knowledge of vertebrate fossils in general and the evolution of various animals in particular. The fauna of the Pinjors) *Equus sivalensis*, *Rhinoceros sivalensis*, *Rhinoceros palaeindicus*, *Chilotherium intermedium*, *Bubalus*, *Bos*, *Hemibos*, *Leptobos*, *Bison*, *Cervus*, *Camelus sivalensis*, *Archidiskoden planiforns*, *Stegodon insignisgenesa*, *Hexaprotodon sivalensis*, *Geoclemys sivalensis*, *Crocodylus biporcatus*, *Crocodylus palaeindicus*. *Gavialis browni* etc.) are significant in that they provide a mixture of the Old World and the New World elements and therefore might point to probable routes of migration to and from the Indian subcontinent.

Furthermore, the Upper Siwalik Subgroup straddles the Plio-Pleistocene boundary. An important feature of the Lower Pleistocene fauna was the absence of certain groups of animals which were conspicuous in the Upper Pliocene times. Along with the disappearance of the archaic groups, the Plio-Pleistocene transition was contemporaneous with the emergence of the progressive forms that have persisted to the present day or at least had a long history in the Pleistocene.

2. Middle Pleistocene (?):

Central Narmada Valley: After the Siwaliks, the Narmada Valley has yielded the richest deposits of mammalian fossils found in India. Many of the fossils are found in association with Stone Age tools which makes the Narmada Valley very significant as far as the origins of man are concerned. The region constitutes one of the great hunting grounds of India. Even today large cats, bear, gaur, deer and black-buck are found in forests. Many of the ancestors of these animals lie buried in the Pleistocene deposits along with other animals such as elephant, hippopotamus, horse and rhinoceros.

The first authoritative list of vertebrate fossils from the Narmada Valley was given by Pilgrim (1905), who had also described the fossil fauna from the Godavari Valley and on the basis of the similarity of species equated the deposits of the two Valleys. The fauna listed by Pilgrim is as follows: *Bos namadicus*, *Bubalus palaeindicus*, *Cervus duvauceli*, *Equus namadicus*, *Hippopotamus namadicus*, *Hippopotamus palaeindicus*. *Leptobos frazeri*, *Pangsura tectum*, *Rhinoceros unicornis*, *Stegodon ganesa*, *Stegodon insignis*, *Sus* sp. and *Ursus namadieus*.

Most of the above mentioned genera still exist at the present day. *Bubalus palaeindicus* and *Cervus duvauceli* seem to be related to the modern Indian buffalo and the barasingha (the swamp deer) respectively. The turtles like *Pangsura tectum* are also identical with the turtles living in Indian rivers today. *Stegodon insignis*, *Stegodon ganesa*, *Equus namadicus* and possibly *Hippopotamus namadicus* are survivals from the Siwalik of North India. *Elephas namadicus* is identical with *Elephas antiquus* of Europe. *Bos namadicus* is profusely represented in the Pleistocene deposits of Peninsular India. In fact *Bos namadicus* survives as late as the Early Holocene. Its bones have been found from excavations at Mehergarh, Pakistan c. 6000 B.C. (Meadow, 1981).

De Terra and Paterson (1939) added two turtles, *Trionyx* sp. and *Emys* sp. to the above list and opined that the fauna of the Upper Narmada Group is similar to that of the Lower Narmada Group and that both carry Middle Pleistocene elements. Colbert (1942) brought to notice two more species from the Narmada viz., *Holarctos namadicus* and *Palaeoloxodon namadicus*. Subsequently *Elephas maximus*, *Elephas hysudricus*, *Bubalus bubalis*, *Equus caballus*, and *Crocodylus Palaeindicus* were rsported from the Narmada by Supekar (1968), Badam (1979a) and Joshi *et al.* (1978) in addition to some of the fossils listed above.

Some fossils found in the Narmada Valley definitely represent the forerunners of the present day animals as indicated by the well preserved features of the dentition and other osteological parts. The total complex of the faunal remains indicates that the Valley was a vast savannah land punctuated by flood plain lakes and swamps in which flourished a rich assemblage of hoofed mammals and reptiles. However, it may be emphasised that there were no significant departures from the existing tropical climate in the area and therefore the valley provided a favourable ecosystem where some of the animals which migrated from the north-west because of climatic rigour in the glacial periods of the early Pleistocene, could survive almost upto 20,000 years ago.

Taking into account the faunal and cultural meterial, different workers have assigned different geological ages to the Narmada Alluvium, eg. Theobald (1960) to Pliocene; Medlicott (1873) to late Pleistocene; and de Terra and Paterson (1939) to Middle Pleistocene.

However on the basis of fauna, Badam (1982) suggested the following litho,,bio- and chrono-stratigraphy from the Narmada Stone Age cultures.

I. The Gravel of the Upper Narmada Group has yielded typical Upper Pleistocene fauna. A single 14-C date from around Devakachar and Nitrogen tests carried out on bones (by Dr. K.P. Oakley of the British Museum of Natural History) from Saguna Ghat and Devakachar confirm this dating. Similarly, a comparative study of faunal material from the Upper Narmada Group with the fauna from the Older Alluvium of the Godavari and Bhima in the Peninsular India also suports the dating of the Upper Group of the Narmada to the late Pleistocene (40,000-10,000 B.P.).

II. In view of the post-diagenetic changes of flood plain silts capping the Boulder Conglomerate of the Lower Narmada Group and the occurrence of a few mammalian species in the Boulder Conglomerate which are totally absent in the Upper Group it appears that the Boulder Conglomerate/Red Clay has a far greater antiquity than the Upper Group. Thus the Lower Group could be tentatively dated as late Middle Pleistocene to early Upper Pleistocene (150,000—40,000 B.P.) The Stone Age tools found in the Boulder Conglomerate belong to this Period and therefore, represent one of the earliest remains of Stone Age Man in Peninsular India.

The cemented sandy gravels around Devakachar (Upper Narmada group) give a 14-C date of $31750 \begin{smallmatrix}+1820 \\ -1625\end{smallmatrix}$ years B.P. (Agrawal and Kusumgar, 1974) as based on fresh water molluscan shells.

3. Upper Pleistocene :

(*a*) *Indo-Gangetic Localities* : A few palaeontological reports occur from the Indo-gangetic alluvium which comprises sands and lenticules of gravels, silts and clays with scattered organic matter. The vertebrate fossils found in the Older Alluvium have affinity with those found along the deposits of the Narmada (Falconer, 1865), whereas those from the younger layers resemble recent ones. Some earlier works are those of Chakravarty (1931, 1935, 1938) who reported the occurrence

Chrono-and Cultural stratigraphy of Central Narmada Valley is tabulated below

Approximate Age	*Lithological Units*	*Approximate Thickness (in metres)*	*Palaeontological and Archaeological materials*
Early-Mid Holocene (10,000 to 4,000 B.P.)	Dark brown moderately consolidated silt and gravel		Semi-mineralised bones. Mesolithic
Late Upper Pleistocene (40,000 to 10,000 B.P.)	Yellowish brown calcreted silts*, sands and gravels	10—13	Middle Palaeolithic tools and Upper Pleistocene fauna
Late Middle Pleistocene to early Upper Pleistocene (150,000 to 40,000 B.P.)	Reddish brown calcareous silt and well cemented boulder gravels	3—8	Early Palaeolithic and Middle Paleolithic (only a few), tools+Middle Pleistocene fauna (?)

*Richest zone in fossils.

of *Stegodon insignis* and *Palaeoloxodon namadicus* from the Upper Pleistocene of the Gangetic alluvium around Varanasi and Allahbad. In 1964, a complete skull of *Elphas antiquus* was excavated from the Older Alluvium near Gurgaon in Haryana (Khan, 1968).

The Belan and the Seoti rivers in Allahabad district have preserved good faunal remains of the Quaternary period. The fauna collected includes *Equus* sp. *Equus onager khur*, *Bos* sp.' *Bubalus* sp., *Gazella* sp., *Antilope* sp., *Cervus* sp., *Elephas* sp., *Govialis* sp. and *Trionyx* sp. Fossils are concentrated in the two lower units viz., the Boulder-clays and Gravel-sands, without any appearent difference in the faunal assemblages from the two units.

Satsangi and Dutta (1968) opined that this faunal assemblage is comparable to that from the Jamuna and the Ganges. The latter have been assigned by Falconer (1865) and Pilgrim (1905) to a horizon of the Pleistocene, slightly younger than the Narmada alluvial deposits. Chakravarty (1931) assigned a Middle Pleistocene age to the Narmada beds and an Upper Pleistocene age to the Gangetic alluvium.

Dassarma (1979) has suggested that the faunal assemblages of the Older Alluvial deposits of the Ganges, Jamuna and the Sone Valleys are comparable to the Upper Narmada Group, characterised by the occurrence of *Bos namadicus*, *Palaeoloxodon* and *Setraprotodon*. This assemblage according to him favours an Upper Pleistocene age.

A Late Pleistocene palaeontological site discovered in the Paikar Valley near Gaya in Bihar yielded fossils of *Cervus* sp., *Axis* sp., *Bos* sp.. *Bubalus* sp., and *Emys* sp. (Badam, 1976). Tools of Acheulian characters (ovates, handaxes, cleavers, scrapers and flakes) were also collected from deposits yielding fossils.

(*b*) *Mahanadi Valley* : A number of vertebrate fossils (*Bos* sp., *Bos namadicus*, *Ovis*/*Capra Equus namadicus*) have, for the first time been discovered in the Upper Mahanadi Valley (Joshi *et al.*, 1980). Middle Palaeolithic tools were generally found associated with the fossils. Though the faunal material is scanty, it helps to fix the Stone Age chronology for the Middle Palaeolithic cultures. The presence of the fossils indicates that the valley was probably a vast savannah land with abundant vegetation and water which supported a variety of these ungulates. During the late Pleistocene the nearby forests must have provided a varied assemblage of wild animals. Even today jackal, wolf, hare, nilgai, chital, antelope, deer, buffalo, bear, lion and leopard abound the hilly and forested areas.

(*c*) *Godavari Valley* : One of the earliest discoveries of fossil vertebrates from the Godavari Valley was made by Pilgrim (1905) who reported the presence of *Elephas antiquus*, *Hippopotamus palaeindicus*, *Equus namadicus* and *Crocodylus*, Tirpathy (1967) collected *Bos namadicus Bubalus palaeindicus*, *Equus namadicus*, *Hexaprotodon namadicus*, *Cervus* sp, *Palaeoloxodon namadicus*. *Stegodon insignis* and *Crocodylus* from the Godavari and its tributaries, the Pravara and the Mula. Subsequently, Sankalia (1964), Joshi *et al.* (1966), Rajaguru (1968-69), Badam (1973) and Joshi *et al.* (1978), discovered from various localities more fossils in association with Early and Middle Palaeolithic tools. These studies made some significant additions to the faunal list, that of

Elephas hysudricus, *Bubalus bubalis*, *Elephas maximus* and *Cervus duvauceli*.

The alluvial deposits of the Godavari Valley were earlier believed to be equivalent to the Narmada deposits (Pilgrim, 1905). However, recent biostratigraphical studies support the general observation that through the Upper Pleistocene alluvia are well preserved in the shallow valleys of the Deccan, there is no convincing evidence for the presence of Middle Pleistocene formations in the Godavari Valley. It is, therefore, necessary to revise our earlier views on the so-called Middle Pleistocene fauna discovered in the Deccan in general and in the Godavary Valley in particular. As far as the Godavari is concerned, so far there is only a single 14-C date of about 19,000 B.P. for the upper part of the calcareous alluvium exposed around Paithan (Corvinus *et al.*, 1972-73). A few semirolled Middle Palaeolithic tools along with the limb bones of *Bos* sp. were collected from the sands and gravels occurring slightly below this well-dated formation (Rajaguru, 1968-69). The author has made a morphological study of fossils collected from the Older Alluvium of the Upper Godavari Valley and assigns this alluvium to the Upper Pleistocene. It is also suggested that *Bos namadicus* (found along with Lower Palaeolithic tools of Late Acheulian characters at Gangapur), *Elephas namadicus*, *Equus namadicus* and *Bos namadicus* (found in association with Lower and Middle Palaeolithic tools in the Older Alluvium around Nevasa in the Pravara Valley and in the Upper Godavari) are in fact the Middle Pleistocene (?) survivors in the Upper Pleistocene period. This hypothesis is supported by a well dated Jaw of *Bos namadicus* (32,000 B.P.) recovered from the buried channel (about 30 m below the surface) of the Mula, a southerly tributary of the Upper Godavari (Rajaguru, 1970). Further, a few 14-C assays on fresh water shells and drift wood found in the Older Alluvial fills from the source region of the Godavari (Rajaguru and Badam, 1976) confirm the general dating to the Upper Pleistocene only of the exposed alluvial fills.

The litho- and bio-stratigraphy of the Central Godavari Valley can tentatively be reconstructed as follows (from top to bottom) :

Litho-and Bio-stratigraphy of the Central Godavari Valley

Lithological Units	*Fauna*	*Probable Age*
1. Less Calcareous brownish silts with occasional patches of gravels and sands.	—	Mid-Holocene (4,000-2,000 yrs. B.P.)
2. Black soil (Vertisol)	—	Early Holocene (10,000-4,000 yrs. B.P.)
3. Calcareous brownish silt with intercelated channel gravels.	*Bos*, *Bubalus*, *Elephas maximus*, *Elephas namadicus*, *Equus namadicus*, *Unio* and other fresh water molluscs.	Late Pleistocene (40,000-10,000 yrs. B.P.)
4. High level gravels resting on rock-cut valley pediment.	A few highly mineralised unidentifiable fragmentary bones.	Late/Mid-Pleistocene (150,000-40,000 yrs. B.P.)
5. Pediplained erosional surfaces (500-600 m) with thin cappings of pedocal soils.	—	Terrtiary to Early Pleistocene.

(*d*) *Manjra Valley** : Recently one of the richest palaeontological treasures in the country, the third in order of importance and abundance after the Siwaliks of NW India and the Narmada Valley in Madhya Pradesh was discovered in the Manjra, a major southerly tributary of the Godavari. The importance of the fossils with regard to provenance is

*Though the Manjra is a tributary of the Godavari, it has been dealt with separately because of the rich palaeontological data that it has yielded.

enhanced by the rich complementary geological and archaeological data that the Valley has yielded. A large number of fossils of *Elephas maximus*, *Elephas hysudricus*, *Stegodon insignis ganesa*, *Sus*, sp., *Bos namadicus*, *Bubalus*, *bubabis*, *Equus namadicus*, *Axis axis*, *Antilope cervicaprà*, *Hippopotamus* sp., *Cervus unicolor*, *Cervus duvauceli*, *Crocodylus* sp. and Chelonia were discovered in the low energy overbank flood deposits of the Upper Manjra at Dhanegaon (18°36′N: 76°10′E), Wangdari (18°35′N: 76°25′E), Tadula 18°35′N: 76°25′E) and Ganjur (18°35′N: 76°24′E). The varied faunal assemblage discovered from the valley has a profound bearing on the palaeoecological conditions of the valley when the late Pleistocene sediments were being deposited. It is of interest to note that fossils of Proboscidea were predominantly found in abandoned ox-bow lake formations near Dhanegaon. The old channel deposits at Wangdari (about 30 km east of Dhanegaon) yielded the maximum number of ungulates out of which fossils of *Bos* account for nearly 75% of the total collection. This situation substantiated by sedimentological studies would probably point to the distribution of these animals being controlled by local ecological foctors. The dominance of elephants suggests a heavily vegetated environment, while that of cattle indicates savannah landscape.

Our investigations have also revealed the existence of several deep water pools in the valley. One such perennially deep water pool at Tadula, which occupied an area of 15 acres, served as what would be the richest Pleistocene animal habitat in the Deccan. During the Pleistocene the Manjra Valley had good vegetation cover, probably a savannah forest, with several deep water pools. The presence of fossil reptiles speaks of abundant water in the channels of the Manjra. On the whole the climate during this period was more humid than prevails today in the region.

Fossils similar to those found in the Manjra have been discovered from the yellowish sandy bed (Upper Group) of the Central Narmada Valley dated to about 31,750 B.P. and from the Godavari and Bhima river valleys from where we have a number of 14-C dates ranging from 40,000 B.P. onwards. The Manjra Valley fossils, on morphological grounds are assigned a late Pleistocene age.

Composite stratigraphy of the Manjra Valley along with the palaeontological data is summed up below:

Litho units	*Plalaeontological findings*	*Probable climate*	*Probable Age*
Non calcareous dark, brown silt and gravels	—	Semi-arid monsoonic	Early to Mid Holocene
Calcareous Brownish silt gravels	*Equus namadicus*, *Bos namadicus*, *Bubalus bubalis*, *Axis axis*, *Antilope cervicapra*, *Sus* sp., *Elephas maximus*, *Elephas hysudricus*, *Stegodon insignis ganesa*, *Crocodylus* sp., Chelonia, *Unio* sp.	Semi-arid monsoonic with frequent storm raids	Late Pleistocene
Laterite	—	sub-humid monsoonic	Late Tertiary to Early Pleistocene

(*e*) *The Krishna Valley* : The Krishna Valley has yielded scantier faunal material than other Peninsular deposits despite similar ecological and geological conditions. Perhaps the earliest record of fossils from the Krishna and its tributaries is by Foote (1876). He discovered fossils of *Bos namadicus* (?) and an upper jaw of rhinoceros, which he described as a new species, *Rhinoceros deccanensis*, from the ossiferous deposits near Gokak in district Belgaum on the Ghataprabha river. After a big lull lasting nearly a hundred years, Paddayya (1969) discovered a fossiliferous Middle Palaeolithic site near Hagargundi on the left bank of the river Bhima. Fossils discovered by him include *Bos namadicus*, *Cervus* sp. and *Elephas* sp. The fossils are found in a clear-cut stratigraphical context. In fact the importance of Hagargundi centres around the occurrence of animal fossils as this is perhaps one of the very few sites in the Krishna Valley where Stone Age tools occur in association with vertebrate fossils. The fossils reported earlier come from non-implementiferous areas. Ansari (1970) reported along with a pebble tool industry (of typical Sohan type) fossils of *Bos namadicus* in Nittur, on the right bank of river Tungabhadra in Mysore State. Recently, fossils of *Bos* sp. were discovered along with Middle Palaeolithic tools in sandy pebbly gravel from the Bhima river valley near Dhond. Borkhal Dam, on the main channel of the Krishna yielded fragments of *Elephas* tusk. Pieces of *Elephas* tusk were also discovered in a gravel bed occurring 20 m below the surface in the cut-off trench of the dam site at Dhom, a place 20 km downstream of Mahabaleshwar. This is the only fossil site in the Krishna where fossils have been dated to $37{,}640^{+9{,}200}_{-4{,}250}$ years B.P. by C-14 method (Corvinus *et. al*.. 1972-73).

On stratigraphical, palaeontological and cultural grounds, therefore, the deposits in the Krishna have been placed in the latter part of the Pleistocene. It is to be admitted, however, that palaeontological work in the Krishna basin needs rigorous attention.

(f) The Ghod Valley: while the only notable occurrence of fossil vertebrates from the Bhima comes from Hagargundi (Paddayya, 1969), the Ghod river, a tributary of the Bhima, has in recent years yielded half a dozen palaeontological sites namely, Inamgaon, Sirasgaon Kanta, Chinchini, Chandoli, Khadki and Kalamb (Kajale, 1979). All the sites are located upstream of Inamgaon—the locality that has yielded the maximum number of fossils from the Ghod. The fossils discovered include *Elephas maximus*, *Elephas* sp., *Bos namadicus*, *Bos/Bubalus*, *Hippopotamus* sp., *Cervus unicolor*, *Equus namadicus*, *Canis* sp., *Leptobos* sp., *Sus* sp., and Chelonia.

Most of the fossils have been excavated from the gravel bed dated to about 20,000 years B.P. by C-14 method on the basis of fresh water molluscan shells. The discovery of hippo which is the first of its kind from the terrain south of the Godavari Valley, has a profound bearing on the palaeo-environmental conditions in the Ghod Valley during late Pleistocene. The sedimentary characters of the formations indicate that they were deposited either as braid bars or point bars with a series of water pools in them. This is evidenced by the occurrence of lenticular bands of silt and clay in the pebble gravel. Such pools probably with tall grass cover, might have provided a suitable habitat for water-loving animals such as the hippo. Though the animal inhabited swampy plain areas where sluggish water predominates, the presence of the remains of elephant, horse, buffalo, cattle, deer, pig and wild bull in the valley indicates a tropical semi-arid savannah type of environment. The region was experiencing warm monsoonic climate with plateaux and lowlands covered by dense tall grass and shrubs. The high crowned nature of the teeth of almost all the animals which wear to a rasp-like chewing surface, indicates a herbivorous diet.

Leptobos and *Sus* are being reported for the first time from the Ghod Valley. While the former, which is the biggest fossil find from the area so far, was excavated from within the yellow silt, the latter came from the underlying gravelly beds.

The litho-bio and chrono-stratigraphic units in the Ghod Valley are tabulated on page 130.

(g) *The Kurnool Caves* : There are several caves in the limestone formations of the Kurnool District in Andhra Pradesh which have been known to palaeontologists and archaeologists since the second quarter of the last century.

The Kurnool Caves have disclosed a rich faunal assemblage which is significant for the reconstruction of late Pleistocene ecology and climate in the area. Some of the fauna may well be the representatives of their living counterparts. Some of the caves have yielded faunal material in association with lithic and bone artefacts ascribed to a phase of Indian Upper Palaeolithic. The dating of the cultural material on palaeontological grounds at Kurnool Caves, therefore, is not as difficult as in some of the river valleys in the Deccan where some fossils are found in association with both Lower and Middle Palaeolithic materials.

A list of the fauna excavated from the caves is given in Table-1. Common names of the species have been added for the benefit of the readers.

The Kurnool fauna helps in understanding the evolutionary processes and migration patterns of some of the animals and as such it is important to add some remarks on individual species connected with migration. As Lydekker (1886) has pointed out, the genera *Cynocephalus* and *Manis* are identical with the living African species while *Rhinoceros*, *Hystrix* and *Viverra* are distinct from the species now living in India. The occurrence of *Cynocephalus*, *Hyaena*, *Equus* and *Manis*

Summary of Pleistocene litho-bio and chronostratigraphic units (After Kajale, 1979)

	Lithological Units	*Biological findings*	*Age*
1.	Calcreted brownish sandy silts or silty sands; intercalated with sandy pebbly gravel particularly in the lower parts, maximum thickness up to 10 m.	*Bubalus* sp., *Bos* sp., *Leptobos* sp., *Canis* sp., *Unio* sp., A few pollen grains of *Acacia* sp., *Eugenia* sp. and abundance of *Holoptelea* sp.	Terminal Pleistocene.
2.	Coarser gravels with subfacies of bouldery pebbly and sandy pebbly gravels and intercalated patches of silt and clays, maximum thickness upto 10 m.	*Canis* sp., *Equus namadicus*, *Bos namadicus*, *Bubalus* sp., *Hippopotamus* sp., *Cervus unicolor*, *Sus* sp., *Elephas* sp., *Unio* sp.	c. 20,000 B.P. (C-14 date obtained on fresh water molluscan shells).
3.	Buried alluvium at the depth of 13 m below the modern bed level.	Dicotyledonous wood in carbonised condition.	c. 39,000 B.P. (C-14 date obtained on carbonised wood).

indicates that many of the existing Ethiopian mammals were derived from India. Interestingly, some of the forms have gradually died out in India to become dominant in Africa. Those which have not totally disappeared are either poorly represented or smaller in size.

In India, species of *Cynocephalus* and *Hyaena* disappeared after the Pleistocene. *Macrotherium sindiense*, the gigantic Siwalki edentate, presents features connecting it with *Manis* and is succeeded by the smaller *Manis gigantea* of Kurnool which has now migrated to Africa. However, all the species of *Manis* now inhabiting Peninsular India are of smaller size. *Atherura* now totally unrepresented in India occurs in Africa. *Equus* which has also died out as a wild genus in the greater part of India, has attained great development in Africa. The lion is a comparatively rare animal in India now but very abundant in Africa. *Felis chaus* is an example of a species which probably originated in India and is still common here. However, it has also extended its range into Africa. The *Viverra* and *Hystrix* of the Kurnool probably provide an evolutionary stage between the Siwalik representatives and existing forms of those genera, possibly the existing *Sus cristatus* was derived from the Siwalik *Sus falconeri* which may also have given rise to the now extinct *Sus karnuliensis*. This group of pigs has also extended into Africa. *Rhinoceros karnuliensis* or even *Rhinoceros deccanensis* have no representatives at present in India. According to Lydekker (1886) the Kurnool species appears to show characters connecting it on the one hand with *R. etruscus* (European) and *R. deccanensis* and on the other with *R. bicornis* (African).

The above account supplements the evidence, also efforded by the Siwalik fauna, that there was a faunal link between Asia and Africa.

As mentioned earlier, the varied assemblage of the Kurnool fauna throws interesting light on the palaeoecology of the area as a whole during the late Pleistocene. Flocking animals like *Antilope cervicapra*, *Gazella gazella*, *Cervus unicolor* and *Boselaphus tragocamelus* indicate a scrub to tree jungle in the hilly and plateau country and a tall grass cover in the plains. The presence of *Bos/Bubalus* suggests that the plateaus and stremsides might have provided a plentiful supply of grass while the hilly slopes had a tree cover. The occurrence of *Presbytis entellus*, the arboreal langur, which moves in packs that can live on rocks and cliffs (provided there are shady groves and accessible water) also points to a small forest-type vegetation (Murty 1975).

Rhinoceroses which have totally disappeared from southern India, must have inhabited this area when the low hills were forested with swamps in the short canyons surrounded by grass. The presence of *Tragulus meminna*, *Tetracerus quadricornis*, *Sus cristatus*, *Hystrix crassidens*, *Lepus nigricollis*. *Felis chaus* and *Viverra karnuliensis* also suggests a scanty bush jungle around

Table-1

Fauna of the Kurnool Caves (after Lydekker, 1886; Murty, 1975), (Nomenclature brought up to date after Ellerman & Morrison-Scott, 1951)

Class/order	*Species/Genus*	*Common name*
Mammalia		
Primates	*Presbytis entellus*	Langur
	Papio sp.	Baboon
Carnivora	*Panthera tigris*	Tiger or Lion
	Panthera cf. *pardus*	Leopard
	Felis chaus	Jungle cat
	Felis rubiginosa	Rusty-spotted cat
	Crocuta crocuta	Spotted hyaena
	Viverra karnuliensis	Civet
	Prionodon sp.	Linsang
	Herpestes edwardsi	Indian grey mongoose
	Herpestes fuscus	Indian brown mongoose
	Melursus ursinus	Sloth bear
Insectivora	*Sorex* sp.	Shrew
Chiroptera	*Taphozous saccolaimus*	Pouch-bearing bat
	Hipposideros diadema	Large Malay leaf-nosed bat
Rodentia	*Sciurus* sp.	Squirrel
	Tatera indica	Indian gerbil
	Bandicota indica	Large bandicoot rat
	Bandicota bengalensis	Lesser bandicoot rat
	Millardis mettada	Soft-furred field-rat; metad.
	Mus platythrix	Indian brown spiny mouse
	Colunda ellioti	Indian bush rat
	Hystrix crassidens	Porcupine
	Atherura karnuliensis	Borcupine
	Lepus cf. *nigricollis*	Black-naped hare
Perissodactyla	*Equus asinus*	Ass
	Rhinoceros karnuliensis	Rhinoceros
Artiodactyla	*Bos* or *Bubalus* sp.	Ox or buffalo
	Boselaphus tragocamelus	Nilgai
	Gazella gazella bennetti	Chinkara
	Antilope cervicapra	Black buck
	Tetracerus quadricornis	Four-horned antelope
	Cervus unicolor	Sambar
	Axis axis	Chital
	Muntiacus muntjak	Barking deer
	Tragulus cf. *memmina*	Mouse deer
	Sus scrofa cristatus	Indian wild boar
	Sus karnuliensis	Pig
Pholidota	*Smutsia gigentea*	Pangolin
Reptilia	*Crocodylus* sp.	Crocodile
	Varanus dracaena	Varanus
	Python molurus	Python
	Ptyas mucosus	Indian rat snake
Amphibia	*Bufo* cf. *melanostictus*	Common Indian toad

in this hilly country. The faunal evidence on the whole, therefore, suggests a thicker vegetation cover in this region during the late Pleistocene times.

Most of the ungulates excepting the domesticated forms (ox, sheep, goat, pig etc,) have disappeared from this region. However, some species of antelopes and cervids still inhabit the forested regions of Nallamalai and other neighbouring ranges. The animals known in the late Pleistocene and inhabiting the cave areas to this day include *Felis chaus, Hyaena hyaena, Viverricula indica, Herpestes edwardsi, Hystrix indica, Lepus nigricollis, Golunda* sp., *Mus* sp., *Rattus* sp., *Bandicoota* sp., and *Manis crassicaudata*. Changed ecology has not threatened the survival of these animals to a great extent.

The total evidence (archaeological, faunal and geomorphological) suggests that these sites (both open-air and cave) represent Upper Palaeolithic way stations or transit sites (Murty 1975).

OTHER DISCOVERIES

In addition to the fossil discoveries mentioned above, several new fossiliferous localities have come to light in recent times. The more important ones are listed below:

1. Numerous vertebrate fossils (belonging to Proboscidea, Rodentia, Carnivora, Equidae, Bovidae, Suidae, Crocodilidae and Chelonia) have been collected from the Gandheswary river valley near Susunia hill in West Bengal (Sastry 1968), Most significant among the collections are *Panthera* cf. *leo* (lion) and *Crocuta* cf. *sivalensis* (spotted hyaena), the former being the first definite record of fossil lion from India and the latter from any Pleistocene deposit in Peninsular India. *Crocuta* had probably migrated from the Siwaliks to Peninsular India during the Pleistocene. It is of interest to note that spotted hyaena now restricted to Africa had its origin in India while striped hyaena mainly restricted to India today, originated in Africa (Kurten, 1968).
2. A third metacarpal of *Equus* cf. *asinus* obtained from the eroded gravel on the left bank of rivar Meshvo in Gujarat, forms the first record of a Middle Palaeolithic fossil from Gujarat (Badam, 1977b).
3. The discovery of a partial skull of *Hypselephas hysudricus* in Tirunelveli District, (Prasad and Daniel, 1968) is of considerable interest as it throws new light on the distribution of Elephantidae during the Pleistocene.
4. A few discoveries of fossils from the Aiyalur region of Tamil Nadu include fossils of *Equus namadicus* (Khan, 1971), *Bos* sp. (Mamgain and Sastry, 1967), *Equus* and *Bos* (Saha, 1976) and a new species of *Bubalus, B. maruva-toorensis* (Ghosh *et al.*, 1972).
5. A partial skull of fossil *Rhinoceros* has recently been discovered from Coimbatore, Tamil Nadu (Jayakaran, 1980).
6. A few discoveries of fossils come from eastern Himalayan (e.g., Trivedy, 1966—from Tripura; Badam, 1974—from Assam; Badam, 1979b—from Garo Hills). The earlier discovery of fossils from Garo Hills is by Pentland (1828).

REMARKS ON THE PLEISTOCENE FAUNA

Great strides have been taken in palaeontological studies in India during the last thirty years. Many new fossiliferous localities have come to light in, for example, the Manjra, Ghod and Mahanadi valleys. Several new species have been discovered from various sites and the geological and geographical ranges of some have been revised e.g. of the hippo and *Sus* in the Ghod. The data obtained has thrown considerable light on the chronology and depositional environment of the Pleistocene deposits of India. Keeping in view the fact that the Pleistocene deposits in the Indian Sub-continent cover roughly an area of 500,000 sq km, the percentage of fossiliferous deposits is meagre. In the Himalayas the absence of the fossils in the post-Villafranchian deposits is an account of torrential rivers and high energy environment. In the Peninsular India there are very few sedimentary troughs suitable for better preservation of fossils. This is also due to strong erosive forces operating on the plateaux of Peninsular India during the vigorous monsoons.

Our recent studies have shown that major part of the exposed alluvium in Peninsular India is not older than the Upper Pleistocene and that the Middle Pleistocene(?) patches may probably be confined to some parts of the Narmada Valley only. It must also be admitted that the Middle Pleistocene deposits have so far only been vaguely dated by palaeontology and not a single absolute date is avaialble.

Until recently, the narmada alluvium and the fossils therein were considered as the standard post-Villafranchian deposits in India. During the last decade, however, palaeontological studies in the Narmada, the Godavari, the Bhima and the Pravara valleys have shown that fossils hitherto considered as index for the Middle Pleistocene (*Equus namadicus, Bos namadicus*) in fact range from early to late Pleistocene. There are reports of the occurrence of *Equus namadicus* even in the Lower Pleistocene deposits of the Upper Siwaliks. *Bos namadicus* survives late enough and is also reported from some Early Holocene deposits. *Stegodon insignis-ganesa* and *Elephas hysudricus* are also present from the Lower to the Upper Pleistocene in India. Species like *Elephas maximus, Cervus duvauceli* and *Rhinoceros unicornis* range from late Pleistocene to Holocene. Their presence in the late Pleistocene deposits of the Deccan river valleys is confirmed by several 14-C dates. The author is of the opinion that only *Hexaprotodon namadicus* and *Sus namadicus* may today be considered as index fossils for the Middle Pleistocene. The latter resembles Middle Pleistocene suids described from China, Burma and Java (Hooijer, 1963). In the light of recent faunal discoveries therefore, our concepts of what constitutes an index fossil assemblage for Lower, Middle and Upper Pleistocene, should be revised.

The upper part of the Upper Pleistocene deposits of the Narmada can be correlated with deposits on the Godavari, the Ghod and the Pravara where we have a score of C-14 dates more or less of the the same range along with identical fauna. Morphologically, the fauna from the Lower Narmada Group, which is associated with the Boulder Conglomerate, appears to be older (Hooijer, 1963) than that received from the Ghod, the Pravara and the Manjra valleys.

The wide distribution in time and space of some fossils may be accounted for by a similarity of ecological niches, climatic conditions and geographical history prevailing in most parts of Central and South India. The animals seem to have had a zonal distribution in these parts without any definite ecological barriers. Most of the forms appear to be late survivals from the Siwaliks, having migrated to other suitable areas in India (especially the Narmada-Godavari complex) when the conditions in northwest became unfavourable on account of glaciation. The ice-sheet as a result of Pleistocene glaciation pushed out repeatedly from the north-west. It acted as a physical and climatic barrier to the movement of animals northwards and forced the animals to move southwards.

However, many of the species became extinct in the course of such migrations due to adverse climatic conditions and allied factors like non-adaptability and hence are not represented in these deposits in such profusion or are totally absent. A few evolved into advanced froms in the Holocene.

The climate during the Pleistocene was at times more warm and humid and at other times much drier and cooler than today. The existence of such widely diverse phenomena gave rise to a profusion of large and varied fauna. However, this magnificant assemblage of animals was not totally indigenous to India. Progressive groups possibly of local origin were the primates, many giraffe-like forms, musk-deer, goats, buffaloes, bovids and pigs. The mammals which were shared with the contemporary fauna of Europe were the sabre-toothed cats, the hyaena, wolves, rhinoceroses, horses of the genus *Equus*, various deer, antelopes and hippopotamus. The migratory routes lay east and west of the Himalayas (Pilgrim, 1925) and most of the larger animals migrated from Egypt, Arabia, Central Asia and N. America through passes across Alaska, Siberia and Mongolia. Hippopotamus and elephants had their early origin in Central Africa from where they migrated outwards and entered India during the Tertiary period through Arabia and Iran. *Rhinoceros*, horse and camel all originating in North America, evolved in some countries of central and western Asia before migrating to India. The elephant and horse have been world travellers and populated almost every country of the world except Australia. Between India and Africa, the interchange of fauna probably took place more easily. There is sufficient evidence for the existence of land-bridge across the straits at the entrance of the Persian Gulf. A corresponding bridge across the Red Sea would have opened up a ready means of communication between India and African through Arabia. Hawever, the problem of animal migrations to and from India needs to be studied in more detail in view of new faunal evidences that have come to light in recent years. Population pressure, evolutionary pressure and slow climatic changes throughout the Tertiary seem to be other cause of animal migrations (Russell 1962) in addition to glaciation. India's population of higher mammals was far greater in the past than it is today. The sudden and widespread reduction of the vertebrates is a most startling event for the geologist and the biologist. In northwest India this reduction in the animal population is generally attributed to the effects of intense cold of glaciation while anthropogenic factors may have been responsible for the reduction of animals in the central and Peninsular India.

The complete absence, so far, of the remains of pre-*Homo sapiens* man excepting *Ramapithecus* in India is undoubtedly the biggest lacuna in Indian pre-historic archaeology. Though the handiwork of man in the form of stone tools and other artefacts is available in profusion, the absence of physical remains of the architects of these tools has been a puzzle alike to palaeontologists, geologists, archaeologists and anthropologists. Primitive man who certainly lived here must have left behind his bones and teeth somewhere and it is certain that with patience and luck they will come to light one day. As rightly pointed out by P.T. de Chardin, between Africa and Java, India happens to hold an exceptionally critical place as far as the origins of man are concerned.

The author feels that the evidence of fossils and Stone Age tools on the Narmada and its tributaries, the presence of a number of rock shelters in the vicinity of the Narmada river and the well preserved terraces make the Narmada Valley an ideal place for the hunt of the primitive man.

In conclusion, Pleistocene studies in India offer a challenging field of investigation to natural scientists, particularly geologists, palaeontologists and anthropologists.

Distribution of important fauna in the Pleistocene deposits of India along with their ages and associated cultural material is tabulated below.

Distribution of Fauna in the Pleistocene Deposits of India and their Probable Ages

Locality	*Important Fauna*	*Associated cultures*	*Probable age*		*Environment*
Kurnool, Ghod, Manjra, Pravara, Godavari, Krishna	*Canis* sp., *Bubalus* sp., *Cervus* ssp., *Bos namadicus*, *Elephas hysudricus*, *Elephas maximus*, *Rhinoceros unicornis*, *Bos Indicus*, *Hexaprotodon Palaeindicus*.	Bone tools, Burins, Blades, points, Scrapers, Flakes, Blades. Points, Borers.	Upper Palaeolithic Late Middle Palaeolithic	Late upper Pleistocene (also dated by C-14: 40,000 to 15,000 B.P.)	Savannah type with pockets of forests and swamps (humid in Kurnool)
Central Narmada (Upper group)	*Equus namadicus*, *Bos namadicus*, *Haxaprotodon*, *Palaeindicus*, *Elephas hysudricus*, *Stegodon insignisganesa*, *Cervus* ssp.	Scrapers, Flakes, Flake-blades, Points, Borers, Handaxes, Cleavers, Polyhedrals, Discoids, Choppers.	Middle Palaeolithic (Late Acheulian)	Early Upper Pleistocene	Savannah grassland interspersed with swamps
Central Narmada (Lower group)	*Sus namadicus*, *Elephas hysndricus*, *Equus namadicus*, *Bos namadicus*, *Hexaprotodon namadicus*, *Stegodon insignisganesa*.	Choppers, Handaxes, Cleavers, Flakes,	Lower Palaeolithic (Acheulian)	Middle Pleistocene (not well established)	Savannah grassland interspersed with swamps
Lower Karewa, Pinjor of Upper Siwaliks	*Equus sivalensis*, *Rhinoceros sivalensis*, *Rhinoceros palaendicus*, *Elephas hysudricus*, *Bos* sp., *Archidiskodon planifrons*, *sivatherium giganteum*.	No stone age tools		Lower Pleistocene	Valley & Open Savannah grassland with lakes and swamps.

Problems and Suggestions:

Inspite of the tremendous work done on the Indian Pleistocene deposits, there are some problems which need our attention:

1. A common agreement has to be reached on the placement of the Plio-pleistocene boundary.
2. The age of the Karewa gravels and that of the Boulder Conglomerate of the Siwalik zone. seems to be disputable in view of the absence in it of in situ organic or other material suitable for radiometric dating. Hitherto this age was generally taken as Middle Pleistocene (Cromerian) on the basis of the dating of the Narmada Boulder Conglomerate.
3. In the Deccan, most of the fossiliferous localities are associated with Stone Age culture. Hence the fossils must not be studied in isolation. An understanding of the stone Age tools manufactured by Early Man and found in association with fossils can add to our knowledge of the man-land relationship in the past.
4. Detailed macro morphological studies of the fossils can help in buliding a relative chronology of the Early and Middle Palaeolithic cultures in the Deccan, particularly in the Narmada and Godavari.
5. In the light of recent faunal discoveries, our concepts of what constitutes an index fossil assemblage for Lower, Middle and Upper Pleistocene should be revised.
6. The exposed alluvium in the Deccan is of late Pleistocene age. The Middle Pleistocene deposits and their faunal assemblages have to be throughly searched for.

REFERENCES

Agrawal, D.P. and S. Kusumgar, 1974. *Pre-historic Chronology and Radiocarbon dating in India*, p. 41, Munshiram Manoharlal, N. Delhi.

Ansari, Z.D., 1970. Pebble tools from Nittur, Mysore State, *Indian Antiquity*, 4 (1-4), pp. 1-7.

Badam, G.L., 1968. Note on the occurence of the fossil vertebrates in the Karewas of Kashmir, *Res. Bull. Punjab Univ.* (N.S.), *19* (3-4), pp. 453-455.

——1972. Additional mammalian fossils in the Karewas of Kashmir, *Curr. Sci.*, *41* (14), pp. 529-530.

——1973. Pleistocene fossil studies, *Bull. Deccan College PRI*, *33* (1-4), pp. 21-40.

——1974. Fossil elephants from the Brahmputra Valley, Assam, India, *Jour. Assam Sci. Soc.*, *17* (1-2), pp. 75-78.

——1976. *Society of Vertebrate Palaeontology, News Bulletin*, *108*, pp. 39-41.

——1977a. The Upper Siwalik mammalian fossils and the problem of Neogene—Quaternary boundary in India, (in Russian), *Bull. Comm. Quat. Res. USSR*, *47* pp. 37-44.

——1977b. Significance of Palaeontological studies in Indian Pleistocene deposits, *Arch. Studies*, *II*, pp. 71-82.

——1979a. Quaternary palaeontology of the Central Narmada Valley and its implications in the Pre-historic studies, *G.S.I. Misc. Publ.*, *45*, pp. 311-320.

——1979b. *Pleistocene Fauna of India*, Deccan College PGRI, India, 250 pp.

——1982. Biostratigraphy of the Central Narmada Valley—A reappraisal, *Indian Archaeology—New Perspectives*, Prachya Niketan, Bhopal, pp. 38-47.

Balasundaram, M.S. & Sastry M.V.A., 1972. Plio-Pleistocene boundary in sediments of the Indian sub-continent, *Inter. Coll. on "The boundary between Neogene and Quaternary"*, collected papers, *3*, USSR.

Chakaravarty, D.K., 1931. On a *Stegodon* molar from the older Gangetic alluvium near Banaras, *Quatar. Jour. Geol. Min. Met. Soc. India*, *3*, pp. 115-125.

——1935. On the discovery of a Pre-historic fossil elephant in the Allahabad distt., *Curr. Sci. 3* (8), pp. 364-365.

——1938. On the *Palaeoloxodon namadicus* mandible, *Quatar, Jour. Geol. Min. Met. Soc. India 10*, pp. 143-149.

Colbert, E.H., 1942. The geological successions of the Proboscidea in India, In: Osborn, H.F.; *Probos cidea, Amer. Mus. Nat. History*, *2*, pp. 1421-1521.

——1951. Discussion on Plio-Pleistocene boundary, *18th Int, Geol. Congress*, *11*, pp. 64.

Corvinus, G.; S.N. Rajaguru & G.G. Majumdar, 1972-73. Some observtiaons on the Quaternary of Western Maharashtra, India, *Quartar.*, *23/24*, pp. 53-69.

Dassarma, D.C., 1979. Some observations on the Quaternary Stratigraphy and mammal assemblages of India, *G.S.I. Misc. Publ.*, *45*, pp. 279-287.

De Terra, H. and Paterson T.T., 1939. *Studies on the Ice age in India and associated human cultures*, *Publ. Carn. Inst. Washington*, *493*, pp. 1-354.

Ellerman, J.R. and Morrison-Scott T.C.S., 1951. *Checklist of Palaearctic and Indian mammals*, Trustees British Museum (Natural History), London, Alden Press, Oxford.

Falconer, H., 1865. Fluviatile deposits of the Ganges, *Quartar. Jour. Geol. Soc. London*, *21*, pp. 311-389.

Foote R.B., 1876. The geological features of South Mahratta Country and adjacent districts, *Mem. G.S.I.*, *12*, (1), pp. 1-256.

Ghosh, R.K.; Paul S.N. and Saha K.D., 1972. A new Pleistocene Buffalo from Tiruchirapalli districts, Tamil Nadu, *Jour. Zool. Soc. India*, *24* (1), pp. 97-102.

Gill, W.D. 1951. The stratigraphy of Siwalik series in the northern Potwar, Punjab, Pakistan, *Quartar. Jour. Geol. Soc., London*, *107* (4), pp. 375-394.

Hora, S.L. 1937. On fossil fish remains from the Karewas of Kashmir, *Rec. G.S.I. 72*, (2), pp. 178-187.

Hooijer, D.A. 1963. Preliminary identification of some fossil mammals from Narmada Valley, India, *Rivista Di Scienze Prehistoriche*, *18*, (1-4), p. 20.

Jayakaran, S.C. 1980. Fosil Rhinoceros from Tamil Nadu, *Curr. Sci. 49*, (9), pp. 346-347.

Joshi, R.V.; Bopardikar, B.P. and Sali S.A. 1966. Animal fossil and early stone age tools from Gangapur on the Godavari river (Nasik distt., Maharashtra State), *Curr. Sci. 35*, (13), p. 344.

Joshi, R.V.; Majumdar, G.G. Rajaguru S.N., Pappu R.S. and Badam G.L. 1978. Late Pleistocene history of the Upper Godavari Valley, India, *Recent Researches in Geology*, *4*, pp. 381-387.

Joshi, R.V.; Badam, G.L. and Pandey R.P. 1980. Late Pleistocene animal fossils and stone age cultures in Upper Mahanadi Valley, M.P., *The Eastern Anthropologist*, *33*, (2), pp. 169-175.

Kajale, M.D. 1979. *Bioarchaeology of the Ghod Valley, Maharashtra*, unpublished Ph.D. Thesis, Poona Univ.

Keller, H.M., Tahirkheli R.A.K.; Mirza M.A.; Johnson, G.D.; Johnson, N.M. and Opdyke, N.D. 1977. Magnetic polarity, stratigraphy of the Upper Siwalik deposits Pabbi Hills, Pakistan, *Earth and Planetry Sci. letters*, *36*, pp. 187-201.

Khan, E., 1968. Pleistocene stratigraphy in India, *Ann. Geol., Dept. Aligarh Muslim Univ.*, 4, pp. 61-72.

——1971. Pleistocene deposits around Ariyalur (Madras), *Curr. Sci. 40*, (2), pp. 37-38.

Kurten, B., 1968. *Pleistocene mammals of Europe*; Weidenfield and Nicholson, London.

Lewis, G.E., 1937. A new Siwalik Correlation, *Amer. Journ. Sci.* Ser. 5, *33*, pp. 191-204.

Lydekker, R., 1886. Fauna of Kurnool Caves, *Pal. Ind.*, Ser. C, *4* (2), pp. 23-58.

Mamgain, V.D. and Sastry, M.V.A., 1967. Note on the occurence of Late Pleistocene fossils near Ariyalur, Tiruchirapalli distt., Madras, *Indian Minerals*, *21* (1), pp. 61-62.

Mathew, W.D., 1929. Critical observations upon Siwalik mammals, *Bull. Amer. Mus. Nat. History*, *56*, pp. 437-560.

Meadow, R.H., 1981. Notes on the Faunal Remains from Mehargarh, Pakistan, with a Focus, on cattle (*Bos*) (in press).

Medlicott, H.B., 1873. Note on the celt found by Mr. Hacket in the ossiferous deposits of the Narmada Valley (Pliocene of Falconer), on the age of the deposits, *Rec. G.S.I.*, *6* (3), pp. 49-57.

Murty, M.L.K., 1975. Late Pleistocene fauna of Kurnool caves, South India, In Clason, A.T. (ed.) *Archaeozoological studies*, North Holland Publishing Co., Amsterdam and New York, pp. 132-138.

Paddaya, K., 1969. Hagargundi: A fossiliferous Middle stone age site on the Bhima river, *Jour. Asiatic Soc. Bengal*, *11*, (1-4), pp. 12-14.

Pentland, J.B., 1828. Description of fossil remains of animals from the northeast border of Bengal, *Trans. Geol. Soc., London*, Ser. 2, *2*, pp. 394-395.

Pilgrim, G.E., 1905. On the occurrence of *Elephas antiquus* (*namadicus*) in the Godavari alluvium with remarks on the species, its distribution and the age of the associated Indian deposits, *Rec. G.S.I.*, *32* (3), pp. 199-218.

——1925. The migration of Indian Mammals, *Presidential Address Section of Geology*, *12th Ind. Sci. Congress*.

——1944. The lower limit of Pleistocene in Europe and Asia, *Geol. Mag. 81*, pp. 28-38.

Prasad, K.N. and Daniel, J.A. 1968. On the occurrence of *Hypselephas hysudricus*, in the Pleistocene deposits of Tirunelveli valley, Madras state, *Curr. Sci.*, *37* (18), pp. 516-517.

Rajaguru, S.N. 1968-69. Some new fossil discovery from Western Maharashtra, India, *Puratattva 2*, pp. 16-21.

——1970. *Studies in the Late Pleistocene of the Mula Mutha Valley*, unpublished Ph.D. Thesis, Poona Univ.

Rajaguru, S.N. and Badam, G.L. 1976. Litho-and Bio-stratigraphy of the Quaternary formations in the Central Godavari Valley, Maharashtra, Symposium on "*Deccan Traps and Bauxites*", G.S.I. Poona, Abst. 45.

Russell, L.S. 1962. Mammalian migrations in the Pleistocene *probleme of Pleistocene Epoch and Arctic area 2*, (2), pp. 48-55.

Saha, K.D. 1976. Fossil Vertebrates from Maruvattor, Tiruchirapalli distt., Madras, *Curr. Sci.*, *45*, (5), p. 18.

Sahni, M.R. and Khan, E. 1964. Stratigraphy, structure and correlation of the Upper Siwaliks, east of Chandigarh, *Jour. Pal. Soc. India*, *4*, pp. 61-74.

Sahni, A. 1981. Report on small collection of Karewa Vertebrates investigated under the Kashimr palaeoclimatic project, *Man and Environment*, *5*, p. 87.

Sankalia, H.D. 1964. Middle stone age culture in India and Pakistan, *Sci. 146*, (3642), pp. 365-375.

Sastry M.V.A. 1968. Pleistocene vertebrates from Susunia, Bankura distt., W. Bengal, *Indian Minerals*, *22*, p. 20.

Sastry, M.V.A. and Dutta, A.K., 1977. Review on Neogene/Quaternary boundary in India, *Annals. of Museum Geol. of Bologna*, Ser. 2a, *41*, pp. 331-340.

Satsangi, P.P. and Dutta, A.K. 1968. Progress report for the field season 1967-1968, unpublished G.S.I. report.

Supekar, S.G. 1968. *Pleistocene stratigraphy, prehistoric archaeology of the Central Narmada Basin*, unpublished Ph.D. Thesis, Poona Univ.

Tewari, B.S. and Kachroo, R.K. 1977. On the occurrence of *Equus sivalensis* from Karewas of Shopian, Kashmir Valley, *Recent Researches in Geology*, *3*, pp. 468-477.

Theobald, W. 1980. On the Tertiary and alluvial deposits of the Central portion of the Nerbudda Valley, *Mem. G.S.I.*, *2*, pp. 279-298.

Trivedy, A.N. 1966. A note on the finding of vertebrate fauna in the Surma Series of Tripura and its bearing on the stratigraphy of the area, *Curr. Sci.*, *35*, (3), pp. 68-69.

Tripathi, C. 1967. The Pleistocene alluvial deposits around Nevesa, Ahmednagar distt., Maharashtra, *Rec. G.S.I.*, *95*, (2), pp. 355-366.

Wadia, D.N. 1951. The transitional passage of Pliocene into the Pleistocene in NW Sub himalayas, *Proc. 18th Int. Geol. Cong.*, *2*, pp. 43-48.

Studies in Ancient Indian Technology: A Review

H.C. BHARDWAJ
Banaras Hindu University, Varanasi

THE technological studies have been neglected in India but recent years have shown the awareness of scientists to this branch. Technological studies require the investigation of the raw materials e.g., (stones, ores, native metals, clay) used by man, the processes innovated by him to extract materials e.g., copper, iron, from their ores and compounding the extracted materials e.g., preparation of arsenical copper and Tin bronzes etc. and making new class of compounds by combining various materials e.g., making of glass by fusion of silica, lime and colouring agents etc. etc.

The aim of the present paper is to survey technological studies of archaeological artifacts since independence. The aspects of stone age technology, agriculture, animal husbandary, irrigation and land utilization have recently been reviewed by Ray and Chakrabarti (1975: 219-232). This paper is confined to metal technology, pottery and glass with an emphasis on the areas not covered in the above cited review and the contradictory findings of the scholars.

Prime importance goes to the advent of copper and the genesis of its technology in Early Copper-bronze age cultures and further developments up to Early Historical Period. A good number of studies have been made (Bhardwaj 1965-66: 57-80, Lamberg-Karlovsky 1967:145-165, Bhardwaj 1970: 229-37, Agrawal 1971a, 1971b, Hegde 1972: 140). These studies have centered around the following problems:

I. Was the origin of copper-bronze technology in India independent or was it influenced from outside ?

II. What are the metallurgical affinities and relations amongst Early Copper-Bronze Age cultures ?

III. What are the main developments in copper-base metallurgy in Early Iron Age and Early Historic Period ?

Origin

Around 4000 B.C., smelting of copper ore is well documented at Tal-i-Iblis (south-east Iran, Kerman range). Lamberg-Karlovsky (1967) traces the diffusion of copper metallurgy in north-western zone comprising Sindh, Punjab and Rajasthan from Tal-i-Iblis. Agrawal (1971) supports this view. It would be too much to say that copper smelting originated here. There is a growing body of data to suggest that smelting of copper was being done by the 7th millennium B.C. in some parts of south-west Asia. Even copper from the neolithic levels of Cayonu Tepesi and Catal Huyuk level IX and Yarim tepe I, level 12 are all smelted Coppers and not native coppers as supposed earlier (Merpert 1977: 65-104, Maddin *et al.* 1980: 211-225). Copper slag has been found from Catal Huyuk VI, dated to late 7th-early 6th millennium B.C. So it must be emphasized that discovery of copper smelting is now datable to 7th millennium B.C. and not to 4000 B.C. as is generally supposed. So it is not reasonable to trace the diffusion in India of such an early discovery (7000 B.C.) in the middle of 3rd millennium B.C. from Iran via Afghanistan (Tal-i-Ablis or for that part from the metallurgical stages discernible at Mundigak in Afghanistan). Lamberg-Karlovsky (1967) attributes copper-bronze metallurgy of Pre-Harappan, Harappan and Post-Harappan Chalcolithic cultures to a closely linked metallurgical tradition. Agrawal *et al* (1971) are of the opinion that:

(i) Harappan metallurgy is a diffusion from West Asia.

(ii) Metallurgy of the central, Deccan and west Indian Chalcolithic cultures was probably largely indigenous: though Harappan influence can not be ruled out.

(iii) North-Eastern Zone copper metallurgy (the Copper Hoards) would have derived its metallurgical know-how from South East Asia.

(iv) Origin of Kayatha and Ganeshwar metal technology looks to be indigenous.

The technology of the copper arrow heads from Bagor datable to 2700-2100 B.C. (Misra 1971: 59-77) has an alleged similarity with Harappan arrow heads and is supposed to be derived from a source that catered to the needs of Harappan Communities.

In this connection it must be said that:

Though primary discovery of metal smelting would have been made in a particular cultural area, yet the idea would spread rapidly and it might be futile to trace simple and straight diffusions. It must be remembered that it is the local genius that has played the most important part in exploiting the discovery to suit his resources—with modifications in the processes according to the raw materials and needs. So the main emphasis of the technological studies has to be: to reconstruct the efforts of the local genius in exploiting, extracting and compounding the raw materials to produce and fabricate newer and better materials and artifacts.

Further, efflorescence of full bloom metallurgy including smelting of copper, lead, silver, use of electrum and wide variety of copper alloys in Harappan culture cannot be explained by diffusion from Tal-i-Iblis and Mundigak. The possibility of indigenous developments as suggested by the present author in 1965 cannot be ruled out. Recent evidence of copper smelting from Ganeshwar datable to *circa* 2700 B.C., from where remains of smelting crucibles and furnaces have been found along with a rich haul of copper celts and arrow heads is a pointer towards indigenous developments (Agrawal *et al* 1982: 127-28). These developments do not substantiate simple and straight diffusion but highlight the efforts of the local genius.

The Harappan Copper-bronze technology differed from the West Asiatic technology and possessed distinctive features of its own; it could have had an independent growth, though possibly sharing a common base with West Asiatic metallurgy.

Metallurgical affinities amongst Early Copper-Bronze Age Cultures

If we study the chemical and metallographic compositions of the various groups we find that Pre-Harappan, Harappan, various Post Harappan—Chalcolithic objects as well as the copper hoard objects have differences and that they should be considered as belonging to different technological categories (Bhardwaj, 1971).

Pre-Harappan Nal axe has 93.05% Cu, 2.14% Pb and 4.08% Ni with only traces of Arsenic and Mundigak I has 98.79% Cu, 1.06% Sn and 0.15% Fe. These do not show any affinity with Harappan Copper. Harappan Copper-bronze specimens show a wide variety of alloying including Copper-Arsenic alloy with upto 6.58% Arsenic from Harappa. Harappan Tin bronzes contain 2 to 26% tin and Copper-Lead alloy with 1 to 14.9% lead and even Copper-Nickel alloy containing 2 to 9.38% Nickel. This wide variety may be a pointer to the fact that Harappan Copper-base material came from various sources both from within India and outside.

So called Ganeshwar-Jodhpura culture (Agrawal *et al* 1982) represents an indegenous copper industry exploiting local mines of Khetri. The limited chemical analysis of the two objects does not show any affinity with that of Indus Culture. Agrawal *et al* (1982) have grounds to prove that Copper technology was well developed from the Pre-Harappan period in the Ganeshwar-Khetri area as early as 2700 B.C. and that they had evolved copper metallurgy in 3rd millennuim B.C. at Ganeshwar.

Table I

Percentage Composition of Ganeshwar Objects

Object and provenance	*Cu*	*Ag*	*As*	*Pb*	*Sn*	*Ni*	*Zn*	*Fe*
Copper celt from Ganeshwar	97.0	0.2	0.3	1.0	0.1	0.6	0.1	—
Copper arrow head from Ganeshwar	96.5	0.3	1.0	0.03	0.2	0.04	0.25	0.2

The impurity pattern of these Ganeshwar samples show that the copper used might have included native copper as it: includes the impurities of Silver, Arsenic and Iron. Further the absence of Sulphur indicates that they had mainly mined the native copper or oxide ores of the surface out-crops and had not mined deep for the ores.

Recent analysis of Harappan, copper hoards and Chalcolithic copper objects by Nautiyal *et al* (1981: 48-51) indicate that:

1. Harappan and Chalcolithic objects invariably show impurity of Nickel and thus may indicate common source of copper.

2. Tin alloying is a common practice of Harappans, while arsenic alloying is also practised by them.

3. Nickel and Tin are absent in Copper Hoards and these can be separated from the others by their arsenic alloying (1 to 8%) which is deliberate and that there is absence of tin alloying in general.

4. In chalcolithic objects pure unalloyed copper is the rule and arsenic and tin alloys look to be imports from other Cultures.

Probable Sources of Ores

Copper Ores: Harappans, and all the Chalcolithic cultures of Rajasthan and Deccan look to have used Khetri copper mines of Rajasthan. But some of the Harappan sites might have obtained their supply from Iran, Afghanistan, and Oman while the ores of Hazaribagh and Singhbhumi districts of Bihar were used by the Copper Hoard people and later cultures.

Tin Ores: Sources of Tin in antiquity have attracted the attention of scholars in India and abroad. Hedge (1979: 39-42) and Chakrabarti (1979: 62-74) mention areas of Hazaribagh-Gaya-Ranchi in south Bihar and Baster in M.P. as most significant. In Rajasthan tin ores are found in the Aravalli Hills, about 27 km north of Shahpura near Paroli in Bhilwara distt. and at Soniana in Udaipur district. In Gujarat the deposits occur within the Aravalli Hills near Hussainpura and Palanpur in Banas Kantha distt.

It is generally believed that Cassiterite in the form of "stream Tin" was exploited by Early metallurgists rather than the vein deposits as the former occurs as surface deposit and is to be just picked up.

Asthana's (1982) article on the Harappan Trade in Metals and Minerals: A regional approach deserves mention. It must be emphasized that many ores and minerals were traded in Early times and the Harappans took active part in the trade. The main sources were located in the high lands of Iran, Soviet Central Asia, Afghanistan, Baluchistan, Oman, Persian Gulf and interior of India.

There has been general shortage of Tin after the Harappan period: Neither the Chalcolithic cultures nor the copper hoards have used tin alloying. Does it mean that tin was coming to India from outside sources which ceased after the demise of Harappan Culture? Probably yes.

We note gradual diminishing of tin content in Ur Bronzes. For example, Bronzes from Royal graves of Ur contain about 8 to 12% tin, but the percentage of tin in Ur bronzes falls from 2500 B.C. to 2200 B.C. and we see gradual diminishing of tin content to 2% and by 2200 B.C. tin content is negligible (0.1%). No wonder tin shortage was a global affair around 2200 B.C.

Flactuations in composition of Indian bronzes might be of archaeological significance.

Arsenical Bronzes

It is now believed that the main alloy for the Near East during the early and middle Bronze Age is in fact not bronze but Arsenical copper and Tin bronze does eventually replace arsenical copper in late bronze Age (Eaton and Mekerrell 1976: 205-227). Agrawal (1978) reported new data on Copper Hoards, and the present author (Bhardwaj 1980: 235-247) discussed Early Indian Arsenical Copper. It is now generally agreed that Arsenical Copper preceded Tin bronze (Easton and Mackarell 1976). But since both the Harappan and Copper Hoard samples show arsenic alloying the precedence of the one over the other on this count cannot be established. While the Arsenical copper from Harappan sites might have been obtained from Tulamessi mines in Iran from where Cu_5As—Algodonite and Cu_3AS (Domeykite) are reported as native alloy. No such deposits are known to occur in India.

However, it must be pointed out both the Rajasthan and Bihar ores are well known to have arsenopyrite as associated mineral. Native Arsenic is conspicuous by its silvery white colour and as such there is a possibility of its having been obtained from long distance trade from Iran. Chitral in Pakistan has ores of arsenic: realgar (AS_2S_2) and orpiment (AS_2S_3). The occurrence of arsenical pyrite is reported from Sampthar hill in Kalimpong sub-division (West Bengal) and that of iron arsenides i.e., lollingite and leucopyrite from mica bearing pegmatites of Hazaribagh distt. of Bihar. Of course these are not of much economic importance today. So the question of the source of arsenic for copper Hoards of the Gangetic valley remains unanswered. However upto 1% arsenic reported from Ganeshwar samples could be the result of use of Khetri copper ores including native copper—and arsenic is known as an impurity therein.

Tin-Bronzes from Archaeological Excavations

The nature of copper-base material from Pre-Harappan assemblage is not known. Harappan sites: Harappa, Mohenjodaro, Rangpur have yielded bronzes, which show that copper-tin alloying was a regular practice and that there is no scaricity of tin in general. But coming to chalcolithic sites of Jorwe (1.78%), Nevasa (2.72%), Navdatoli (upto 4.37%) tin show a general scarcity of the metal. However, Somnath axe with 12.82% tin in Post-Harappan Chalcolithic is also reported. Sonepur rod show meagre 1.39% tin.

Daimabad Bronzes

Analysis of Daimabad bronzes by Archaeological Chemist, Government of India and Physical Research Laboratory Ahmedabad are contradictory (Chakrabarti 1979: 62-74). Former reports 0.85% to 6.51% tin in these bronzes, the latter finds tin to be absent and instead reports the presence of arsenic.

Copper-Hoards

Earlier analysis reported by Smith show a few of the copper hoard specimens to contain upto 13.3% tin. However, recent analysis by Agrawal (1978) show absence of tin and presence of arsenic instead.

So the picture that emerges is that tin is a scarce metal after the Harappan till we come to Early Historic period when we get high content tin bronzes from Taxila. Bronze is also reported from Prakash (Period II 600 B.C. and onwards) in Maharashtra and Sonepur II showed 32.42% Tin. Kausambi (5th-6th cent. B.C.) copper fragment showed 19.13% tin and Rajghat (Pd. IC—400-200 B.C.) show 13.99% Tin.

Copper-base metallurgy of Early Iron Age-Early Historic Period

A few analyses of P.G.W., copper objects reveal them to be of unalloyed copper. That by and large unalloyed copper was used in Early Iron age as attested by analysis of Rajghat Pd. I B copper objects (Bhardwaj 1969: 188-192). Similar position is revealed from the analysis of copper objects from Kausambi and Prakash.

However, tin alloying is again practised around 500-400 B.C. as revealed from Kausambi, Rajghat, Taxila and Prakash. Another feature worth noticing is the introduction of brass: Copper-Zinc alloy is attested both at Taxila around 300 B.C. and at Prakash in the late phase of NBP. The brass from Prakash is either copper-zinc alloy (17.75% Zinc, remainder copper) or leaded brass (25.86% Zn, 8.34% Pb and remainder copper).

Early Iron Technology

Upto about 1000 B.C. the various cultures had satisfied their needs for tools and weapons with either copper or Arsenic-copper alloy or copper-tin bronzes. But toxic nature of arsenic and general shortage of tin caused disturbance and thus gradually gave rise to the beginning of iron—followed by carburising and finally steel in various cultural horizons.

The beginning of the Iron age in India has been discussed by various authors and special mention may be made of Pleiner (1971). Technological studies have been limited mainly because of the hesitation of the archeologists to spare early samples and lack of laboratory facilities. The present author (Bhardwaj 1973: 391-400) reported the chemical, spectrographic and metallographic analyses of iron samples from Rajghat material dated to 600-400 B.C. The study concluded that—

1. There is no evidence of the use of meteoric iron.
2. The iron of these samples is slag bearing wrought iron which could be welded and forged.
3. It would not harden much on cooling.
4. Some of these objects might have been carburized during forging in charcoal fire.
5. The presence of small amount of iron carbide at the grain boundries shows that carburization was coming into vogue during NBP phase.
6. No flux was used.
7. Furnaces available at that time could not produce temperature much above 1180°C.
8. Banded structure shows that iron objects were forged stage by stage from a bloom to a bar then thining, pointing, folding and forged welding.
9. The Rajghat iron might have been obtained from Titaniferous ores with apatite complex, probably from Bihar.

Similar studies have been made on iron samples from Prakash (Athavale 1967) and Kausambi (Prakash and Singh 1968), Hegde (1975b) and Mahurjhari (Deo 1973: 77). The result of the main findings of these are reported in table II.

These studies confirm the evidence that wrought iron was the main material used in the Early days—with case hardening here and there. Forge welding of carburized iron plates is evidenced from the excavation of Dhatva iron hoe datable to the middle of the first millennium B.C. (Hegde 1975b: 48-56).

Steel Making

Some evidence of steel making has been reported by

Table I

Analysis of Ancient Indian Steel Objects

No.	*Date*	*Provenance*	*Object*	*Carbon %*	*Micro-structure*	*Hardness*	*Remarks*
1.	600 B.C.	Rajghat IB (Ancient Varanasi) U.P.	Nail	1.10	Equiaxed ferrite grains; small amount of iron carbide at the grain boundaries		Case hardened steel (Bhardwaj 1973)
2.	Circa 500 B.C.	Dhatwa, Distt. Surat, Gujarat	Hoe	—	—	Surface: 117-123 Inside: 99-107	—do— (Hegde 1975)
3.	700-600 B.C.	Mahurjhari, Distt. Nagpur	Axe	0.90	—	—	Steel (Dec. 1973)
4.	600 B.C.	Wurrigaon, M.P.	fragments of cast steel weapons	—	—	—	Cast steel These objects are housed in British Museum (Forbes 1964)
5.	100 B.C.	Prakash, Distt. Dhulia, Maharashtra	Axe	0.90	Equiaxed ferrite grains with small amount of pearlite at grain boundaries. Amount of pearlite is fairly constant over the whole area examined.	—	Low grade steel (Athavale 1968)
6.	125 B.C.	Besnagar, District Vidisha, M.P.	Piece of a broken sword	0.70	Elongated and irregularly disposed crystals of pearlite upon ferrite ground mass	Brinell hardness 146	Steel after quenching from 850°C in water specimen becomes martensitic (Marshall 1951)
7.	100 A.D.	Taxila, W. Punjab, (Pakistan)	Double edged sword	1.3-1.5	Slightly elongated grains of ferrite and spheroidal carbide, the result of decomposition of cementite	Brinell hardness 235	High Carbon steel (Marshall 1951)
8.	100 A.D.	Taxila, W. Punjab (Pakistan)	Carpenter's adze	1.23	—	—	High Carbon steel (Marshall 1951)
9.	100 B.C.	Kausambi U.P.	Arrow head	0.74	Grains of pearlite throughout the section	—	Steel (Prakash & Singh 1968)

the present author (Bhardwaj 1981). Presence of 0.9% Carbon has been taken as steel (Deo 1975). Kausambi arrow-head datable to 100 B.C. to 500 A.D. has been confirmed by metallographic studies as made of steel (Prakash and Singh 1968). Metallographic examination (Marshall 1951) of a broken sword from Besnagar, Distt. Vidisha and some tools from Taxila datable to 125 B.C. to 100 A.D. (confirm the use of steel making in ancient India).

This may be taken as an indication that after a few centuries of the carburization Process—a process for making homogenous steel-popularly known as Wootz might have been innovated in India and this process continued till modern times. My premise is that Chalybes, Greeks, Parthians and Chinese never, made real homogenous steel but only carburized iron and Indians deserve the credit for innovating steel by crucible process (Bhardwaj, 1981).

Quarrying and Mining

Quarrying of stones and mining of metalliferous ores has been practised since Pre-historic period in India. In the Indus civilization slabs of hammer-dressed limestone are found covering brick drains. In the granite regions of south we get slabs of granites detached with considerable skill-towards the end of Chalcolithic Period and increasingly during iron age. (Iron age graves from Brahmagiri-Mysore). Mining of native gold and copper followed by mining of different ores has been practised since Pre-Harappan period. At present showing only a few 14-C dates of early mining activity are available, according to which copper mining activity at Dariba goes back to 360 B.C. (Agrawal 1976) and that of gold mining at Hutti goes back to Christian era—1890 ± 70 and 1810 ± 70 B.P. (Allchin 1962), 14-C dates from Kolar gold mines are still later i.e. 5th cent. A.D. (Agrawal 1975-76: 138-39).

Notwithstanding these dates, Allchin (1962) rightly concludes that gold mining was current during neolithic period datable to the end of 3rd millennium B.C. Mining was mainly on the surface. There was search for suitable rock, its smashing by fire setting. The tools were limited to stone picks. However, copper chisel is reported from Piklihal. Seeing common nature of electrum type of gold it is probable that gold from these mines was exported to Harappans. However, intensive mining might have been started only with coming of the iron age specially first with carburized iron and then steel. This is corroborated by the finding of crow bars, gouges and pick axes from the Iron age graves. This large scale mining coincides with the period of Mauryan colonisation of Deccan by the end of 4th cent. B C. and the South Indian iron age. Evidence from Arthashastra supports this. The mines were being worked up to the depth of 640 feet during the first centuries of Christian era, is supported by the survey of ancient mines at Hutti.

Bose (1968: 83-89) describes ancient mining practices in some detail. He emphasises that early mining was handicapped due to non-availability of better mining tools and ancient miners limited themselves to surface alluvial deposits or shallow vein deposits occuring at surface. The mines were opened by adits 0.9 m × 0.9 m to 1.8 m × 1.2 m or by shallow shafts 1.5m × 1.2 m or 1.2 m × 0.9 m Small pillers of rock were left to support the ground and in some case timbers of babul (*Acacia arabica*) 15-18 Cm in diameter were used to support the stoped out areas. About 4 to 12 persons were involved in the process. They sat upon their haunches in the gallaries or stood on the niches cut in the shaft. Chisel and hammer were the main tools and bamboo basket was used for collecting and moving out the ore from the mine. There is some evidence of the use of rope and windlass for this purpose at the gold mines at Hutti (Allchin 1962: 105-211). The water collected in the mines was baled out by means of earthen pots. Nothing is known about lightening devices employed in this underground work, in the absence of any finds of lamps, we may assume that torches of some kind were used. The bamboo ladders are also suggested as an accessory equipment for mining. There is good evidence of ancient copper mining in Khetri (Rajasthan), Rakha (Bihar) and Sikkim, and Gold mining at Hutti and Kolar. Similarly Lead and Zinc mining in Rajasthan and mining of diamonds at Golcounda and Panna are of great antiquity. There is great need to date more samples from these mines by 14-C.

Pottery

Though pottery is the most prolific object found in archaeological excavations, yet most of the potteries have not received attention in the laboratory. Even recent works on potteries (Deo 1961-62, Manchanda 1972) do not report on the composition of the clay, identification of associated minerals, degraissant material, nature of the slip or glaze. Thin section studies, differential thermal analysis, porosity study etc. could throw light on the technique of pottery making and the raw materials used for it. Result of some of the scientific studies on pottery has been summarized by Sankalia

(1970). Work of Lal (1969) on O.C.P. (Ochre colour pottery) proves that it has a fine texture and is made from well levigated clay. It is mostly red or ochre coloured, of course, the core is grey. The red colour is indicative of the fact that it has been fired under oxidizing conditions at a sufficiently high temperature and that it is wrong to allege that it is ill-fired. It is a ware of usual hardness. The friability of O.C.P. is due to long burial in contact with saline moisture. Lal (1969: 83-94) opines that O.C.P. horizon witnessed a period of prolonged exposure and had deposition over it of wind borne silty sand and that its weathering is not due to rolling in water or water logging. Recent work of Agrawal *et al.* (1978) shows that O.C.P. associated sediments have been deposited by fluvial rather than aeolian activity. Thus there is need of checking the discrepency in these views. However, the fact remains that O.C.P. is a well fired pottery.

About the technique of manufacture of Painted Grey Ware (PGW) Bhallabh Saran (1969) suggests that P.G.W. has a superior quality of paste, formed from well levigated clay and that the pot was twice on the wheel, first for throwing the pot and secondly when it was leather hard it was returned to the wheel or attached to the lathe on which its walls were reduced in thickness with a scraper both from inside and outside. The pots were fired in a kiln with a well distributed heat under reducing conditions resulting in a smooth grey surface. Such 'open type' vessels with egg shell thickness are made at Azamgarh (U.P.).

According to Hegde (1975a: 187-190) black paintings were executed over P.G.W. by the same type of material as was used for the slip of N.B.P. and pot fired in a similar manner.

Technique of firing of black-and-red ware was studied by Majumdar (1968: 90-93). His experiments show that the black-and-red ware could be made by one of the three methods.

1. Single firing: in which inner surface and the rim portions of the outer surface are subjected to reducing condition, turning them black, while the rest of the portion is fired in oxidising condition, making it red.

2. Alternatively black-and-red ware could be made by double firing in which the whole pot is (i) either first fired under reducing condition so that the whole of it is black and in the second firing the portion to be made red is fired second time in oxidizing condition, (ii) or the pot is first fired in oxidising condition when whole of it fires red and in the second firing the portion desired to be black is fired in reducing conditions.

Regarding N.B.P., though notable experiments have been made by Sanaullah (1946: 58), Lal *IAR* (1955-56: 56-57), Bimbson (1959: 30), Bhardwaj (1969: 188-192), and Hegde (1972: 140) in understanding the technique of providing exquisite slip to this pottery, yet there is great discrepency in the views as is well known to the scholars and it will be futile to repeat them here.

Glass Technology

Advent and development of ceramic and glass technology has been discussed by present author in a number of papers and compiled in the monograph "Aspects of Ancient Indian Technology" (Bhardwaj 1979). The study shows that Harappans exploited and experimented with various siliceous raw materials and tried to transform them into useful objects by proper admixture and manipulation, utilizing high temperature of about 1200°C making faience, glazed pottery and other ceramic materials. They manipulated many a shades in ceramics by use of Iron and Copper compounds in reducing and oxidising conditions. Though no true glass objects are reported from Harappan levels, yet they had compounded glass as proved from glazed pottery.

Use of regular glass objects in the form of beads and bangles is reported from PGW levels at Hastinapur, Alamgirpur and Ropar. Qualitative analysis by Lal shows proper formulation, fabrication and careful annealing. As far as I could see the literature the earliest use of glass bangles in Old World is met from PGW levels in India. But this has to be confirmed. Detailed chemical analysis of glass beads from Period I (600 B.C.-200 B.C.) of Rajghat (Bhardwaj 1967-68: 42-46) shows that various constituents of the glass as revealed by the chemical analysis are quite compitible for producing good quality of glass, however, majority of glass beads lack transparency and show air bubbles, these facts point out their technological limitations, specially in obtaining higher temperature required for plaining.

Colouring agents were confined to the use of Copper and Iron. Though Soda was the main alkali, which might have been obtained from crude natron. Potash (derived from plant ashes) might have also been used. Use of Manganese as a decolouriser or as a tinctorial agent was not known. Copper-red glasses of the colour of sealing wax were made and their formulation looks indigenous. High content of alumina in Rajghat glasses has parallel only in Central Asian glasses (Bhardwaj, 1979). Critical examination of the composition of Taxila glasses shows introduction of new ingredients like Lead, Manganese, Tin and Antimony used either as tinctorial agents or opacifiers.

Introduction of Phosphorus and Manganese and shifting from Soda to Potash is noted during early centuries of Christian era as evidenced from Kausambi, Ahichchhatra, Ter and Arikamedu.

Chemical analysis of Kopia glasses by the author do not prove them to be an ancient industry as hitherto believed.

Metal Technology of Lead and Silver

Both of these metals have been used since Harappan period. Result of their technological studies has been summarized by Bhardwaj (1979). Silver of the Harappans and later cultures was obtained from argentiferous galen; basically an ore of Lead. Such ores occur in Bihar, Orissa, Rajasthan, Karnataka, Burma, Afghanistan and Iran. Bawdwin mines of Burma are very rich and show evidence of ancient mining. Impurity of Lead in Harappan silver supports this. Further it shows that:

1. Harappans were aware of the basic principles of smelting galena and extraction of lead which could have been done by simply heaping the ore on the charcoal fire in a pit. Fused metal which melts at a low temperature of 327°C runs and is collected. Separation of Lead and Silver was done by desilvering process akin to Pettinson process.

2. Use of silver is scarce after the Harappans till the heralding of Punch Marked coins around 600 B.C. Metallurgical studies of these Coins (Bhardwaj *et al.* 1968) also show that argentiferous galena was used for extraction of Silver. Low percentage of lead indicates that cupellation process which was also known was carried with great perfection. Debasement of silver coins by copper is deliberate and has dual purpose of (i) economising Silver, and (ii) providing strength and wear resistance.

3. The Gungeria Silver pieces recovered along with Copper hoards indicate a different source and method of extraction of Silver. These have impurity of Gold (3.7%).

4. Hegde observes that Lead coins of the Kshatrapa period were extracted from the Zawar mines in the Aravallies but Silver coins of the Kshtrapa cannot be linked to the same source (Hegde 1972: 140).

Gold Metallurgy

Gold has been reported from Harappan sites as well as Neolithic-Chalcolithic levels in Deccan. Small pure metallic nuggets collected from the mining ores could be hammered and directly shaped into simple ornaments and should not have needed the expertize of a goldsmith. This accounts for the use of Gold in Neolithic cultures. However Gold mined from quartz veins had to be obtained by crushing the ore into fire powder, which was washed and Gold particles were separated. Alluvial Gold was obtained by agitating with water in pans, cradles and sluices and earthy matter was flacted off and Gold particles were retained. Gold particles separated from either source were fused into small ingots in clay crucibles over charcoal fire and a temperature of 1063°C was necessary. Gold objects from Harappan levels show good craftsmanship—including hammering, annealing and casting and drawing Gold wares. Soldering of Gold and making of hollow and solid ornaments shows their high skill.

Gold is a bit scarce after the Harappan period. Gold foil beads and Gold objects are reported from the Early Historic period. From the Kushan period onwards the metal is not scarce. It is mainly used for coinage. The Gold coins of Gupta Period show excellent metallurgy.

The above is a very limited and brief survey. It brings to light a number of contradictory results and large gaps in our knowledge of Ancient Indian technology. The need of the day is to take up chronologically ordered and problem oriented laboratory studies of the archaeological artifacts from various cultural horizons. Let us hope that in coming years efforts will be made to pool various resources to take up laboratory studies of archaeological materials.

A number of studies await : There is a great need of analyses of metal artifacts from archaeological sites. Chemical and metallographic analyses are available only from a few selected sites and as such it is not possible to arrive at any viable results.

The great need of correlation of artifacts from different sites, as well as ore-artifact correlation on the basis of trace element concentration has not been appreciated despite some preliminary work done by B.A.R.C. (Iyer 1971). These analyses could solve some of the theoretical problems associated with the Early copper bronze cultures (both in space and time). The problem, of the genesis of NBP and its relation with Black slipped Ware or Painted Grey Ware could also be investigated by trace element concentration analyses.

There is great need of documentation of industrial equipments, furnaces, crucibles, and tools from archaeological excavations.

The study of the surviving ancient industries whether tribal smithy or ancient potters art could provide valuable help in reconstruction of Ancient Indian Technology.

REFERENCES

Agrawal, D.P., et al. : 1969. "The Copper Hoard Problem : A Technological Angle, *Asian Perspective*, XII, pp. 113-119.

——1971(a). *The Copper and Bronze Age in India*, New Delhi.

——1971(b). The diffusion of metallurgy in Prehistoric India, *28th International Orientalists Conferences*, Canberra Mimeographed.

——1975-76. Ancient Gold Working : Some New 14-C Dates, *Puratattva*, No. 8, pp. 138-39.

——1976. Ancient Copper Workings : Some New 14-C Dates, *I.J.H.S.*, Vol. II, No. 2, pp. 133-36.

——1977. The ambient environment of the Gangetic Sediments of Chalcolithic Period, *Proc. Indian Acad. Sci.*, Vol. 87A (E & P Sciences), pp. 23-28.

——1978. "New Data on the Copper Hoard and Daimabad Bronzes", *Man and Environment*, Vol. II.

Agrawal, R.C., et al. : 1982. Ganeshwar-Jodhpura Culture : New Traits in Indian Archaeology, in *Harappan Civilization* (Ed. Possehl, G.L.), pp. 127-28, Delhi.

Allchin, F.R., 1962. Upon the Antiquity and Methods of Gold Mining in Ancient India, *J.E.S.H.O.*, Vol. 5, pp. 105-211, London.

Bhardwaj, H.C., 1965-66. "Some Technical Aspects of Indus Valley Copper", *Bharati*, No. 9, pp. 57-80, B.H.U., Varanasi.

——1967-68. "A Note on Chemical Composition of Some Glass Beads from Rajghat, *Puratattva*, No. 1, pp. 42-46.

——1969. "Some Technical Observations on N.B.P. Ware slip," in, *Potteries in Ancient India*, pp. 188-192 (Ed. Sinha, B.P.), Patna.

——1970. "Problem of Advent of Copper in India", *Indian Journal of History of Science*", Vol. 5, No. 2, pp. 229-37, Delhi.

——1973. Aspects of Early Iron Technology in India, in *Radio Carbon and Indian Archaeology* (Ed. Agrawal and Ghosh), pp. 391-400, Bombay.

——1979. *Aspects of Ancient Indian Technology*, Delhi.

——1980(a). Early Indian Arsenical Copper, *Vijnan Parishad Anusandhan Patrika*, Vol. 23, No. 3, pp. 235-247.

——1980(b). An Assessment of Science and Technology during Harappan Phase, Proc., *12th Ind. Arch. Congress, Allahabad* (in Press).

——1981(a). "Impact of Development of Science and Technology on the environment of man as revealed through archaeological excavations of Harappan sites, *Proceedings of Indian Science Congress* (68th Session).

——1981(b). Indian Contribution to Steel Making in Antiquity, *Proceedings of the XVIth International Congress of History Science*, Bucharest.

Bimbson, 1959. In, *Early India and Pakistan*, (Wheeler, R.E.M.), p. 30, London.

Bose, H.K., 1968. "Mining in Ancient India," *Transactions of Mining, Geology and Metallurgical Institute of India*, Vol. 65, No. 1, pp. 83-89.

Chakrabarti, D., 1979. "The Problem of Tin in Early India—a Preliminary Survey, *Man and Environment*, Vol. III, pp. 62-74.

Deo, S.B., 1961-62. The Potters Technique of Prehistoric Ahar, *B.D.C.R.I.*, Vol. 22, pp. 105-111.

——1973. *Mahurjhari, Excavations* (1970-72) Nagpur, p. 77.

Eaton, E.R. and McKerrell, 1976. Near Eastern alloying and some taxual evidence for the early use of Arsenical Copper, *World Archaeology*, Vol. 8, No. 2, pp. 205-227.

Forbes, R.J., 1964. *Studies in Ancient Technology* IX, p. 164, Leiden.

Hegde, K.T.M., 1972. Physics and Chemistry in Indian Archaeology, *Archaeological Congress and Seminar papers* (Ed. Deo, S.B.) Nagpur, p. 140.

——1975(a). The Painted Grey Ware of India, *Antiquity*, XLIX, pp. 187-190.

——1975(b). Iron Metallurgy at Dhatva in *Excavations at Dhatva*, pp. 48-56, Baroda.

——1979. Sources of Ancient Tin in India, in *Search for Ancient Tin* (Eds. Wertime and Olin), pp. 39-42, Washington.

Iyer, R.K., 1971. Criteria for Correlation of Trade element concentration in Archaeological Specimens, *Publication No. B.A.R.C./I-104*, Bhabha Atomic Research Centre, Bombay.

Lal, B.B. (Dr.), 1955-56. in *Indian Archaeology*—A Review, pp. 56-57.

——1957. in *Ancient India*, No. 13. pp. 20, 106-113.

——1969. The Ochre-Coloured Pottery, in *Potteries in Ancient India*, (Ed. Sinha, B.P.), pp. 83-94, Patna.

Lamberg-Karlovsky, C.C., 1967. "Archaeological and Metallurgical Technology in Prehistoric Afghanistan, India and Pakistan, *American Anthropologist*, Vol. 69, pp. 145-165.

Maddin, R., et al. :1980. Distinguishing Artifacts made of Native Copper, *Journal of Archaeological Science*, Vol. 7, pp. 211-225.

Majumdar, G.G., 1968. The problem of the Black and Red Ware—A Technological approach, *Indian Megalith Seminar*, pp. 90-93, B.H.U., Varanasi.

Manchanda, O., 1972. *A Study of Harappan Pottery*, Delhi.

Marshall, J., 1951. *Taxila*, An illustrated account of archaeological excavations at Taxila, Cambridge.

Merpert, N.I., et al.: 1977. The investigation of the Soviet expedition in Iraq (1974) *Sumer*, pp. 33, 65-104.

Mishra, V.N., 1971. Two late Mesolithic Settlements in Rajasthan, A Brief Review of Investigations. *Journal of the University of Poona* (Humanities Section), No. 35, pp. 59-77.

Munn, L., 1936. Observations and notes on the method of ancient Gold mining in Southern India. *Tr. Min. Geol. Inst. India*, XXX, pp. 103-116.

Nautiyal, V., *et al.* : 1981. "Some new analyses on the Protohistoric Copper artifacts". *Man and Environment*, Vol. 5, pp. 48-51.

Pleiner, R., 1971. The Problem of the beginning of Iron Age in India. *Acta Pre-historica et Archaeologica*, 2, pp. 5-36.

Ray, A. and Chakrabarti, D., 1975. "Studies in ancient Indian Technology and production—A Review, *J.E.S.H.O.* Vol. XVIII, Pt. II, pp. 219-232.

Sana Ullah, 1946. "*Ancient India*", No. 1, New Delhi, 58.

Sankalia, H.D., 1970. *Some Aspects of Prehistoric Technology in India*, Delhi.

Saran Ballabh, 1969. Technology of Painted Grey Ware, *Potteries in Ancient India*, pp. 124-28 (Ed. Sinha, B.P.).

Atmospheric Pollution and Cultural Property

O.P. AGRAWAL

IT is now well established that atmospheric pollution has an adverse effect on cultural property including stone monuments. This adverse effect has been shown to exist on monuments in Venice, in Rome, in London, in the U.S.A. and in other parts of the world.

With the rapid industrialization, the threat of atmospheric pollution in India also is now becoming real. However, so far enough attention has not been paid to this aspect of deterioration of cultural property. In real terms attention to the dangers of pollution were highlighted by the establishment of the Mathura Oil Refinery which, it was pointed out, was too near the Taj Mahal and could pose a serious threat to its preservation. The Government of India appointed a High Powered Committee under the chairmanship of S. Varadarajan to study the problem. Tecnco, an Italian institution was invited to assist in the investigations. The Varadarajan Expert Committee which submitted the report in December 1977 came to the conclusion that after proper control of exudations from the Mathura Refinery there will be no threat from this source to the Taj Mahal. More pollution, according to the Committee, was emitted by the Thermal Power Stations and iron foundries which existed in Agra and by the coal-burning locomotive engines.

Apart from this indepth study at the Taj Mahal, so far much has not been done in our country to survey and to assess the impact of atmospheric pollution on materials of cultural property. It is hoped that effective steps will be taken to tackle the issue at various levels.

It is proposed to review in this article the implications and the dimensions of the problem of atmospheric pollution in relation to cultural property.

What is Pollution ?

Before any type of discussion on the effect of atmospheric pollution on cultural property can take place, it is necessary to define what is pollution and what are the materials which can be called *'pollutants'*. The term *'pollutant'* has often been defined as any material, solid, liquid, or gas, which changes the natural composition of the environment. However, in this definition a question arises as to how shall we define the natural composition of the environment, because the environment is continuously changing. Man being the major source which brings about a change in the environment, the term *'pollutant'* also means a substance that is present in the environment mainly as a result of human activity.

In relation to conservation of cultural property a better definition is given by Garry Thomson (1965: 148). He defines pollution as follows:

"For our purposes the easiest approach is to regard any minor constituent of the atmosphere, whether man-made or not, which might do harm to the common museum materials as a pollutant. Oxygen, though responsible for much damage, is not a minor constituent and cannot obviously be regarded as a pollutant."

Types of Pollutants

The pollutants present in the atmosphere are in the form of solid particles, like dust in varying grain sizes, aerosols and gases, like sulphur dioxide, hydrogen sulphide, ozone, nitrogen oxide, ammonia, halogen compounds, carbon dioxide and carbon monoxide. Near the industrial establishments there could be several other different types of gases. Then also there is the microbiological pollution present in the air, particularly in relation to micro-climate inside museum building.

Pollutants are sometimes classified as primary and secondary : primary pollutants being those which are emitted directly from identifiable sources, and secondary pollutants are those which are produced in the air by the interaction of two or more primary pollutants or by reaction with normal atmosphere constituents, for example, sulphur dioxide, a primary product, in contact with atmosphere and water is changed to sulphur trioxide and sulphuric acid which are termed secondary pollutants (Chambers, 1976: 3-22).

In relation to monuments and other cultural materials, the substances considered air-pollutants may be categorized as follows:

(i) Sulphur compounds,
(ii) Nitrogen compounds,
(iii) Carbon compounds,
(iv) Halogen compounds, and
(v) Particulate matter.

The last mentioned term, i.e. air-borne particulate matter describes several types of substances, namely the following (Scienfeld, 1975: 7).

(i) *Dust* : Dust is the term used to describe solid particles dispersed in the atmosphere by the mechanical disintegration of material. Dust itself may contain several different types of particles, for instance clay, sand, carbon, metal compounds, etc.
(ii) *Smoke* : The most common form of smoke is particulate suspension produced by the combustion of fuels. Smokes are small particles resulting from condensation of supersaturated vapour composed of material of low vapour pressure in relatively high concentrations.
(iii) *Mist* : Mists are formed by suspension of liquid droplets which in turn are produced by condensation of vapour. Normally a mist is composed of fairly large particles (exceeding 10 micrometres) in diameter at relatively low concentrations.
(iv) *Fog* : When the concentration of liquid droplets is so high that visibility is affected, the mist is called a fog.
(v) *Smog* : This is a term used to describe an air pollution situation which is associated with decreased visibility and presence of smog and fog.
(vi) *Aerosol* : Aerosol is the term used to describe a cloud of microscopic and sub-microscopic particles in air, for instance, smoke, fume, mist or fog.

Sources of Air Pollution

There are several contributors to the total atmospheric pollution, for example, combustion of fossil fuels, coal, refining of oil, diesel engines, automobiles, furnaces, etc. In India, industries like foundries and brick kilns use large amounts of fossil fuels which often are rich in sulphur content and thereby are a major source of sulphur gases. Incomplete combustion of these fuels emit copious amounts of smoke. Locomotives in our country use coke for production of steam. Thermal Power Stations use large quantities of fossil fuels for production of electricity. Automobile exhaust gases contain a good percentage of nitrogen oxides. This source is all the more dangerous because the gases emitted remain near to the ground. Another major source of pollution is an oil refinery, unless precautions have been taken to control the pollution at the source. Domestic *chulhas* in which wood and coal are burnt also contribute to the overall pollution level to a very great extent.

The extent of the deterioration of cultural property due to pollution ultimately depends upon the type and severity of pollution and the nature of cultural property.

Nature of Cultural Property

Cultural property was the term coined to describe the remanents of the products of human achievements in the past, available now in the form of monuments, art objects, archaeological materials, ethnographical objects, archival materials, and so on. It will be appreciated that cultural property is not one single type of material; its constituents are made of diverse substances like stone, metal, clay, paper, textile, wood, fibres of different types, etc. For this reason deterioration of cultural property is a complex phenomenon and for understanding of which study of different types of materials have to be taken into account.

Basically all matter, including cultural property can be divided into two main categories:

(i) Inorganic substances,
(ii) Organic substances.

Stone, ceramics and metals are of inorganic origin. Wood, paper, textiles, leather, ivory, bone, feathers and other similar objects, the material for which was derived from living beings, animals or plants are examples of organic materials.

It is obvious that pollution will affect all types of materials whether inorganic or organic. As stated earlier, the extent of decay will depend upon the nature of the material and the nature and the extent of the pollution combined with other factors like temperature and rainfall.

Effect on Materials

Most of the studies pertaining to the effect of pollution have been in relation to human health or to plant and animal life. There are very few efforts to assess the impact of air pollution on materials, particularly of cultural significance. This view was confirmed by the participants of the Third Indo-U.S. Conservation Workshop on the "Effect of Air Pollution on cultural Property" held in the U.S.A. in 1982.

Nevertheless, it is known that pollutants do have an effect on various materials.

Effect on Stone

Stone, which normally is a durable and strong material, is also damaged by air pollution. The decay of monuments and buildings in Venice, in London, in Rome and many other cities of Europe is attributed to the effect of air pollution. The rapid deterioration of the Acropolis in Greece is also due to the pollution present in the air. Stone monuments which withstood the vagaries of nature for centuries have now started to wither because of rising pollution level in the atmosphere.

The extent of the effect of air pollution on stone depends on the nature of the stone and the nature of the pollutants present in the atmosphere. What is the precise effect of the pollutants on materials is still not fully understood. The problem has attracted the attention of scientists all over the world and several studies have been done on the subject. But these studies are not enough and further work, particularly in Indian conditions is to be undertaken.

The pollutants mainly responsible for deterioration of stone are said to be sulphur dioxide, carbon dioxide, soot and dust. In urban areas the disfiguration of monuments takes place largely because of the accumulation of soot, which due to the presence of tarry matter in it, adheres tenaciously to any material. The soot fills the pores of the stone and blackens it quite often forming thick crusts. The analysis of soot from various sources show the presence of salts which may initiate chemical weathering of stone.

Adherence of dust on stone is also a major cause of deterioration. The analysis of dust has revealed the presence of calcium, potassium, chloride, sulphur and silicon in it (Kodokura, 1980: 29-34).

Dust and other particulate matter being of minute size become easily air-borne and thus get dispersed and remain suspended in the air for long periods. Dust particles attract water vapour and dust, the upper layers of the dust which get deposited on the surface of the stone start dissolving in the water vapours and depending upon the nature of the substrate the dissolved constituents behave either as acid or alkali and a chemical action starts to take place.

Sulphur dioxide is said to be the most potent pollutant present in the atmosphere and its effects are far more severe than possibly of any other pollutant (Manganelli and Gillardi 1966, Kirsch and Moeller 1972: 915-917). Sulpher dioxide in contact with air is converted to sulphur trioxide which in its own turn coming in contact with water vapour is changed to sulphuric acid (Bufalini 1971: 685-700). A large number of studies have been carried out to understand the mechanism of sulphur dioxide attack on stone. Studies of the deterioration of sandstone at the Cologne Cathedral indicate that they were deteriorated mainly because of the effect of sulphur dioxide. (Luckat 1976: 37-43, 1980: 149-153). However, Riederer was of the opinion that air pollution was not responsible for the decay of Cologne Cathedral (Riederer 1974: 42-43). He attributed this decay to inferior stone and to the use of concrete. On the other hand, Luckat's studies, show that there is a direct correlation between the amount of pollutant in the air and the decay of stone on the buildings.

De Henau *et al*. studying the alteration of Acropolis monuments concluded that the acidity of rain water enhanced by industrial air pollution have led to the erosion of marble (De Henau and Dupas 1976: 310-325). Similar observations were done by Yocu who showed that the damage to the historical buildings of Acropolis was due to abrasion and chemical attack from air pollutants, namely sulphur dioxide and sulphur trioxide. (Yocum 1979: 333-338).

Studies on Venetian marbles by several workers showed that the decay is because of pollution. (Fassina *et al.* 1981: 401-416).

In India, the effect of sulphur dioxide on the world famous monument, the Taj Mahal has been a matter of discussion, particularly because of the setting up of Mathura Oil Refinery. (Anon 1977: 6, 1978: 5; Rao *et al.* 1978: 663-674; Gauri and Holdren 1981: 386-390). The Varadarajan Committee studied the problem in great detail and came to the conclusion that the marble of the Taj will not be affected by the Oil Refinery at Mathura provided sufficient precautionary measures were taken.

It has been shown that with the action of sulphur gases hard permeable skins of calcium sulphite and calcium sulphate which tend to blister and exfoliate are formed on calcareous stones. According to Hampel (1968: 34-44) sulphur dioxide affects the marble in three ways:

(i) Loss of high polish,
(ii) Gradual growth of calcium sulfate, and
(iii) Shedding of this layer.

Effect on Metal

Like stone, metals are also affected by pollution in the atmosphere. The tarnishing of silver objects due to the presence of hydrogen sulphide in the air is well-known. Sulphur dioxide in the presence of high humidity forms salts of sulphates with metals. Near the sea coast, where the air is laden with chlorides, metal chlorides are formed. Electrochemical corrosion of metals is accelerated greatly when dust and other particulate matter are present on the metal surface. These particles adhering to the metal surface absorb moisture and pollutants like sulphur dioxide to become the seat of corrosion.

Iron is particularly attacked by sulphur dioxide. Rusting of iron is an electrolytic process for which moisture and an electrolyte should be present on the iron surface (Thomson 1978: 139). Sulphuric acid formed in the atomophere because of the converison of sulphur dioxide acts as an electrolyte and causes rusting.

Effect on Paper

Acidity deteriorates rapidly all cellulosic meterial including paper. Thus sulphur dioxide and the presence of moisture weakens the paper materials. It has been noticed that in the urban atmosphere the edges of the books get more damaged than the inside

Like paper, cellulosic textiles, for example cotton and linens are also damaged by atmospheric pollution. This is to be expected bacause acids are known to degrade cellulose and therefore, they are damaged by acid pollutants such as sulphur dioxide.

Monitoring of Pollution

In order to keep a check over the pollution levels at various sites, air monitoring is very necessary. Normally, air monitoring is done by various agencies keeping human health in consideration. However, the requirements of pollution levels for the protection of cultural property might not be the same as for man Furthermore, in order that measurements have some fruitful application to conservation of cultural property, the monitoring stations have to be located in relation to the monuments or museums concerned.

Some very important questions for monitoring of air pollution are:

(i) Where should the monitoring points be located?
(ii) What should be the frequency of measurements?
(iii) Which of the pollutants should be monitored?

There are several techniques of monitoring devices ranging from automatic constant monitoring techniques to manual measurement procedures. Constant reading measurements can be programmed to give hourly readings. The frequency of measurements with manual devices will be much less. This question was also discussed at the Indo-U.S. Workshop of 1982 on the Effect of Air Pollution on Cultural Property. One of the questions raised at the Workshop was whether it was necessary to measure pollution levels at all the sites of cultural property or only at a selected few. The opinion expressed was that to have a precise idea of levels of air pollution it would be necessary to make measurements at the site. Measurements inside museum buildings would also be necessary because they could radically differ from outside conditions.

The Indo-U.S. Workshop recognised three important situations for monitoring of pollution levels in relation to sites of cultural property, namely:

(i) Highly important cultural property sites where fairly intensive monitoring would be required.
(ii) Normal sites where simpler methods could be used for record and subsequent check up with more reliable data.
(iii) Research sites where again more detailed data and reliable monitoring would be needed.

It is evident that monitoring requirements are to be decided individually for each site depending on its importance and the type of information that is required. However, in each case the minimum data required would be :

(i) Measurement of particulate matter.
(ii) Sulphur dioxide level.
(iii) Acid deposition—both wet and dry.
(iv) Meteorological data giving wind direction, temperature, rainfall and humidity levels.

As to the question whether continuous monitoring was required or could simple methods suffice, it may be stated that each method has its own merit and could be used for a specific purpose. Simple chemical methods like lead peroxide method or acid gas plate method gave average sulphation rates for the collection periods and do not give information on short-term fluctuations to measure which continuous monitoring was necessary.

Techniques of Pollution Monitoring

It is not intended to discuss here the details of monitoring because that is a subject in itself and very good works are available on the subject. In this article only a basic outline of the techniques will be presented.

Sampling and Analysis

There are two important areas from where sampling for pollution analysis can be done. These are :

(i) Sampling of stack gases : For this type of analysis, gases being emitted in a stack or flue of an industrial furance are sampled. Obviously, there are a number of problems in this method : The stack is not easily approachable, the gases are too hot and several points of the stack are to be tapped.
(ii) Open air sampling : In this technique the pollutants present in the air at a particular site are analysed.

For actual analysis, as already indicated, the chemist can use either continuous recorders or methods which give intermittent readings.

Automatic samplers and recorders are useful in situations where a number of analysis are required either for research or for monitoring air quality levels continuously. Gases as well as particulate matter can be measured by this technique.

On the other hand, the pollutants after sampling by suitable techniques are chemically analysed with the help of instruments like X-ray Diffraction, X-ray Fluorescence Spectrometer, Emission Spectrograph, Ultra-violet Spectrophotometer, Infra-red Spectrophotometer and other analytical tools. Each technique is to be employed according to the need of estimation.

Control Measures

When we speak of control of pollution our main intention is to protect the objects of cultural property from the adverse effects of atmospheric pollution. Obviously, the problem outdoors is much more acute than indoors because the atmosphere is not confined within a room or a showcase. A monument, for example is exposed to the atmosphere from all the sides and is subjected to other natural degradation factors like rain and sun. Because the atmosphere around a monument cannot be changed, except to a minor degree by plantation of trees and like, the only solution available is the control of pollution at the source. In other words, the control has to be done, or should be done by the factories, oil refineries, automobiles, thermal power stations, and so on. This is an area in which the Departments of Environment of the Government of India as well as of the State Governments can play a significant role. The Environmetal Protection Agency in the U.S.A. is constantly studying the problem of environmental control as related to the conditions in the U.S.A. In our country too such measures are required.

In case of important monuments, several steps ought to be taken for protecting the monument against pollution effects. These steps can be enumerated as follows :

(i) The industries in the vicinity likely to have an effect on the monument should use only low sulphur coal.
(ii) No industry including small industries.
(iii) Which can cause pollution are to be located near the monument. This was one of the important recommendations of the Varadarajan Committee in relation to the Taj Mahal. The two Thermal Power Stations working near Itmat-ud-daulah have already been closed down. Furthermore, on the advise of the Committee, Railways were advised to replace the present coal based locomotives with diesel based locomotives at the Marshelling Yard at Agra.

It is often argued that a protective coating may be applied on the monument as a protection against pollution. However, such a practice will be full of dengers, because unlike museum objects, a monument is a part of the ground on which it is built with its foundation in it. There are several factors like capillary action of water and rain acting on the monument and it cannot, therefore, be sealed completely. Where-ever such a step of appliyng a thick resinous coating on the surface of the monument had been taken, results have been disastrous. Therefore, even if such a step was to be taken, it must be after very careful study and taking into consideration all the pros and cons.

Conclusion

It is obvious that the problem of atmospheric pollution is tremendous and vast. The studies conducted so far are rather sporadic and not intensive. There should be all efforts to study the effect of pollution on the materials of cultural property and to study the control methods. As has been stated earlier, the problem outdoors is much more severe. But even indoors the problem is not so simple. Air-conditioning which is often recommended for museums is not feasible for our countries. This is so, not only because of the high cost of the equipment but also because of the high maintenance and running cost. Some simple techniques have to be devised for effective pollution control.

REFERENCES

ANON., 1977. Rain on the Taj, *Chemistry*, 50, No. 9, 6.

——1978. Concern Over Taj Continues, *Chemistry*, 51, No. 9, 5.

Bufalini, M. 1971. Oxidation of Sulfur-dioxide in Polluted Atmoshere—A Review, *Environ. Scie. Tehnol.*, 5, No. 8, 685-700.

Chambers, L.A., 1976. Classification and Extent of Air Pollution Problems, in *Air Pollution* (ed.) by A.C. Stern, Vol. 1 (Academic Press, New York, 3rd ed.) Chapter 1, 3-22.

De Henau, P. and Dupas, M. 1976. Study of the Alteration in Acropolis Monuments, *Proceedings of the II International Symposium of Deterioration of Building Stones*, 319-325.

Fassina, V. Bonarrigo, A. and Ongaro, A. 1981. An Air Pollution Survey inside the Basilica of Tor cello in relation to the deterioration of mosaics, *The Conservation of Stone II*, Pt. A, Bologna, 401-416.

Gauri, K.L. and Holdren, G.C. 1981. Pollutants Effects on Stone Monuments, *Environ. Sci. Technol.*, 15, No. 4, 386-390.

Hempel, K.F.B., 1968. Notes on the Conservation of Sculpture, Stone, Marble and Terracotta, *Studies in Conservation*, 13, 34-44.

Kirsch, H. and Moeller, R., 1972. Sulfur dioxide emissions and their destruction of marble buildings, *Z. Ges. Hyg. Ihre Grenzgebiets* (Berlin) 18 (12), 915-917.

Kodokura, T., 1980. Studies on Air Dusts around Cultural Property (III), Chemicals in Dust, *Science for Conservation*, 19, 29-34.

Luckat, S. 1976. Stone Deterioration at the Cologne Cathedral due to Air Pollution, *The Conservation of Stone, R. Rossi-Manaresi* (ed.) (Proc. Int. Sym.), Bologna, 37-43.

——1980. Analysis of Air Pollutants and their influence on works of art on stone shown on the example of the Cathedral of Cologne. *Arbeitsblaetter fur Restauratoren*, gr. 6, 149-153.

Manganelli, R.M. and Gilardi, E.F., 1966. Absorption of atmospheric sulphur dioxide by clay brick and other building materials, *Rutgers Univ.*, *Terminal Progress Rept.*, (May 1, 1962—Apr. 30, 1966).

Riederer, J. 1974. Decay of Stone without Smog, *Unwelt*, No. 1, 42-43.

Rao, K.S., Sain, R.S. and Rao, T.S. 1978. Air Pollution threat to the Taj Mahal and its environs due to Mathura Oil Refinery, *Chem. Age India*, 29, No 8, 663-674.

Scienfeld, John, H. 1975. Air Pollution—Physical and Chemical Fundamentals, McGraw-Hill, New York, 7.

Thomson, Garry 1965. Air-Pollution—A Review for Conservation Chemists, *Studies in Conservation*, 10, 148.

——1978. The Museum Environment, London, 139.

Yocum, J.E., 1979. Air Pollution Damage to Buildings on the Acropolis, *J. Air. Pollut. Control. Assoc.*, 29, No. 4, 333-338.

Excavations at Rojdi: 1982-83

GREGORY L. POSSEHL, Y.M. CHITALWALA, PAUL RISSMAN, GAIL WAGNER

THE Harappan site of Rojdi (70°55′E—21°52′ N)[1] is located in Gondal Taluka, Rajkot District in the State of Gujarat (Figures 1 and 2). The village, on whose tax rolls Rojdi is found, is now known as Shrinathgarh. Rojdi was first excavated in the 1950's (Indian Archaeology, A Review, 1957-58: 18; Indian Archaeology, A Review, 1958-59: 19-21). Later work undertaken in 1964-65 (Indian Archaeology, A Review, 1964-65: 12) is referred to only obliquely. None of this material from Rojdi has been published in any substantial way (Possehl, 1980). During January and February of 1983 a joint team from the United States and India began the re-excavation of the Harappan town of Rojdi on the Saurashtran Peninsula of Gujarat. This is a preliminary report on this work.

Rojdi is situated on the northern bank of the Bhadar River which flows into the Arabian Sea. The settlement is a long oval with an area of ca. seven hectares, (Figure 3), all within what appears to have been an ancient stone wall. Some background to the archaeology of the site can be found within the 1958-59 report on the excavations there. This is quoted in full as follows:

The Harappan occupation of the site (Period I) fell into three Phases, A, B, and C. The first settlers on the site, in Phase A built a 2 ft. high mud platform, capped by rammed earth and lime, to carry their mind and mud-brick houses. Their pottery consisted of the convex-sided bowl, handled bowl, perforated jar, square-rimmed jar, vase with a beaded rim and round belly, dish-on-stand, trough, etc. The pots were generally made of well-levigated clay and were uniformly fired. They were treated with a red, and rarely with a chocolate, slip and were mostly unpainted except for a few horizontal bands in black. Crude and ill-burnt pottery was, however, not absent; it was sometimes treated with a greyish slip and was decorated with wavy incised lines or concentric corrugations.

Blades, trapezes, and lunates of chert and pipes, rings and celts of copper were in use. The personal ornaments were spiral gold rings, terracotta, etc.

Phase B, which arose after the destruction of the previous Phase by fire, was characterized by rubble and mud structures plastered with lime and rammed-earth floors. The ceramics of the Phase represented two traditions, red ware and buff ware, the latter in lesser quantities than the former; a few green sherds were also found. The main types were the convex-sided bowl, perforated jar, dish with a flared rim and dish-on-stand. The designs painted in black on a red, buff or chocolate slip included the fish, leaves, hatched triangles and lozenges, intersecting loops, roundels, wavy lines, vertical bands, etc. Two black-and-red sherds, one with painting in white consisting of concentric circles and the other of a bowl, were interesting. The corrugated grey ware occurred in much greater proportions than in the previous Phase. While the treatment of some specimens in this ware was similar to that of Period I of Prabhas Patan, the incised decoration characteristic of that site was absent.

Small blades and other microliths in geometric shapes were common. Copper was represented by chisels, rods and bangles. Beads of faience, banded agate and etched carnelian, gold ear-ornaments, cubical weights of chert and gamesmen were the other note-worthy finds on the Phase.

1. These geographic coordinates are accurate to within one minute. The coordinates given by S.R. Rao (1963: 206) are incorrect.

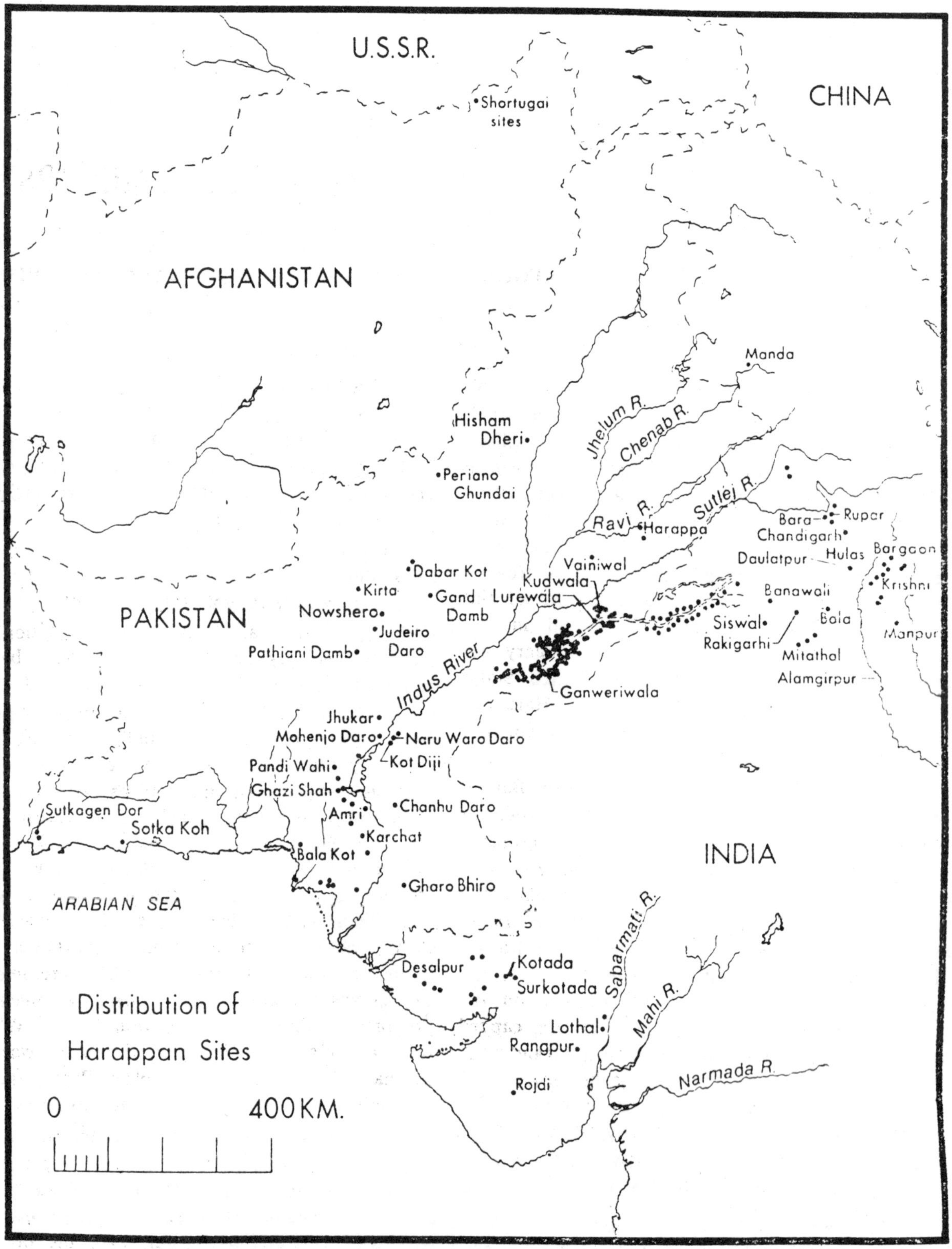
U.S.S.R.
CHINA
•Shortugai sites
AFGHANISTAN
PAKISTAN
INDIA
ARABIAN SEA
Manda
Hisham Dheri•
•Periano Ghundai
Jhelum R.
Chenab R.
Ravi R.
Sutlej R.
•Harappa
Bara
Rupar
Chandigarh•
Daulatpur
Hulas
Bargaon
Krishni
•Dabar Kot
•Kirta
•Gand Damb
Nowshero•
•Judeiro Daro
Pathiani Damb•
Vainiwal
Kudwala
Lurewala
Banawali
Siswal•
Bala
Rakigarhi
Mitathal
Manpur
Alamgirpur
Ganweriwala
Indus River
Jhukar•
Mohenjo Daro•
Naru Waro Daro
Kot Diji
Pandi Wahi•
Ghazi Shah
Sutkagen Dor
Sotka Koh
Amri
•Chanhu Daro
•Karchat
Bala Kot
•Gharo Bhiro
Sabarmati R.
Desalpur
Kotada
Surkotada
Mahi R.
Lothal•
Rangpur•
Rojdi
Narmada R.
Distribution of Harappan Sites
0 400 KM.

Fig. 19.1.

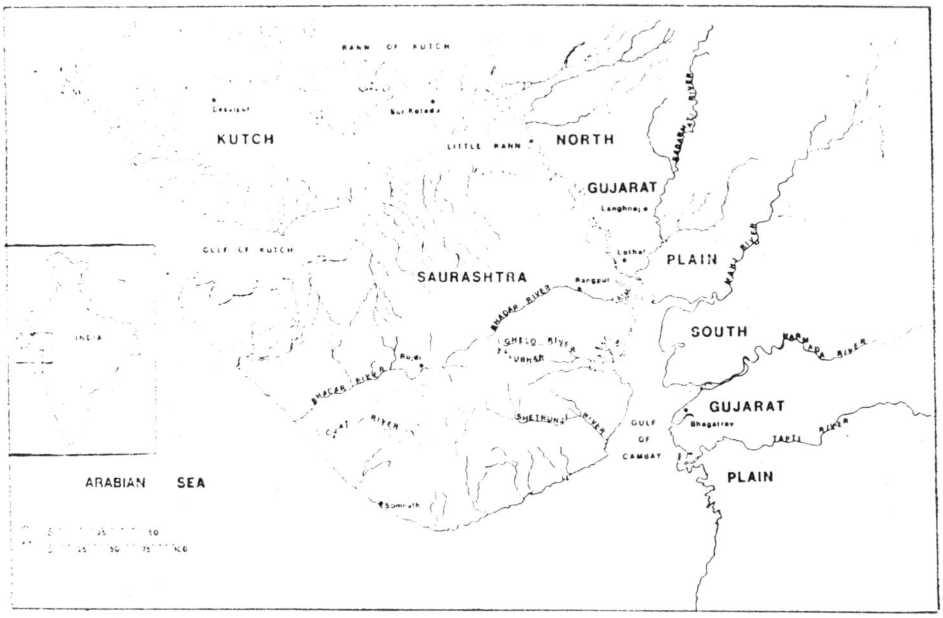

Fig. 19.2.

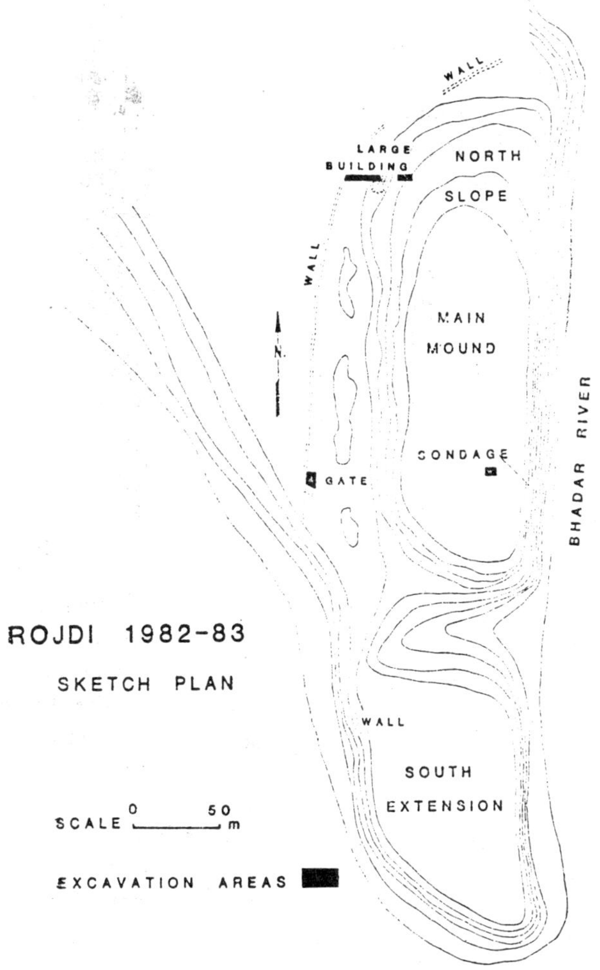

Fig. 19.3.

In Phase C only rubble structures were encountered. Along with the late Harappa red ware, in which, however, the perforated jar and square-rimmed jar were absent, the characteristic pottery of Period II of Prabhas was introduced. The painted designs were mainly horizontal bands, but slanting bands, wavy lines and intersecting loops were not absent. Crude ware decreased in number. Beads of carnelian, shell and terracotta were recovered.

After a long desertion, a part of the site was re-occupied in the early historical period (Period II) by a people using the Red Polished Ware and coarse grey and black pottery. Though the structural remains of the Period were scanty, it could be seen that the alignment of the houses was entirely different from that of the preceding Period." (Indian Archaeology, A Review, 1958-59: 19 & 21).

The 1982-83 Field Season

Three separate operations were undertaken during the first season of renewed work at Rojdi (Figure 3).

Operation 1

The most extensive excavation and clearing was undertaken in the vicinity of a gateway through the perimeter wall that surrounds Rojdi. This gateway, a surface feature of the site, consists of a series of large boulders apparently *in situ*, if judged by the patterning of their placement (Figure 4; Plate 1).

The gateway ties into what was once a wall that apparently surrounded the entire site, save possibly for the river side (Figure 3). All that can be seen today of this feature is a series of large foundation stones, often in what seems to be their original position. In one section of the wall these foundations can be traced for over 200 meters.

The excavation of the gateway area enabled us to understand the foundation architecture and stratigraphic position of this feature and wall. As can be seen from the accompanying illustration (Figure 5) the foundations of the wall and flanks of the gate were large boulders, in this case a fine grained, good quality basalt. The exact source of this stone is not known; however, local bedrock of the district is basaltic and we can fairly presume that these large boulders were not transported great distances. It appears that a single course of large stones was laid end to end with a minimum of excavation for foundations. This formed the lowest portion of the wall. Smaller basalt boulders may form a second foundation course. Smaller stones and rammed earth filled the interstices between these courses of foundation. The substance of the wall itself was earth. Toward the bottom there was an additional filling of baseball-sized stones. These latter stones seem to be mostly a low quality amygdeloidal basalt which is found in substantial quantity along the river side of the site.

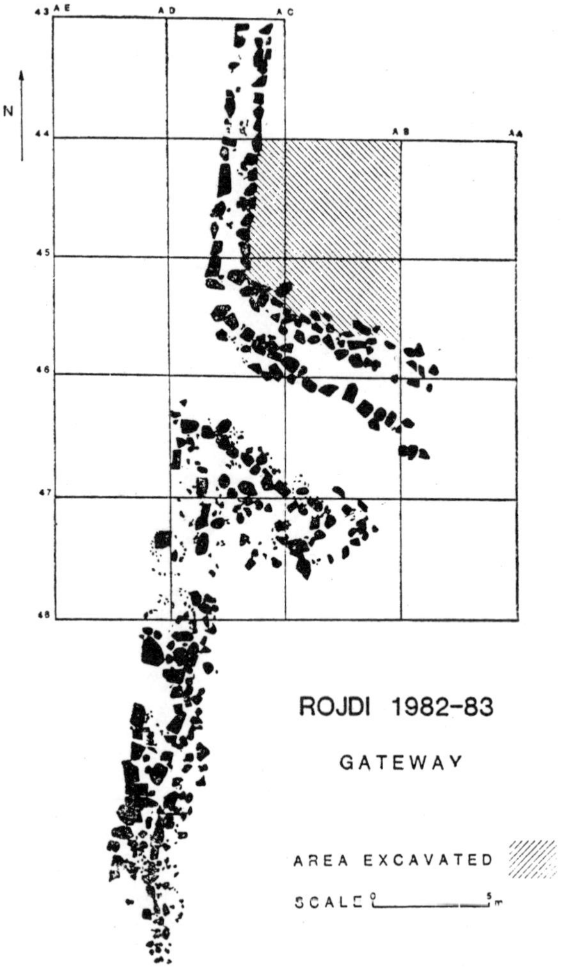

Fig. 19.4

The wall is an average of 60 to 80 cm in thickness at its base. Assuming that a wall of this construction would be extremely unstable if its height was more than four times the thickness of the base, we can assume that our structure was not higher than about 3.2 meters or 10 feet. It could have been somewhat lower.

The function(s) of this feature are not known. It can be fairly doubted that it was primarily a fortification emplacement. There are no bastions anywhere along its course and it hardly seems to be of a size and

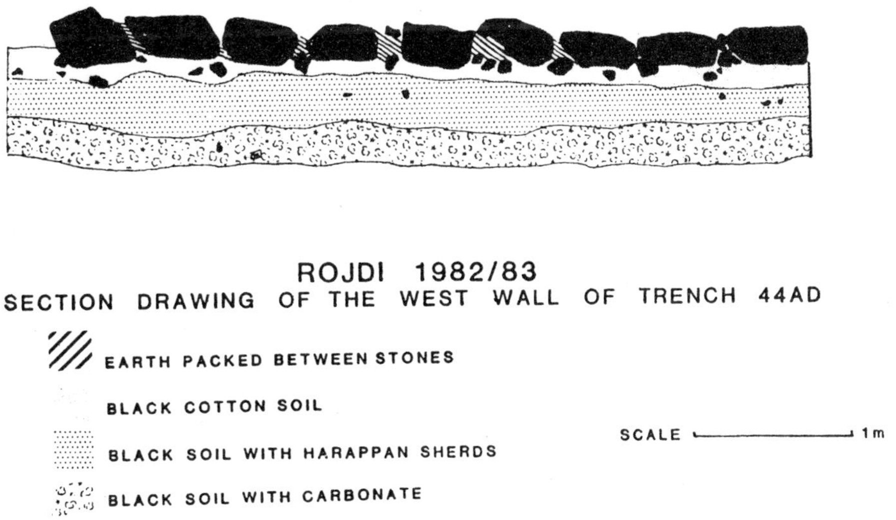

Fig. 19.5.

thickness to withstand concerted attack. Also note on Figures 2 and 3 that the flanks of the gateway face into the settlement. While we recognize incomplete understanding of the wall and gateway, we tend to think that it was erected to form a perimeter to the settlement and control the movements of people and animals. It would have also offered some protection against flood and preditory beasts.

Stratigraphy at the gateway shows that the course of large foundation stones was set on the local black soil which in turn sits directly on a fine white sandstone. It was observed that it is stratigraphically above the amygdeloidal basalt. In the southeastern corner of trench 45 A.D. a single microlithic lunate was found sitting directly on the sandstone.

The black cotton soil under the gate was found to contain small numbers of "rolled" or abraided Harappan redware pottery sherds. Thus we are certain that the wall cannot be associated with the initial period of Harappan occupation at the site (see below).

Operation 2

The second operation took place at the geographic summit of the site where we began what was to be a deep stratigraphic *sondage*. Previous work at the site, and our own careful survey of the surface, indicated that we could expect between three and four meters of cultural deposit in this area. The operation could not go beyond minus 1.75 meters, as the stratigraphy is complex and the presence of a number of structures, or fragments of structures, demanded a great deal of photography and recording.

Operation 3

The third operation at Rojdi took place at the northern end of the site in the vicinity of what we originally thought was an intramural tower (Figure 3). As our cleaning and excavation proceeded it became clear that the building was rectilinear in plan and that there may be interdigitated structures or articulated rooms (Figure 6).

A row of trenches each five meters with one meter baulks was laid along the northern side of this building. These were placed so that we could investigate the outside stratigraphy of this building and connect this to the surrounding wall. It was discovered that both the northern walls of the building and the wall surrounding the settlement were built on the same very hard, compact stratum four in this area. Moreover, the engineering of the building foundations and that for the wall is the same.

We are thus in a position to infer quite positively that the large building, whose function has yet to be determined, and the wall are of the same date, sometime during the Harappan tradition. We hold the latter as reasonable conclusion at this time since the wall surrounded the entire settlement at Rojdi. The only period of occupation on the site that is so extensive is the earliest one—that associated with the Harappan material. The Red Polished Ware and Medieval occupations are both small, covering only 20% to 30% of the total area.

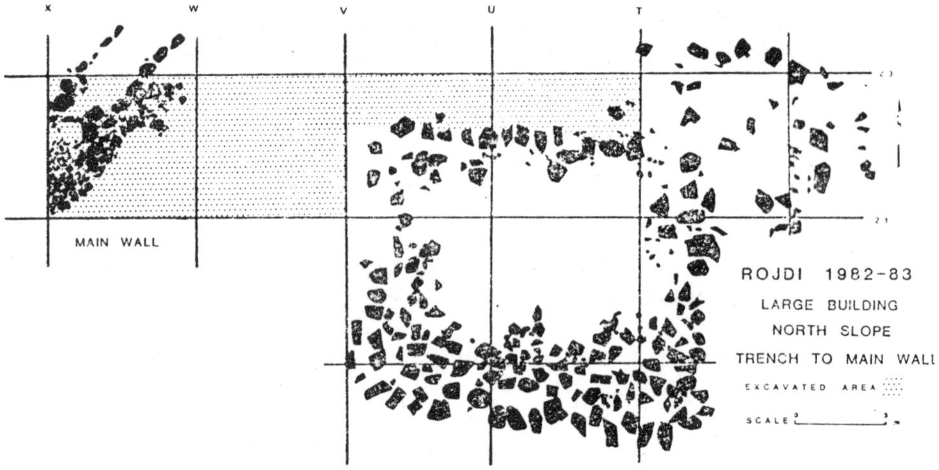

Fig. 19.6.

To the east of the excavation at the building, two-five by five meter trenches were opened by the Gujarat State Department of Archaeology as a part of Operation Three. The ceramics that came from the approximately meter and one-half of deposit at this point are later than those from other parts of the site. They look much like the kind of material that came out of S.R. Rao's Rangpur IIC and may have a small amount of the important Lustrous Red Ware. This material is currently under study.

Probably ephemeral floors and two or three possible post holes were also uncovered in this part of Operation Three. Nothing could be made of the pattern of these features, nor could we fit the large amount of architectural debris into definite patterns. We did not find bricks, foundation stones and the like but rather lumps of dried mud plaster and flooring material with reed and wattle impressions all through them (Plate 2). This is the kind of material that occurs at chalcolithic sites on the Deccan Plateau. For understanding the plan, we will continue our excavation in this part of the site next season.

Lateral Stratigraphy

Excavation at Operations Two and Three, and some attention to surface survey on the southern end of the site, called the South Extension, have led us to suggest the following stratigraphic time sequence for Rojdi. These tentative inferences, not final are all based on ceramic typology and comparative study and are therefore, useful to us in focusing our research.

The South Extension seems to have the earliest ceramics. The material from Operation Two, at the summit of the mound appears to represent a subsequent phase of Harappan occupation at Rojdi. Our *sondage* in Operation Two did not penetrate a sufficient depth for us to determine whether the early South Extension material extends to this part of the site. The material from the Gujarat State Department of Archaeology trenches in Operation Three represents the latest Harappan occupation.

The fact that the circumvallation seems to have encompassed the South Extension leads us to suspect that it should be associated with a relatively early part of the Harappan occupation at Rojdi.

Ceramics

The pottery which was recovered from the site is currently under detailed analysis. A fair sample of Harappan red ware was recovered, none of which had the characteristic black painting of the Mature, or Urban Phase. In fact, painted sherds were only infrequently encountered. One piece of the distinctive Ahar Black and Red Ware was found, with characteristic white paint.

Methodological Aspects of the Rojdi Excavations

We want our work at Rojdi to be methodologically innovative. During the first season of work we employed both magnetometers and resistivity survey techniques in subsurface prospecting. We believe that this is the first time that such equipment has been used on an Indian archaeological project. We also continued our work with water flotation and designed a special wet screening "machine" built from materials available in almost any Indian bazaar.

Subsurface Prospecting : 1982-83

A complete report on the geophysical survey of Rojdi undertaken by Bruce Bevan is under preparation. The magnetometer survey produced three strong anomalies which are of interest to us. The resistivity survey proved to be a less successful endeavour due to the lack of moisture in the soil.

One of the magnetic anomalies was near the gateway. This was a long ridge of high magnetic potential which crossed the wall, and ran in an east-west direction from the gateway toward the Main Mound. A trench was laid across this feature and we determined beyond reasonable doubt that it was not cultural.

Two very strong point anomalies were located near the *sondage* in Operation Two. The difficulties we faced in making progress at completing this operation prevented our complete investigation of these features. We do plan to lay trenches in these parts of the Main Mound at some later point in time and will determine the nature of these features at that time.

Palaeobotany, 1982-83

The 1982-83 season at Rojdi focused on the creation of an efficient recovery system for the macrobotanical remains that are of significance to our problem orientation. Very little analysis was completed.

The preliminary examination of our light fractions indicates that the sample is likely to be a diverse one. Grass 'A', also found at Oriyo, is probably at Rojdi as well. Seeds of the Indian jujube (*Zizyphus jujuba*) are there as well. We are anticipating the presence of one of the millets. (Possehl, in the press).

We feel that considerable progress has been made in this important part of the Rojdi project. Further details on our methodology and sampling are to be found in Ms. Gail Wagner's report which follows :

Palaeobotany at Rojdi : Methodology

During the 1982-83 field season at Rojdi, 99 samples totalling nearly 650 liters of unscreened dirt were processed through water flotation. Approximately four samples per stratum or one from each quadrant of the trench were collected from trenches 43K and 20P (49 and 21 samples, respectively). The remaining 29 miscellaneous samples were taken from trenches 200, 20T, 20V, 20W, 36L, 42K, and 42AC. The archaeological context of each sample was recorded in the field by the trench supervisor, and the designated dirt was sent to flotation. At flotation, the sample was immediately poured into one of ten plastic buckets marked in liters. The empty field container was sent back to the trench. The number of incoming samples rarely exceeded the number of available plastic buckets.

A mechanical flotation system similar to the SMAP machine (Shell Mound Archaeological Project) (Watson 1976) was built from locally available materials This system, named "Piyush one," consisted of a 55-gallon oil drum with the top removed, a metal screen-bottomed insert, a small wooden screen-bottomed light fraction box, and a constant supply of water. The barrel was modified by rewelding the bottom to form a baffle sloping down to a capped drainage pipe nine centimeters in diameter. Four horizontal inner struts of 3/4-inch pipe were welded inside the barrel at 33 cm below the top to support the bottom of the insert (See Plates 3 throuth 13). A rectangle was cut out of the lip of the barrel, where the sluiceway of the insert rested during operation ; two 3/4-inch pipe elbows were welded to the outside of the barrel below this opening. During operation, two eleven centimeter lengths of pipe were screwed into the elbows, and along with two removable wooden bars supported the small wooden light fraction box.

Water entered the barrel through an upward-pointing shower head located several centimeters below the level of the internal struts. The flow of water was controlled by a valve outside the barrel. A separate valve controlled the flow of water through a short length of hose used to rinse the equipment. All of the water was supplied by a four-inch PVC pipe connected to a local irrigation system powered by a single-stroke diesel engine. The pump was shut down only for maintenance or repairs, but the water supply to the barrel could be shut off either at the barrel or where the PVC pipe joined the irrigation system.

The insert, similar in appearance to a wash tub, was made of galvanized tin 45 cm in diameter and 31 cm deep. At one side, a sluiceway 15 cm wide and 9 cm deep slanted outward and slightly downward for 21 cm. The bottom of the insert consisted of window screen (1.5 mm^2) supported by sturdy 1/4-inch wire cloth. The wooden light fraction box was an open rectangle 25 cm long by 15 cm wide by 8 cm deep with brass 30 mesh wire cloth (0.6 mm^2) nailed to the bottom. During flotation, this box supported a 30 cm square piece of fine-mesh cotton cloth used to catch the light fraction.

Each sample required 15 to 20 minutes to process through flotation. In preparation, the surface of the water was cleaned, the insert was placed in the barrel, and the water pressure was adjusted to show a slow roil on the surface. A clean piece of cloth was loosely tacked to the wooden light fraction box, the cloth was thoroughly wetted, and the light fraction box was positioned to catch all of the water from the sluiceway. Several newspapers were opened to half-page size and the sample number written on the top page.

As the bucket of dirt was slowly added to the insert, the light fraction rose to the surface, washed through the sluiceway, and was caught in the open cloth bag. The operator agitated the sample by hand, breaking up dirt lumps, throwing away non-artifactual rocks, and herding the light fraction toward the sluiceway. When the sample was cleaned of all dirt, the insert was tilted up with the sluiceway resting on top of the barrel so that no more water could run into the light fraction box. It was this feature of the design more than any other that allowed "Piyush One" to be operated by a single person.

The light fraction was washed gently into the center of the cloth square and the cloth removed from the light fraction box. The edges of the cloth were brought together to form a bag and were tied shut with the label. The light fraction bag was clipped to a clothesline hung in the shade and the heavy fraction was deposited on newspapers and spread on to dry. The insert and light fraction box were washed with a strong spray of water before the next sample was begun. The barrel was emptied and cleaned of dirt after approximately 14 samples or 95 liters of dirt.

If the sample was floated in the morning, the heavy fraction was often dry by that afternoon. The light fraction usually took one or two days to dry. The heavy fraction was sorted later that day or the next day by sifting it through two geological sieves, a 4 mm^2 and a 2 mm^2. All diagnostic sherds as well as fragments larger than 2×2 were saved and sent to the sherd yard. All of the bone, shell, gastropods, artifacts, and charred plant remains were removed and the remainder of the heavy fraction was discarded. After the light fraction was dry, it was placed into a labeled plastic vial along with any plant remains from the heavy fraction. The relatively few plant remains recovered in the heavy fractions were mostly charred wood or jujube fragments. Bone was a common component in the heavy fractions, whereas beads and micro-beads were not common.

Flotation recovery tests run on two separate days returned counts of 92% and 98% recovery of floating seeds between 0.7 and 1.4 mm in size. During both tests, fifty carbonized poppy seeds (*Papaver somniferum*) were mixed in with the dirt of an archaeological sample prior to flotation. The results of the tests are consistent with recovery rate figures from similar mechanical flotation systems in North America (Wagner 1982).

The amount of time required to process each sample stretched along a continuum : small samples or those with few bones or plant remains took the least amount of time, whereas samples with a lot of bone or plant remains took longer. Flotation invariably took 15 to 20 minutes per sample, regardless of sample size. Most of the heavy fractions required 10 to 20 minutes to sort, although those with a great deal of bone took much longer. The greatest variability in time spent on each sample occurred during analysis. Most samples could be scanned in less than one hour, but those with a lot of modern debris (such as rootlets) took much longer. Finally, the identification and description of the seeds generally took at least as long to accomplish as did the scanning.

The first step in analysis was to scan each sample for seeds and identifiable wood. This was done by thinly spreading the sample in a shallow box lid marked with lines and examining it under a binocular dissecting microscope at 10x. During analysis, movement of the box was guided by the lines to ensure that all of the sample was examined. Seeds and large pieces of wood were removed and then identified under higher magnification by comparing them with a modern comparative collection. The Rojdi samples were scanned immediately whenever specific questions about recovery arose during excavation.

During the 1982-83 field season at Rojdi, the 103 samples from the 1981-82 excavation at Oriyo Timbo were scanned and all the seeds were identified and described. A representative sample of 64 of the 99 samples from Rojdi were scanned. Although all the seeds were removed from these Rojdi samples, there was insufficient time to complete their identification and description.

Nevertheless, it is already evident that plant remains from Rojdi will represent not only the cultivated crops, but also the seedy components of the local flora. Small grass seeds are particulary abundant. Although a number of seeds occur in the horizontal strata representing various surfaces in Trench 43K, a greater number and variety of seeds consistently occur in the pit features within that same trench.

Stalk and seed impressions in burnt daub were recovered from trenches 20P and 200. The seed impressions were not detailed enough to permt identification, and no identifiable nodes occurred in the stalk impressions. A pollen wash was taken from the inside of a small but complete black and red ware pot from Trench 20P; this sample has yet to be analyzed.

Modest progress was made in the collection of a modern comparative collection of seeds and woods with voucher herbarium specimens. As effort was made to collect plants—particularly grasses—from the area of the site. Positive identification of the modern grasses and sedges was kindly supplied by Mrs. Deshpande of the Botanical Survey of India, Poona. The village women willingly supplied seeds of various local crops, and a collection was made of the grains sold at a local market. Samples of each were carbonized by wrapping them in aluminium foil and roasting them in the hot coals of a chullo or outdoor oven. Carbonizing made the samples more directly comparable to the archaeological remains which were preserved in part because they, too, had been carbonized, either by accident or by deliberate burning. Efforts in future years will be directed toward expanding the modern comparative collection and eliciting information on plant uses from ths local villagers.

Faunal Studies

The recovery and analysis of macro-fauna was undertaken by the Rojdi team. Our zooarchaeologist, Pamela Crabtree, could not join us in the field during the first season for work. We did, however, recover all of the bone from our dry screening operations. Preliminary examination of the material by Paul Rissman indicates the presence of an equid, cattle, pig, sheep and goats. All of these are presumably domesticated. A surprisingly wide variety of wild ungulates also seem to be present, as well as substantial numbers of tortoise, fish, and crustaceans.

Summary of the 1982-83 Field Season

The excavation at Rojdi is, we hope, a very sound beginning to a long-term investigation of this site. The technical studies are well along and an overall approach to the project has been established. This first season of excavation also provided us with a series of reasonably established conclusions about Rojdi:

1. This wall around the settlement is a part of the Harappan occupation. It was thought by many who had seen the site, even excavated there, that this feature should be associated with one of the two historical periods represented there.
2. The building on the North slope once thought to be an intramural tower, is instead a building built on a rectilinear plan.
3. Stratigraphic evidence demonstrates that the large building on the North slope and the settlement are coeval. This is corroborated by evidence related to certain shared features of their engineering.
4. Evidence for lateral stratigraphy in the settlement suggests that all of the area within the wall may not have been settled at one time. We have also expanded the presumed chronology of the site into the Rangpur IIC possibly Rangpur III range of time.
5. Evidence for an area of temporary habitations on the North slope was obtained.
6. Palaeobotanical evidence points to a diversity of resource use. The same is true for preliminary work with faunal remains.

REFERENCES

Indian Archaeology: A review 1957-58. Exploration in Districts Gohilwad, Halar, Jhalawar, Madhya Saurashtra and Sorath. Delhi: Government of India: 18.

——1958-59. Excavation at Rojdi, District Madhya Saurashtra. Delhi: Government of India: 19-21.

Possehl, Gregory L. 1980. *Indus Civilization in Saurashtra*, Delhi: B.R. Publishers.

——In press. The Status of African Millets in South Asian Pre history. In, *Essays in Indian Archaeology*. Jerome Jacobson, editor Delhi: American Institute of Indian Studies.

Rao, S.R. 1963. Excavations at Rangpur and Other Explorations in Gujarat. *Ancient India*, Nos. 18-19: 5-20.

Watson, Patty Jo, 1976. In Pursuit of Prehistoric Subsistence: A Comparative Account of Some Contemporary Flotation Techniques, *Midcontinental Journal of Archaeology* 1: 77-100.

The Cult Object on Unicorn Seals : A Sacred Filter ?*

IRAVATHAM MAHADEVAN

I. The Harappan Cult Object

1.1 The most characteristic artefact of the Indus Civilization is the square stamp seal made of stone, featuring a one-horned bull (the so-called 'unicorn') with a cult object placed in front of the animal and a brief inscription above (Fig. 1). The cult object is depicted as a device consisting essentially of two parts, namely a generally cylindrical upper vessel and a hemispherical lower vessel with a long stem at the base. It has been variously identified as an incense burner or a bird-cage, or a crib and stable rack or as a calendar system to indicate the Jovian cycle of sixty years. The present paper suggests a new identification of the cult object as a 'Sacred Filter' on the basis of pictorial representations of the object on Harappan artefacts as well as parallels from the Soma ritual in the Ṛgveda (*RV*).

1.2 The Harappan cult object appears as a pictorial symbol on seals, sealings, miniature tablets and a few other miscellaneous objects. No actual object resembling this symbol has so far been found from any Harappan site and it is thus likely that the original was made of some perishable material like wood. The following Table summarises the statistics of frequency and distribution of this symbol :

Sites	*Occurrences of the cult object symbol on*			
	seals	*sealings*	*miniature tablets*	*Total*
Mohenjodaro	658	12	—	670
Harappa	187	19	4	210
Chanhudaro	37	—	—	37
Lothal	31	26	—	57
Kalibangan	22	9	—	31
Other sites	7	3	—	10
Total	942	69	4	1,015

Note : The statistics relate only to inscribed objects with texts included in my book, *The Indus Script: Texts, Concordance and Tables* (*IS*).

The cult object is the third most frequent symbol depicted on the Harappan inscribed objects, next only to the JAR sign (*IS*, sign 342) of the Indus Script (1395 times) and the unicorn among the field symbols (1159 times). The cult object appears almost always paired with the unicorn (985 times). The most common arrangement of this classic Harappan motif has the

* Paper read at the 31st International Congress of Human Sciences in Asia and North Africa held at Tokyo, Japan, in September 1983.

unicorn facing right (as seen in impression) with the cult object placed in front under the head of the animal (e.g *MIC* 38). In a few cases the unicorn faces left and the cult object is also found at the left (e.g. *FEM* 8).

1.3 There are a few exceptional cases where the cult object is associated with animals other than the unicorn. Such cases include the two-horned urus ox, probably identical with the 'unicorn', though this is not certain, as the horns are of different types (e.g. *FEM* 234); a fabulous animal resembling in parts both rhinoceros and urus ox (*FEM* 140); the long-tailed ox-antelope on a seal from Chanhudaro (*CE*, LI: 21); the short-tailed goat-antelope on a seal from Lothal (*IS* 7025); and the horned tiger on a seal from Banawali (*IS* 9201). It is noteworthy that with the two partial exceptions listed first above, only the unicorn is accorded the honour of being accompanied by the cult object at Mohenjodaro and Harappa, and the rare association of this object with other animals on seals found at other Harappan settlements may perhaps represent local or later developments.

1.4 The cult object also appears a few times as the sole pictorial motif on inscribed objects indicating its status as an object of veneration in its own right. A unique seal from Harappa (*EH* 256) depicts the cult object on the left half of the field and a two-line text on the right half (Fig. 2). A few sealings (*EH* 320, 321, 652, 665, and duplicates in *IS*) and miniature tablets (*EH* 440, 441, 443, 533) depict the cult object as the sole motif on one side and carry the text on the other side (or sometimes on both sides).

1.5 Three sealings which depict the cult object as part of ritual scenes are of special interest as they provide an insight into the true nature and function of this enigmatic device :

(i) *Cult object in procession* (Fig. 3)

Two identical prismatic sealings from Mohenjodro (*MIC*, CXVI: 5, 8) depict four persons in procession, each carrying a tall standard with a different cult object on the top. One of these objects appears to be the cult object studied here (with only the lower vessel visible) and another, probably the unicorn (with the horn missing). The third object appears to be some kind of a cloth banner, while the fourth has been obliterated. The other two sides carry a text of six signs. Marshall (*MIC*, p. 69) compares these standards with the sacred Nome standards of Egypt. Mackay (*MIC*, p. 384) compares the scene with the one found on the mace of Narmer of Egypt.

(ii) *Cult object as a standard* (Fig. 4)

An oblong sealing from Harappa (*EH* 309) depicts the cult object on both sides. On one side, the object is drawn on an immense scale in comparison with the person who holds it aloft with both hands as a ceremonial standard. One line of inscription is found by the side of the stem of the cult object. On the other side the cult object occupies the field flanked by one line of text on either side of the stem.

(iii) *Cult object as part of a frieze* (Fig. 5)

Three identical oblong sealings from Harappa (*EH* 322; *IS* 5243, 5244) depict a frieze on one side and a text of four signs on the other. The frieze consists of alternate representations of the cult object and small circles arranged in vertical columns. The exceptional importance of the motif which is one of the major clues to the identification of the cult object will be considered presently.

1.6 We may also notice here the occurrence of the cult object on three other interesting artefacts not bearing any inscriptions:

(i) A gold fillet from Mohenjodaro depicting the cult object at both ends (*MIC*, p. 219; pl. CXVIII: 14);

(ii) A circular steatite pectoral of exceptional workmanship from Mohenjodaro depicting the unicorn facing right with the cult object in front and a vase above the animal. (For a beautiful colour reproduction see, *Civilizations of the Indus Valley and Beyond*, Mortimer wheeler, ill. 44);

(iii) An unpublished oblong sealing from Harappa

depicting the cult object on one side and a tree within a railing on the other (*ASI* 63.11.226; *Pu.* 63.4394-95).

1.7 Marshall (1931: 69) identified the cult object as an incense-burner which possibly served simultaneously as a lamp also. According to him the object consisted of two vessels fixed on to a short central staff and was intended to be carried in hand. The lower bowl carried the fire as indicated in some cases by short thin lines rising from its upper surface indicating flame (e.g. *EH* 3). The upper vessel appeared to be of open metal work, possibly revolving on a stem, and containing incense. He suggested that incense played a prominent part in the cult of the one-horned ox. Vats (1940: 321-22) agreed with Marshall on the identification of the cult object as an incense-burner and expressed the view that as it was depicted alone on sealings and tablets from the lower levels of Harappa, it was worshipped even before it came to be associated with the cult of the unicorn.

1.8 Marshall's identification of the cult object however suffers from a fatal flaw. One would expect any representation of an incense-burner to indicate smoke rising from the incense, rather than flame. In more than a thousand representations of the cult object available to us, there is not a single instance indicating smoke or fumes arising from the incense supposed to be contained in the upper vessel. Even if the short lines appearing above the lower vessel in a few instances could possibly indicate flame, this explanation cannot be valid for the rows of small circles or lines arranged radially below the lower vessel in a much larger number of specimens. Marshall's explanation of these as "points" representing "small flames rising above the sides of the vessel" (Marshall 1931: 69, 383) is not convincing.

1.9 Mackay (383-84) regarded the upper vessel as more likely to be made of basket-work with varying coarse or loose weaves as suggested by the grid-like lines appearing on its surface. He thought that the lower vessel was made of leather or wood, as some specimens seem to show embossed rosette-like marks on the sides, while other specimens resemble basket-work. He also thought that the upper and the lower vessels are held together by a staff made of wood or metal running through both. He suggested 'with diffidence' that the cult object was a cage and that it held a bird.

1.10 It is surprising that if the upper vessel were indeed a cage made of loosely woven open-type basket-work as suggested by Mackay, the bird inside is never once visible! However, it is only fair to add that Mackay himself implicitly withdrew this somewhat odd suggestion when he later admitted that "no really satisfactory explanation of the meaning or purpose of these cult objects has yet been recorded" and added that "this cult-stand presents a problem which one day, no doubt, will be satisfactorily solved" (Mackay, *CE*, 147).

1.11 H.F. Friederichs, in a paper mainly devoted to the identification of the animals appearing on the Harappan inscribed objects (*Der Alte Orient*, Vol. 32, 1933, pts. 3 & 4, pp. 1-120) identified the lower receptacle of the cult object as a crib, the upper one as a stable rack and the upper projecting lines from the edge of the lower basin as representing fodder. I have had no access to the original paper, but I am inclined to agree with Mackay's comment (670) that "this particular object cannot be so easily explained", as it seems to be a ritual object carried in procession and venerated in its own right. There is no recorded tradition of cribs or racks being objects of worship.

1.12 After a long interval of four decades, the challenge of identifying the mysterious cult object was again picked up, this time by a group of Soviet scholars working on the decipherment of the Indus Script (Volchok in Knorozov et al., *Proto-Indica*: 1972; Knorozov et al., *Proto-Indica*: 1979). In brief, the Soviet scholars regard the cult object as a combination of two symbols, the top portion appearing in five variants and the bottom portion in twelve variants. The variants are distinguished by means of minor differentiation in the number and treatment of details like vertical strokes and horizontal lines of the upper part and the ornamentation of the lower part with curved lines, small circles etc. The Soviet scholars interpret the upper part as representing a five-year cycle based on solar-lunar correlation, and the lower part as representing a twelve-year cycle based on the correlation of the courses of the Sun and Jupiter. The combination of the five-year and the twelve-year cycles formed the sixty-year cycle, pictorially represented by the combination of the upper and the lower parts of the cult object into a single device. Thus according to the Soviet interpretation, the cult object is a symbol representing, through variations of design, each of the sixty years of the Jovian Cycle, and usually used for dating the seals.

1.13 The problem with the Soviet theory of Maya-like calendar glyphs is that the variations in the details or ornamentation of the Harappan cult symbol are simply too many to admit of a precise total of sixty types only. Volchok herself admits that there are many variations not included in the 'recognized' list of sixty types, but explains, rather unconvincingly, that these may be "stylistic differences which are perhaps characteristics of certain twelve-year periods only" (*Proto-Indica*: *1972*). Again as Volchok herself points out, there are many cases where the representations are too small to admit of much detail. The beautifully carved and well-preserved steatite pectoral from Mohenjodaro delineates only the contours of the cult object without any inner ornamentation, showing that such details (while they may not be devoid of significance) are not essential to the recognition of the symbol. It is difficult to explain why dates were represented on objects like the golden fillet and the steatite pectoral. For these reasons I feel that the Soviet interpretation of the Harappan cult object as a calendar device is not convincing.

1.14 The new interpretation of the Harappan cult object proposed here is based on a close study of over one thousand representations of the symbol seen by me in originals or photographs when I was engaged in copying the texts in the Indus Script. As I was looking closely at the unicorn seals in the magnificent collections of the Archaeological Survey of India and the National Museum, New Delhi, it occurred to me that the two basic elements pictorially emphasised most in the Harappan cult symbol, namely the '*flow*' depicted by the parallel zigzag lines drawn through the upper vessel and the '*drops*' depicted in and around the lower bowl, correspond rather precisely to the two central features of the Soma sacrifice as described in the *RV*, namely *pavamāna*, the 'flowing (one)' and *indu*, the 'drop' mentioned in almost every hymn of the Ninth Maṇḍala dedicated wholly to Soma. These are the two clues which gradually led to the recognition that the Harappan cult object is in fact a filter device, the upper vessel acting as a strainer and the lower perforated bowl as a sieve.

1.15 I shall first describe the component parts of the Harappan cult object and then proceed to explore the close parallelisms between the pictorial representations of this object and the rich and varied imagery of the Soma ritual in the *RV*. A representative selection of the main variants of the cult object depicted on the larger and better preserved unicorn seals from Mohenjodaro and Harappa is reproduced in Fig. 6 from the plates of *MIC*, *FEM* and *EH*. The illustration in Fig. 7 is a composite drawing bringing together twelve distinct features of the cult object depicted on different seals. The features (serially numbered 1 to 12 from top to bottom in Fig. 7) are described below in detail. In dealing with each feature, I shall cite the best examples from the plates of *MIC*, *FEM* and *EH* for comparative study.

Features of the Harappan cult object (Fig. 7).

(1) *Ring or handle at the top of the upper vessel*

This feature is seen clearly in *MIC* 3, 15, 17, 19; *EH* 2, 3, 5, 17. Its purpose is resumably to serve as a handle to carry the upper vessel by hand or for suspension from above. Thus it appears that the upper and the lower vessels were not joined to each other and were independently supported.

(2) *The body of the upper vessel*

The upper vessel is generally cylindrical in shape and often slightly flared at the top and the bottom. Excellent examples may be seen in *MIC* 9, 18, 38; *FEM* 149, 422; *EH* 1, 3, 6. A major variant depicts the upper vessel as hemispherical in shape giving it the appearance of an 'inverted basket'. This shape may be seen clearly in *MIC* 36, 88, 92; *FEM* 11, 398, 644; *EH* 72, 256. The upper vessel appears to be a hollow container.

(3) *Schematic depiction of the downward flow of liquid through the upper vessel*

The most conspicuous feature of the upper vessel

is a series of close parallel lines, drawn vertically or in a wavy zigzag fashion, traversing the length of the vessel Straight vertical lines may be seen in examples like *MIC* 2, 18, 37; *FEM* 11, 225; *EH* 4, 6, 10. Good examples of the wavy or zigzag lines will be found in *MIC* 9, 38; *FEM* 19, 69, 149, 396, 436; *EH* 1, 3, 9, 12. The clue to the true function of the upper vessel is provided by the wavy, zigzag lines which represent schematically the downward flow of some liquid through the vessel.

(4) *Schematic depiction of filtering medium in the upper vessel*

The upper vessel is generally marked by a series of two to five parallel horizontal lines. These lines are straight when the shape of the vessel is cylindrical (e.g. *MIC* 9, 18; *FEM* 149; *EH* 4, 6), and generally curved or convex when the shape of the vessel is hemispherical (e.g. *MIC* 90, 100; *FEM* 11, 74, 147; *EH* 256). In some specimens the horizontal lines are arranged in three or four pairs giving the distinct impression of separate layers of some thick material (e.g. *MIC* 39, 69; *EH* 50, 256). Since the zigzag lines appear to indicate the downward flow of some liquid through the upper vessel, I interpret the horizontal lines (straight or curved) as schematically depicting successive layers of some kind of porous filtering medium placed inside the upper vessel.

(5) *Schematic depiction of the streaming of liquid from the upper vessel into the lower vessel*

Many of the larger seals depict realistically the stream of liquid pouring from upper vessel through the intervening space into the lower vessel. (See especially the examples in *MIC* 18, 38; *FEM* 149, 422, 616; *EH* 3, 6). Depiction of this feature as a thin straight column is to be regarded as conventional (e.g. *MIC* 19, 22, *FEM* 14; *EH* 693).

(6) *A small circular device between the two vessels*

Just above the upper rim of the lower vessel, a small circular device sometimes with slightly upturned ends is seen on some specimens (e.g. *MIC* 9, 18, 38, 66; *EH* 693). This is probably a channel or funnel-like device to receive the liquid flowing from the upper vessel and to regulate its flow into the lower vessel.

(7) *Splash of liquid above the top of the lower vessel*

In some examples short, thin and sometimes curved lines are shown rising from the top of the lower vessel (e.g. *MIC* 38; *EH* 3). These short lines depict the splash of liquid as it pours in a stream from the upper vessel into the lower vessel.

(8) *The lower vessel*

The lower vessel is a hemispherical bowl (e.g. *MIC* 9, 18, 38; *FEM* 616; *EH* 1, 3, 6). Occasionally the bowl is shown with a concave upper rim giving it a crescent-like appearance (e.g. *MIC* 8; *FEM* 422), or with a conical projection at the middle point where the liquid flows into vessel (e.g. *MIC* 126; *FEM* 74, 644; *EH* 256).

(9) *Perforations on the sides of the lower vessel*

The most conspicuous feature of the lower vessel consists of the markings seen on its sides. These are of three main types :

(a) 'eyes' or 'rosettes' formed by small circles with central dots (e.g. *MIC* 16, 38; *FEM* 422, 616; *EH* 4, 7, 8);

(b) 'knobs' or 'bosses' which appear as round projections from the sides of the vessel (e.g. *MIC* 9, 18, 29, 124; *FEM* 19, 26, 149, 340; *EH* 6, 17, 40);

(c) curved, wavy or circular lines (e.g. *MIC* 30, 33, 40, 61, 66, 92; *FEM* 33; *EH* 1, 3, 9, 12, 24, 30).

The feature in type (a) above, namely circles with small central dots, provides the clue to the real function of the lower vessel which appears to be a perforated bowl. It acts as a sieve receiving the filtered liquid from the upper vessel and allowing the clear filtrate to trickle out as drops through the orifices on the sides, while impurities still remaining after filtration would settle at the bottom of the vessel. What makes this interpretation very likely is the depiction of 'drops' actually emerging out of the sides of the lower vessel and also surrounding it. This feature is dealt with in (10) below.

As regards type (b) above, I suggest that what appear to be 'knobs' or 'bosses' are in fact a schematic representation of 'drops' of liquid inside the lower vessel, as if the bowl holds a collection of 'drops' rather than the liquid in mass. The reason for this unusual representation seems to lie in the ritual importance attached to 'drops' of the liquid in the filtering ceremony, judging from the parallelism of the role of *indu* ('drop') in the Soma ritual to be considered more fully in the next section.

The design in type (c) above, namely the curls or circular or wavy lines may be interpreted as artistic depiction of the swirl or eddy of the liquid or the waves on its surface generated by the streaming of the liquid from the upper vessel into the lower bowl. In general, wavy lines represent conventionally water or any other liquid.

(10) *Drops of liquid around the lower vessel*

The most vital clue to the true function of the Harappan cult object is the depiction of 'drops' of liquid emerging through the perforations on the sides of the lower vessel and also surrounding the vessel in a symbolic manner. There are several examples which depict the drops in the actual process of trickling through the orifices on the sides of the vessel. These drops have the characteristic hemisherical or elongated shapes with 'waists' or shown as thin lines radially arranged around the lower sides of the bowl suggesting the spurting of the liquid in jets.

Examples of the motif of 'emerging drops' can be seen in :

MIC 2, 35, 36, 37, 54, 64, 70, 77, 84, 90, 91, 101, 166, 236, 237;

MIC 41 shows thin pin-like lines radially arranged around the bottom of the bowl. (See also the eye-copy of G.R. Hunter, 1934, pl. I, 322).

FEM 2, 11, 225, 312, 351, 412, 578;

EH 10, 35.

A very common motif is a semi-circular row of small circles surrounding the sides of the lower vessel. I interpret the motif as drops of liquid surrounding the bowl in a symbolic manner. Good examples of this arrangement can be seen in

MIC 8, 15, 18, 23, 24, 29, 40, 52, 61, 67, 88, 126, 168, 214, 245.

MIC 3 shows two parallel rows of 'drops' around the bowl.

FEM 7, 68, 80, 141, 147, 233, 348, 398, 492, 585, 644.

EH 68, 73, 78, 195, 256.

The interpretation of the small circles around the lower vessel as 'drops' of liquid is supported by several lines of evidence, namely the flow of liquid through the upper vessel, the pouring of liquid as a stream into the lower vessel, perforations on the sides of the lower vessel, the depiction of emerging 'drops' through the orifices, and wave-like lines on the sides of the lower bowl. It is also significant that while the circles on the bowl may or may not have central dots (representing respectively orifices or 'drops'), the circles around the bowl are never shown with the central dots as they can represent only the 'drops'. Futher the drops surround even those bowls in which perforations are not depicted (e.g. *MIC* 40, 61; *EH* 10, 256). This is evidence to show that the lower bowl was perforated in all cases and the artistic convention permitted the depiction of different aspects of the liquid as 'drops', 'waves' etc.

(11) *The stem attached to the lower vessel*

The lower bowl is supported by a slender vertical stem attached to its base (e.g. *MIC* 38; *FEM* 422; *EH* 1). The stem is generally thicker at the lower end. The purpose of the stem is presumably to hold the lower bowl by hand as in fact shown on some sealings (*MIC*, CXVI; 5, 8; *EH* 309). I venture to suggest that the stem was perhaps not a part of real life-size filter device and was attached only to small-scale hand-held models used in processions or for symbolic ritual purposes.

(12) *The pin-like device on the stem*

There is a short pin-like device inserted horizontally in the vertical stem just below the base of the lower vessel, probably to prevent the bowl from slipping down the stem. The pin is thicker or slightly bent at one end. Examples of this device can be seen in *MIC* 38, 66: XCVI: 5, 8; *EH* 2). This feature appears to indicate that the lower bowl had a hole at the bottom into which the stem was inserted tightly (at least in the hand-held models seen in the pictorial representations).

II. Parallelism with the Soma Ritual of the Ṛgveda

2.1 Before I proceed further with a comparative study of the Harappan cult represented by the Filter symbol and the Soma ritual of the *RV*, I must emphasise that I shall be dealing only with the physical or naturalistic aspects of Soma as the pressed juice and with the mechanical details of its purification through a filter device. Soma is also of course one of the most important deities of the Vedic religion; and the Soma poetry, no less than the other parts of the *RV*, is often couched in metaphysical language with deeper mystical significance. I have no competence to go into these aspects, but happily this is not necessary for the present purpose.

2.2 Soma sacrifice forms the main feature of the ritual of the *RV*. The Ninth Maṇḍala of the *RV* is entirely dedicated to the praise of Soma. The word *soma* means 'pressed (juice)'. The Soma ritual consists essentially of three stages, namely

(a) PRESSING (*savana*) the stalk (*aṃśu*) of the Soma plant between stones (*adri, grāvan*) or in a mortar (*ulūkhala*) to extract the juice;
(b) PURIFYING (*punāna*) the Soma juice by allowing it to flow (*pavamāna*) through a strainer (*pavitra*) made of wool (*vāra, roman*) of sheep (*avya, meṣya*) and through a sieve (*aṇvī*) before collecting the filtered juice in wooden vessels (*kalaśa, kośa, droṇa*);
(c) MIXING (*āśir*) the purified juice with milk curds or barley and offering it to the gods, especially to Indra, the Soma drinker *par excellence* (*somapāḥ*).

2.3 A comparative study of the pictorial variants of the Harappan Filter symbol and the descriptions of the Soma ritual in the *RV*, especially in the Ninth Maṇḍala, has led to the identification of five principal features which appear to be common to the Harappan and the Ṛgvedic rituals, namely

A. The Śtrainer (*pavitra*)
B. The Sieve (*aṇvī*)
C. The Flow (*pavamāna*)
D. The Drop (*indu*)
E. The Bull (*vṛṣan*)

These parallalisms are considered below in detail.

A. *The Strainer* (*pavitra*)

Components of the Filter Device

2.4 The filter and its component parts are very frequently mentioned in the Soma verses of the *RV*. (For a list of the 'filter' words see *Vedic Index*, I.508; Hillebrandt, *Vedic Mythology* Eng. tr., I.297.) The *RV* does not however describe how the filter apparatus was assembled. In the absence of this information the technical terms associated with the filter have been interpreted by the commentators in the light of the later ritual practices which differed in many respects from those of the Ṛgvedic times. Modern scholars are also not in agreement as to the significance of several of these expressions. The translators in English (Wilson, Griffith and Bhawe) employ the terms 'filter', 'strainer' or 'sieve' generally as synonyms. I shall translate *pavitra* as 'strainer' and *aṇva* or *aṇvī* as 'sieve', reserving the term 'filter' to denote the composite device consisting of both the elements. The necessity for this distinction will become clear as I proceed with the argument. We shall see presently that the identification of the Harappan cult object as a *filter* with a two-tier arrangement consisting of a *strainer* above and a *sieve* below provides us with new insights into the significance of several technical terms, metaphors and allusions in the Soma verses of the *RV*, which have so far remained obscure.

Sheep wool (avyaḥ vāram)

2.5 Sheep wool was used for straining the Soma juice. This is very often mentioned in the *RV*:

tiraḥ pavitraṃ vi vāram avyaṃ (9.109.16).
"Through the sheep wool strainer".

The association between the strainer and the sheep wool was so close that the *RV* often uses the terms 'sheep wool' or even merely 'sheep' to stand for the 'strainer' in the Soma verses:

pavate vāre avyaye (9.36.4).
"(Soma) flows into the sheep wool (strainer)".
somaḥ punāno arṣati sahasradhāro aty aviḥ (9.13.1).

"Soma, being purified, flows thousand-streamed, beyond the sheep (wool) (strainer)".

It appears that loose woollen fibres were employed for straining as there is no mention of woven or plaited fabrics in this context. The words *vāra* and *roman* both mean 'hair' and it is unlikely that they were used in the sense of 'cloth'. (The term *daśāpavitra*, 'fringed woollen strainer cloth' cited in the commentaries occurs only in the later texts).

'Top' of the filter device (sānu)

2.6 The loose woollen fibres must have been supported by being placed or packed inside a container or vessel through which the raw juice must have been strained into the receptacle placed below. This arrangement is in fact suggested by the term *sānu*, interpreted by Macdonell as the 'top of the contrivance' (*Vedic Mythology*, p. 106). The two words *avya* and *sānu* occur so often together as to suggest that the sheep wool was placed at the top of the filter device:

yad avya eṣi sānavi (9.50.2).
"When (thou) goest into the top of the sheep (wool) (strainer)".
pavitre adhi sāno avyaye (9.86.3).
"At the top of the sheep (wool) strainer".

Translations of the phrase *sānau avye* (9.97.3) as "elevated fleece" (Wilson) or "fleecy summit" (Griffith) have tended to obscure its simple and natural meaning. A comparison of the Harappan Filter symbol with the Ṛgvedic expressions cited above indicates that the upper vessel corresponds to *sānu*, the 'top' of the Vedic filter device, and the horizontal bands of lines drawn across the upper vessel represent layers of some porous medium for straining (probably sheep wool as described in the *RV*).

B. The Sieve (aṇvī)

2.7 The terms *aṇva* and *aṇvī* generally denote a 'fine sieve' in the Soma verses of the *RV*:

sūro aṇvam vi yāti (9.91.3).
"Soma (lit., the sun) goes through the fine sieve".

Both Veṅkaṭa Mādhava and Sāyaṇa explain *aṇvam* here as '*sūkṣmacchidram pavitram*', 'a sieve with fine holes'. Sāyaṇa also connects *aṇvam* with the *uparava* holes (dug into the ground in later ritual). Sāyaṇa again refers to 'holes in the filter cloth' in his gloss on 9.14.4. Wilson translates *aṇvam* in 9.91.3 as 'filter'. Griffith translates *aṇvam* in 9.10.5 as 'through the openings of cloth' and *aṇveṣu* in 9.16.2 as 'through the sieve'. Bhawe generally renders *aṇva, aṇvī* and related forms as 'thin (strainer)' (9.10.5), 'sieve' (9.14.6), or 'fine strainer' (9.26.1). The commentators however, mostly translate *aṇva* or *aṇvī* as 'slender fingers', probably taking their cue from 9.1.7 where *aṇvīḥ* definitely refers to the 'slender (maidens),' a metaphor for the 'fingers' of the Soma presses. Bhawe (*SH*, 1.66) refers approvingly to Grassmann's view that *aṇva* (*aṇvī*) in the singular stands for the 'fine soma-sieve' while the plural forms refer to the 'fingers'. However Bhawe himself interprets the plural *aṇveṣu* in 9.16.2 as 'fine (strainer chords)'. After a careful review of the occurrences of *aṇva, aṇvī* and the related grammatical forms, I consider that with the exceptions of 9.1.7 where *aṇvīḥ* refers to the 'slender (maidens)', 9.86.47 and 9.107.11 where *aṇvāni meṣyaḥ* refer to the 'fine (hairs) of the sheep', all other occurrences can be interpreted as 'fine (sieve)' in the singular or as 'fine holes (of the sieve)' in the plural (cf. 1.3.4; 9.10.5; 14.6; 15.1; 16.2; 26.1 and 91.3). It now appears likely that the lower perforated bowl of the Harappan Filter device corresponds to *aṇva* or *aṇvī*, the 'fine Soma sieve' of the *RV*. This means that the Ṛgvedic filter device was, like its Harappan prototype, an assemblage of two vessels one below the other, an upper vessel (*sānu*) filled with sheep wool (*avyaḥ vāram*) acting as a strainer (*pavitra*) and a lower perforated bowl acting as a fine sieve (*aṇva* or *aṇvī*).

The Sieve as Soma's place of birth (yoni)

2.8 The receptacle in which Soma 'settles down' or is 'seated' is offen referred to as the *Yoni* in the *RV*:

ā yonim somaḥ Sukṛtam niṣīdati (9.70.7).
"Soma sits on the well-made place".

Yoni means literally the 'womb', but conventionally translated in this context as 'place', 'seat' etc. The problem here is why the Soma receptacle is called the *yoni,* rather than the mountain, the pressing stones or the sheep wool strainer where the Soma plant, its raw juice and the purified drink respectively arise. Bhawe suggests a solution to this puzzle on the basis of the later ritual practice in which the *droṇakalaśa* is placed on wooden pressing boards which may be regarded as the place of birth of the Soma juice (*SH,* I, pp, 9-10). Quite apart from the fact that there is no mention of the pressing boards in the *RV*, this interpretation is somewhat contrived and does not really explain why the vessel is called the *yoni.* I suggest that the expression makes sense once it is interpreted in the light of the Harappan cult object. The Soma vessel which is perforated and functions as a sieve produces clarified Soma juice through its orifices. Thus it is here that Soma, the sacrificial drink, is 'born'. Hence the Soma receptacle is in fact literally the *yoni,* the womb, place of birth or origin of Soma.

Interpretation of legends of Indra based on the Soma sieve

2.9 This new interpretation leads in turn to the recognition that the fine, sieve of Soma is the physical basis of three legends connected with Indra, one of them being mentioned in the *RV* itself :

(a) *Indra's birth through the 'side' of his mother*

Indra is often spoken of as 'having been born'. In a hymn dealing with his birth (4.18) he is described as wishing to be born in an 'unnatural' way through the side' of his mother, says Indra :

> *nāham ato nirayā durgahaitat*
> *tiraścatā pārśvān nirgamāni* (4.18.2).
> "Not this way go I forth : hard is the passage.
> Forth from the side obliquely will I issue" (Griffith).

The key word here is *tiraścatā*, 'obliquely', 'slantingly' or 'transversely'. The same word is used once again in the Ninth Maṇḍala where it describes the path of the Soma juice through the sieve (*aṇvyā*) :

> *ati śritī tiraścatā gavyā jigāty aṇvyā* (9.14.6).
> "For the sake of resort. he (Soma) goes over the slanting (path) through the sieve towards the cows' (milk)" (Bhawe).

Now we can solve the mystery of both the allusions. The Soma sieve was a vessel perforated on its sides, through which the drops of the filtered juice came out (as vividly represented on many Harappan seals). While it is natural for a liquid to be poured out of the top or even the bottom of a vessel, it is quite unusual (and hence unnatural) for a liquid to come out of the sides of the vessel. It is this unusual course that is referred to in 9.14.6 with the expression *tiraścatā* ('obliquely, slantingly or transversely'). This confirms that the *RV* did indeed know of a sieve-like Soma bowl perforated on the sides (*aṇva, aṇvī*) as represented by the lower vessel in the Harappan Filter symbol. By a well-known process in the Vedic hymns, the traits of Soma are transferred to its greatest drinker, Indra. The physical basis of the myth about Indra's birth through the 'side' of his mother now becomes clear. Indra is so depicted because this is how *indu,* the 'drops' come out of the Soma sieve, through the orifices on the sides of the vessel, obliquely, slantingly or transversely.

(b) *Soma coming out of every pore on Indra's body*

According to a later legend, Indra drank pure Soma which pressed forward again through all the openings of his body so that the gods had to cure him by means of the *sautrāmaṇī* ceremony (*ŚBr.* V.5.4.9.ff). Hillebrandt (*VM*, I. 423, n. 238) points out that this ceremony was known by name as early as in *AV.* III.3.2, and expresses his conviction that the ritual was still older. Here again the physical basis of the myth is the equation of Indra's body with the Soma sieve. The trickling of Soma drops through the orifices on the sides of the Soma sieve suggested the image of Soma pouring out of all the openings of Indra's body.

(c) *The 'thousand holes' on Indra's body*

The *RV* often compares the flowing of the Soma juice into the receptacle with the flow of Soma into the stomach or heart of Indra :

> —*indrasya hārdi somadhānam ā viśa* (9.70.9).
> "(O Soma) enter the Soma-vessel, the heart of Indra"
> —*indrasy endo jaṭharam ā pavasva* (9.70.10).
> "O Indu, flow into the stomach of Indra".
> *endrasya kukṣā pavate madintama* (9.80.3).

"He (Soma) flows into Indra's stomach for his food."

We can see now that the constant comparison of Indra's stomach, heart or body with the Soma vessel, a sieve with numerous fine holes on its sides, is the physical basis behind the post-Vedic myth of Indra's body being marked with a thousand holes. According to later legends, Indra seduced Ahalyā, the wife of Gautama, and the sage laid upon Indra a curse which covered Indra's body with a thousand orifices (eyes or *yoni*-s according to different accounts).

Harappan perforated ware

2.10 The identification of the lower vessel of the Harappan filter device as a perforated bowl naturally invites comparison with perforated pottery which is one of the most characteristic of the ceramic ware of the Indus Civilization (Manchanda, *A Study of the Harappan Pottery*, p. 141). The perforated vessels are mostly cylindrical jars (unlike the hemispherical bowl seen on the Harappan seals) of widely varying sizes (1.4 to 22 inches in height). The holes on the sides of the vessel are pierced from outside, leaving the inner edges ragged. There is generally a large hole at the bottom centre of the perforated jar. It has been suggested that the vessels were used as braziers or ritualistic incense-burners or lamp-shades etc. In West Asia, perforated vessels were used as strainers or colanders. But Manchanda thinks that such use "cannot be so unequivocally vouched for the tall cylindrical perforated vases of the Harappan type". While perforated ware was known to several ancient cultures, its abundant use is a characteristic feature of the Indus Civilization, perhaps in a ritualistic context as suggested by the perforated bowl seen in the Harappan Filter symbol.

Perforated vessels in later tradition

2.11 A sacrificial vessel called *sata* used in ritual is mentioned in later Vedic literature and the ritual texts (*Vedic Index* II.419). Śabaraswāmin in his commentary on *Mīmāmsa Sūtra Bhāṣya* (I.3.10) describes *sata* as 'a wooden vessel round in shape and perforated with a hundred holes' (*sata iti dārumayam pātram parimaṇḍalam śatacchidraṁ*). He cites the term as an example of words of *mleccha* origin without etymology in Sanskrit. The description bears a striking resemblance to the pictorial representation of the hemispherical perforated bowl seen in the Harappan Filter symbol.

The Twin Soma vessels of the RV

2.12 The *RV* often refers to some Soma vessels in the dual number. According to the traditional interpretation, the twin bowls stand metaphorically for 'heaven and earth'. We are concerned here with the physical basis of this description. Now that there is evidence that the filter device in the *RV* was an assembly of *two* vessels, one functioning as a strainer and the other as a sieve, it is instructive to re-examine the references to the twin Soma vessels in the *RV*.

(a) *oṇyoḥ* : This expression in the ablative dual form occurs thrice in the Ninth Maṇḍala and refers, in its primary sense, to some parts of the Soma filter (9.16.1; 65.11; 101.14). Griffith points out (in his note on 9.16.1) that the term signifies apparently an implement or a vessel, consisting of two pieces used in the preparation of the Soma juice. He translated the word as 'Soma-press' and Bhawe as 'pressing boards' (9.16.1) as they probably considered that the only twin objects involved in the Soma ritual were the two pressing boards. However, there is no evidence for the existence of the pressing boards in the *RV*. In the light of the new evidence furnished by the Harappan Filter symbol we can interpret *oṇī* (dual) in its primary sense as the twin vessels (strainer and sieve). While the filter vessels support the flowing Soma, verse 9.65.11 reverses the situation for poetic surprise, and describes Soma Pavamāna as the supporter of the *oṇī* (*dhartāram oṇyoḥ*), literally the two (filter) vessels, but metaphorically 'heaven and earth'.

(b) *camvoḥ* : The use of the locative dual in the phrase *camvoḥ sutaḥ*, 'pressed in the (two) *camū*-s' (e.g. 9.36.1) has caused a problem in interpretation because Soma is not pressed in vessels but between stones. According to Hillebrandt (*VM*, I.280), *camvoḥ* is probably one of the elliptical duals and denotes the mortar as well as the pestle at the same time. Bhawe has followed the traditional interpretation and translated the phrase *camvoḥ sutaḥ* as 'pressed out on the (two) wooden boards' (9.36.1). We may now consider the possibility that *camū* in the dual form stands for the twin vessels of the filter device as in the following verse:

> *mahī samairac camvā samīcī*
> *ubhe te asya vasunā nyṛṣṭe* (3.55.20).
> "He (Tvaṣṭar) united the (two) great Bowls that face each other; both of them being packed full with his treasure".

The term *camvā* can be interpreted in its primary sense to stand for the twin vessels (of the filter device) which face each other as represented in the Harappan symbol. The expression *camvoḥ sutaḥ* can be understood to mean 'pressed *into* the (two) vessels'.

(c) *dhāmanī* : There is an interesting reference in the *RV* to the two abodes of Soma 'which stand facing' (the priests):

> *tābhyām viśvasya tājasi ye pavamāna dhāmanī*
> *pratīcī soma thasthatuḥ* (9.66.2).
> "By means of those (two) abodes which stand facing (us), thou rulest over all, O Pavamāna Soma."

The word *dhāmanī* (in the dual) has been variously interpreted, as the two lunar halves of the month (by Venkaṭa Mādhava), as the stalk (*aṃśu*) and the juice (*soma*) (by sāyaṇa), as heaven and earth (by Ludwig) or as Soma, the deity and the juice (by Bhawe). Gordon Wasson (*Soma*, pp. 25-34) has suggested a novel interpretation of the two forms of Soma as the juice itself and the urine of the Soma-drinker, which again intoxicates those who consume it, as a psychotropic metabolite. None of these interpretations is in accordance with the specific requirement in the verse that the two forms should actually 'stand facing' (*pratīcī*) the priests. We can now interpret *dhāmanī* as the 'two Abodes' of Soma, that is, the two prominent vessels of the filter apparatus (the strainer and the sieve) facing the priests during the ritual. Alternatively, if *dhāman* is taken to mean 'form' (rather than 'abode'), the expression *dhāmanī* can also be interpreted to stand for the two most important forms of the Soma juice, namely *pavamāna* (the 'flowing one') and *indu* (the 'drop'), both actually seen during the filtering ritual.

(d) *dhiṣaṇe* : *dhiṣaṇā* is also a Soma bowl and the word is often used in the dual as in the other instances noticed above to represent 'heaven and earth' as the 'two great bowls' which close upon each other at the horizon:

> *samīcīne dhiṣaṇe vi ṣkhabhāyati* (10.44.8).
> "He props apart the (two) Bowls (*dhiṣaṇe*) that face each other".

It appears likely that like *camū*, *dhiṣaṇe* also in its primary sense refers to the two bowls (of the filter device) which stand apart but facing each other as depicted by the Harappan Filter symbol.

(e) *Other references to the Twin Vessels*:

> *vi yo mame yamyā saṃyatī madaḥ* (9.68.3)
> "(He) who, (as) the exhilarating juice, has traversed the united twins".

In the context of the Soma ritual and the flow of Soma Pavamāna, the 'twins' (*yamyā*) which are 'united' (*saṃyatī*) and which are 'traversed' (*mame*) by the 'juice' (*madaḥ*) refers, on the physical plane, to the twin vessels of the filter. In the next verse (9.68.4), the phrase *sa mātarā vicaran* 'he (Soma) wandering through (his) (two) mothers' makes sense only when related to the twin filter vessels through which the juice flows. As in the case of the twin vessels discussed above, the traditional interpretation of 'heaven and earth' need not be excluded in these two cases also, but are to be regarded as metaphorical suggested by the twin bowls of the filter, the most prominent objects associated with the Soma ritual.

The Three Filters of Soma

2.13 The *RV* mentions *trī pavitrā*, 'three filters' of Soma twice:

> —*trī ṣa pavitrā hṛdy antar ā dadhe* (9.73.8).
> "He (Soma) carries three filters inside his heart".
>
> *sam trī pavitrā vitatāny eṣy anv ekaṃ dhāvasi pūyamānaḥ* (9.97.55).
> "Thou comest unto the three filters stretched out; and runnest through each clarified".

Veṅkaṭa Mādhava and Sāyaṇa identify the three filters as Agni, Vāyu and Sūrya, the three purifying deities. Sāyaṇa also suggests that these filters are different from the strainer made of sheep wool. Bhawe (*SH*, III.101) has proposed that the doctrine of the three *pavitras* refers to the three forms of Soma viz., heavenly, mid-regional and earthly. Gordon Wasson (*Soma*, pp. 51-58) identifies the three filters in the order of their function, with (i) the Sun's rays which 'filter' the celestial ambrosia as Soma juice into the plant, (ii) the woollen strainer, and (iii) Indra's belly where Soma is said to be clarified prior to its being filtered out through the bladder into the urine.

I believe we can identify the physical basis for the three filters of Soma when we read the relevant passages in the *RV* keeping in view the construction of the Harappan Filter in which the liquid can be seen to pass through three distinct stages in the course of its downward flow:

FIRST, through the upper vessel corresponding to the sheep wool strainer (*pavitra*) of the *RV*;

SECOND, through mid-air in the intervening open space between the two filter vessels, corresponding to Soma's passage through *antarikṣa* (mid-region) or Vayu's place (mid-air) as often referred to in the *RV*;

THIRD, through the lower perforated bowl corresponding to the fine Soma sieve (*aṇva* or *aṇvī*) of the *RV*, before finally emerging as drops of Soma (*indu*).

This sequence is clearly referred to in the *RV*:

somaḥ punāno arṣati sahasradhāro aty aviḥ
vāyor indrasya niṣkṛtam (9.13.1).

"Soma, being purified, flows thousand-streamed,
beyond the sheep (wool) (strainer),
To Vāyu's and Indra's place".

The sequence is obvious when we understand 'Vāyu's place' to be the mid-air (between the strainer and the sieve) and Indra's place to be the receptacle of Soma, often identified with Indra's heart or stomach. again Soma is described,

antarikṣena rārajat (9.5.2).

"(Soma) shining through the mid-rigion".

Sāyaṇa's gloss *droṇakalaśam prati gacchati* makes it clear that the reference to the mid-region here is to the space between the strainer and the receptacle, from the naturalistic point of view, the concept of the three filters is based on the successive filtering action of

(i) the sheep wool strainer which removes the solid matter;
(ii) the passage through the air (in between the two vessels) which purifies the stream; and
(iii) the fine sieve which further filters off the remaining impurities before the pure drops of Soma energe through the orifices on the sides of the vessel.

The Three Filters as interpreted here may also be the 'three abodes' of Soma (*triṣadhastha*, 8.94.5) though Sāyaṇa identifies them with three Soma vessels of later ritual.

C. The flow (pavamāna)

2.14 The presiding deity of the Ninth Maṇḍala of the *RV* is Soma in the form of Pavamāna. The word *pavamāna* means 'the flowing one'. The supreme moment of the Soma ritual is reached when the juice starts flowing through the filter. The flow of Soma is "the all-absorbing them of the Soma-poetry" (Bhawe). The flow is referred to virtually in every verse of the Ninth Maṇḍala and is extolled with endlessly varying imagery invoking movement of waters in varied forms, as rains falling, rivers streaming or waves billowing. The Soma verses are a veritable cornucopia of 'flow' words, verbs describing movement, adjectives emphasising swiftness, and nouns providing similes of speeding objects like birds, race horses or chariots. As Bhawe points out, the Ṛgvedic poets appear to take an almost sensuous pleasures in the running of Soma Pavāmana.

2.15 The flow of Soma as *pavāmana* is the first and most important clue I have to identify the function of the upper vessel of the Harappan cult object as a strainer. The series of parallel lines placed closely together and drawn vertically or in zigzag fashion through the length of the upper vessel depict pictorially the flowing of a liquid and correspond to the imagery of Soma as *pavāmana* in the *RV*.

2.16 The flow of Soma is also frequently described

as *dhārā*, a 'continuous system'. The expression is often used to depict multiple streams as in *śata-dhārāḥ*, 'hundred streams' (9.86.27), or *sahasra-dhārah*, 'thousand-streamed' (9.13.1). The thin stream of Soma is described as a 'thread' (*tantu*) stretched out and extending to the highest place (9.22.6). The streams passing through the filter are also described as *asaścataḥ*, 'several, separate' (9.57.1; 62.28 etc.). Bhawe's comment (*SH* III.15) is apt: "Every observer of the Indian monsoon knows that the rain falls in continuous yet *separate* thin streams. Soma also flows in the same way". The pictorial depiction of flow by means of a series of thin vertical or slanted parallel lines drawn across the upper vessel of the Harappan cult object fits in exactly with these descriptions in the *RV*.

2.17 One of the more frequent verbs employed to describe the flow of Soma is *dhāv*, 'to run'. An interesting feature here is the use of the verb in two distinct forms, *dhāv* and *vi-dhāv* in different contexts. While either form is used (but *vi-dhāv* more frequently) to describe the flow of Soma through the sheep wool strainer, only *dhāv* is used to refer to the flow beyond the strainer into the receptacles. Similarly the form *vi-dhāv* occurs with *pavamāna* (the 'flowing one') but never with *indu* (the 'drop'):

—*(a)vyo vāram vi pavamāna dhāvati* (9.74.9).

"O Pavamāna, (thy juice) runs diversely through the sheep wool (strainer)".

abhi droṇāni dhāvati (9.28.4).

"(Soma) runs towards the wooden vessels".

ete dhāvant-īndavaḥ somā indrāya ghṛṣvayaḥ (9.21.1).

"These drops, the strong Soma (juices), run for Indra".

It appears that the poets intended a distinction here, *vi-dhāv* representing (optionally) the 'diverse' or 'meandering' flow through the sheep wool strainer, while *dhāv* describes (invariably) the straight flow thereafter. Veṅkaṭa Mādhava and Sāyaṇa interpret *vidhāvati* as *vividham dhāvati* in a few places. Wilson and Griffith translate *vidhāvasi* (9.16.8) as '(thou) wanderest' and Bhawe translates *vidhāvati* (9.37.3) as 'diversely runs'. There is a remarkably close correspondence between the Ṛgvedic imagery of the 'diversely' running flow of *pavamāna* and the zigzag or wavy lines depicted on the upper vessel of the Harappan Filter symbol.

2.18 The word *hvarāmsi* occurs thrice in the Soma verses (9.3.2; 63.4; 106.13) and has been variously rendered as 'declivities' (Benfey), 'plaited cloth' (Zimmer), 'winding ways' or 'twisted obstacles' (Griffith) or 'impediments' (Bhawe). Bhawe considers that the term stands for the obstruction caused by the hairs of the strainer. While this meaning is not unlikely, it is more apt in the context of the flow of Soma to translate the word as 'diverse or winding ways'. (The root meaning of *hvar* is 'to deviate or diverge from the right line, to go deviously'; Monier Williams). The serpentine or winding paths of the Soma juice flowing across the sheep wool strainer correspond to the wavy, zigzag flow lines on the upper, vessel of the Harappan Filter symbol.

D. The drop (indu)

2.19 While *pavamāna* (the 'flowing one') is regarded as the most important aspect of Soma, *indu* (the 'bright drop') is the most frequently applied epithet to the juice. Another term for 'drop' is *drapsa* which is used less often than *indu*. In their naturalistic aspects, *pavamāna* is the *flowing* stream of Soma, and *indu* is the *drop* coming out of the sieve. Both are deified and constitute together the core of the Soma ritual. Griswold put it well when he wrote, "As agni's theophanic moment is when the gheefed altar-flame blazes up, so the theophanic moment of Soma is when the round drops fall from the sieve into the wooden vat below" (*Religion of the RV*, p. 230). Even as the 'flow' of Soma as *pavamāna* was the first clue to identify the flow lines drawn through the upper vessel, the second clue is furnished by the 'drops' of Soma (*indu*) which correspond to the small circles or droplets surrounding the lower vessel and indicating its function as a sieve. The representations of the 'flow' through the strainer and the 'drops' in and around the sieve appear to symbolise the Sacred Elements of the Harappan ritual and correspond exactly to the concepts of *pavamāna* and *indu* in the *RV* respectively.

2.20 The sealing from Harappa (*EH* 322; duplicates in *IS* 5243, 5244) illustrated here in Fig. 5 is of exceptional importance in confirming my interpretation.

This sealing is a frieze of alternate representations of the filter device and the falling drops (small circles arranged in a vertical column). This motif of 'Filter and the Falling Drops' can now be interpreted as depicting the Harappan equivalents of *pavitra* and *indu* of the *RV*.

Pictorial parallels for metaphors of Indu

2.21 I shall now present three cases where the pictorial parallels from the Harappan seals help us to understand the metaphors of Indu in the *RV* which have hitherto remained obscure:

(a) *Embrace of Soma by Indu*

One of the Soma verses refers to the embracing of Soma by Indu:

> *yaḥ somaḥ kalaśeṣv ā antaḥ pavitra ā hitaḥ*
> *tam induḥ pari ṣasvaje* (9.12.5).
>
> "The Soma who is placed in the pitchers (and) in the strainer; him the drop has embraced". (Bhawe)

Commenting on this verse, Bhawe (*SH*, I.63) points out the 'peculiar distinction' between *soma* and *indu* here and draws attention to Sāyaṇa's gloss according to which Indu is the god who embraces Soma, the physical juice. When we look at the Harappan seals (e.g. *MIC* 3, 15, 18) showing the Filter with round drops of liquid surrounding the lower bowl, we realise what the poet meant when he sang of *indu*, the 'drop' embracing *soma*, the 'pressed juice' within the bowl!

(b) *The 'shining knots' of Soma*

The following Soma verse has caused considerable problems in interpretation mainly because the physical phenomenon alluded to in it has not been understood so far:

> *eṣa vasūni pibdanā paruṣā yayivān ati; ava sādeṣu gacchati* (9.15.6).
>
> "This (Soma) having gone beyond the shining (crushed) twig-knots sticking to (him), goes down into the pitchers." (Bhawe)

The problem has been to identify what are the shining (*vasūni*) knots (*paruṣā*) sticking to (*pibdanā*) Soma's body (or the sieve). With the help of Bhawe's interpretation (*SH*, I.71), Wasson (*Soma*, pp. 59-60) identifies the 'knots' with the scales of the white cap of the mushroom (fly-agaric) left behind in the strainer. However, in this case the thin wispy matter would be buried in the layers of the sheep wool strainer and would hardly be prominent enough to merit the description of 'knots' or 'knobs'. Here again the Harappan seals help us to understand the poetic metaphor with a precise pictorial parallel. As described earlier several seals depict drops of liquid in the process of emerging out of the orifices of the sieve (e.g. *MIC* 2, 36). These hemi-spherical drops, still sticking to the sides of the bowl and glistening in the sunlight, create the illusion of shining knots, knobs or studs on the sides of the sieve (or, metaphorically the body of Soma). On the basis of this parallel, we can now attempt a more meaningful translation of this verse:

> "This (Soma) having gone beyond the shining knots (lit., drops) sticking to (the sieve), goes down into the pitchers."

Notice how all the obscurities have vanished and the poem emerges as a natural and beautiful description of shining droplets of the juice sticking to the sides of the sieve.

(c) *The 'thousand knobs' of Soma*

Two nearly identical verses refer to Soma as *sahasrabhṛṣṭi*, '(he) with a thousand studs' (9.83.5; 86.40). One of the verses is given here:

> *rājā pavitraratho vājam āruhaḥ*
> *sahasrabhṛṣṭir jayasi śravo bṛhat* (9.83.5).
>
> "King, on thy chariot sieve thou goest upto war, and with a thousand weapons (lit. sharp points) winnest lofty fame". (Griffith)

The word *bhṛṣṭi* means, 'spike, point, top, corner, edge' etc., (Monier Williams). The metaphor of *bhṛṣṭi* here is very similar to the one of *paruṣā*, 'knot', noticed earlier. Some of the Harappan seals (e.g. *MIC* 9, 18) depict the lower bowl with 'bosses' covering the whole surface giving the vessel the appearance of 'knobbed' ware. Mackay drew attention to this feature, but

Marshall pointed out that bowls made of knobbed ware were not found at Mohenjodaro (*MIC*, p. 383). Manchanda (*A Study of the Harapyan Pottery*, p. 124) has surveyed the occurrence of knobbed ware at Mohenjodaro and Harappa and points out that the specimens are all very small jars with narrow mouths, and appear to be 'luxury ware' for keeping 'expensive liquids'. As we have seen there is clear evidence that the lower hemispherical bowl of the Harappan filter device was a perforated vessel and could not have been made of knobbed ware. I interpret the round globular projections as a pictorial rendering of the concept that the bowl is filled with 'drops', as it were, rather than liquid in the mass, an idea which accords with the Ṛgvedic imagery of Soma as *indavaḥ*, 'drops'. It is however interesting that the 'drops' did suggest the imagery of 'knobs' even to the Ṛgvedic poets as seen in the verse cited here. The 'thousand knobs' refer to the drops formed on the Soma-sieve on the one hand, and the 'thousand-spiked weapon' of king Soma on the chariot-sieve, on the other.

E. The Bull (vṛṣan)

2.22 Soma is frequently compared to a bull (*ukṣan, vṛṣan, vṛṣabha*) in the *RV*. In the following verses there is a characteristic word-play on *vṛṣan* which is unfortunately lost in translation:

vṛṣā soma dyumān asi vṛṣā deva vṛṣavrataḥ
vṛṣā dharmāṇi dadhiṣe (9.64.1).
vṛṣṇas te vṛṣṇyam śavo vṛṣā vanam vṛṣā madaḥ
satyam vṛṣan vṛṣed asi (9.64.2).

O Soma, bull, (thou) art full of lustre;
O god, bull, (thou) art possessed of manly wonder-deeds;

(As) a bull thou holdest sacred activities;
The strength of thine, the bull, is manly;
Strength-giving (is) thy worship, manly thy exhilaration;

O virile one, thou art indeed a Bull.
(Adapted from Bhawe)

Soma as the bull has far-gazing eyes (*vicakṣana*) and sharp horns (*tigmaśṛṅga*). He is fond of sharpening his horns (*śṛṅge śiśāno*) and bellowing loudly (*ruvati*).

ruvati bhīmo vṛṣabhas taviṣyayā
śṛṅge śiśāno hariṇī vicakṣaṇaḥ (9.70.7).

"He (Soma) bellows, terrifying bull, with might,
sharpening his shining horns, gazing afar" (Renou).

2.23 It is somewhat strange that Soma, the juice extracted from a plant, should be so often campared with the bull, with which it has little in common. It is probable that the traits of Indra as a manly warrior stand transferred to Soma. When we turn to the Harappan seals we find the same association represented by the almost constant pairing of the unicorn and the Sacred Filter. The wide staring eye and the sharp horn of the unicorn so prominently depicted on the Harappan seals recall at once the epithets *vicakṣana* and *tigmaśṛṅga* applied to Soma, the bull in the *RV*. As pointed out in the earlier section, the Filter seldom appears with other animals on the Harappan seals. It is therefore likely that the unicorn-bull (or the deity represented by the animal) occupied the same special position in the Harappan religion in respect of the Sacred Filter ritual as Indra did in respect of the Soma ritual in the religion of the Ṛgveda.

III. Evidence for Soma-like Ritual in the Indus Script

3.1 The very high frequency of the Sacred Filter symbol and the special place accorded to it on the unicorn seals indicate that it represents one of the most important, if not the central cult of the Harappan religion. It is therefore quite likely that inscriptions in the Indus Script may have references to this ritual. The Indus Script has not yet been deciphered; but it may be possible to identify the ideograms connected with the ritual by utilising the pictorial clues furnished by the signs themselves and the evidence of the *RV* describing a similar ritual. In the light of the new evidence provided by the Sacred Filter symbol, I have provisionally identified fifteen signs in the Indus Script (Fig. 8) as dealing with a Soma-like cult of the Harappan religion. The signs appear to cover all the stages of the ritual as described in the *RV*, namely

(a) Pressing in a mortar;
(b) Flow of the juice (through a strainer);
(c) Filtering through a sieve;
(d) Offering to the gods in sacrifice.

The evidence from the Indus Script thus Supplements the information from the Sacred Filter symbol which depicts only the most important aspect of the ritual.

Mortar in the Soma Ritual in the RV

3.2 The common method of extracting the Soma juice in the *RV* was by crushing the stalks between 'stones' (*adri*, *grāvan*) which were pleced on ox-hide or held in hand by the officiants. The 'stones' are not described further, but there are reasons to believe that the most ancient method of extraction of the juice was by using mortar and pestle. The ancient Avestan and the modern Parsi rituals employ only a mortar to extract the Haoma juice proving that this custom goes back to the Indo-Iranian period. The use of the mortar (*ulūkhala*) is specifically mentioned only in a single hymn in the *RV* (1.28) with the following refrain in the first four verses:

ulūkhalasutānām aved v indra jalgulaḥ.

"O Indra, drink with eager thirst the droppings which the mortar sheds". (Griffith)

This hymn from the First Maṇḍala may be a late one; but it appears to preserve an archaic tradition as seen from the unique references in it to the pestle being worked by a woman (*nārī*), who otherwise takes no part in the Soma ritual, and to the mortar as operating in every house' (*gṛhe gṛhe*). Hillebrandt (*VM*, I.272) infers from this evidence that the Soma ritual was in the earliest period a domestic or household observance and that extraction by the mortar was the original method. Hillebrandt also cites the study of S.G. Oliphant (*studies in honor of Maurice Bloomfield*, 1920, p. 325) according to whom the term *grāvan* even in the Vedas stood for mortar and pestle, while the term *adri* meant 'press stones' of the type described in the later ritual texts. Hillebrandt adds (*VM*, I.451, n.21) that the term *adrī* (when used in the dual) could also denote stone mortar and pestle. According to Griswold (*Religion of the RV*, p. 226) there is nothing in the description of the press-stones which would not be appropriate for mortar and pestle except the multiplicity in number. I think however that the idea of duality is so inherent in the act of pressing with any implement that grammatical number is not very material to decide the issue. The use of singular or plural could well be meant to indicate the mortar or the presence of large numbers of the pressing implements. My suggestion is that just as *vana*, 'wood', and *vanya*, 'wooden' are used in the Soma verses in a generic sense to denote wooden vessels, even so the 'stone' words (*adri*, *grāvan*) could have been used generically for the stone mortar and pestle. It is also likely that the Soma mortar and pestle were small stone implements (somewhat like the ones used by the modern apothecary) judging from the fact that they were 'held in hand' (*grāva-hastāsah*; 1.15.7).

***'Mortar' signs in the Indus Script* (*IS* 34, 335-337)**

3.3 Sign *IS* 336 is a self-evident pictogram depicting mortar and pestle. It is one of the dozen most frequent signs in the Indus Script occurring 236 times (*IS*: Concordance, pp. 585-95). The sign is found engraved singly on the boss at the back of a unicorn seal (*MIC* 18) indicating its character as a meaningful word-sign by itself. The identification of the cult object symbol on the unicorn seals as a Sacred Filter makes it likely that the 'mortar' sign is connected with the ritual pressing and extraction of the juice as in the Soma sacrifice of the *RV*. The sign may stand for 'mortar and pestle' or 'pressing' or even 'presser'.

3.4 The 'mortar' sign (*IS* 336) occurs as two main variants (*IS*: List of sign variants, p. 791). In one of them the pestle appears as a straight staff of uniform thickness (e.g. *MIC* 30); in the other, the lower end has a bulbous attachment as in a churning staff (e.g. *MIC* 38). This unusual combination has an exact parallel in a verse in the *RV*, which associates the mortar with a churning staff:

Yatra manthām vi badhnate raśmīny amitavā iva
ulūkhalastutānām aved v Indra jalgulah (1.28.4)

"Where, as with reins to guide a horse,
they bind the cnurning-staff with chords,
O Indra, drink with eager thirst
the droppings which the mortar sheds." (Griffith)

Several explanations have been offered for this apparently ill-fitting combination. According to Oldenberg (*RV*, *Noten*, I, 24, note 2) the combination refers to the production of fire as an integral part of the Soma ritual. Hillebrandt (*VM* I.274) has suggested that the twirling stick and the mortar formed a 'single apparatus' a kind of 'manual grinder' for crushing Soma. Griswold (*The Religion of the RV*, p. 223, n. 5) refers to the Parsi practice of turning round the pestle in the mortar to extract the juice further, and suggests, by analogy, that after Soma was crushed, the whole was churned by the 'regular Indian twirling apparatus' the better to secure the juice. It is indeed remarkable that the Indus Sign (*IS*. 336) offers an exact pictorial parallel to this unusual combination proving that this sign depicts no ordinary mortar and pestle (such as the one used for pounding corn).

3.5 One of the verses in the *RV* refers to the pressing stones as 'Some times pierced and other times not pierced with holes' (*tṛdilā atṛdilāsaḥ*; 10.94.11). The Same hymn refers in another line to a 'hole' (ākhara) in the stones (10.94.5). Hillebrandt (*VM*, I.271) wondered whether occasionally holes were made in the stones 'in order to tie them to straps and thus to hold them better'. The true explanation becomes clear from the pictorial parallels offered by two Indus signs of the 'mortar' group (*IS*, 335 and 337). It appears now from these signs that the Soma mortar had perhaps a variant form combining the functions of a mortar and a sieve in one vessel. The sign *IS* 337 depicts a mortar (either with a pestle or with a churning staff) perforated at the bottom with five holes through which the liquid spurts out in thin jets. (*IS*: List of Sign Variants, p. 791). Another sign *IS* 335 depicts a mortar with a long stem at the base and streams of liquid spurting out as thin jets through two holes at the bottom of the vessel on either side of the stem. The sign appears to depict a mortar-cum-sieve to be held in hand, probably in a symbolic ritual. (cf. the hand-held filter depicted on the sealings *MIC*, CXVI:5, 8 and *EH* 309). The anthropomorphic sign *IS* 34 showing a person holding a mortar and pestle in his hand may represent an officiant connected with the ritual of pressing.

The 'Flow' signs (IS, 119-121)

3.6 Signs *IS* 120 and 121 are composed respectively of 9 or 12 short parallel strokes arranged in three tiers. Sign *IS* 119 has varying number of strokes (from 6 to 10) in different variants. (*IS*: List of sign variants, p. 787). These signs have sometimes been regarded as 'numerals', from which however they are clearly distinguishable by the following characteristics:

(i) The numerals have invariably vertical strokes, while these signs have characteristic variants with zigzag lines;
(ii) Sign 119 with variable number of strokes cannot represent a numeral;
(iii) Sign 121 occurs sometimes doubled unlike the numeral signs;
(iv) No sign for 'eleven' has been found to connect the two series;
(v) The present group of signs does not occur in numerical sequences.

G.R. Hunter (1934: p. 98) while concluding that these signs are not numerical also pointed out their close similarity with the flow lines depicted on the upper vessel of the cult object symbol on the unicorn seals (*Ibid*, pl. I). Hunter regarded the signs *IS* 120 and 121 as simple variants. I consider that all the three signs of this group (*IS* 119-121) are most likely to be simple variants of single ideogram representing the 'flow' of a liquid. In other words, they represent in the Indus Script the same concept of 'flow' as depicted by similar lines on the upper vessel (strainer) of the Sacred Filter symbol on the unicorn seals.

The 'SIEVE' signs (IS 332 to 334)

3.7 The sign *IS* 332 depicts a hemispherical bowl with a perforated bottom with four or five holes through which a liquid issues in jets. (*IS*: List of variants, p. 792). The vessel is therefore a sieve exactly like the one forming the lower half of the Sacred Filter symbol on the unicorn seals. Compare this sign especially with the lower bowl depicted on the seal *MIC* 41 (reproduced by G.R. Hunter, 1934, pl. I, No. 322), showing the spurting of liquid by thin lines radiating from the bottom of the vessel. The next sign (*IS*: 333) is an even closer approximation to the lower perforated bowl of the Filter device since the long stem attached to the bowl at the base is also shown along with streams of liquid spurting out as thin jets from two holes at the bottom of the vessel on either side of the stem. The stem served the purpose of holding the perforated bowl in hand or carrying it aloft as a standard in procession, as suggested by the hand-held filter symbols on some sealings (*MIC*, CXVI: 5, 8 and *EH* 309). Compare also the closely analogous sign *IS* 335 depicting a mortar-cum-sieve with a stem. The third sign in the 'sieve' group (*IS* 334) is a modification of the 'sieve with stem' sign (*IS* 333) with the addition of a mark above which probably has the meaning 'celestial' or 'divine'.

The 'offering' signs (IS 32, 44-46, 328)

3.8 The sign *IS* 328 depicts a small vessel resembling the ordinary drinking cup (*IS*, List of sign variants, p. 790). We can infer that the cup stands for a ritual offering from the following anthropomorphic 'cup-bearer' signs:

- *IS* 32: A standing adorant holding a cup;
- *IS* 44: A dancing adorant (shaman?) holding a cup;
- *IS* 45: A kneeling adorant holding a cup;
- *IS* 46: A kneeling adorant (female?) with bangles on one arm holding a cup.

It is also instructive to compare the frequent texts from Harappa consisting of the 'cup' sign and one to four long strokes preceding it (*IS*: concordance, pp. 565-82) with the unique text (*EH* 372) in which the simple 'cup' sign is replaced by the sign of the kneeling female (?) adorant with the cup (*IS* 46), there by indicating that the simple 'cup' sign itself stands for 'offering' as well as 'the person who makes the offering (worshipper or officiant)'. The signs with the kneeling cup-bearers (*IS* 45, 46) may also be compared with the kneeling priest depicted on a seal (*FEM* 430) and with the kneeling adorants on a sealing (*MIC*, CXVI: 29).

IV. **Implications of the Parallelism**

Is the Harappan Culture Indo-Aryan?

4.1 A new theory has been put forward in this paper that the Harappan religion had a central cult or ritual closely resembling the Soma sacrifice of the *RV*. The implications of the parallelism are far-reaching. The first question that will arise obviouly is: can we not now consider that the Harappans were none other than the Vedic Aryans, as that would most naturally account for the resemblances between the Harappan pictorial motifs and the Soma ritual as described in the *RV*? We cannot however consider this question in isolation, but take into account other relevant circumstances. The Filter symbol occurs from the lowest levels at Harappa as pointed out by Vats. The date of the Aryan settlement of the Indo-Iranian regions is unknown, but unlikely to have been so early as to be contemporary with the beginnings of the Indus Civilization (c. 2800 B.C). The *RV* describes many other features of the Aryan society, such as for example the light horse-drawn chariot with spoked wheels, which is not represented in the Harappan art. Soma is often compared in the *RV* to a speeding horse; but the horse is not among the many animals featured on the Harappan seals and sealings. On the whole it is still difficult to associate the largely pastoral way of life of the Vedic Aryans with the urban polity of the Indus Civilization. It is more likely that Soma (Avestan Haoma) was one of the elements taken over from the earlier Harappan culture and assimilated by the Indo-Iranians. In this context we briefly consider Gordon Wasson's theory regarding the identity of the Soma plant as it has a vital bearing on the problem considered here.

Wasson's identification of Soma

4.2 It is well known that the use of the original Soma was discontinued even by the time of the later Vedic Age and the knowledge of its real identity was totally lost. The later descriptions of the plant are based on substitutes having little or no resemblance with the original Soma. During the last two centuries of modern scholarship several attempts were made to identify the original Soma plant, but without success because, as it now turns out, no trained botanist investigated the problem. Gordon Wasson, a gifted amateur botanist achieved a major breakthrough in 1968 when he published his finding that Soma was a psychotropic mushroom, *Amanita Muscaria* or the fly-agaric (*Soma: Divine Mushroom of Immortality*, New York, 1968). Wasson marshalled evidence from the *RV* itself to show that the original Soma plant had 'neither seed, nor blossom, nor leaf, nor root', and therefore not a chlorophyll-bearing plant. It grew only on the mountains, but there was no record of its cultivation even in the highlands. It had a 'head' and fleshy stalk, was red in colour and yielded a tawny yellow extract. The juice could not have been alcoholic as it was pressed thrice a day and consumed immediately; but it was an inebriant which sent those consuming it into divine raptures, an indication that the juice was hallucinogenic. The evidence clearly points out to the fly-agaric as the original Soma plant. Wasson's brilliant discovery, based on cogent and irrefutable reasoning, holds the field, even though one may not agree with all the details of his theory, for example, his interpretation of the Two Forms of Soma or the Three Filters, involving the drinking of urine as psychotropic metabolite. I wish to clarify that I am not disputing Wasson's well-documented finding that the practice of urine-drinking went along with the consumption of fly-agaric. I am on the narrower ground that the two concepts of the *RV* mentioned above can be interpreted more plausibly, as I have done, with reference to the filter device in the light of the new evidence from the Harappan Filter symbol.

Fly-agaric and the Uralic Tribes

4.3 Gordon Wasson has pointed out that the fly-agaric is a mycorrhizal mushroom growing only in association with the birch trees and occasionally with the pines and the firs, which are found at sea-level in Northern Eurasia, but only at great heights in the mountains south of the Oxus. The fly-agaric had long been the Sacred Element in the Shamanic rites of the Uralic tribes of Northern Eurasia. These tribes must have been familiar with the use of the fly-agaric from at least 6000 B.C., judging from the linguistic evidence connecting the words for 'mushroom' and 'inebriation' in the Uralic languages. Wasson has suggested that as there is no evidence for the presence of Soma in the undivided Indo-European Period, the Aryans must have acquired the fly-agaric from the Uralic tribes with whom they lived in long and intimate contact in Northern Eurasia before moving down to the Iranian plateau and into India sometime in the second Millennium B.C.

4.4 The new evidence for the presence of a Soma-like cult with a Filter ritual in the Indus Valley during the Harappan Age indicates however that the Aryans did not bring the Soma cult with them but took it over from the Harappans. The Harappans in turn probably acquired the fly-agaric habit from Uralic-speaking North Eurasian tribes at a much earlier period in history. The recent discoveries of seals with legends in the Indus Script at Shortugai on the south plains of the Oxus in North-east Afghanistan and at Altin Depe in Soviet Central Asia strengthen such a possibility.

Uralian and Dravidian Inter-connection

4.5 Burrow (*Dravidian Studies IV*) compared the most primitive vocabulary relating to parts of the human body in the Uralian and Dravidian languages and concluded: "It would not be possible to produce between any two languages the same amount of detailed comparisons as can be made between Dravidian and Uralian without giving reason to believe that those languages were themselves related". Andronov investigated the comparative morphology of the languages (*Proceedings of the Second International Seminar on Tamil Studies*, 1968, Vol. I, p. 267) and observed: "If double and triple coincidences in the morphology of Dravidian and Uralian pointed out above are not accidental and, apparently, we have reasons to think they are not—they must testify to some remote relationship between the two families (as simultaneous borrowing of two or three inflexional suffixes in each case looks improbable).' Andronov concluded that the remote Dravidian-Uralian ties should be regarded as a vestige of their pre-historic connection rather than as genetic relationship in the normal linguistic sense. The ancient inter-relationship between the Uralian and the Dravidian makes it probable that the cult of Soma, Wasson's 'Divine Mushroom of Immortality', was passed on by the Uralians to the Dravidians long before the advent of the Aryans into the Indo-Iranian regions.

Soma Ritual from the Harappan Substratum

4.6 The evidence discussed above leads to the conclusion that the Soma (Haoma) rituals of the Indo-Iranian religions are based on a pre-Aryan Harappan substratum and that this is the reason for the remarkable resemblances between the Harappan symbolism of the Sacred Filter and the Soma ritual as described in the Ṛgveda.

1

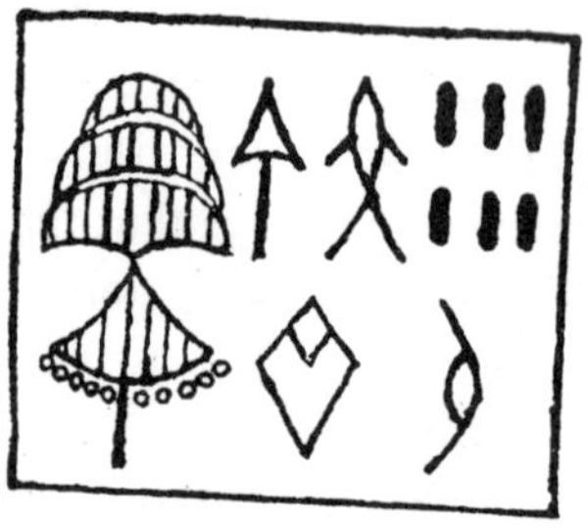

2

3

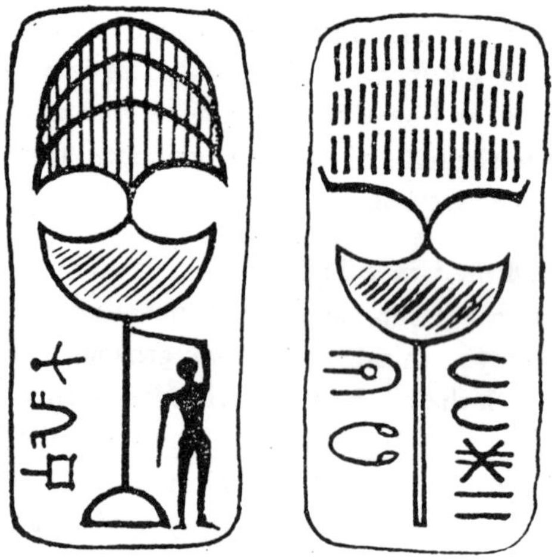

4

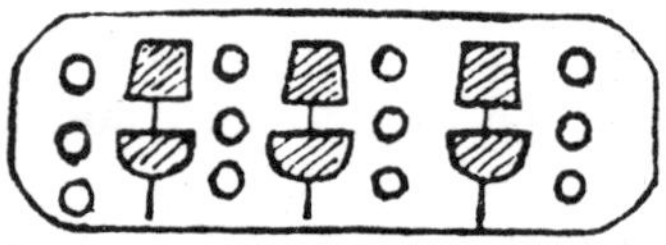

5

Pl. I : *Harappan Inscribed Objects with the 'Sacred Filter' Symbol:*
Fig. 1: *MIC* 38
Fig. 2: *EH* 256
Fig. 3: *MIC*, pl. CXVI: 8
Fig. 4: *EH* 309
Fig. 5: *EH* 322

6

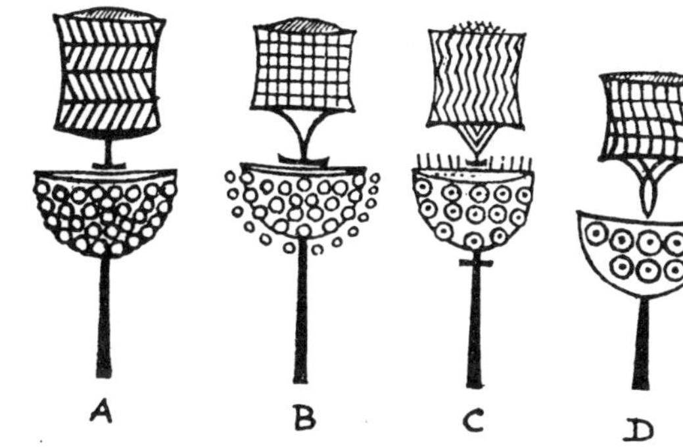

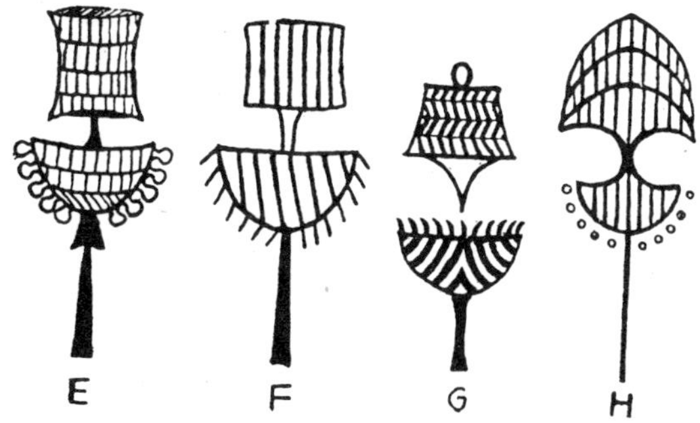

7

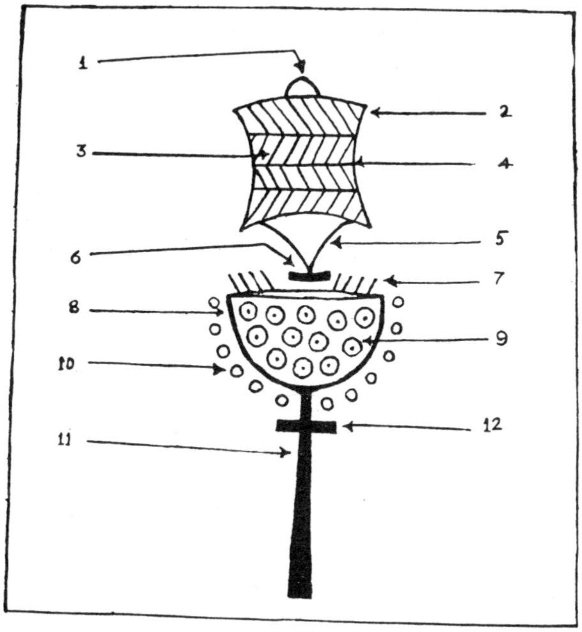

Pl II: *'Sacred Filter' Symbols on Unicorn Seals:*
Fig. 6: A. *MIC* 9; B. *MIC* 18; C. *MIC* 38; D. *FEM* 422; E. *MIC* 2; F. *MIC* 41; G. *EH* 3; H. *EH* 256.
Fig. 7: A Composite Drawing of the Harappan Sacred Filter.

A. 'MORTAR' SIGNS

B. 'FLOW' SIGNS

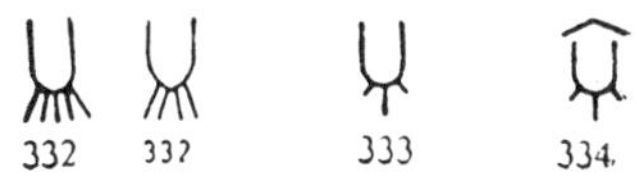

C. 'SIEVE' SIGNS

D. 'OFFERING' SIGNS

Pl. III: *Signs of the Indus Script connected with the Sacred Filter:*
Fig. 8: A. 'Mortar' Signs: *IS* 335-337; 34.
B. 'Flow' Signs: *IS* 119-121.
C. 'Sieve' Signs: *IS* 332-334.
D. 'Offering' Signs: *IS* 328, 32, 44-46.

REFERENCES

Frankfort, H.P., 1978-79. Shortugai, *Puratattva*, 10, 91; pl. VIII-C.

Gupta, S.P. 1978. Archaeology of Soviet Central Asia, 2 Vols., New Delhi, (The Indus seal found at Altin Depe in Turkmania is ill. in Vol 2, 168-69.)

Hunter, G.R. 1934. The Script of Harappa and Mohenjodaro and its connection with other scripts, London.

Knorozov, Y.V., B.Y. Volchok et al. 1972. Proto-Indica: Moscow, 1979. Proto-Indica: Moscow.

Mackay, E.J.H. 1937-38. Further Excavations at Mohenjodaro, 2 Vols., New Delhi, (FEM).

Mackay, E.J.H. 1943. Chanhudaro Excavations (1935-36), New Haven, (CE).

Mahadevan, I. 1977. The Indus Script: Texts, Concordance and Tables, New Delhi, 1977 (IS).

Manchanda, O. 1972. A study of the Harappan Pottery, New Delhi.

Marshall, J. 1931. Mohenjodaro and the Indus Civilization, 3 Vols., London, (MIC).

Punjab, Punjab Series (Photographic Albums), Photo Library, Archaeological Survey of India, New Delhi, (PU).

Vats, M.S. 1940. Excavations at Harappa, 2 Vols., Calcutta, (EH).

Wheeler, R.E.M. 1966. Civilizations of the Indus Valley and beyond, London.

The Ṛgveda (RV):

Bhawe, S.S. 1957, 1960, 1962. The Soma-Hymns of the Rgveda, A fresh interpretation, (RV. 9-1-70), in 3 pts., M.S. University of Baroda, (SH).

Griffith, R.T.H. 1963. The Hymns of the Rgveda, English translation, 2 Vols., Indian reprint, Banares.

Griswold, H.D. 1971. The Religion of the Rgveda, Indian reprint, New Delhi.

Hillebrandt, A. 1980-81. Vedic Mythology, 2 Vols., English translation of 2nd rev. edn. in German, S.R. Sarma, New Delhi, (VM).

Macdonell, A.A. 1981. Vedic Mythology, Indian reprint, New Delhi, (VM).

Macdonell, A.A. and A.B., Keith, 1967. Vedic Index of Names and Subjects, 2 Vols., Indian reprint, New Delhi.

Max Muller, F. 1966. Rig-Veda Samhita, with the Commentary by Sayana, 4 Vols., Indian reprint, Banares.

Vishva Bhandhu, 1964. Rgveda (with commentaries by Venkata Madhava and others), 8 Vols., Vishveshvaranand Vedic Research Institute, Hoshiarpur.

Wasson, R.G. 1968. Soma, Divine Mushroom of Immortality, Ethno-Mycological Studies, No. 1, New York.

Wilson, H.H. 1977. Rig-Veda Sanhita, Engl. tr., ed. by E.B. Cowell and W.F. Webster, 6 Vols., Indian reprint, New Delhi.

Uralian-Dravidian Studies:

Andronov, M.—Comparative Studies on the nature of Dravidian-Uralian parallels (A peep into the pre-history of Language Families).

1971. Proceedings of the Second International Conference-Seminar of Tamil Studies, 1968, Vol. 1, p. 267, Madras.

Burrow, T. 1971. Dravidian studies IV: The Body in Dravidian and Uralian, Collected Papers on Dravidian Linguistics, Annamalai University.

MODE OF CITATIONS

Harappan Inscribed Objects: The numbers immediately following *MIC, FEM, EH* and *IS* refer to the continuous serial numbers of inscribed objects as given in these publications. (Text numbers in *IS* are always in four digits). In other cases, plates (pl.), pages (pp.) or illustrations (ill.) in the source publications are cited.

Signs of the Indus Script: Numbers in one to three digits immediately following *IS* refer to signs. (See *IS*: Sign List, pp. 32-35).

Hymns from the RV: Relevant passages alone are cited from the samhita text, giving Mandala, sukta and mantra numbers separated by dots (e.g. 9.70.7).

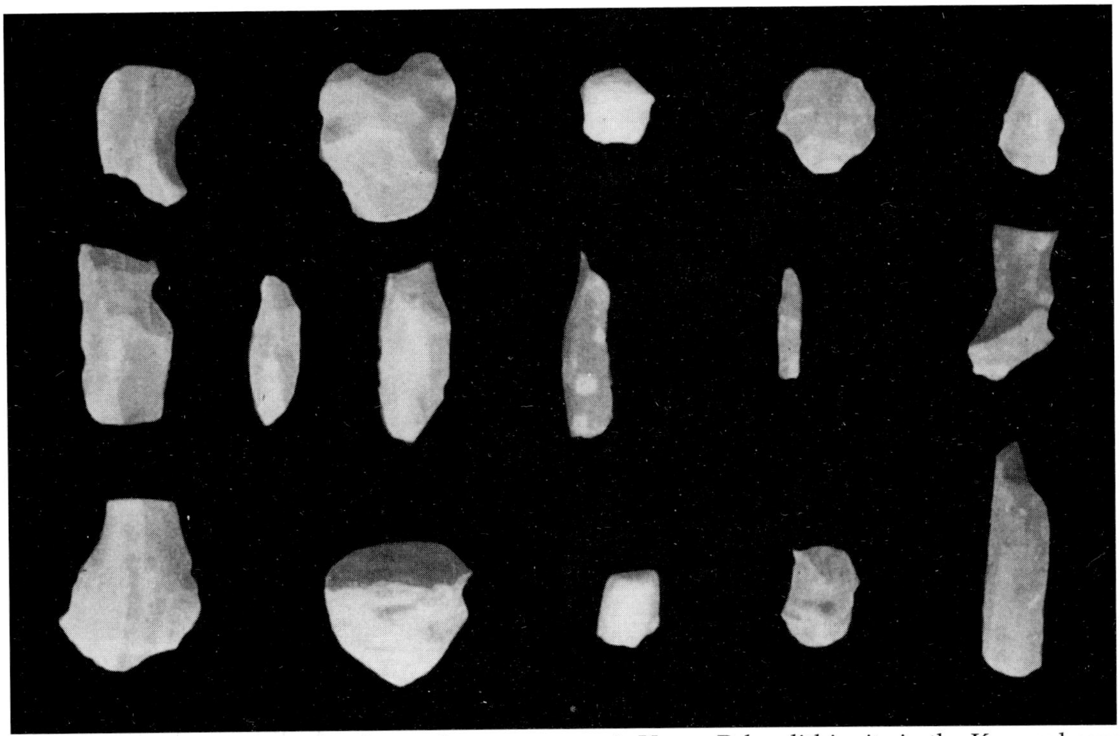

I. M.L.K. Murty: Blade tool industry from an open-air Upper Palaeolithic site in the Kurnool cave areas. 1-2, notched scrapers; 3-4, steep scrapers; 5, burin; 6-10 blades; 11, pluging flake; 12 and 15, flakes; 13-14, blade cores; 16, awl.

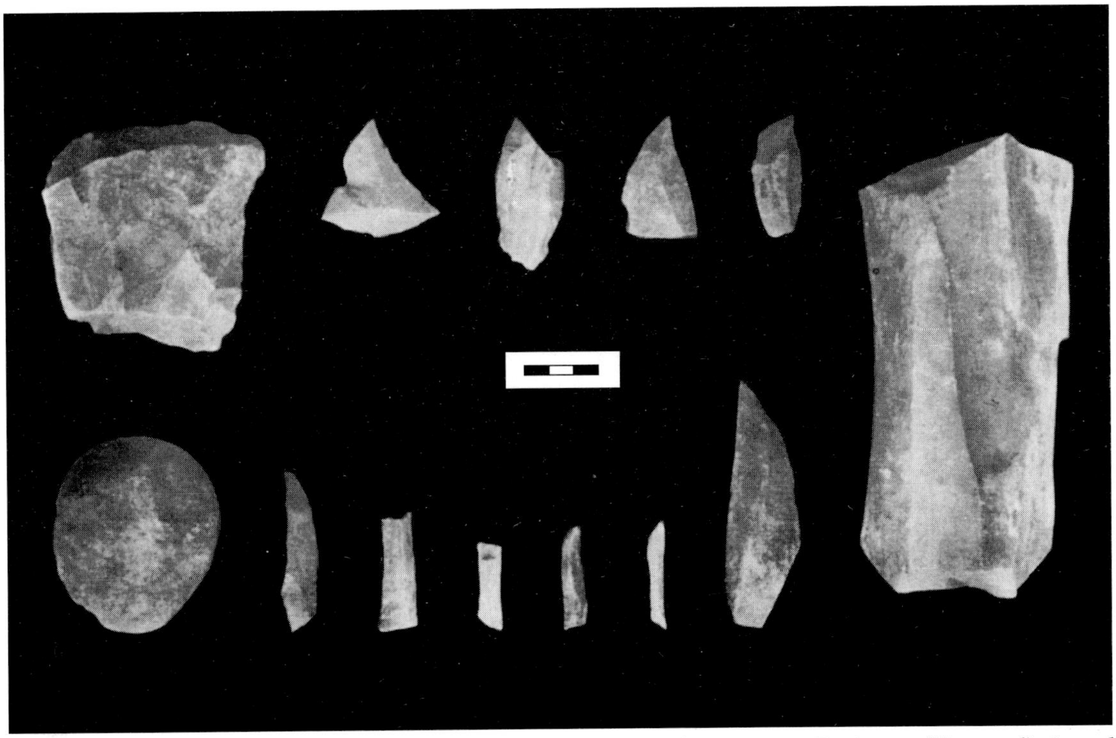

II. M.L.K. Murty: Blade tool industry from Muchchatla Chintamanu Gavi cave (Kurnool). 1, end scrapers; 2, burin; 3, side scraper; 4-5 and 7-12, blades; 6, hammerstone; 13, blade core.

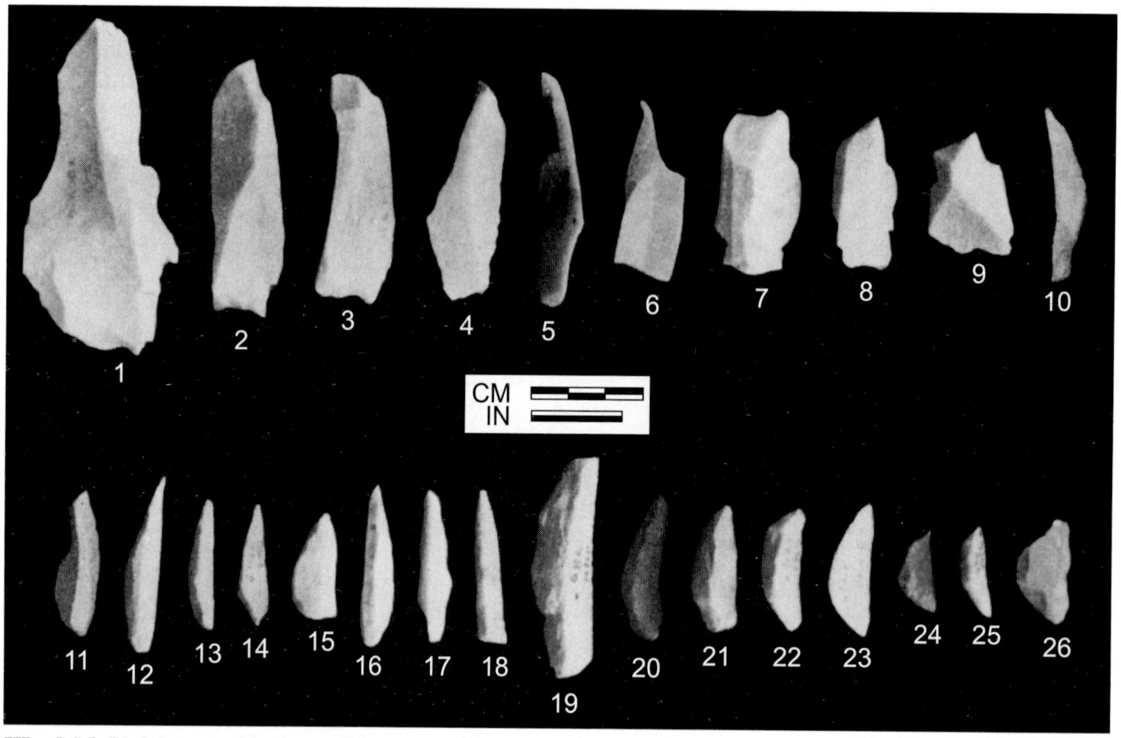

III. M.L.K. Murty: Blade and burin industry from Renigunta, 1-9, burins; 10-16, curved back points; 17-18, straight back points; 19, backed penknife; 20-24, elouera type backed blades; 25-26, macro-triangles.

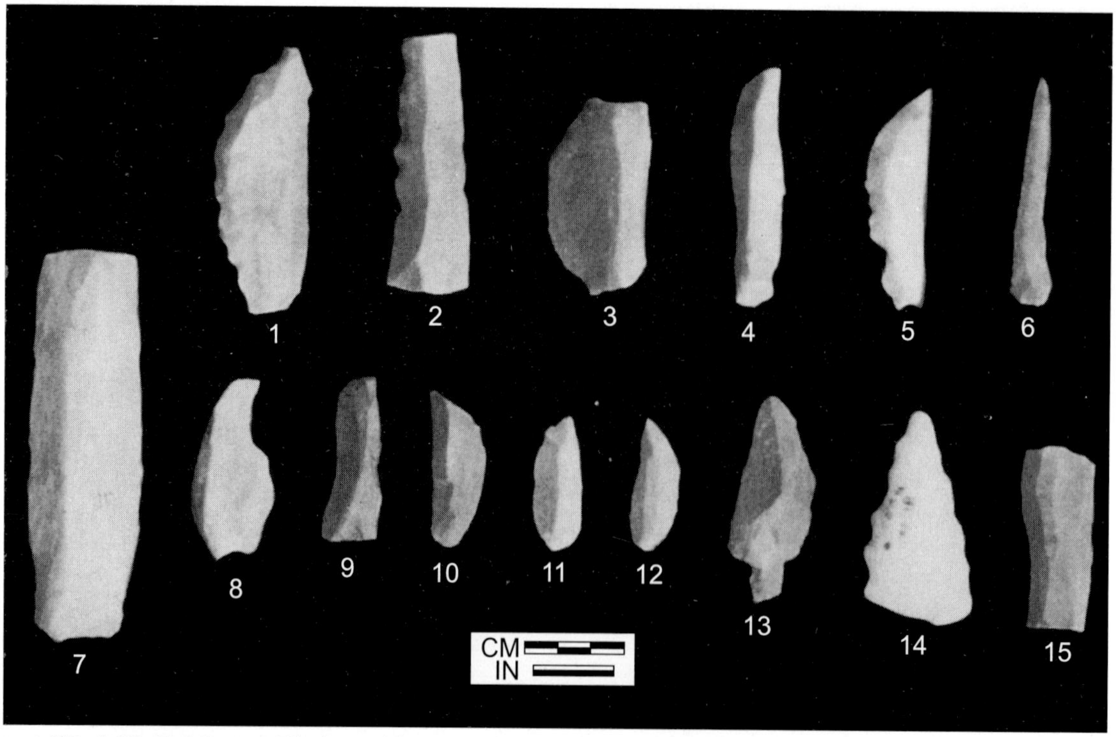

IV. M.L.K. Murty: Blade and burin industry from Renigunta. 1-2, scrapers; 3-12, blades; 13, tanged point; 14, bifacial point; 15, blade core.

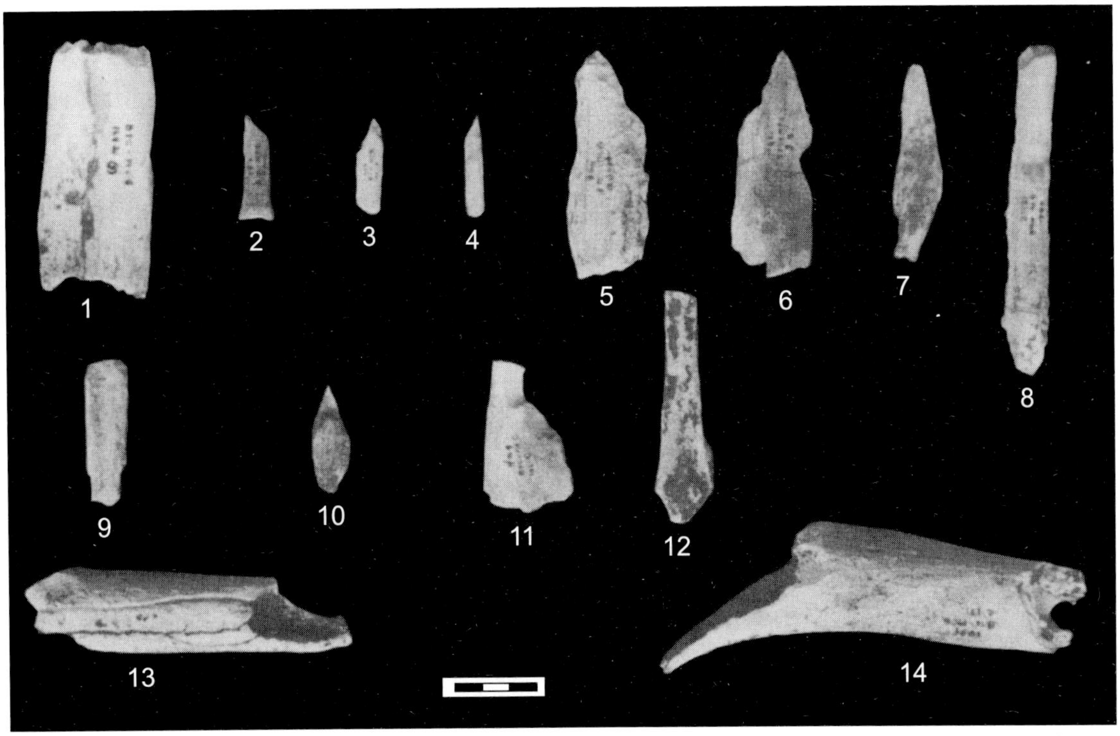

V. M.L.K. Murty: Bone tool industry from Muchchatla Chintamanu Gavi cave (Kurnool). 1, scraper; 2-4, perforators; 5, chisel; 6, unfinished tanged point; 7, tanged point; 8-9, spatulae; 10, barb; 12, bone blank; 11 and 13-14, worked bones.

I. K.N. Dikshit : Hulas, Mud-walled room with a furnace — Late Harappan.

II. K.N. Dikshit : Hulas, Mud-brick room — Late Harappan.

III. K.N. Dikshit : Hulas, Painted red ware pottery — Late Harappan.

I. M.K. Dhavalikar : Inamgaon, a Late Jorwe hut, *circa* 800 B.C.

II. M.K. Dhavalikar : Inamgaon, A Malwa house containing a pottery kiln, *circa* 1500 B.C.

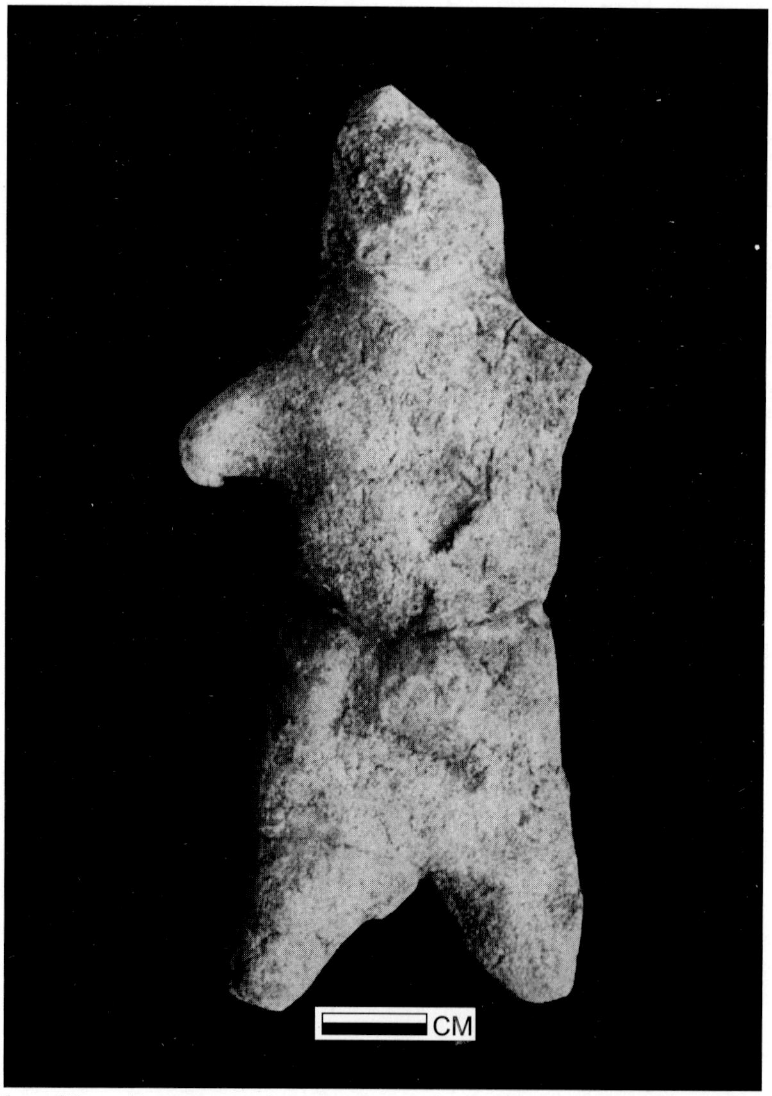

III. M.K. Dhavalikar : Inamgaon, A terracotta male figurine, Period II, *circa* 1400-1000 B.C.

I. G.L. Possehl *et al.* : The Gateway at Rojdi.

II. G.L. Possehl *et al.* : *Lumps of flooring and other architectural material from Operation 3.*

III. G.L. Possehl *et al.* : The flotation machine showing the barrel and plumbing.

IV. G.L. Possehl *et al.* : Detail of the flotation machine. Plumbing for internal shower head and wash-down hose are in the foreground. Pipes extending to the left hold the light fraction box when the machine is in operation. Basket insert is in the 'rest' position.

V. G.L. Possehl *et al.* : The interior of the flotation machine showing the internal shower head.

VI. G.L. Possehl *et al.* : A sample being poured into the floatation machine. The basket is in place and a thin stream of water is coming over the lip and into the light fraction box on the left.

VII. G.L. Possehl *et al.* : Agitating the floatation sample in the wire basket.

VIII. G.L. Possehl *et al.* : Agitating the floatation sample.

IX. G.L. Possehl *et al* : Skimming the light fraction into the light fraction box.

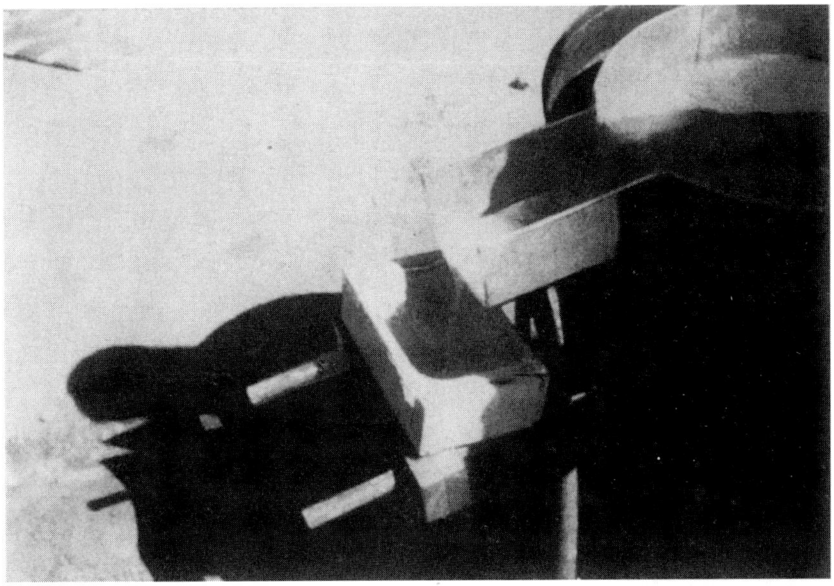

X. G.L. Possehl *et al.* : The light fraction flowing off the top of the wire basket.

XI. G.L. Possehl *et al.* : The heavy fraction in the bottom of the wire basket.

XII. G.L. Possehl *et al.* : Heavy fractions drying in the sun.

XIII. G.L. Possehl *et al.* : Light fractions wrapped in fine cloth drying on a line.